We Were There

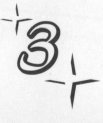

Story & Art by
Yuki Obata

Contents

Characters

Yuri Yamamoto
*Nanami's classmate.
Nana-san, who dated Yano,
was her older sister.*

Motoharu Yano
*Nanami's classmate.
He's a popular guy who
gets good grades.*

Nanami Takahashi
*She's earnest but a bit
forgetful at times.*

Story

Nanami tells Yano that she has a crush on him, but when
he asks her to go out with him, she declines because
he doesn't know if he truly likes her or not in return.
As the months go by, the two gradually become closer.
Then Yano tells Nanami that he likes her, marking
the beginning of Nanami's blissful days, but...

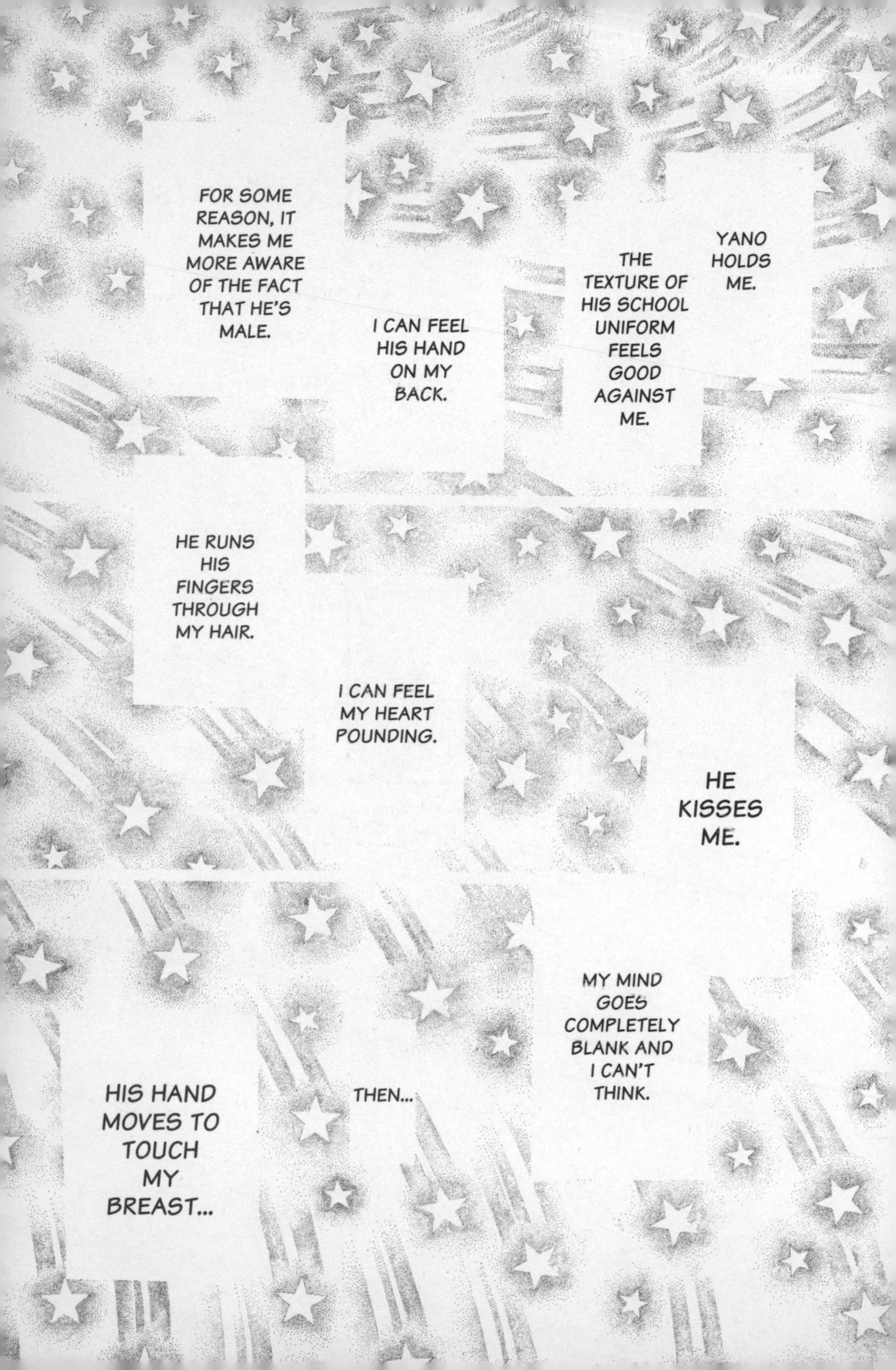
YANO HOLDS ME.
THE TEXTURE OF HIS SCHOOL UNIFORM FEELS GOOD AGAINST ME.
I CAN FEEL HIS HAND ON MY BACK.
FOR SOME REASON, IT MAKES ME MORE AWARE OF THE FACT THAT HE'S MALE.
HE KISSES ME.
I CAN FEEL MY HEART POUNDING.
HE RUNS HIS FINGERS THROUGH MY HAIR.
MY MIND GOES COMPLETELY BLANK AND I CAN'T THINK.
THEN...
HIS HAND MOVES TO TOUCH MY BREAST...

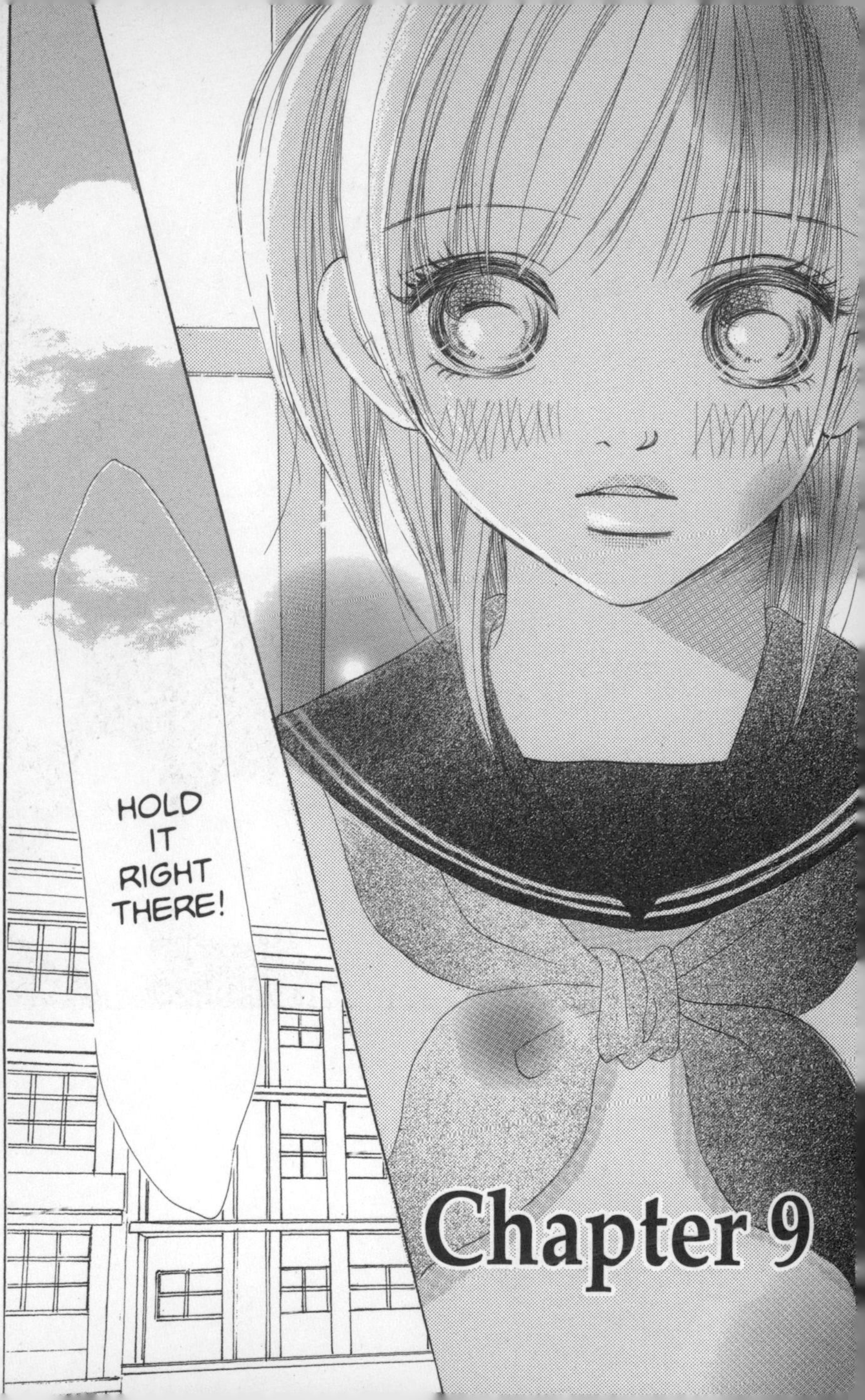
HOLD IT RIGHT THERE!
Chapter 9

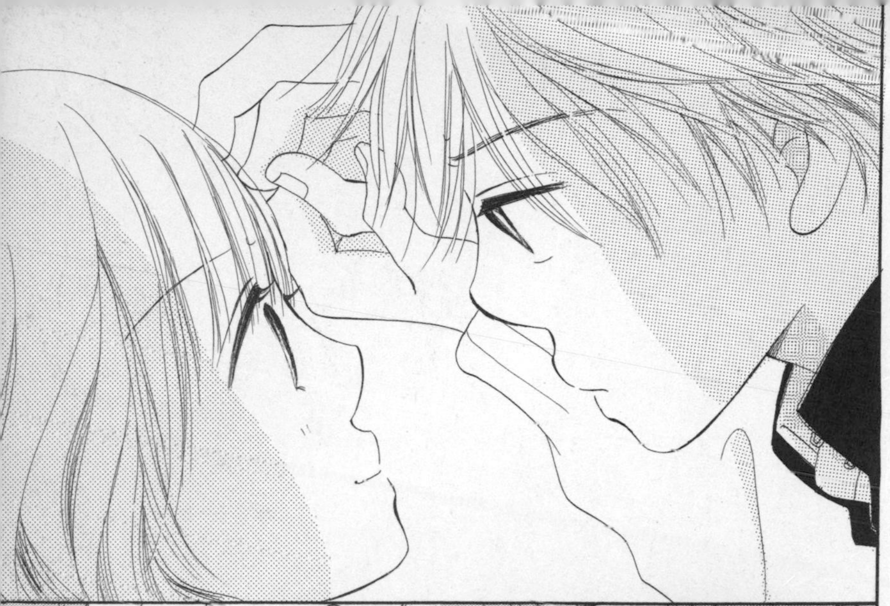

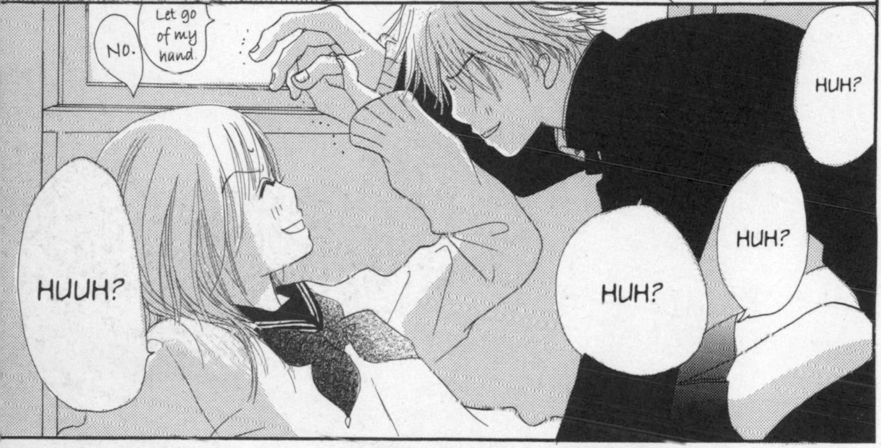
Let go of my hand.
No.
HUH?
HUH?
HUH?
HUUH?

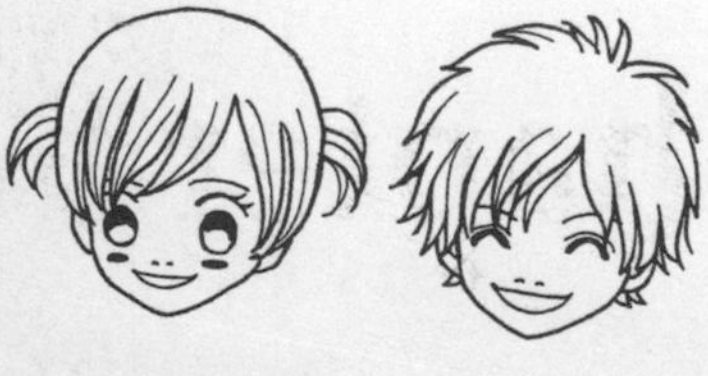

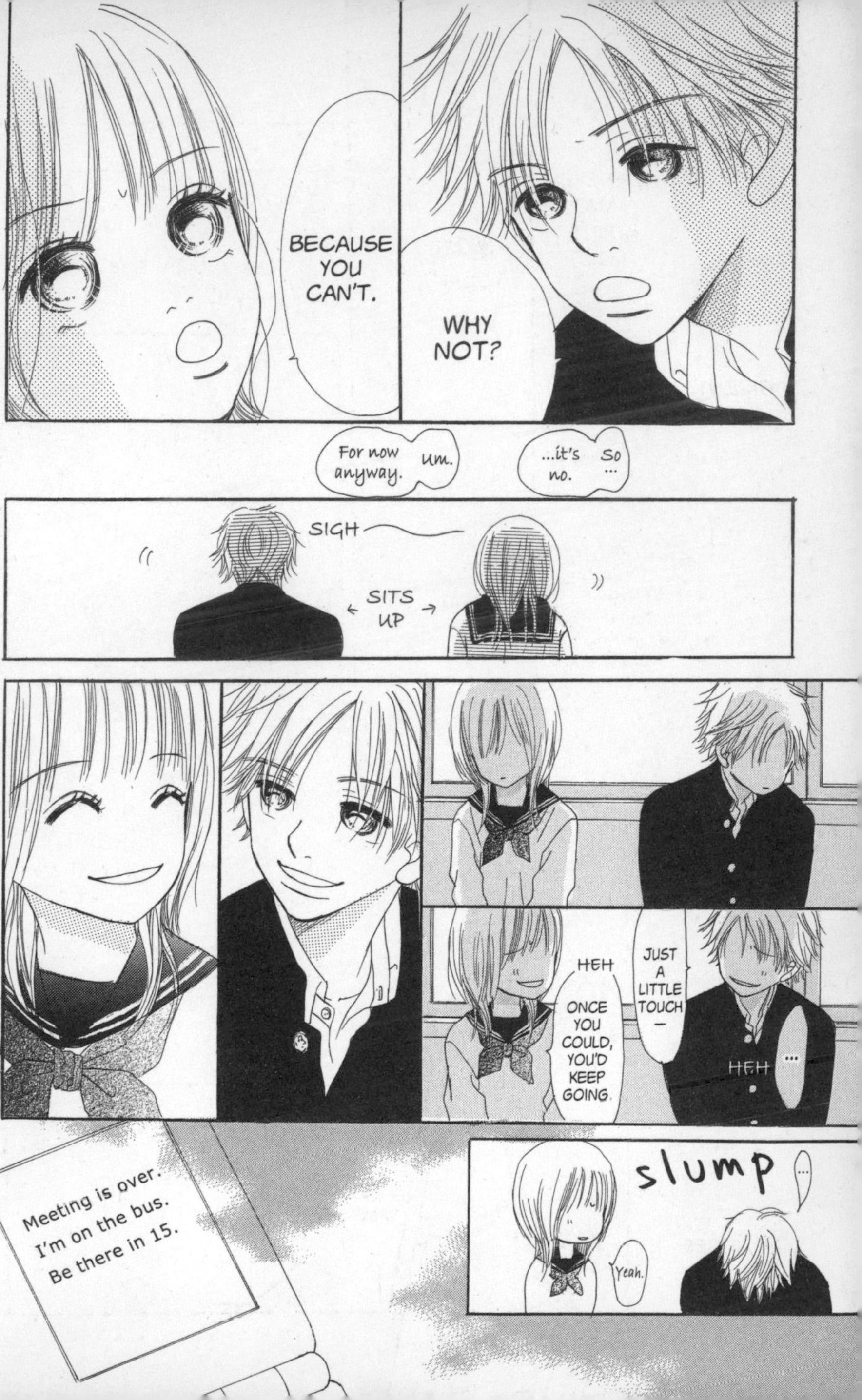
WHY NOT?
BECAUSE YOU CAN'T.
So ...
...it's no.
Um.
For now anyway.
SIGH
SITS UP
JUST A LITTLE TOUCH—
HEH ...
HEH
ONCE YOU COULD, YOU'D KEEP GOING.
slump
...
Yeah.
Meeting is over.
I'm on the bus.
Be there in 15.

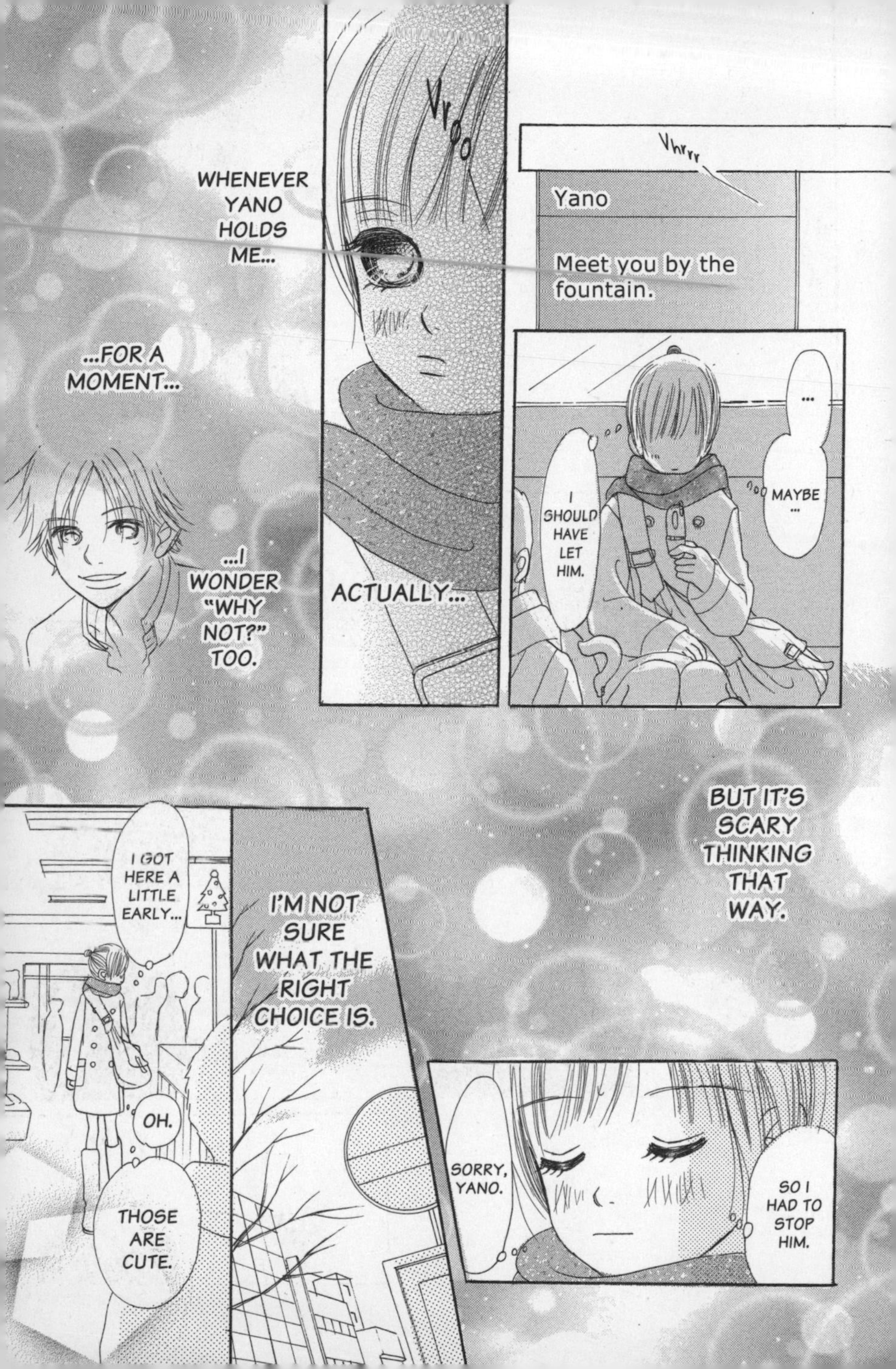
Vhrrr
Yano
Meet you by the fountain.
...
MAYBE...
I SHOULD HAVE LET HIM.
Vroo
ACTUALLY...
WHENEVER YANO HOLDS ME...
...FOR A MOMENT...
...I WONDER "WHY NOT?" TOO.
BUT IT'S SCARY THINKING THAT WAY.
SO I HAD TO STOP HIM.
SORRY, YANO.
I'M NOT SURE WHAT THE RIGHT CHOICE IS.
I GOT HERE A LITTLE EARLY...
OH.
THOSE ARE CUTE.

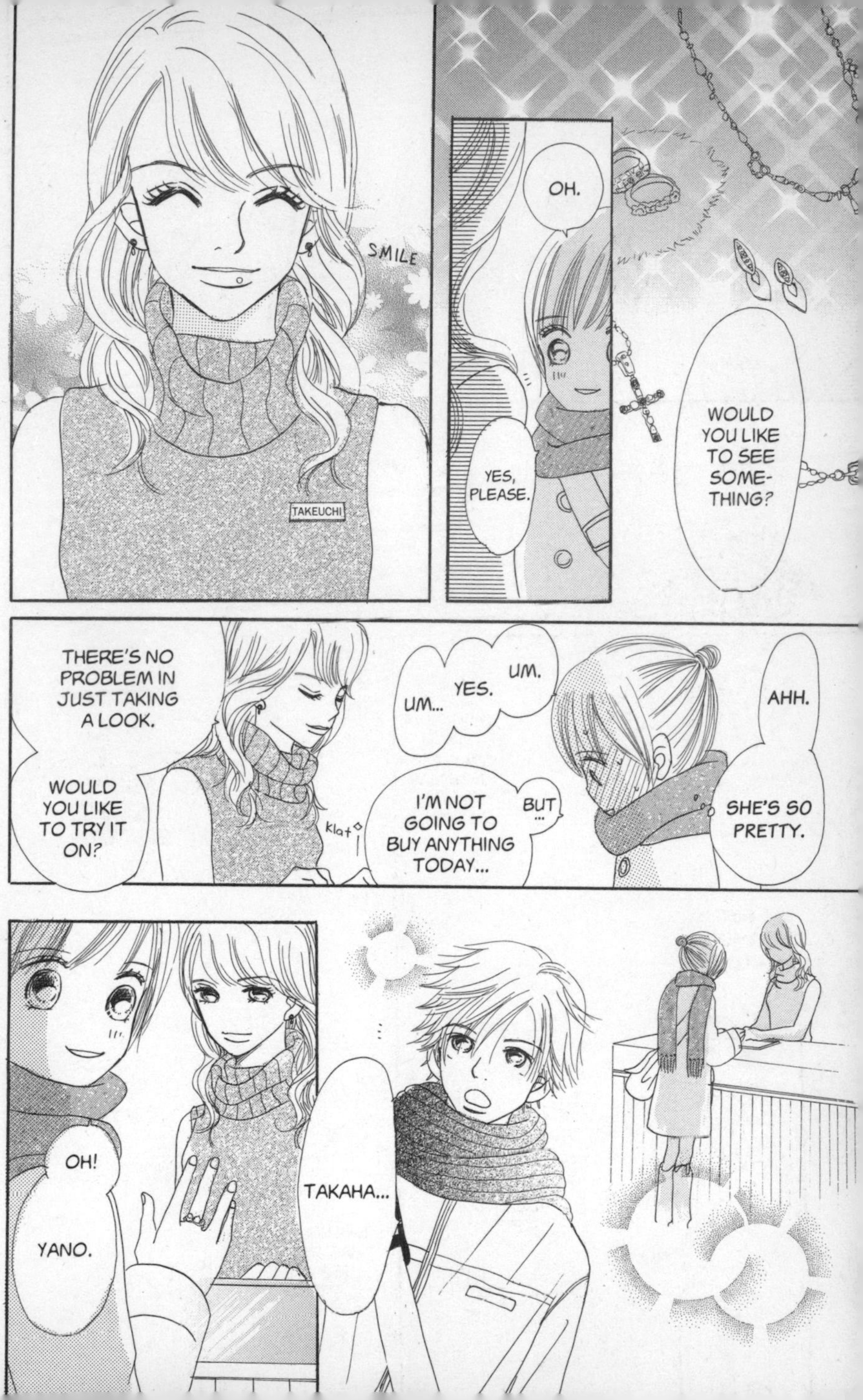
WOULD YOU LIKE TO SEE SOME-THING?
OH.
YES, PLEASE.
SMILE
TAKEUCHI
AHH.
SHE'S SO PRETTY.
UM.
YES.
UM...
BUT...
I'M NOT GOING TO BUY ANYTHING TODAY...
klat
THERE'S NO PROBLEM IN JUST TAKING A LOOK.
WOULD YOU LIKE TO TRY IT ON?
TAKAHA...
OH!
YANO.

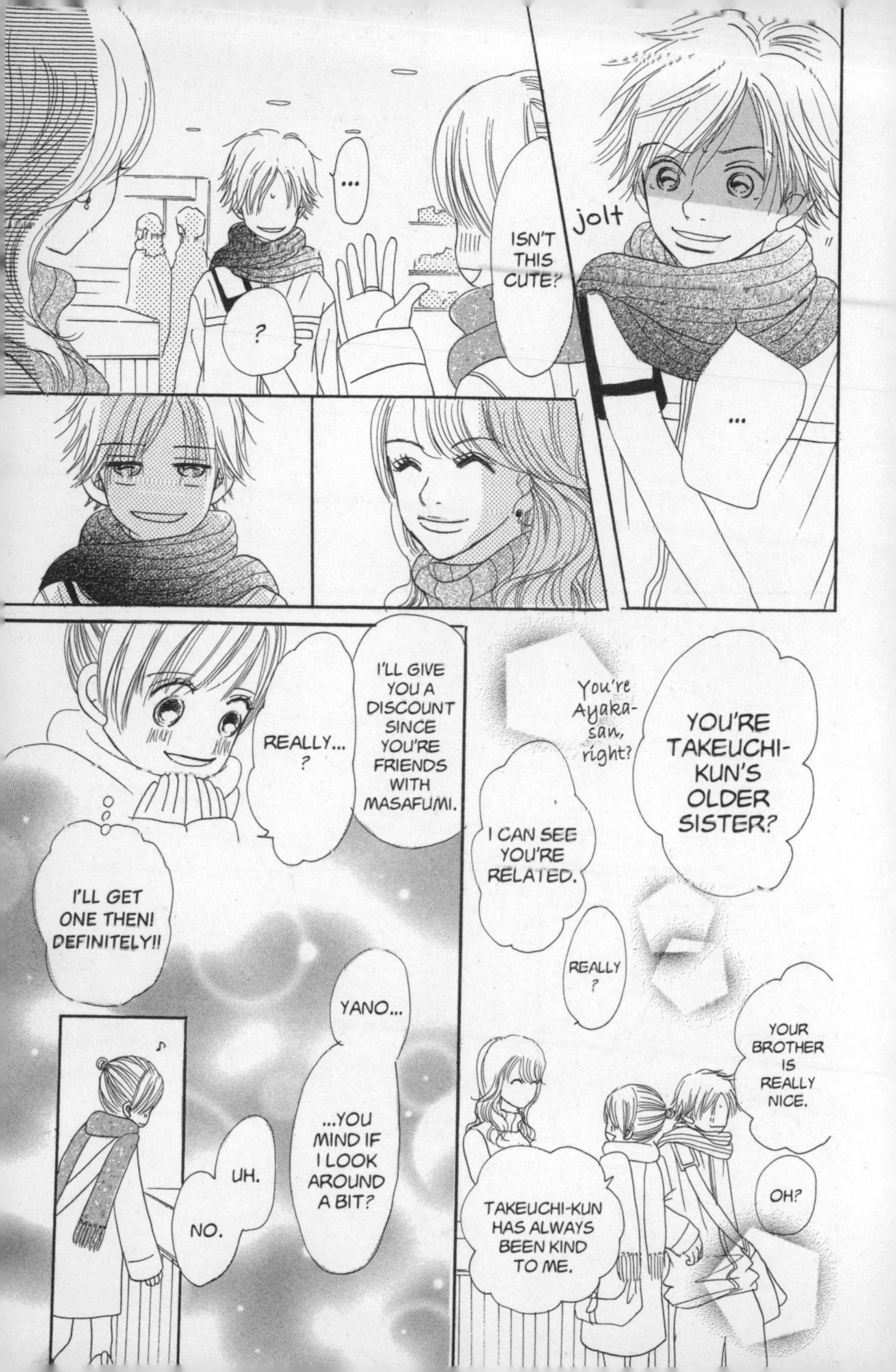
jolt
...
ISN'T THIS CUTE?
...
?
YOU'RE TAKEUCHI-KUN'S OLDER SISTER?
You're Ayaka-san, right?
I CAN SEE YOU'RE RELATED.
REALLY?
YOUR BROTHER IS REALLY NICE.
OH?
TAKEUCHI-KUN HAS ALWAYS BEEN KIND TO ME.
I'LL GIVE YOU A DISCOUNT SINCE YOU'RE FRIENDS WITH MASAFUMI.
REALLY...?
I'LL GET ONE THEN! DEFINITELY!!
YANO...
...YOU MIND IF I LOOK AROUND A BIT?
UH.
NO.

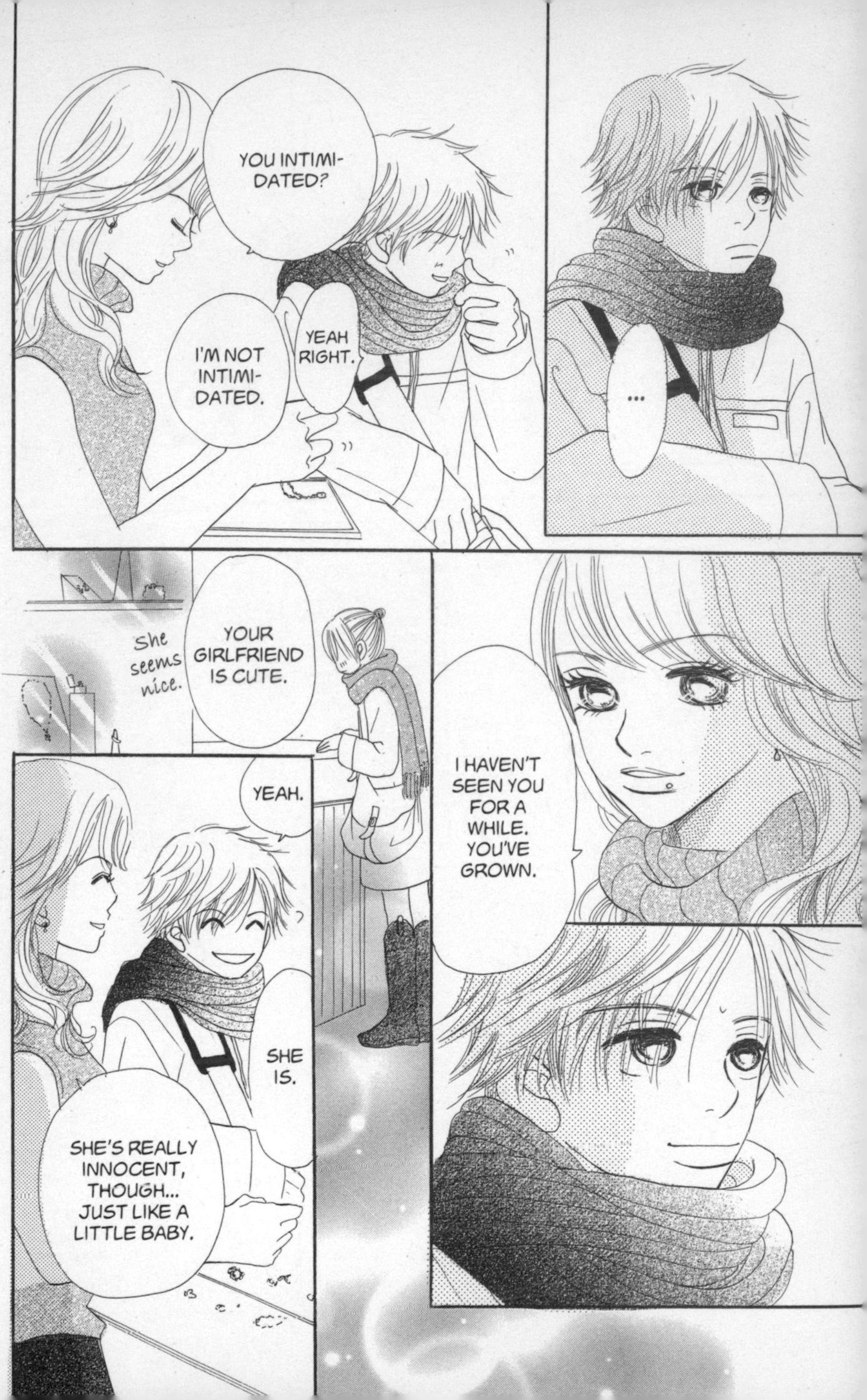
...
YOU INTIMI-DATED?
YEAH RIGHT.
I'M NOT INTIMI-DATED.
I HAVEN'T SEEN YOU FOR A WHILE. YOU'VE GROWN.
YOUR GIRLFRIEND IS CUTE.
She seems nice.
YEAH.
SHE IS.
SHE'S REALLY INNOCENT, THOUGH... JUST LIKE A LITTLE BABY.

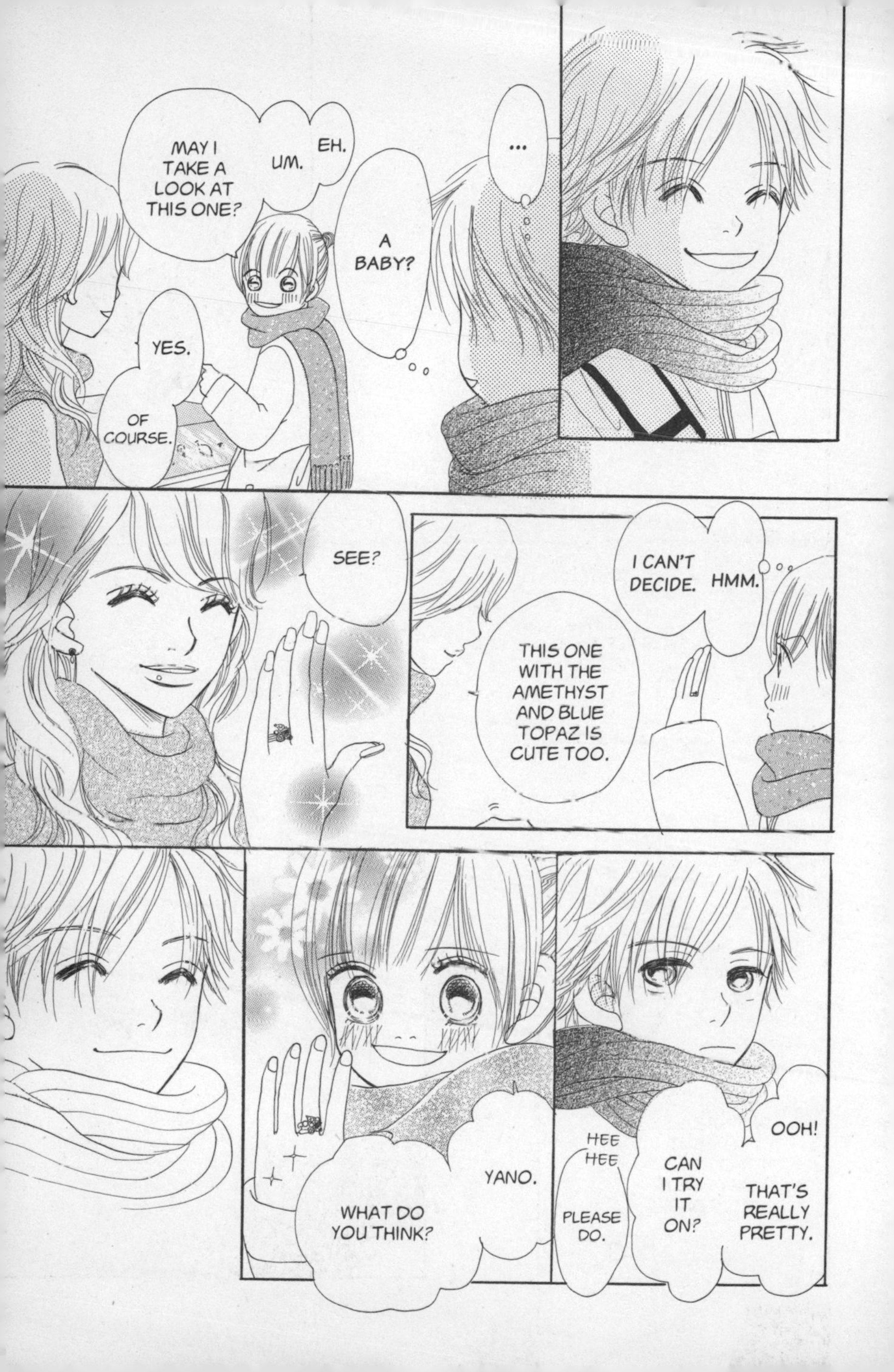
...
EH. UM.
MAY I TAKE A LOOK AT THIS ONE?
A BABY?
YES. OF COURSE.
HMM.
I CAN'T DECIDE.
THIS ONE WITH THE AMETHYST AND BLUE TOPAZ IS CUTE TOO.
SEE?
OOH!
THAT'S REALLY PRETTY.
CAN I TRY IT ON?
HEE HEE
PLEASE DO.
YANO.
WHAT DO YOU THINK?

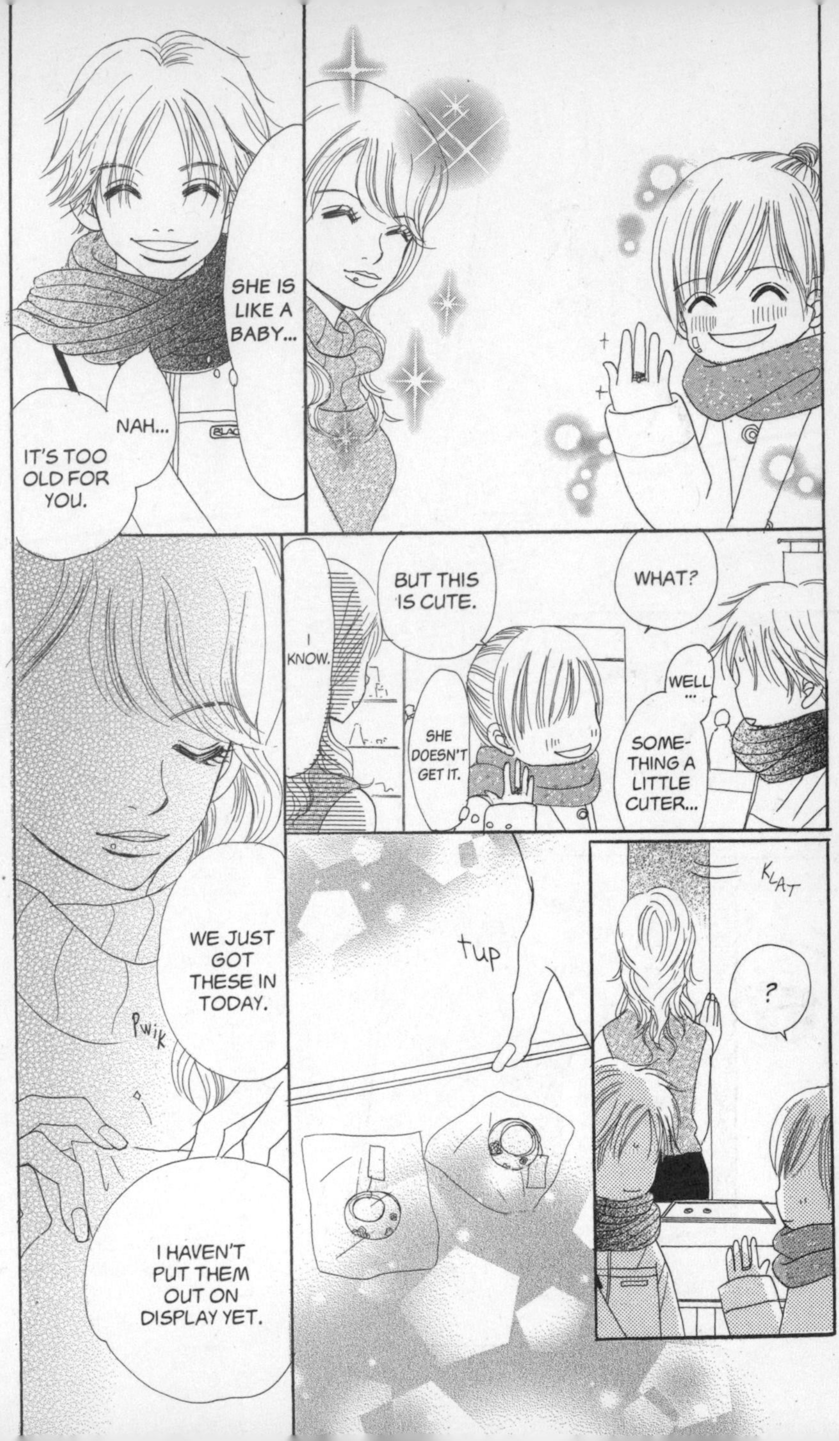
SHE IS LIKE A BABY...
NAH...
IT'S TOO OLD FOR YOU.
WHAT?
WELL...
SOME-THING A LITTLE CUTER...
BUT THIS IS CUTE.
SHE DOESN'T GET IT.
I KNOW.
KLAT
?
tup
WE JUST GOT THESE IN TODAY.
Pwik
I HAVEN'T PUT THEM OUT ON DISPLAY YET.

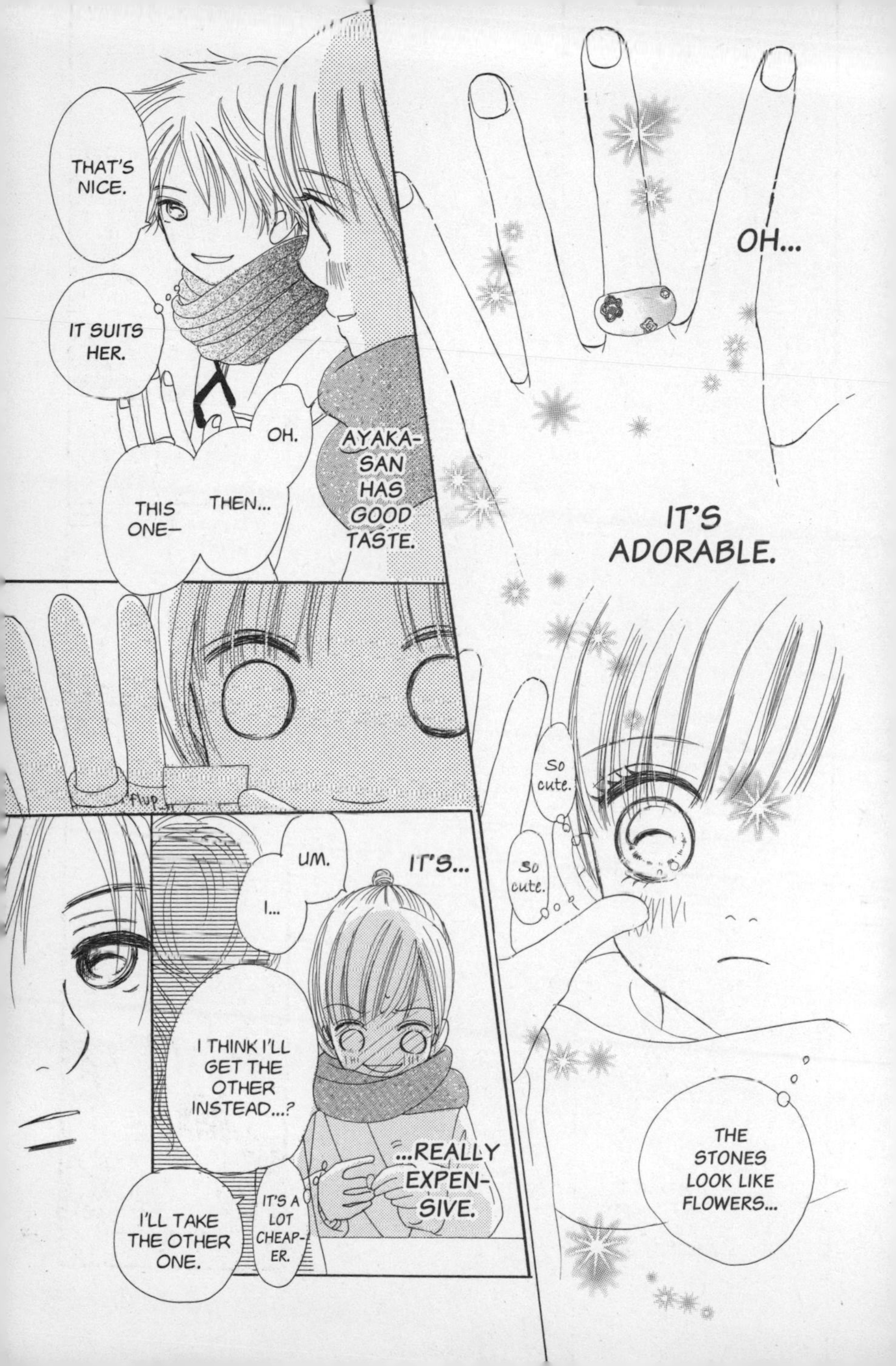
OH...
IT'S ADORABLE.
So cute.
So cute.
THE STONES LOOK LIKE FLOWERS...
AYAKA-SAN HAS GOOD TASTE.
THAT'S NICE.
IT SUITS HER.
OH. THEN... THIS ONE—
flup
IT'S...
UM. I...
...REALLY EXPENSIVE.
I THINK I'LL GET THE OTHER INSTEAD...?
IT'S A LOT CHEAPER.
I'LL TAKE THE OTHER ONE.

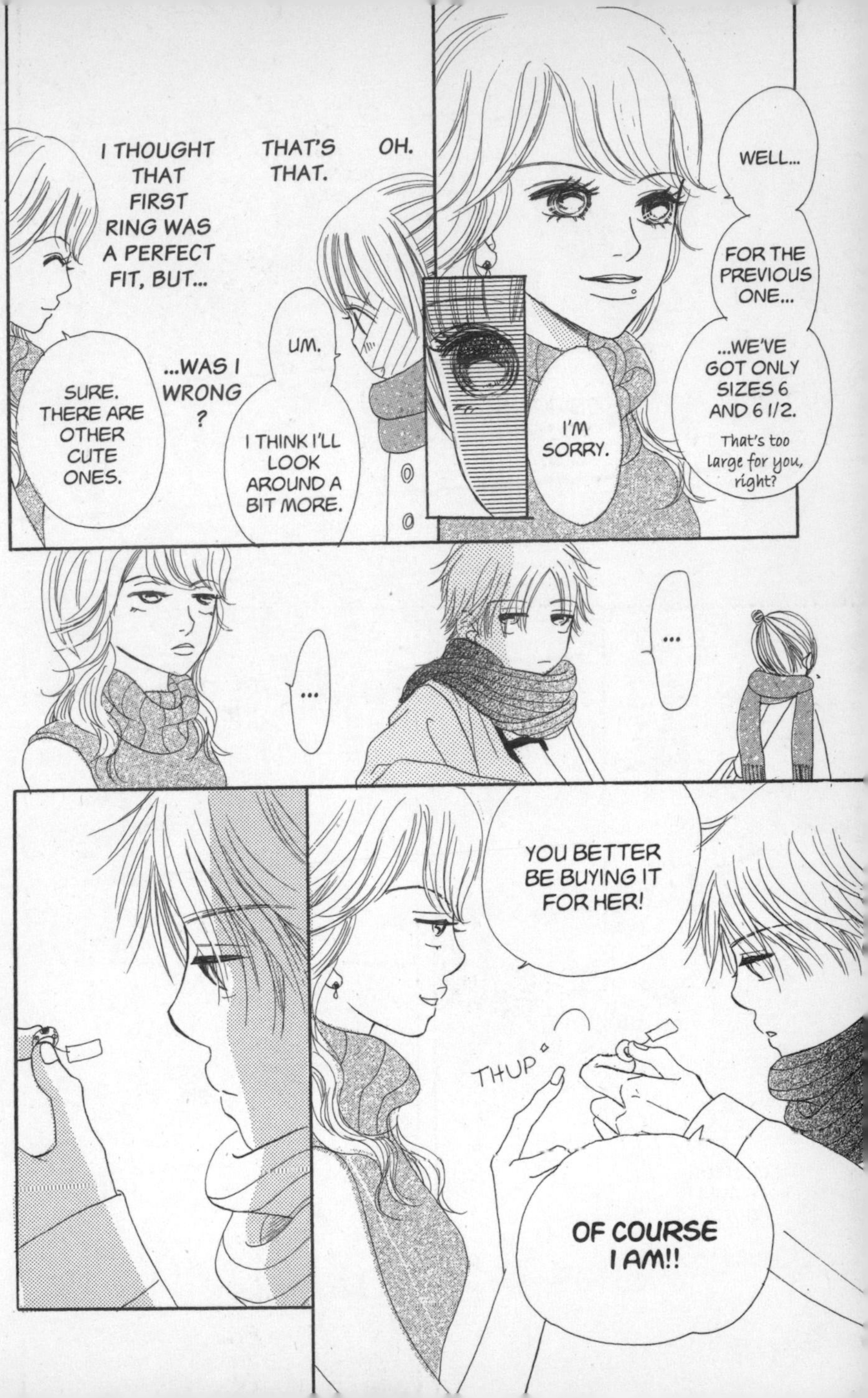

WELL...
FOR THE PREVIOUS ONE...
...WE'VE GOT ONLY SIZES 6 AND 6 1/2.
That's too large for you, right?
I'M SORRY.
OH.
THAT'S THAT.
I THOUGHT THAT FIRST RING WAS A PERFECT FIT, BUT...
...WAS I WRONG?
UM.
I THINK I'LL LOOK AROUND A BIT MORE.
SURE. THERE ARE OTHER CUTE ONES.
...
...
YOU BETTER BE BUYING IT FOR HER!
THUP
OF COURSE I AM!!

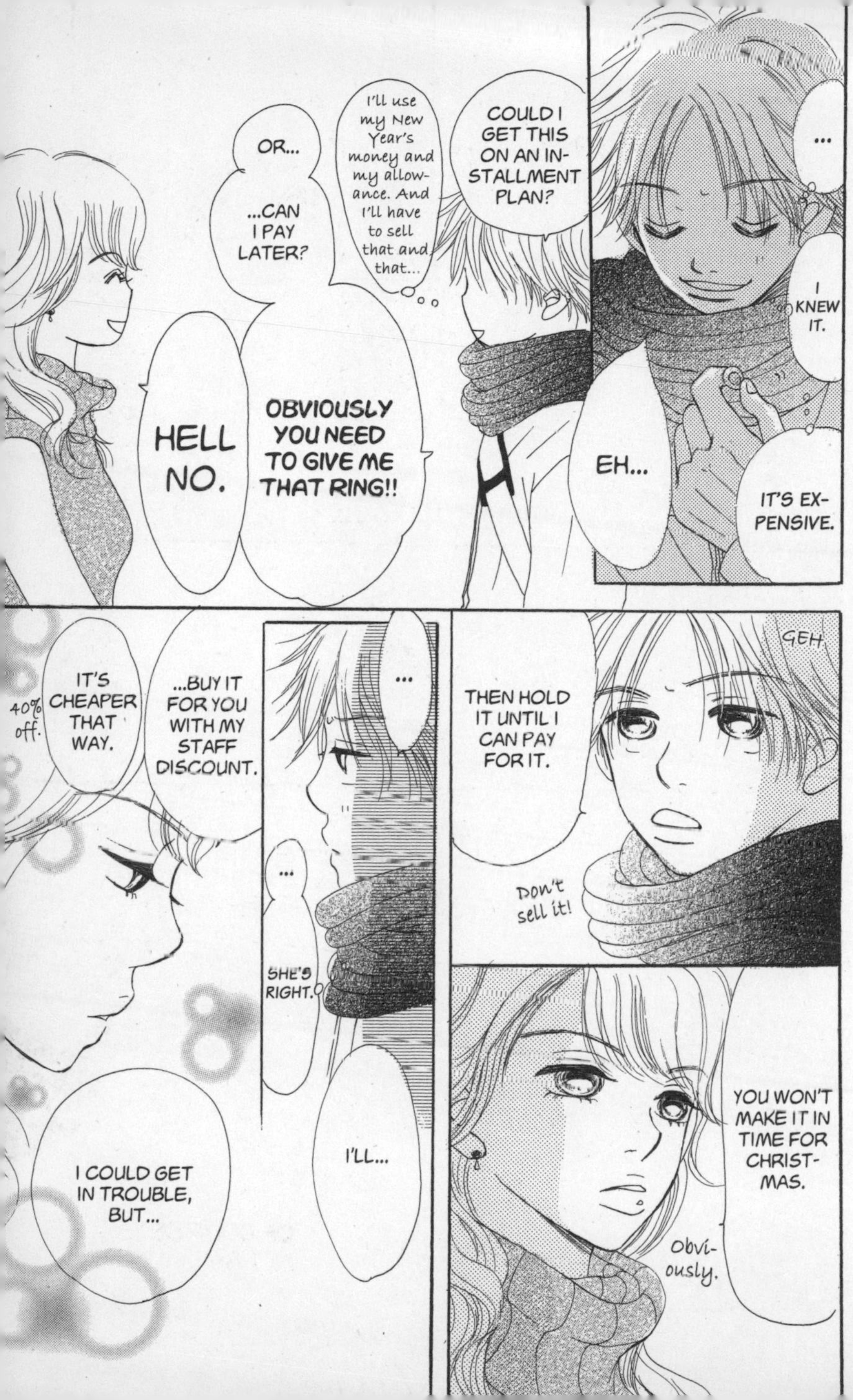
...
I KNEW IT.
EH...
IT'S EX-PENSIVE.
COULD I GET THIS ON AN IN-STALLMENT PLAN?
I'll use my New Year's money and my allow-ance. And I'll have to sell that and that...
OR...
...CAN I PAY LATER?
OBVIOUSLY YOU NEED TO GIVE ME THAT RING!!
HELL NO.
GEH.
THEN HOLD IT UNTIL I CAN PAY FOR IT.
Don't sell it!
YOU WON'T MAKE IT IN TIME FOR CHRIST-MAS.
Obvi-ously.
...
...
SHE'S RIGHT.
I'LL...
...BUY IT FOR YOU WITH MY STAFF DISCOUNT.
IT'S CHEAPER THAT WAY.
40% off.
I COULD GET IN TROUBLE, BUT...

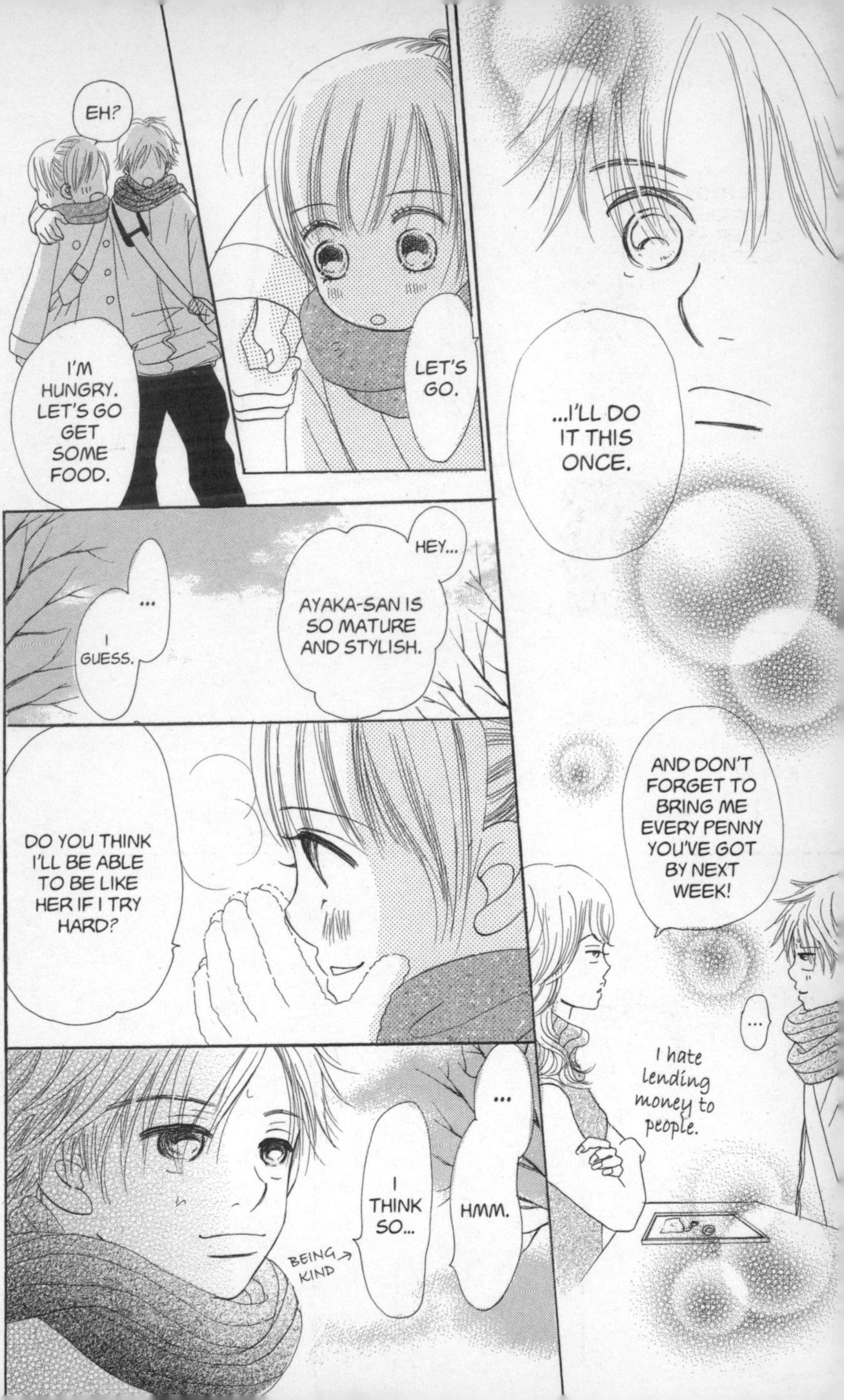

...I'LL DO IT THIS ONCE.
AND DON'T FORGET TO BRING ME EVERY PENNY YOU'VE GOT BY NEXT WEEK!
...
I hate lending money to people.
LET'S GO.
EH?
I'M HUNGRY. LET'S GO GET SOME FOOD.
HEY...
AYAKA-SAN IS SO MATURE AND STYLISH.
...
I GUESS.
DO YOU THINK I'LL BE ABLE TO BE LIKE HER IF I TRY HARD?
...
HMM.
I THINK SO...
BEING KIND

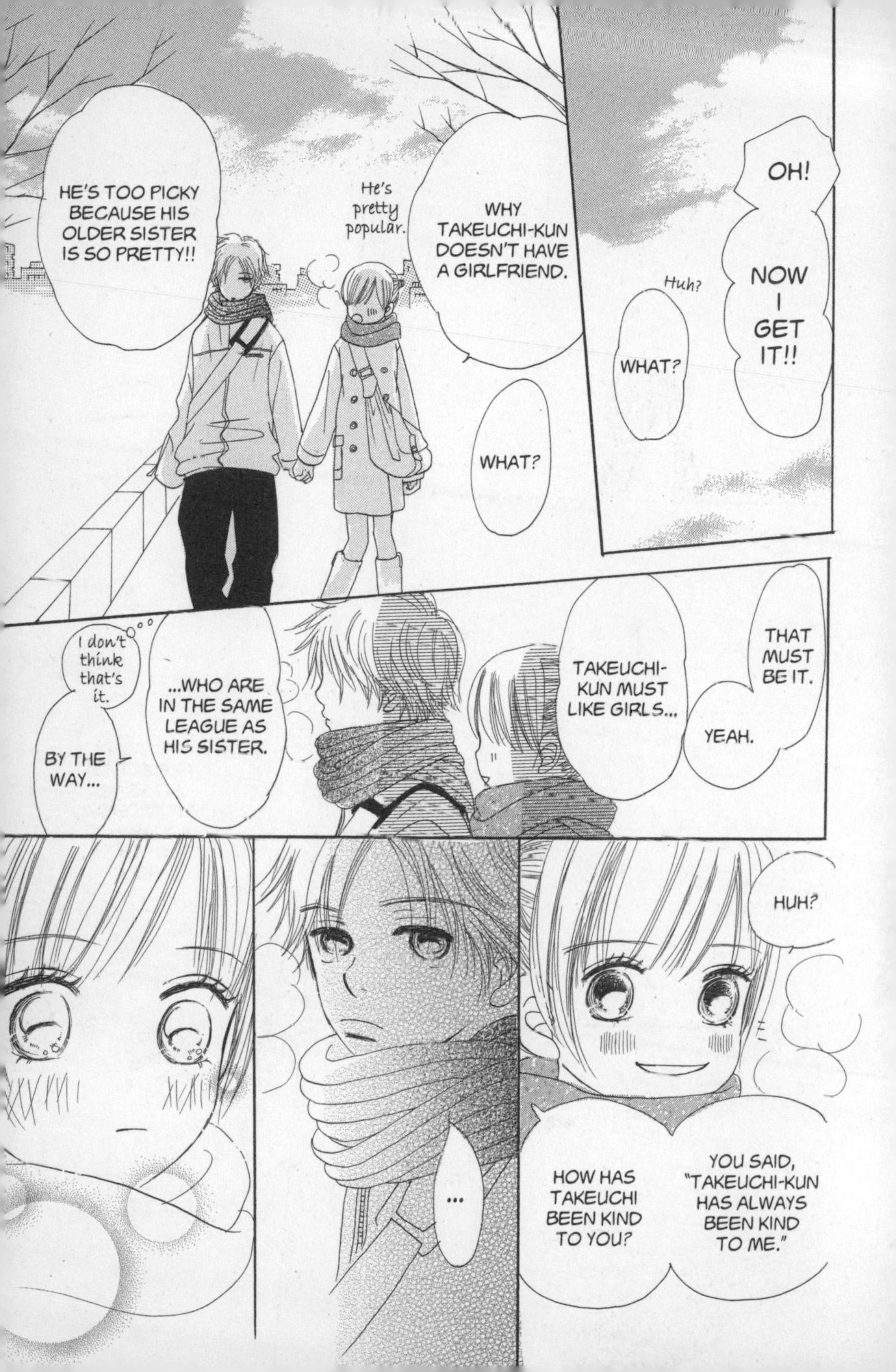
OH!
NOW I GET IT!!
Huh?
WHAT?
WHY TAKEUCHI-KUN DOESN'T HAVE A GIRLFRIEND.
He's pretty popular.
WHAT?
HE'S TOO PICKY BECAUSE HIS OLDER SISTER IS SO PRETTY!!
THAT MUST BE IT.
YEAH.
TAKEUCHI-KUN MUST LIKE GIRLS...
...WHO ARE IN THE SAME LEAGUE AS HIS SISTER.
I don't think that's it.
BY THE WAY...
HUH?
YOU SAID, "TAKEUCHI-KUN HAS ALWAYS BEEN KIND TO ME."
HOW HAS TAKEUCHI BEEN KIND TO YOU?
...

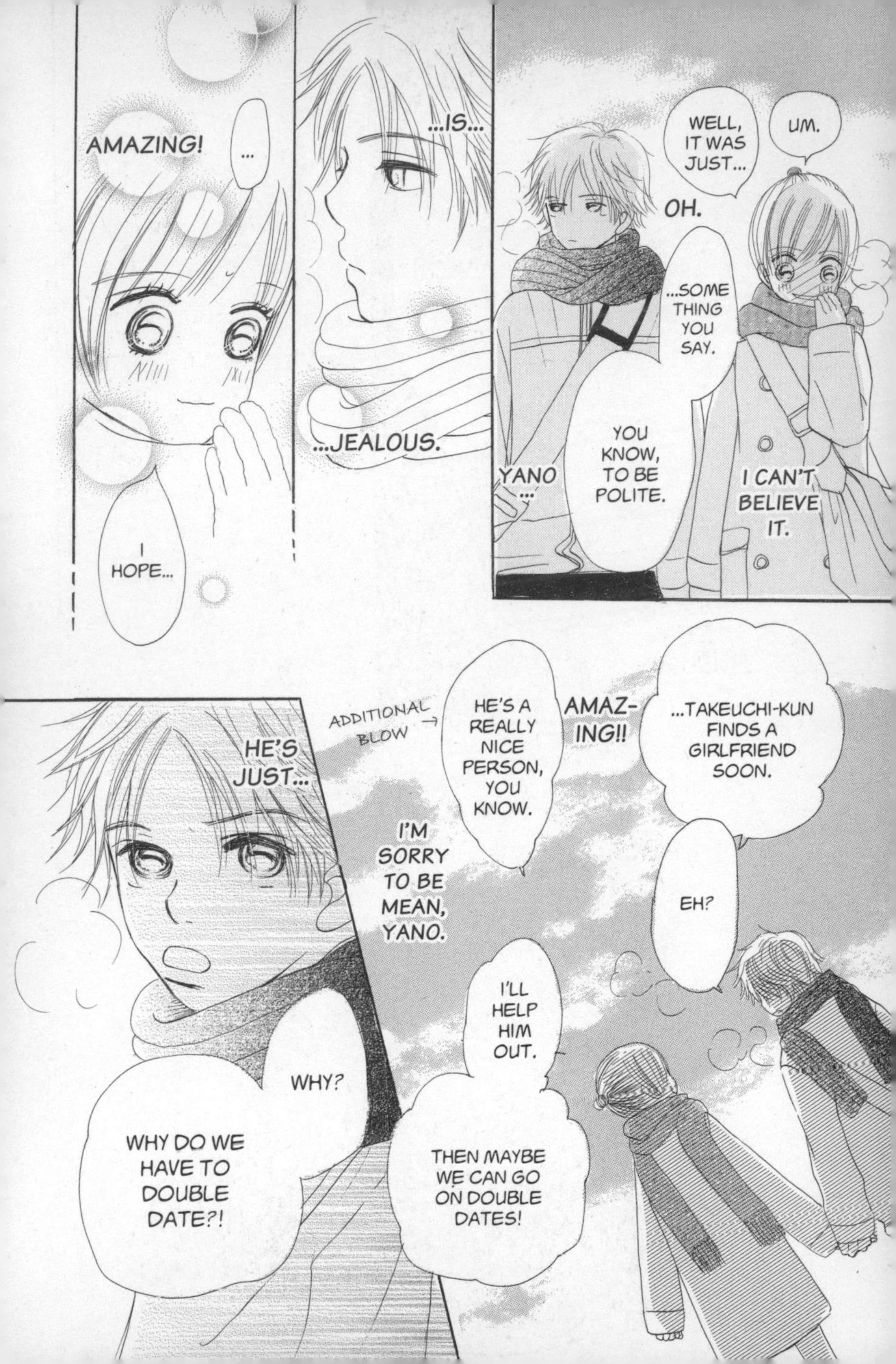
UM.
WELL, IT WAS JUST...
OH.
...SOME THING YOU SAY.
I CAN'T BELIEVE IT.
YOU KNOW, TO BE POLITE.
YANO...
...IS...
...JEALOUS.
...
AMAZING!
I HOPE...
...TAKEUCHI-KUN FINDS A GIRLFRIEND SOON.
AMAZ-ING!!
HE'S A REALLY NICE PERSON, YOU KNOW.
ADDITIONAL BLOW →
EH?
I'M SORRY TO BE MEAN, YANO.
I'LL HELP HIM OUT.
THEN MAYBE WE CAN GO ON DOUBLE DATES!
HE'S JUST...
WHY?
WHY DO WE HAVE TO DOUBLE DATE?!

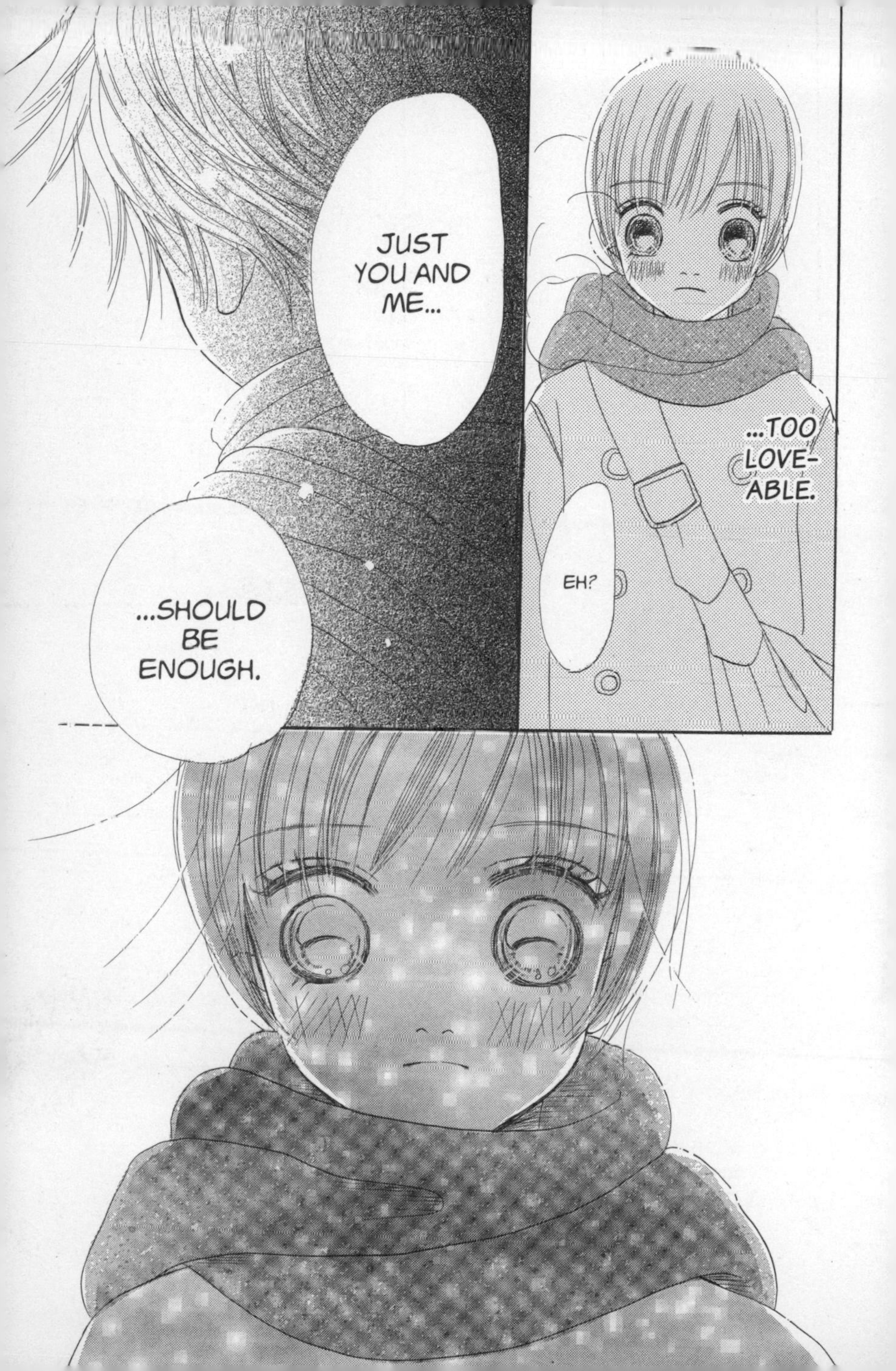
...TOO LOVE-ABLE.
EH?
JUST YOU AND ME...
...SHOULD BE ENOUGH.

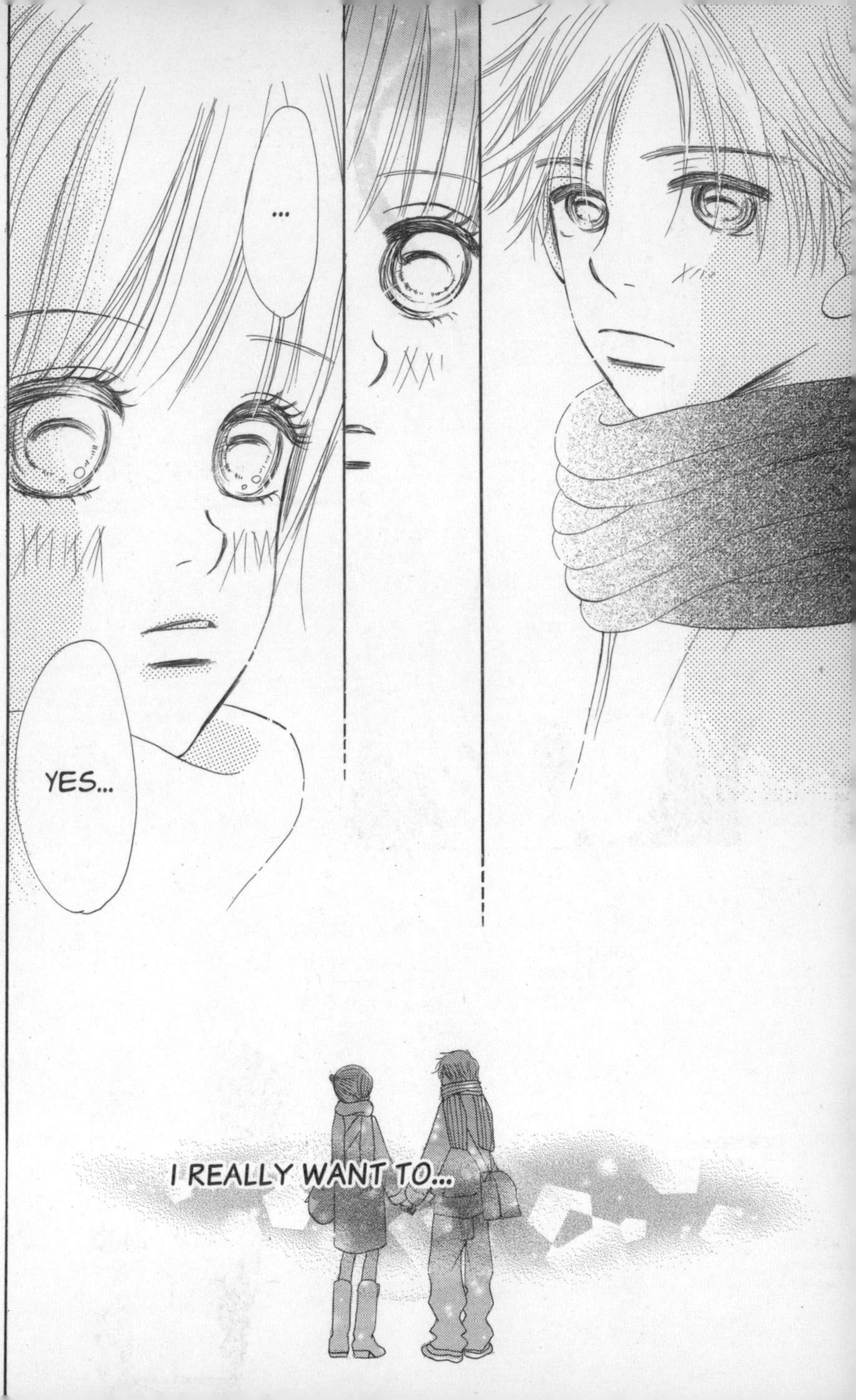
...
YES...
I REALLY WANT TO...

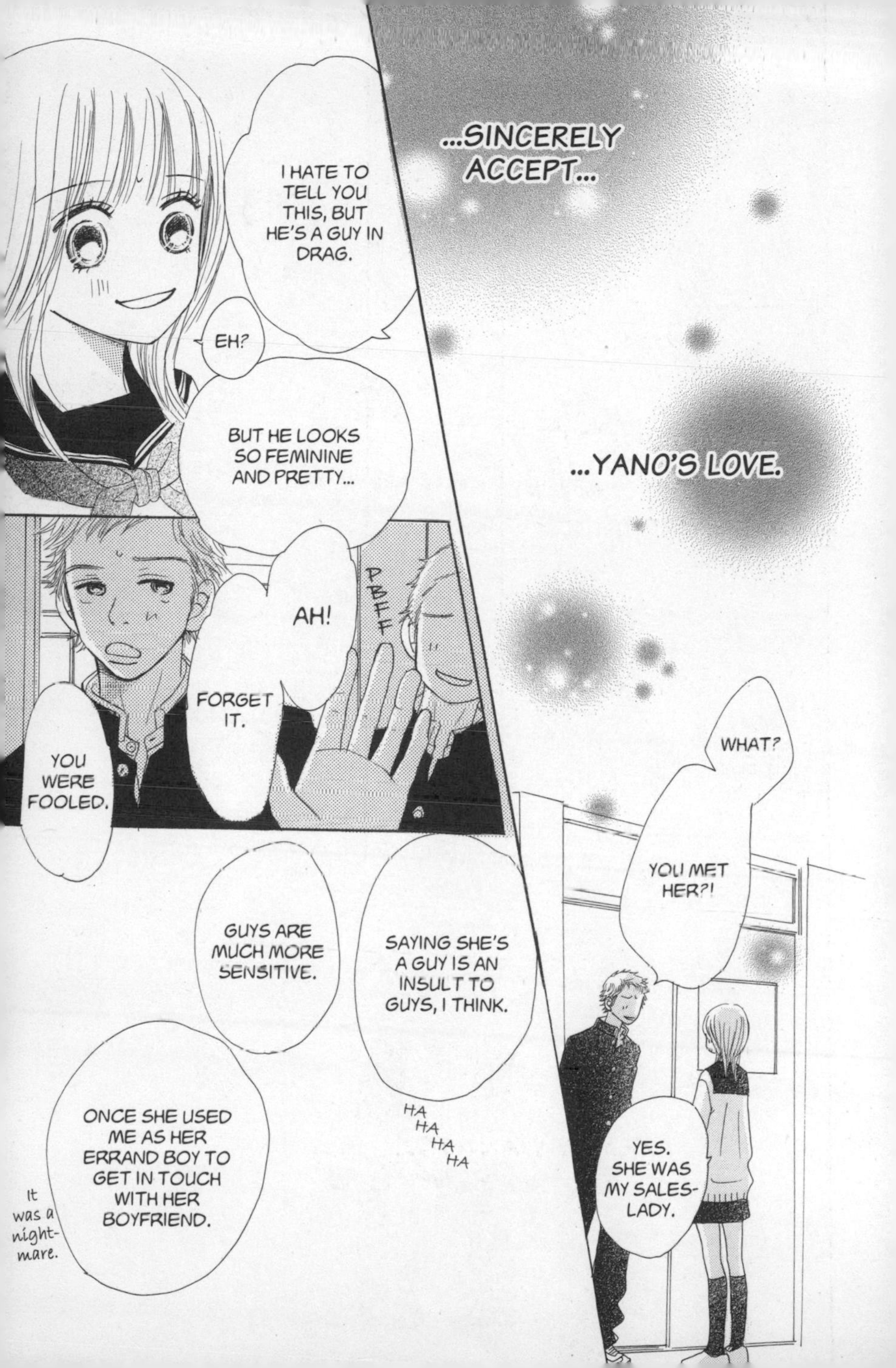
...SINCERELY ACCEPT...
...YANO'S LOVE.
WHAT?
YOU MET HER?!
YES. SHE WAS MY SALES-LADY.
I HATE TO TELL YOU THIS, BUT HE'S A GUY IN DRAG.
EH?
BUT HE LOOKS SO FEMININE AND PRETTY...
AH!
PBFF
FORGET IT.
YOU WERE FOOLED.
SAYING SHE'S A GUY IS AN INSULT TO GUYS, I THINK.
GUYS ARE MUCH MORE SENSITIVE.
HA HA HA HA
ONCE SHE USED ME AS HER ERRAND BOY TO GET IN TOUCH WITH HER BOYFRIEND.
It was a night-mare.

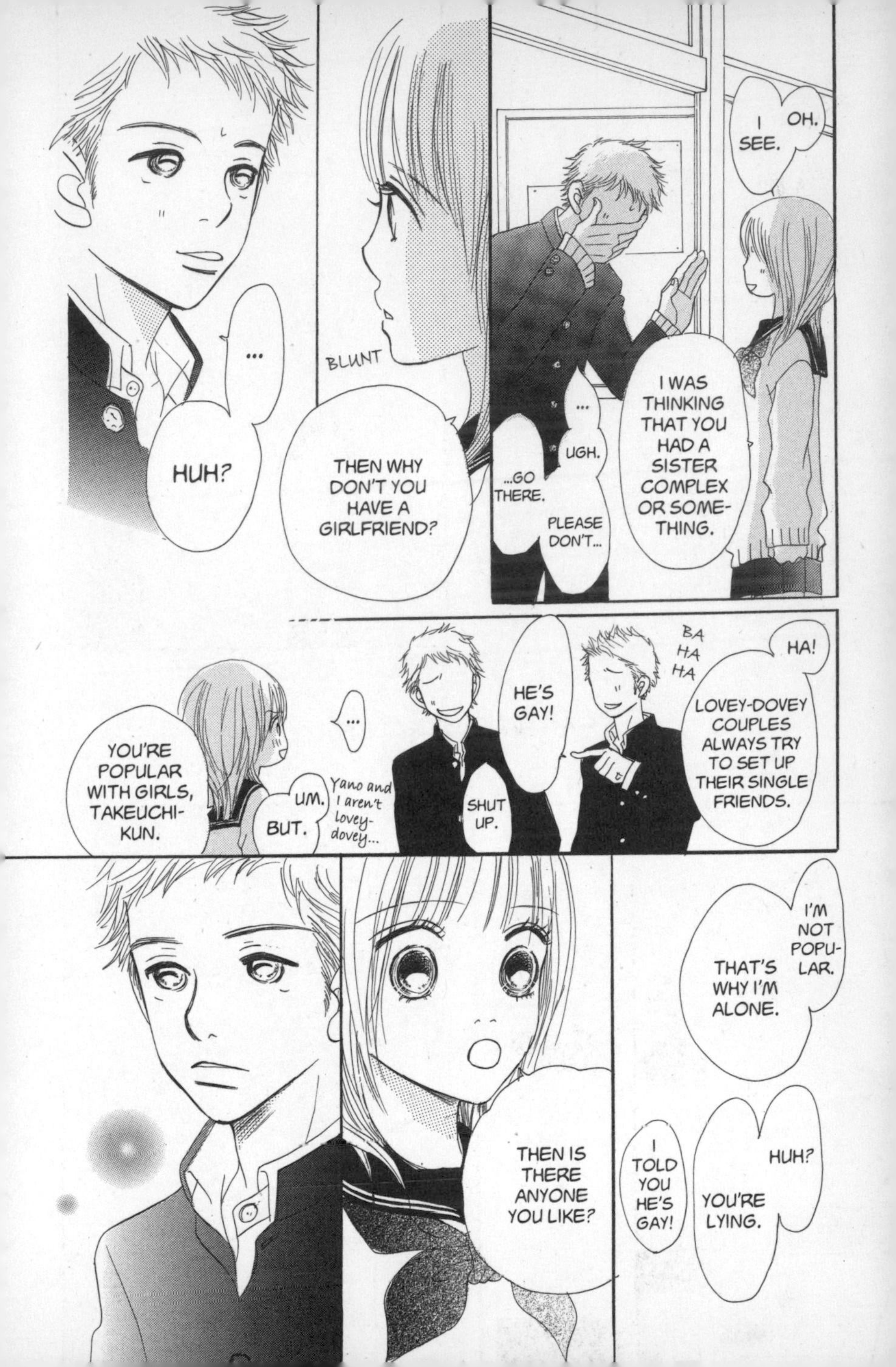

OH.
I SEE.
I WAS THINKING THAT YOU HAD A SISTER COMPLEX OR SOME-THING.
...
UGH.
...GO THERE.
PLEASE DON'T...
BLUNT
THEN WHY DON'T YOU HAVE A GIRLFRIEND?
...
HUH?
HA!
BA HA HA
LOVEY-DOVEY COUPLES ALWAYS TRY TO SET UP THEIR SINGLE FRIENDS.
HE'S GAY!
SHUT UP.
...
Yano and I aren't lovey-dovey...
UM.
BUT.
YOU'RE POPULAR WITH GIRLS, TAKEUCHI-KUN.
I'M NOT POPU-LAR.
THAT'S WHY I'M ALONE.
HUH?
YOU'RE LYING.
I TOLD YOU HE'S GAY!
THEN IS THERE ANYONE YOU LIKE?

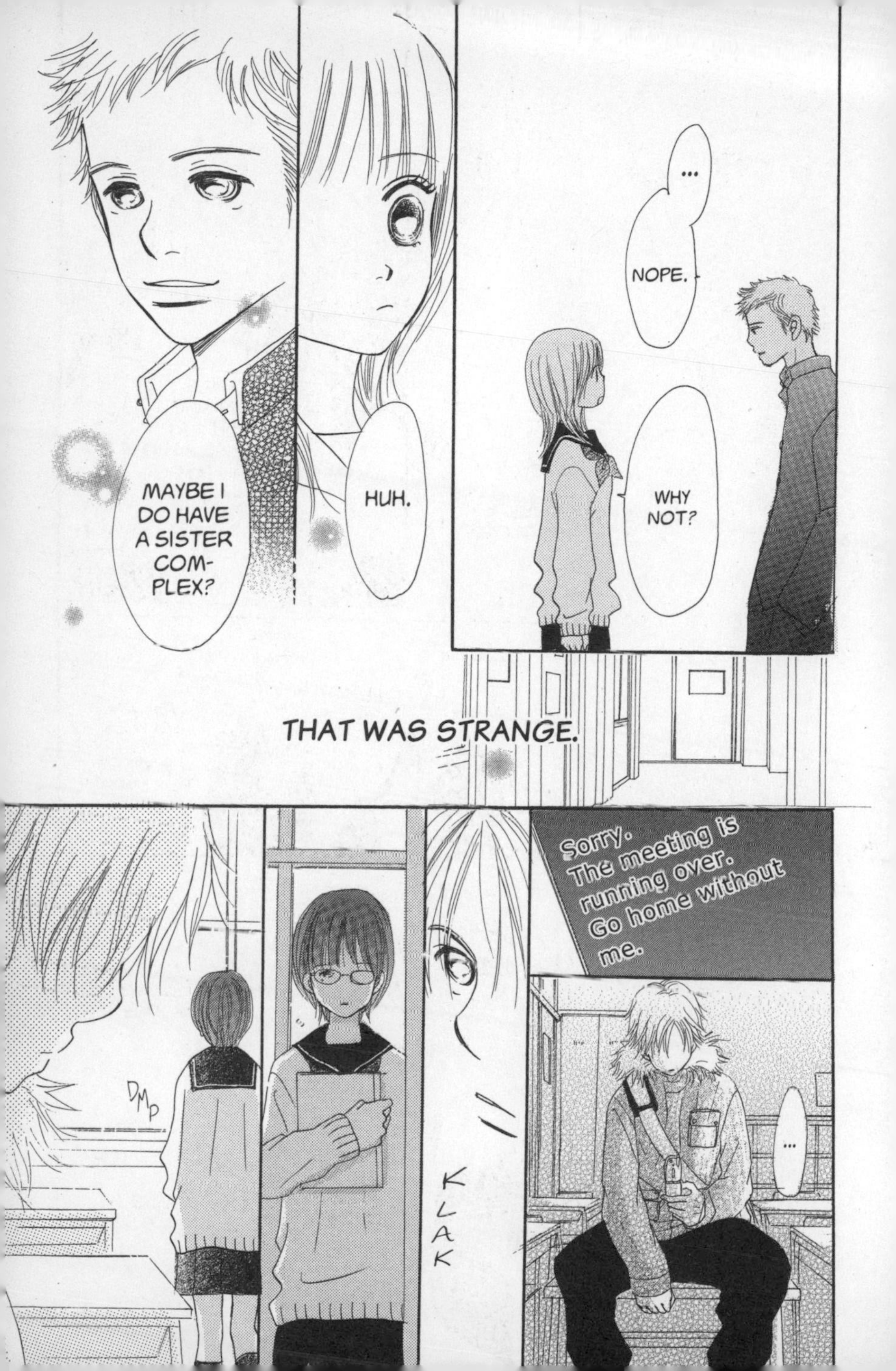
...
NOPE.
WHY NOT?
HUH.
MAYBE I DO HAVE A SISTER COMPLEX?
THAT WAS STRANGE.
Sorry. The meeting is running over. Go home without me.
...
KLAK
DMP

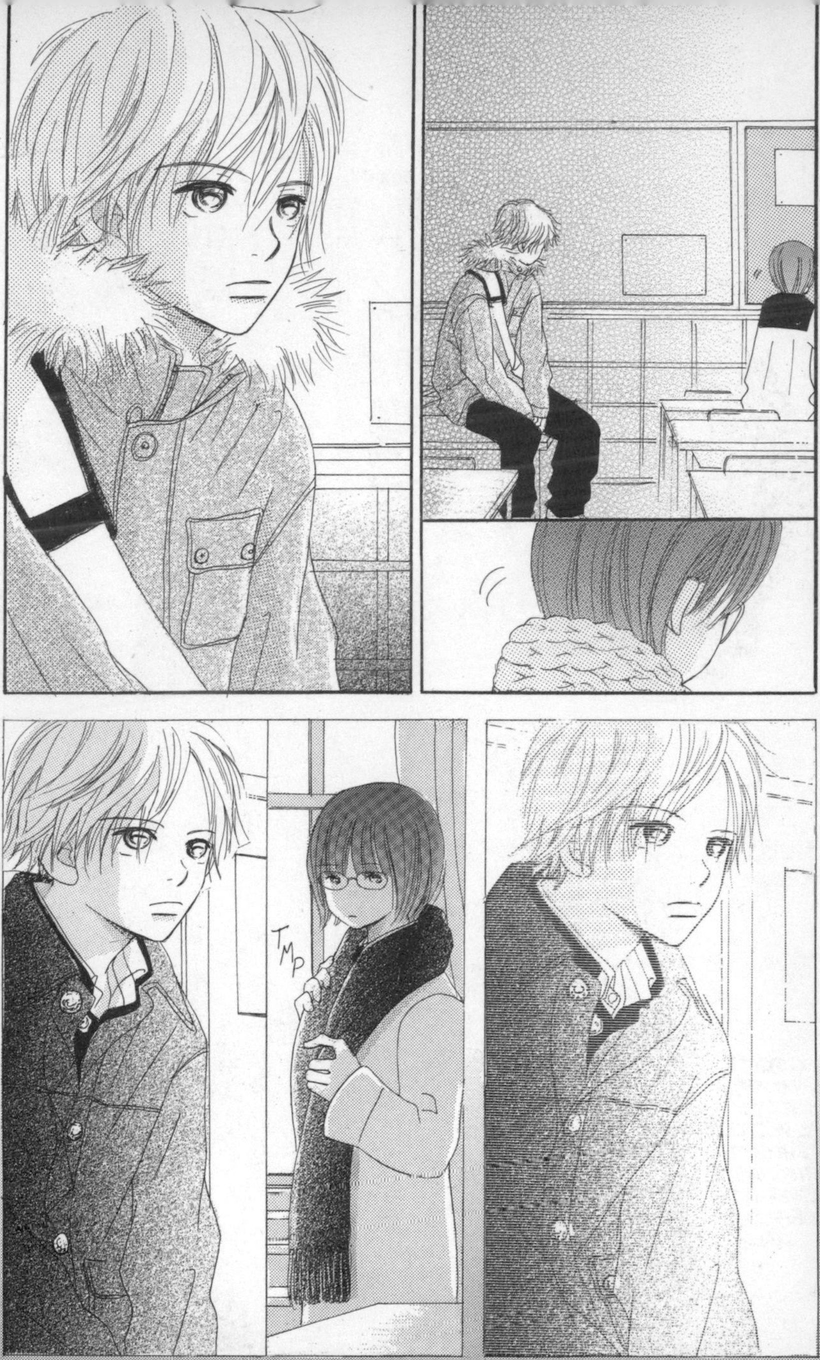
TMP

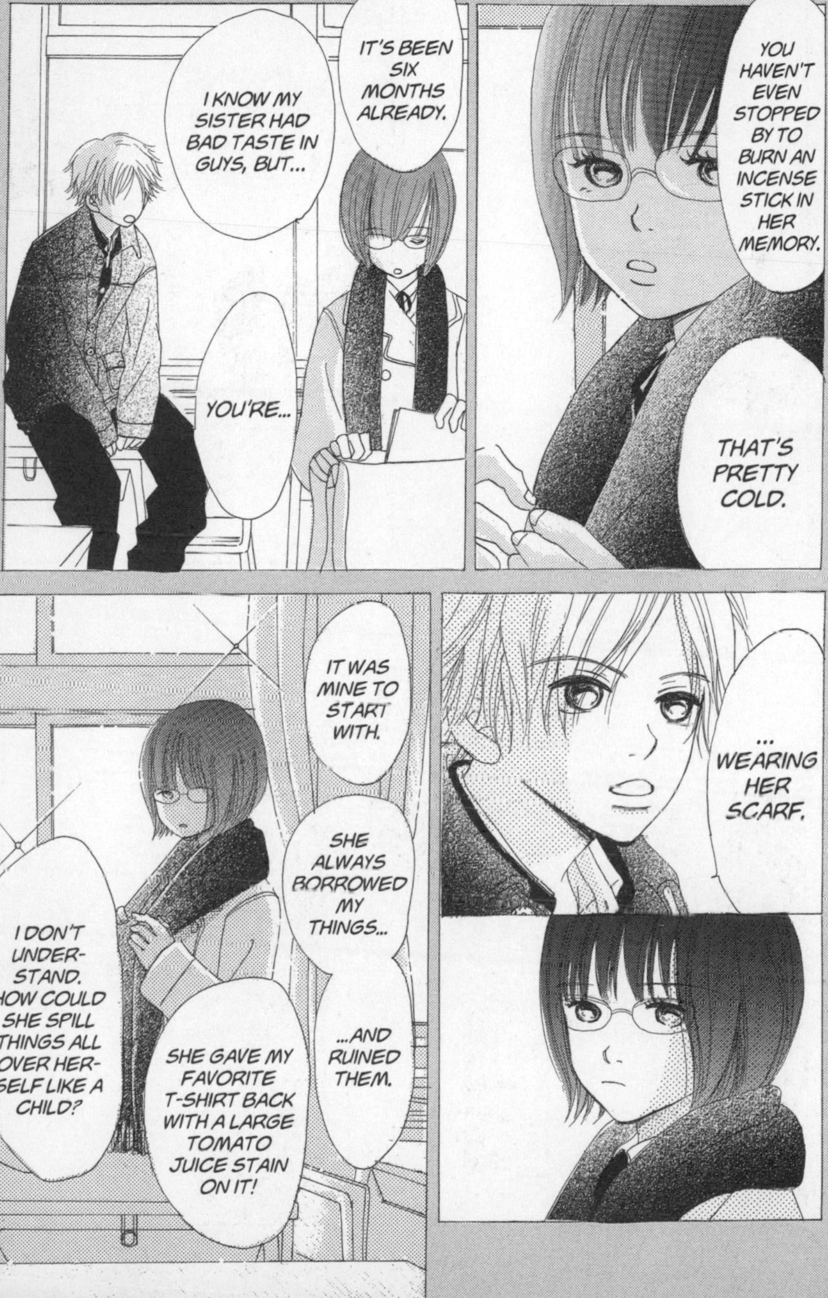
YOU HAVEN'T EVEN STOPPED BY TO BURN AN INCENSE STICK IN HER MEMORY.
THAT'S PRETTY COLD.
IT'S BEEN SIX MONTHS ALREADY.
I KNOW MY SISTER HAD BAD TASTE IN GUYS, BUT...
YOU'RE...
... WEARING HER SCARF.
IT WAS MINE TO START WITH.
SHE ALWAYS BORROWED MY THINGS...
...AND RUINED THEM.
SHE GAVE MY FAVORITE T-SHIRT BACK WITH A LARGE TOMATO JUICE STAIN ON IT!
I DON'T UNDER-STAND. HOW COULD SHE SPILL THINGS ALL OVER HER-SELF LIKE A CHILD?

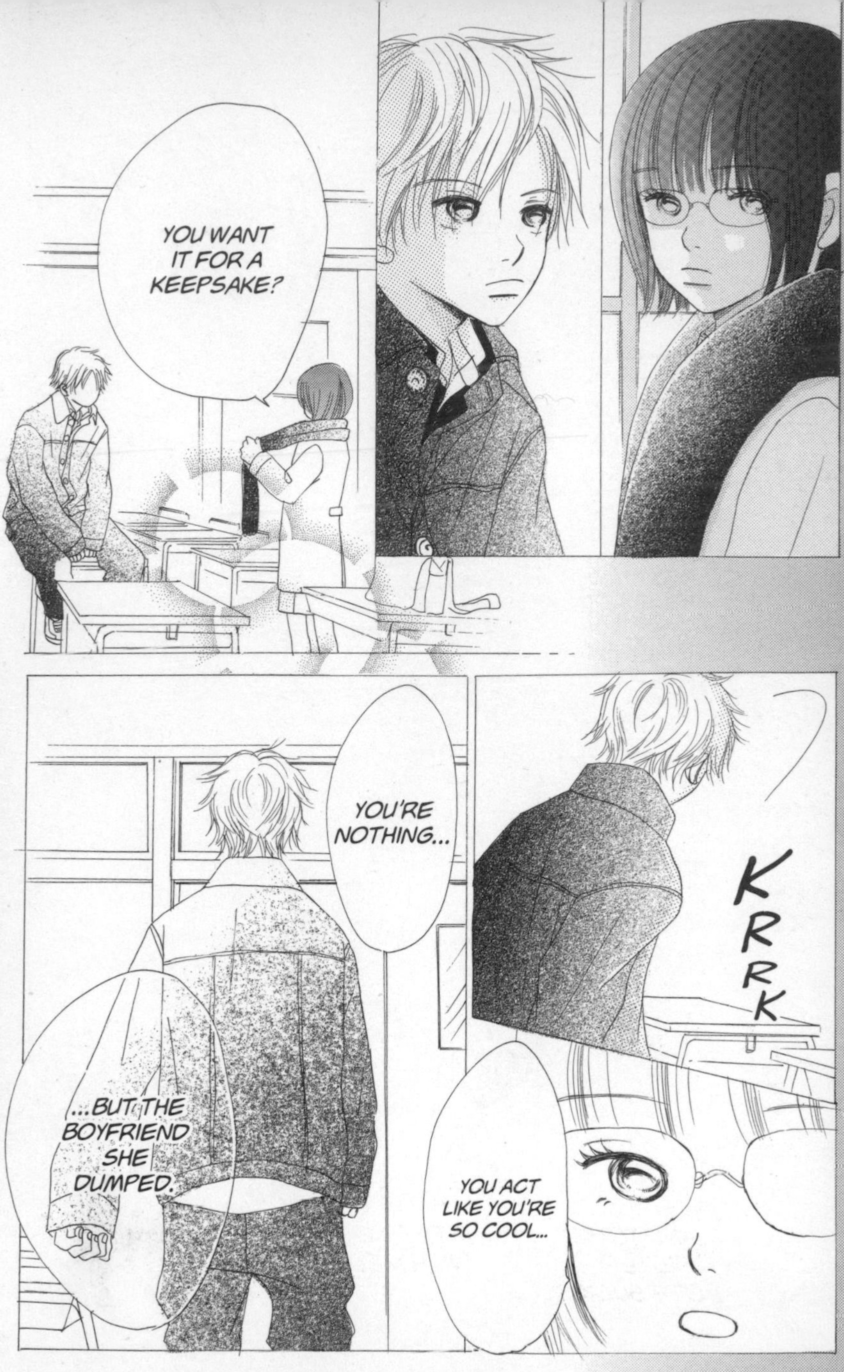
YOU WANT IT FOR A KEEPSAKE?
KRRK
YOU ACT LIKE YOU'RE SO COOL...
YOU'RE NOTHING...
...BUT THE BOYFRIEND SHE DUMPED.

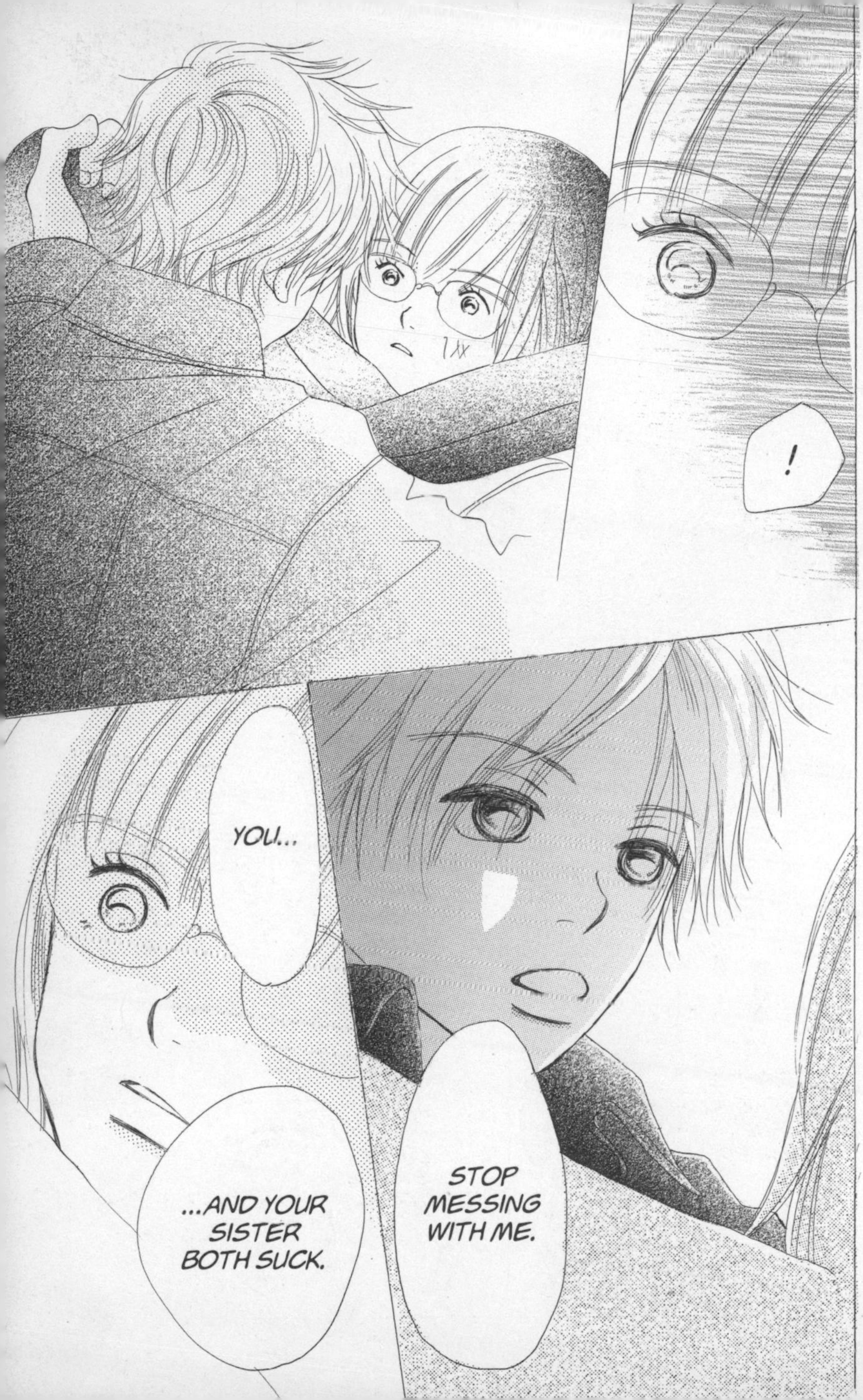
!
STOP MESSING WITH ME.
YOU...
...AND YOUR SISTER BOTH SUCK.

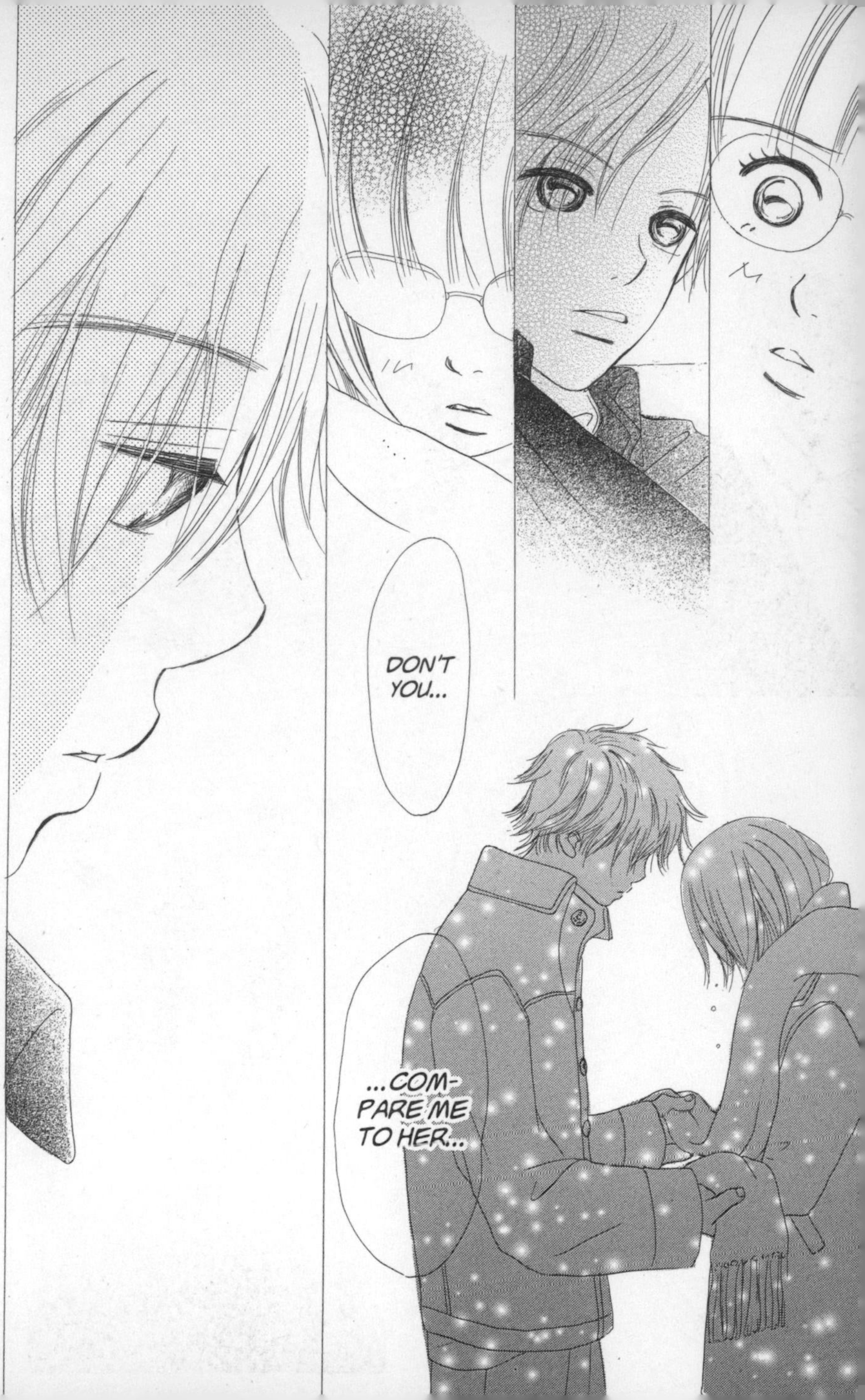
DON'T YOU...
...COM-PARE ME TO HER...

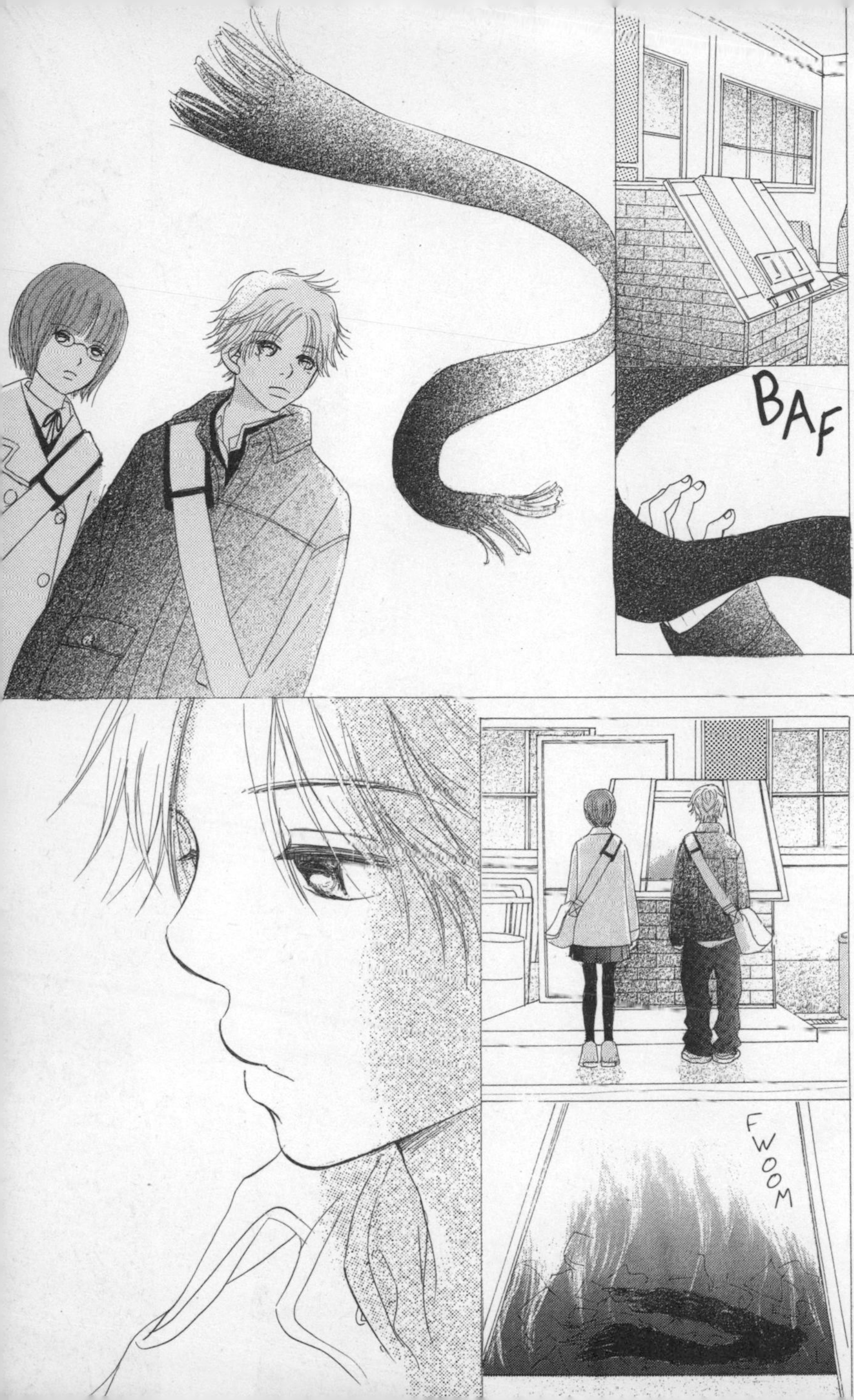
BAF
FWOOM

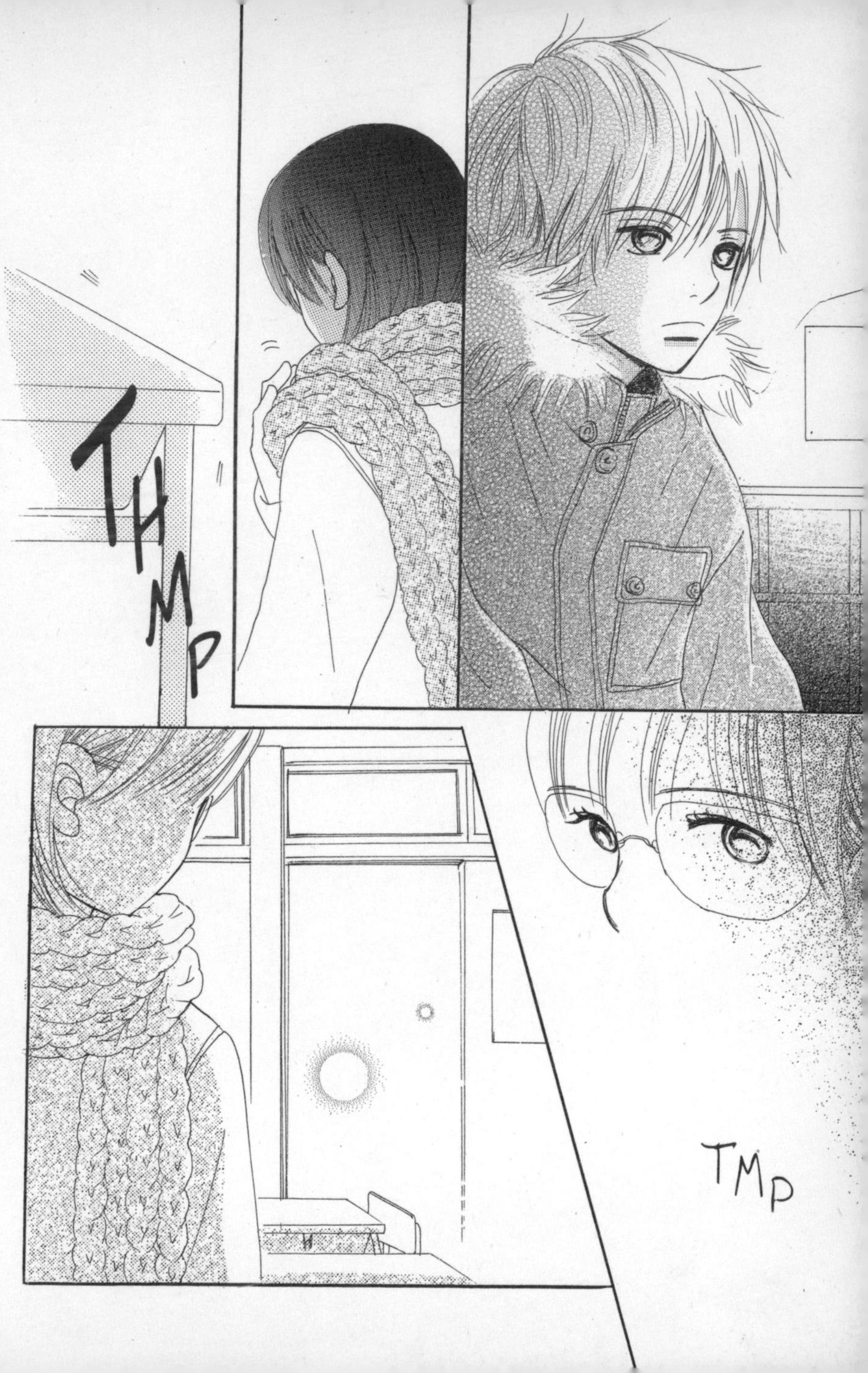
THMP
TMP

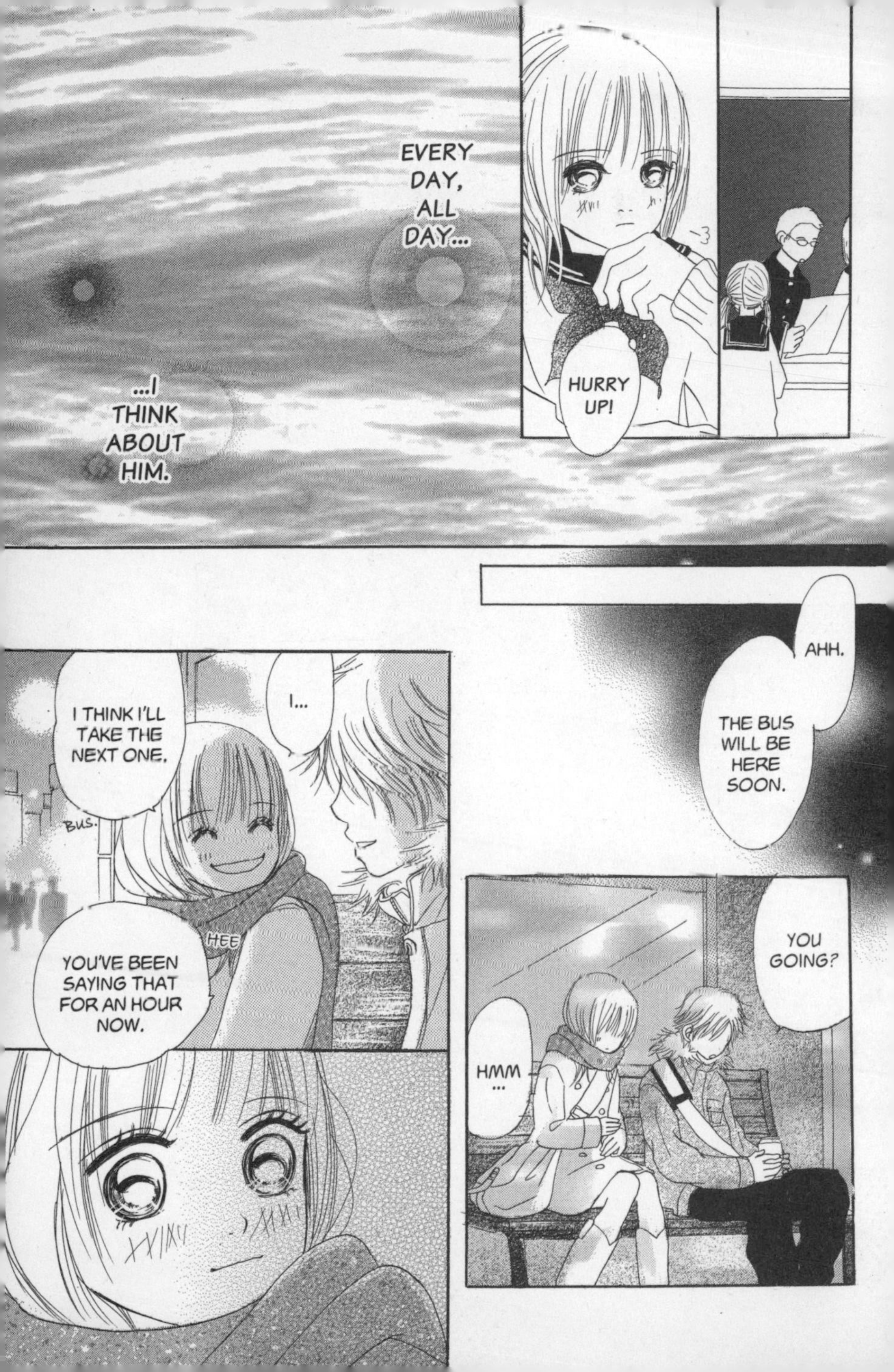
HURRY UP!
EVERY DAY, ALL DAY...
...I THINK ABOUT HIM.
AHH.
THE BUS WILL BE HERE SOON.
YOU GOING?
HMM...
I...
I THINK I'LL TAKE THE NEXT ONE.
BUS.
HEE
YOU'VE BEEN SAYING THAT FOR AN HOUR NOW.

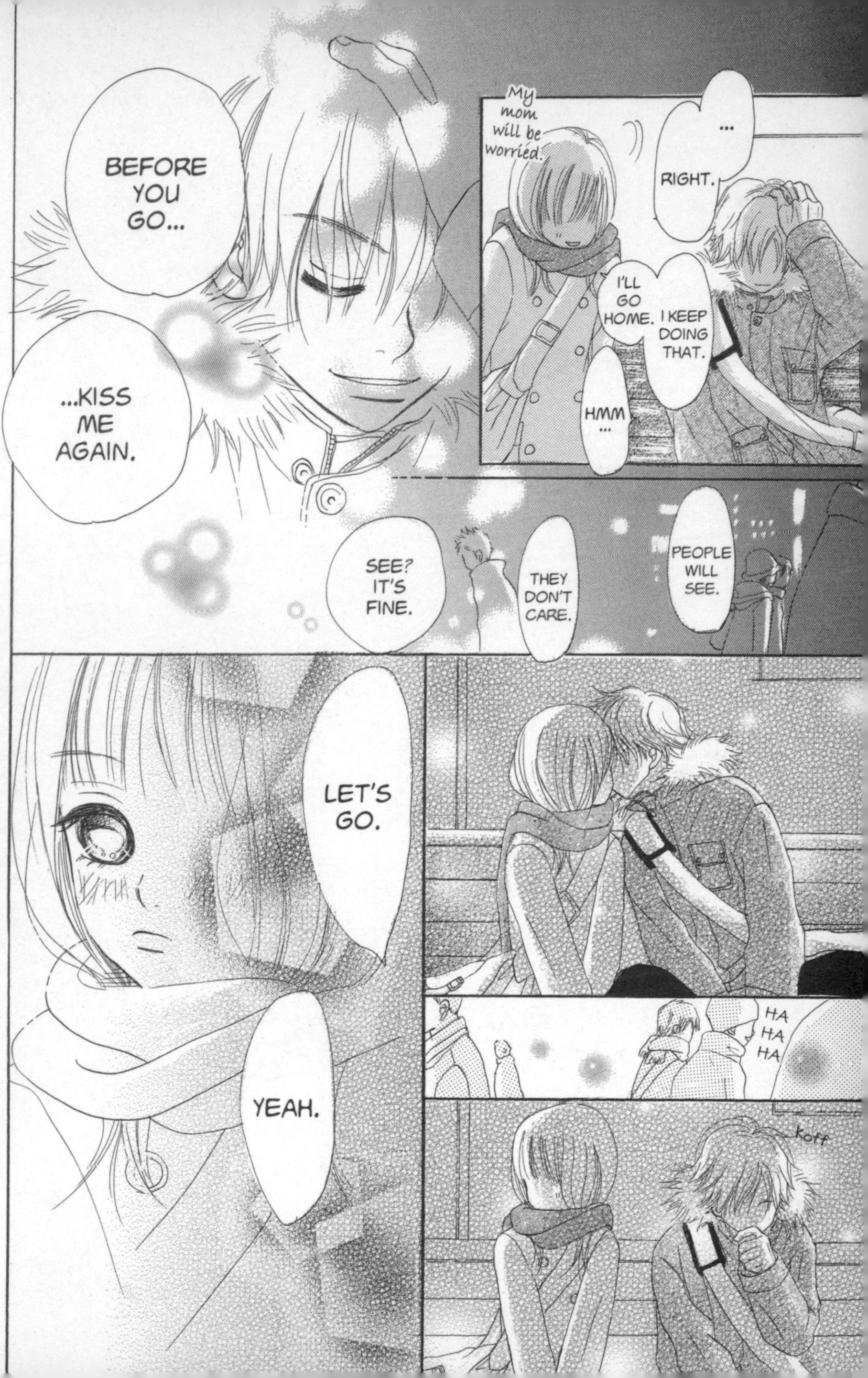
...
RIGHT.
My mom will be worried.
I KEEP DOING THAT.
I'LL GO HOME.
HMM...
BEFORE YOU GO...
...KISS ME AGAIN.
PEOPLE WILL SEE.
THEY DON'T CARE.
SEE? IT'S FINE.
HA HA HA
koff
LET'S GO.
YEAH.

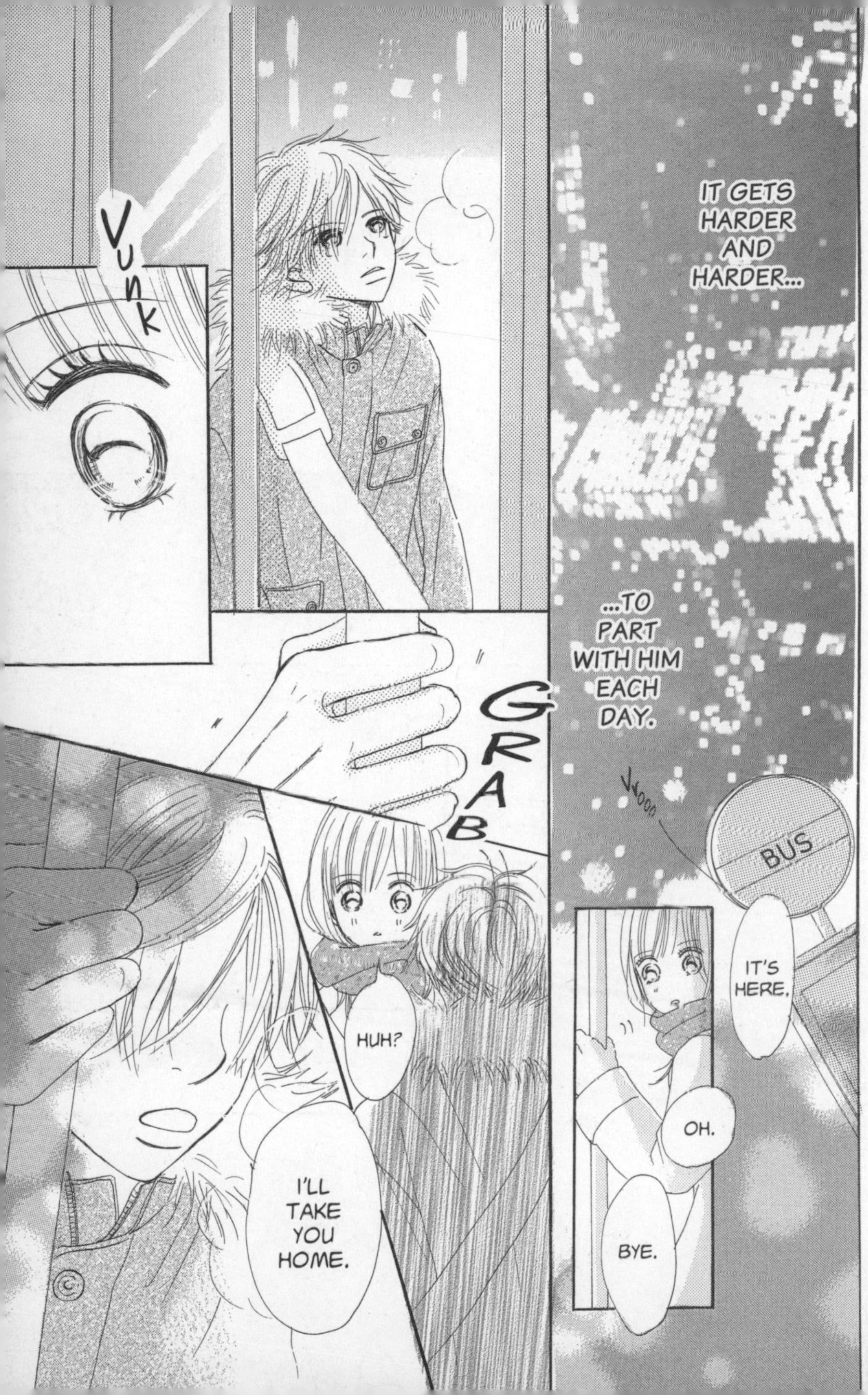
IT GETS HARDER AND HARDER...
...TO PART WITH HIM EACH DAY.
Vwooo
BUS
IT'S HERE.
OH.
BYE.
VUNK
GRAB
HUH?
I'LL TAKE YOU HOME.

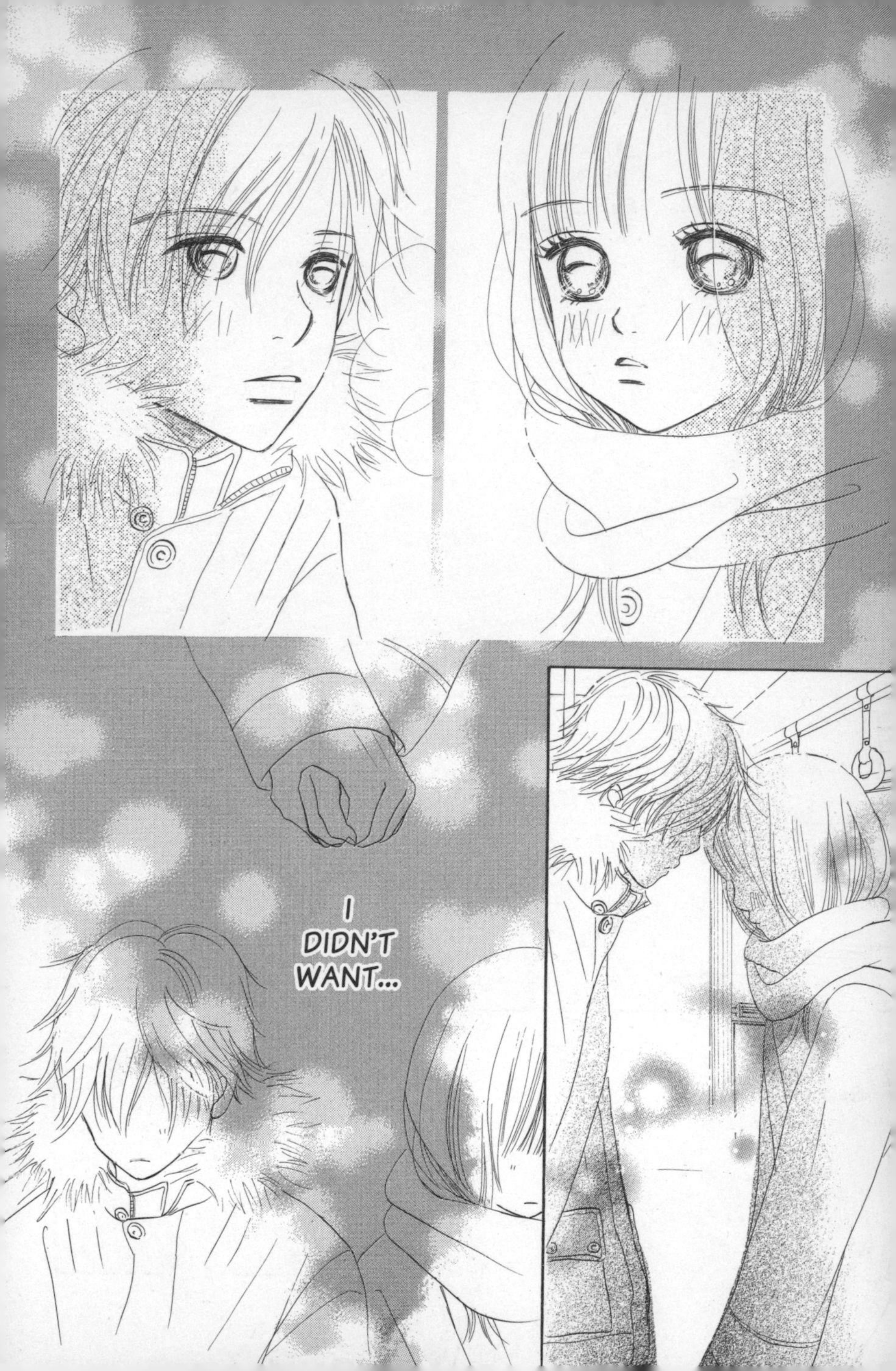
I DIDN'T WANT...

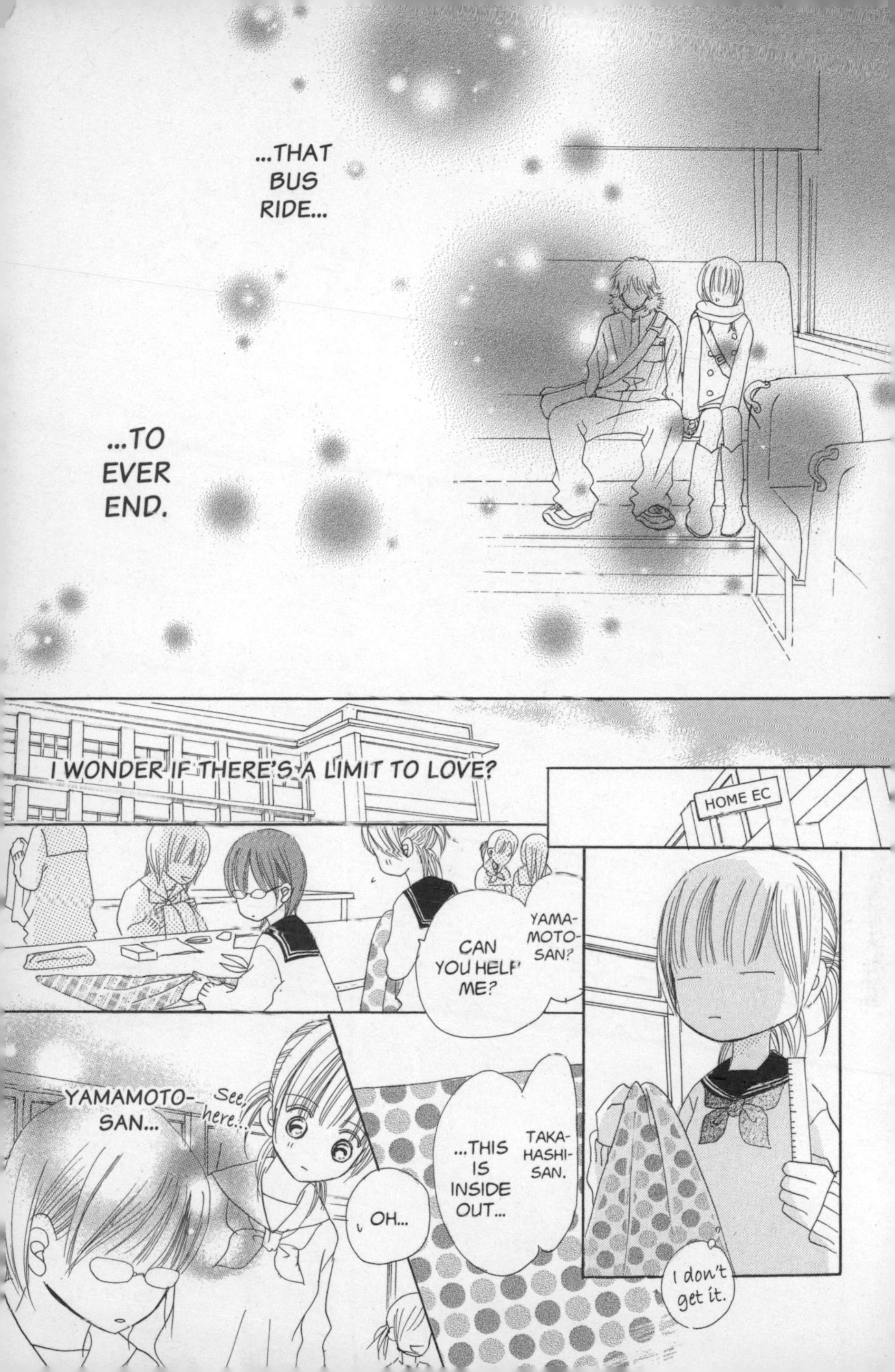
...THAT BUS RIDE...
...TO EVER END.
HOME EC
I WONDER IF THERE'S A LIMIT TO LOVE?
YAMAMOTO-SAN?
TAKAHASHI-SAN.
I don't get it.
CAN YOU HELP ME?
...THIS IS INSIDE OUT...
OH...
See, here...
YAMAMOTO-SAN...

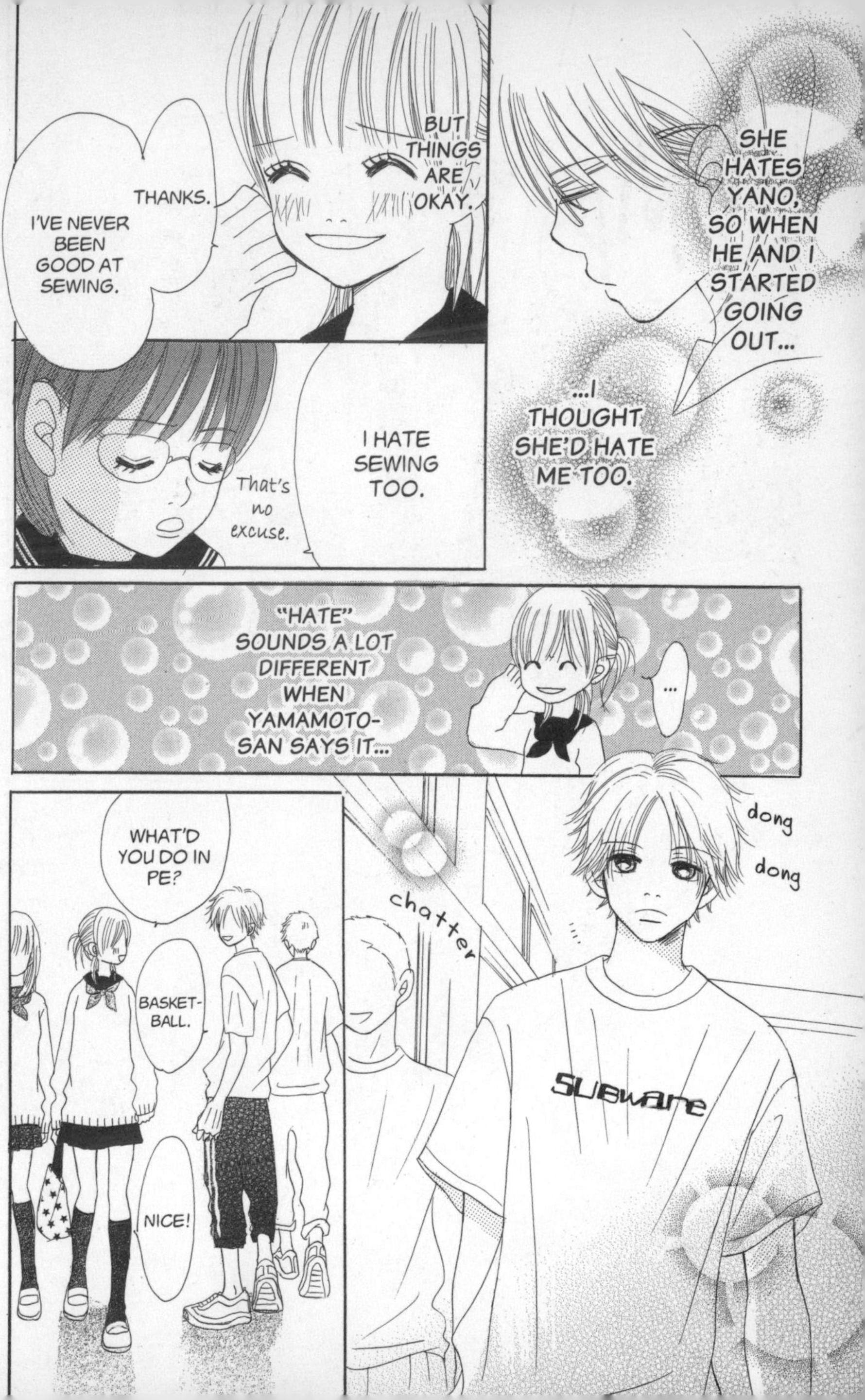
SHE HATES YANO, SO WHEN HE AND I STARTED GOING OUT...
...I THOUGHT SHE'D HATE ME TOO.
BUT THINGS ARE OKAY.
THANKS.
I'VE NEVER BEEN GOOD AT SEWING.
I HATE SEWING TOO.
That's no excuse.
...
"HATE" SOUNDS A LOT DIFFERENT WHEN YAMAMOTO-SAN SAYS IT...
dong
dong
chatter
WHAT'D YOU DO IN PE?
BASKET-BALL.
NICE!

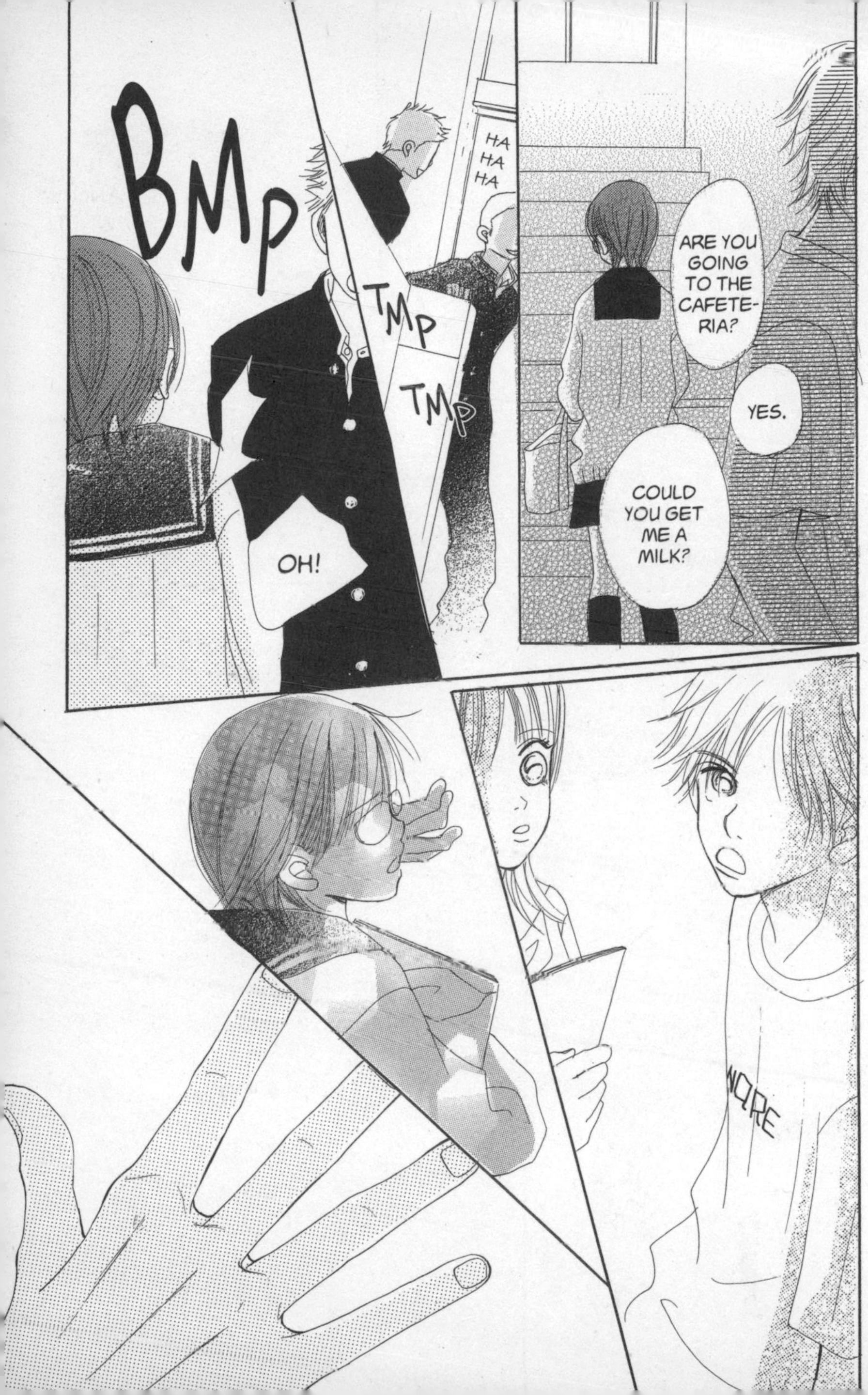
ARE YOU GOING TO THE CAFETERIA?
YES.
COULD YOU GET ME A MILK?
HA HA HA
TMP
TMP
BMP
OH!

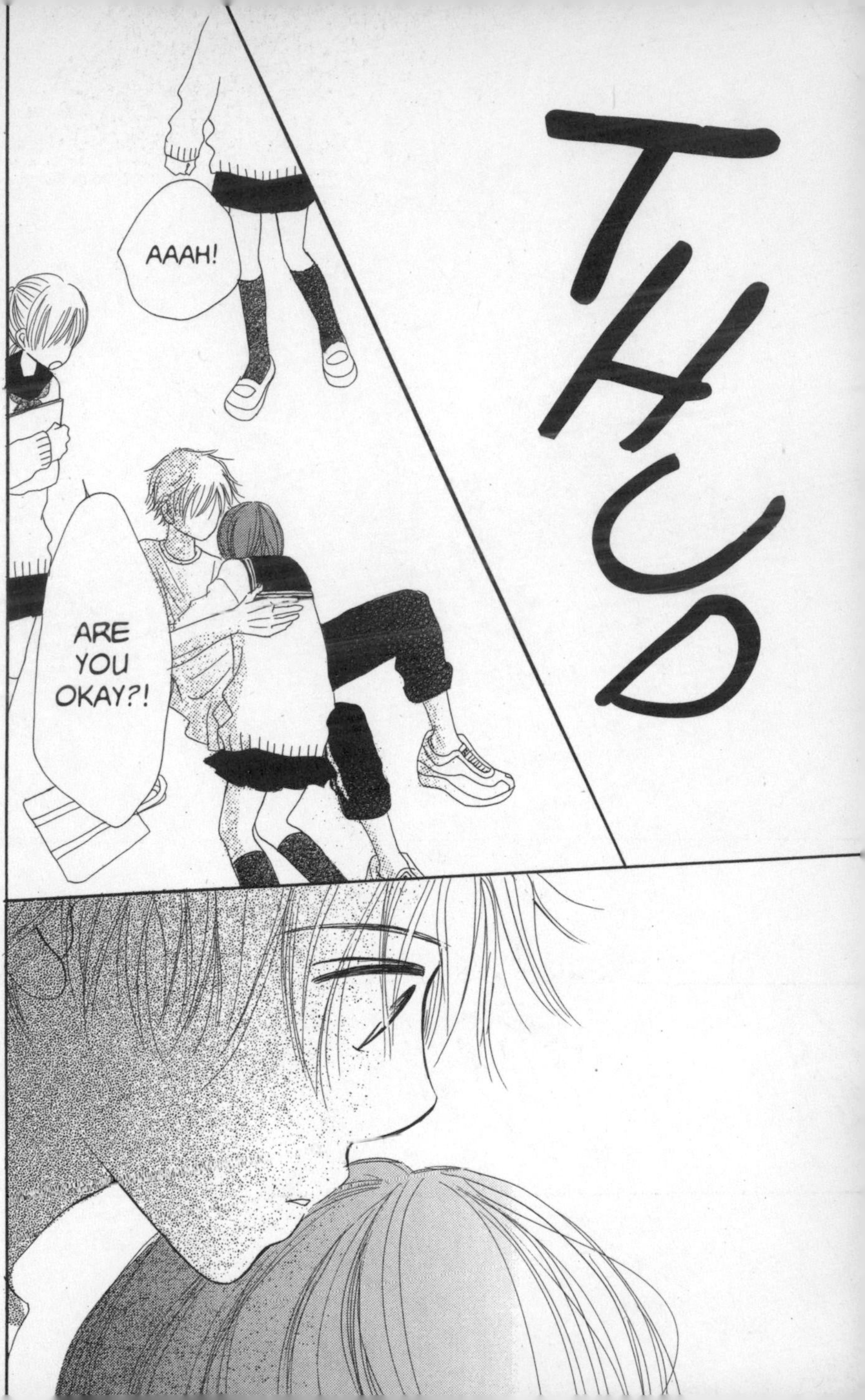
THUD
AAAH!
ARE YOU OKAY?!

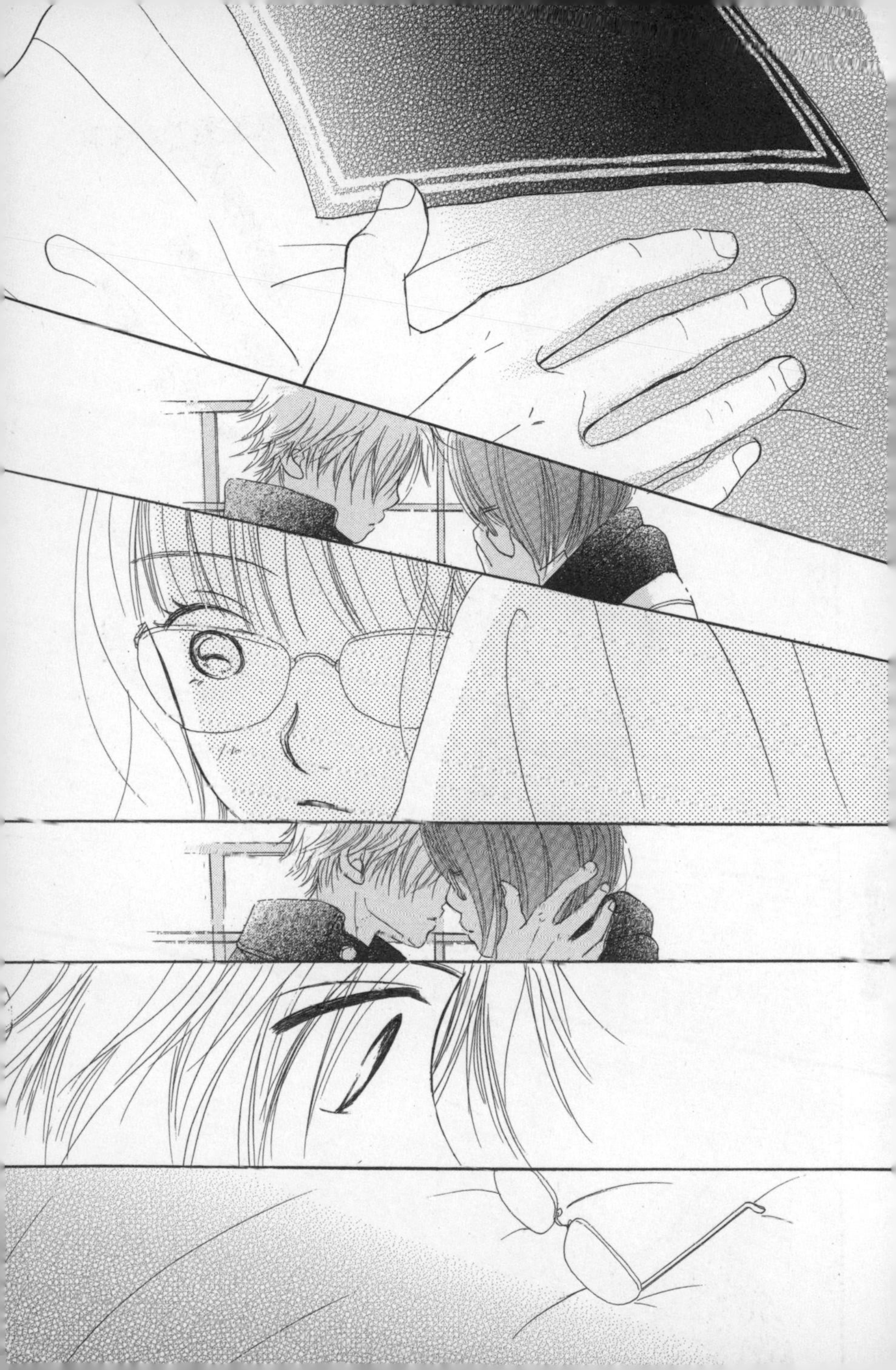

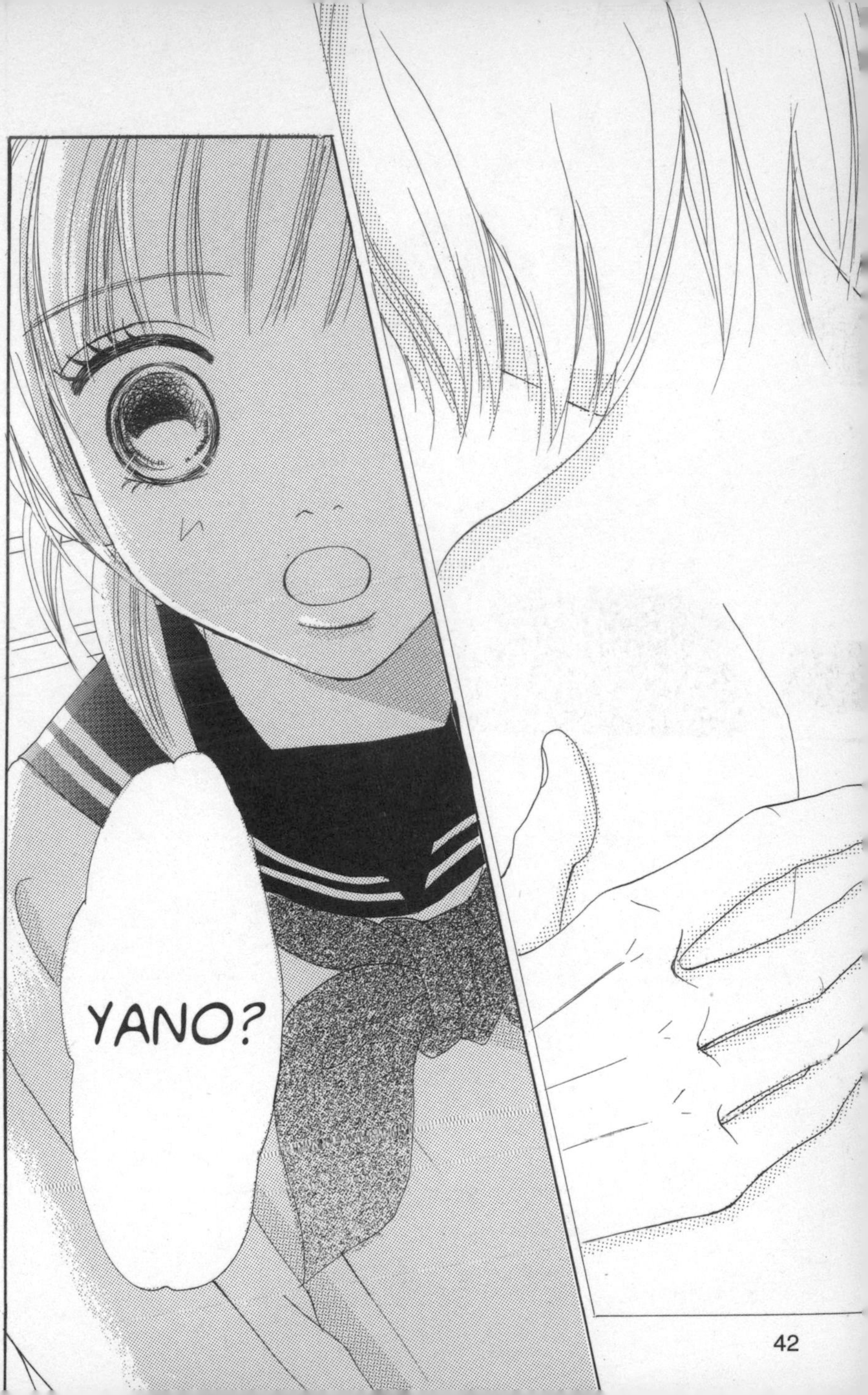
YANO?

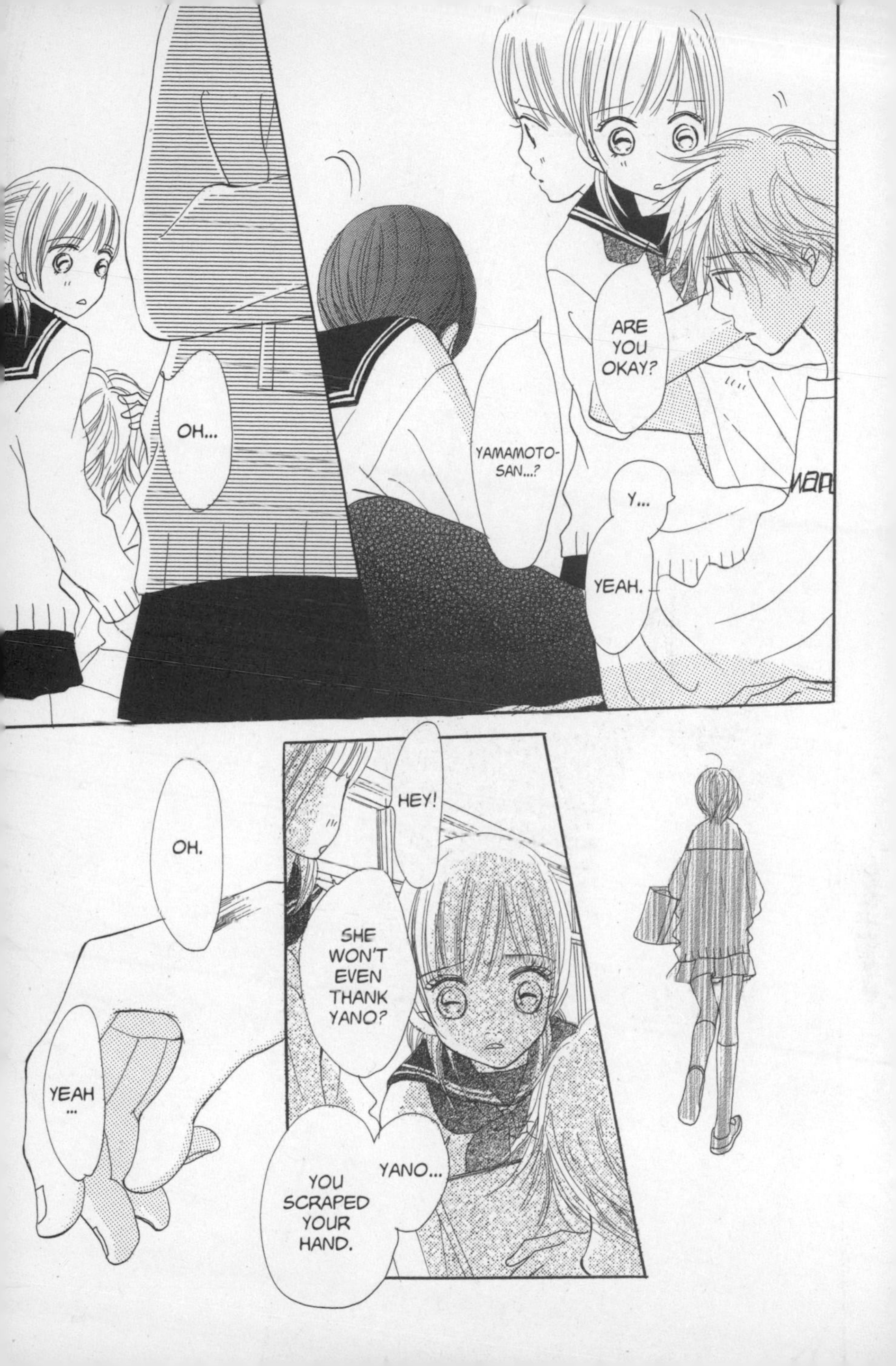
ARE YOU OKAY?
Y...
YEAH.
YAMAMOTO-SAN...?
OH...
HEY!
SHE WON'T EVEN THANK YANO?
YANO...
YOU SCRAPED YOUR HAND.
OH.
YEAH ...

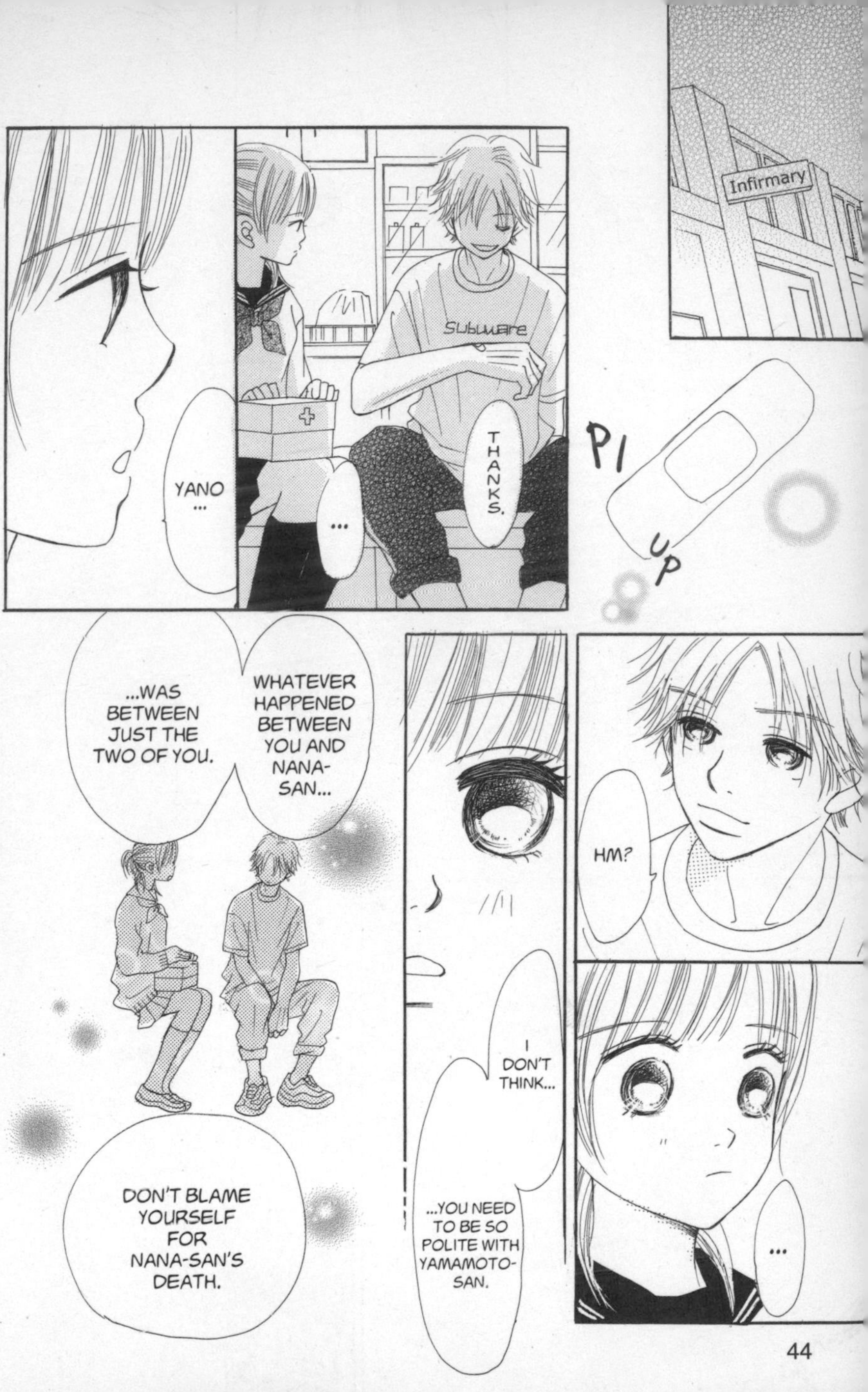
Infirmary
PI
UP
THANKS.
...
YANO
...
HM?
...
I DON'T THINK...
...YOU NEED TO BE SO POLITE WITH YAMAMOTO-SAN.
WHATEVER HAPPENED BETWEEN YOU AND NANA-SAN...
...WAS BETWEEN JUST THE TWO OF YOU.
DON'T BLAME YOURSELF FOR NANA-SAN'S DEATH.

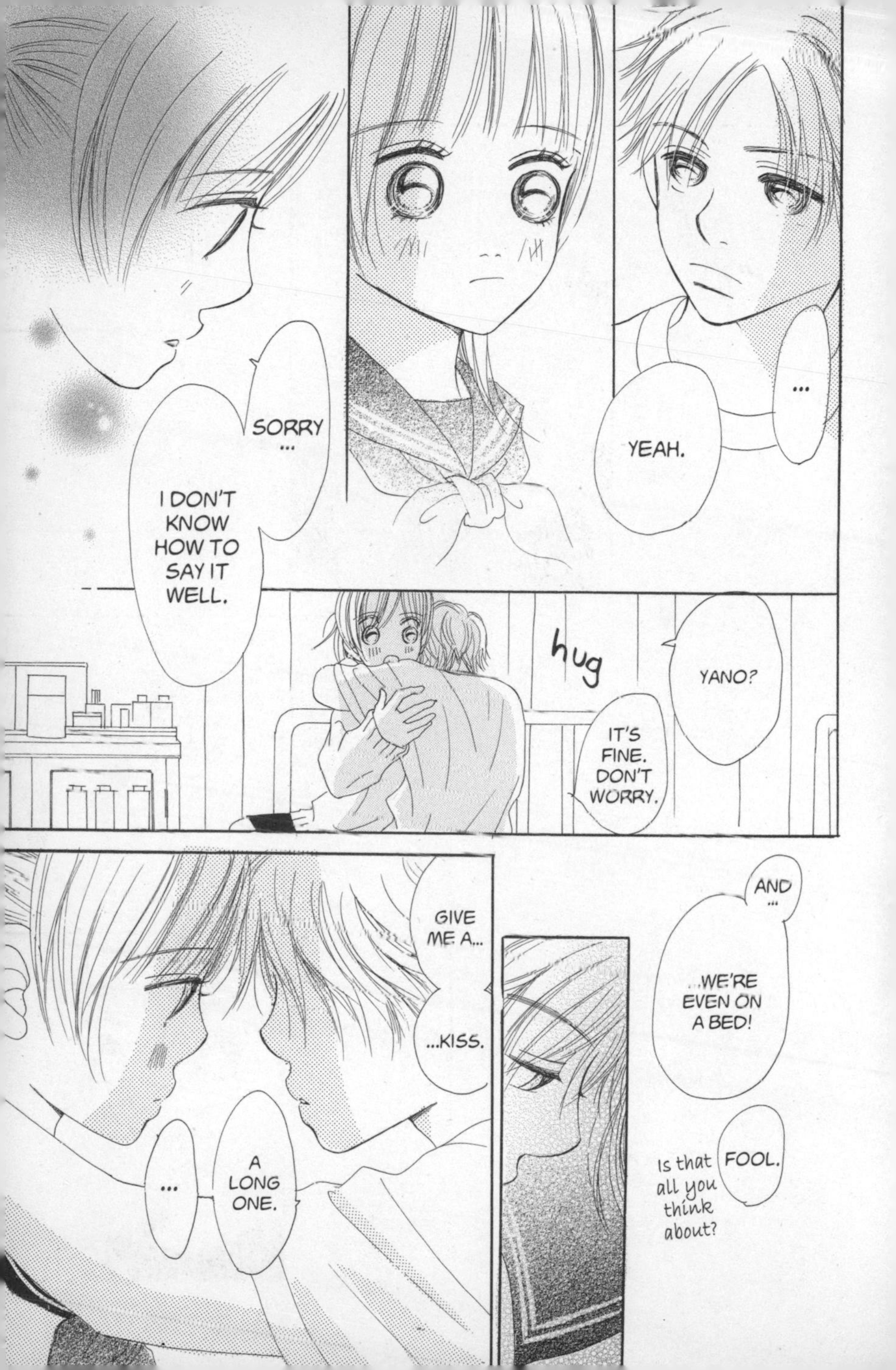
...
YEAH.
SORRY ...
I DON'T KNOW HOW TO SAY IT WELL.
YANO?
IT'S FINE. DON'T WORRY.
hug
AND ...
...WE'RE EVEN ON A BED!
FOOL.
Is that all you think about?
GIVE ME A...
...KISS.
A LONG ONE.
...

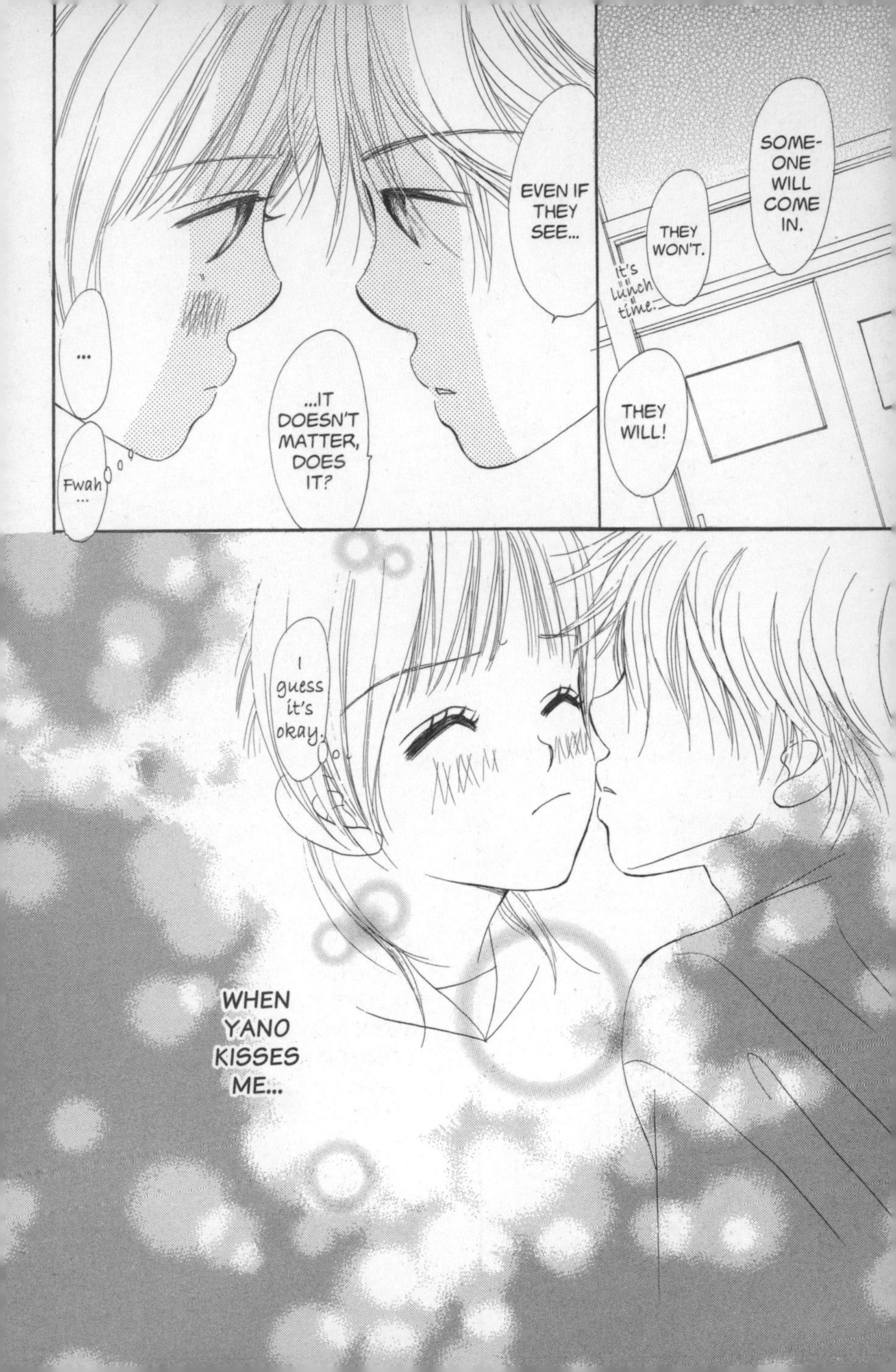
SOME-ONE WILL COME IN.
THEY WON'T.
It's lunch time.
THEY WILL!
EVEN IF THEY SEE...
...IT DOESN'T MATTER, DOES IT?
...
Fwah...
I guess it's okay.
WHEN YANO KISSES ME...

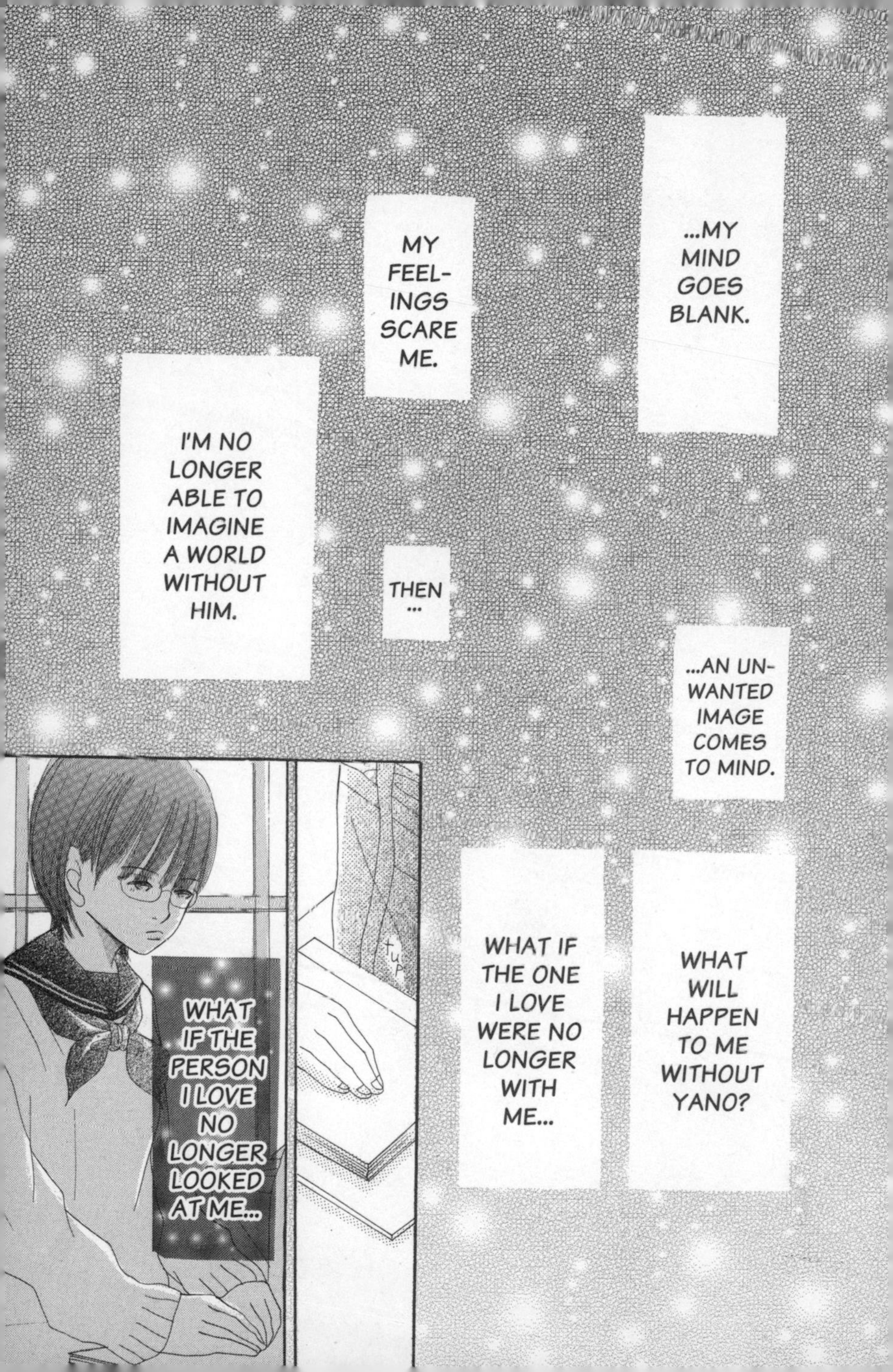
...MY MIND GOES BLANK.
MY FEEL-INGS SCARE ME.
I'M NO LONGER ABLE TO IMAGINE A WORLD WITHOUT HIM.
THEN...
...AN UN-WANTED IMAGE COMES TO MIND.
WHAT WILL HAPPEN TO ME WITHOUT YANO?
WHAT IF THE ONE I LOVE WERE NO LONGER WITH ME...
WHAT IF THE PERSON I LOVE NO LONGER LOOKED AT ME...

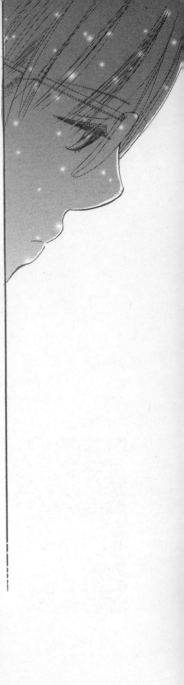

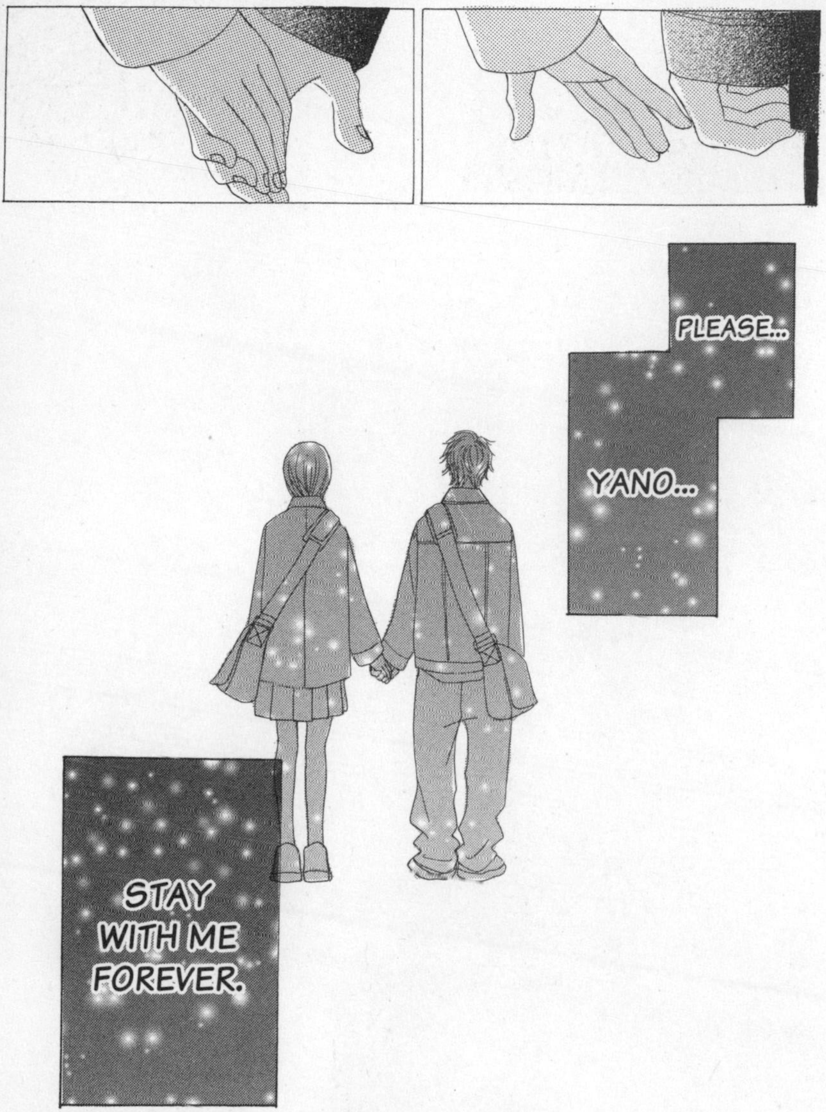
PLEASE...
YANO...
STAY WITH ME FOREVER.

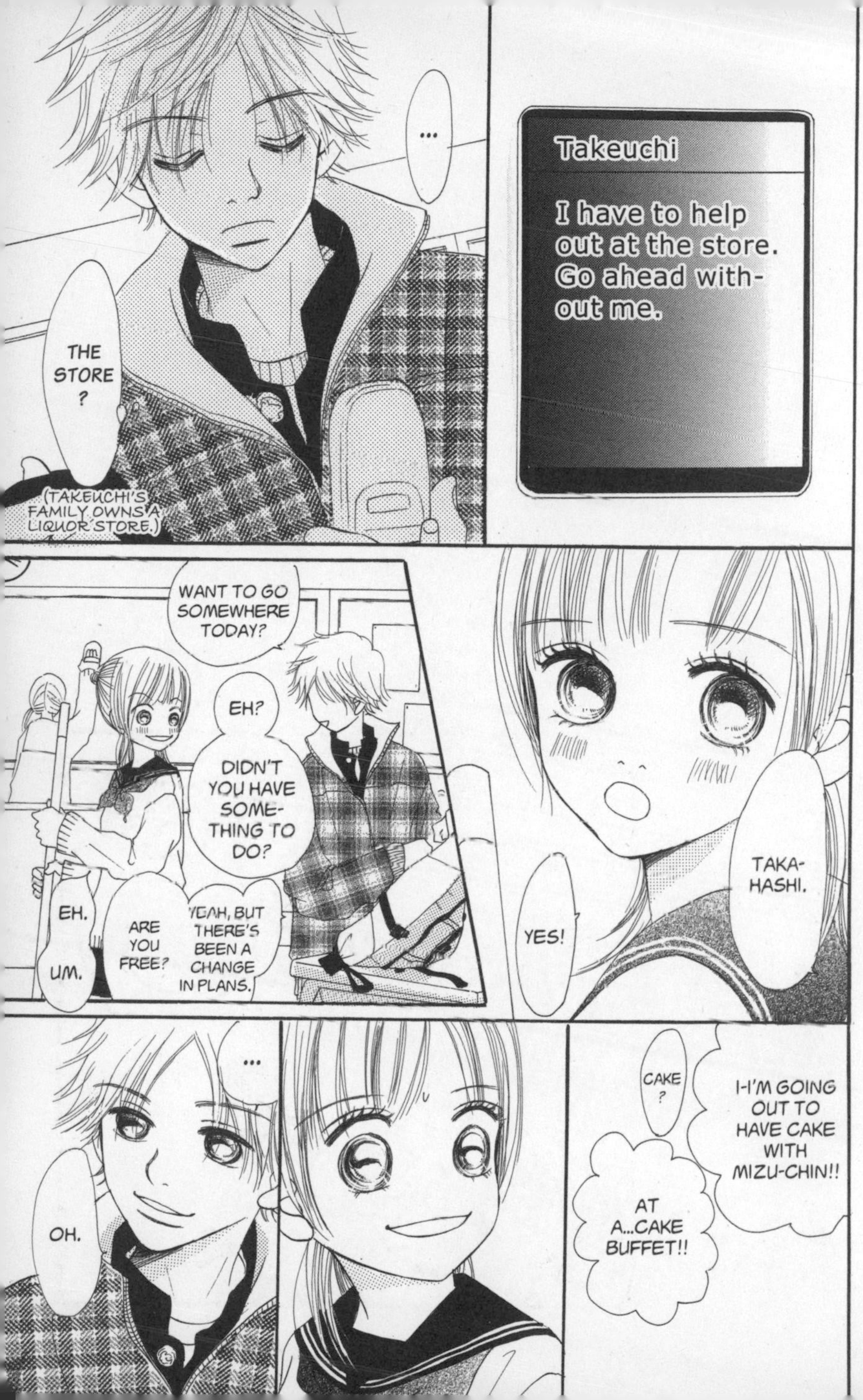
Takeuchi
I have to help out at the store. Go ahead without me.
...
THE STORE?
(TAKEUCHI'S FAMILY OWNS A LIQUOR STORE.)
TAKAHASHI.
YES!
WANT TO GO SOMEWHERE TODAY?
EH?
DIDN'T YOU HAVE SOMETHING TO DO?
YEAH, BUT THERE'S BEEN A CHANGE IN PLANS.
ARE YOU FREE?
EH.
UM.
CAKE?
I-I'M GOING OUT TO HAVE CAKE WITH MIZU-CHIN!!
AT A...CAKE BUFFET!!
...
OH.

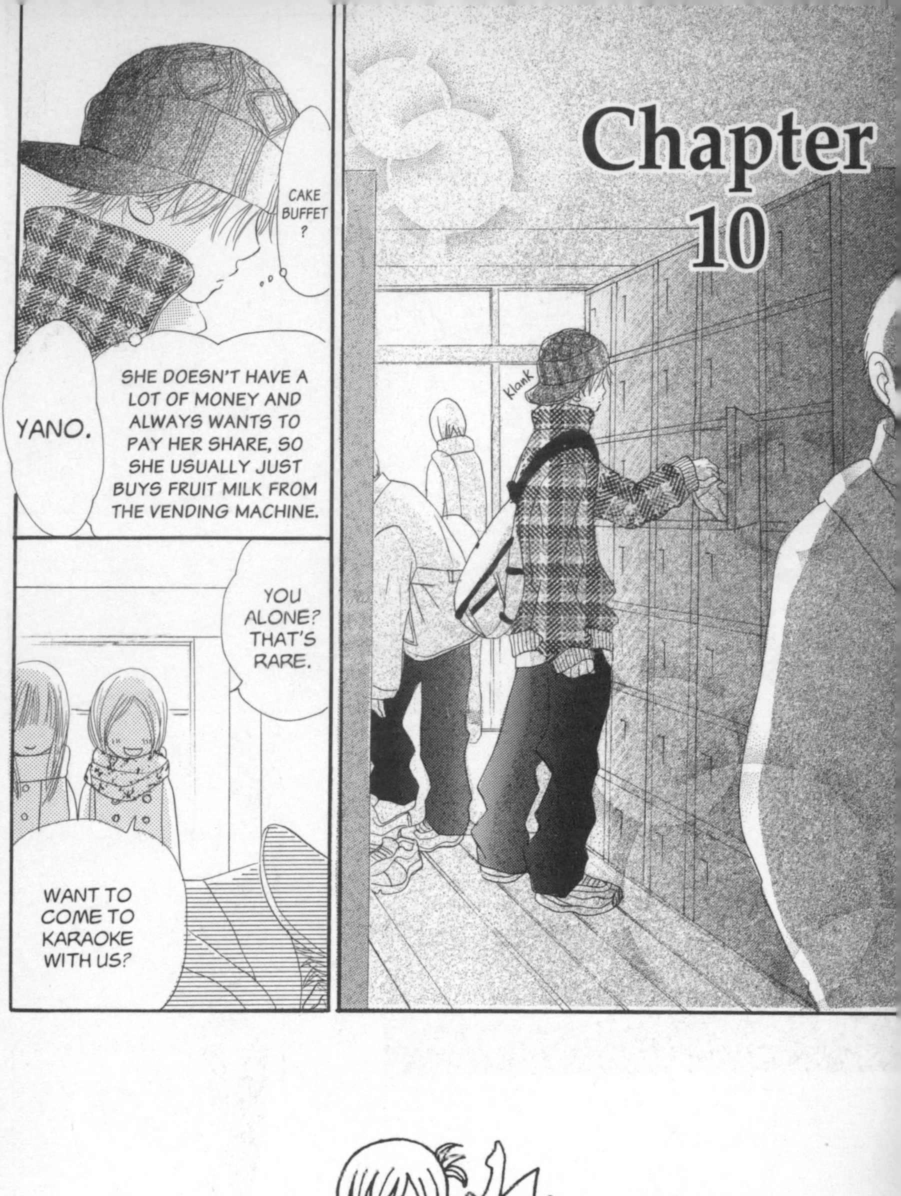
Chapter 10
Klank
CAKE BUFFET ?
SHE DOESN'T HAVE A LOT OF MONEY AND ALWAYS WANTS TO PAY HER SHARE, SO SHE USUALLY JUST BUYS FRUIT MILK FROM THE VENDING MACHINE.
YANO.
YOU ALONE? THAT'S RARE.
WANT TO COME TO KARAOKE WITH US?

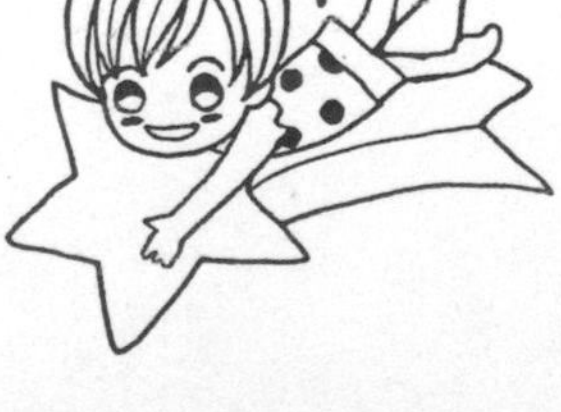

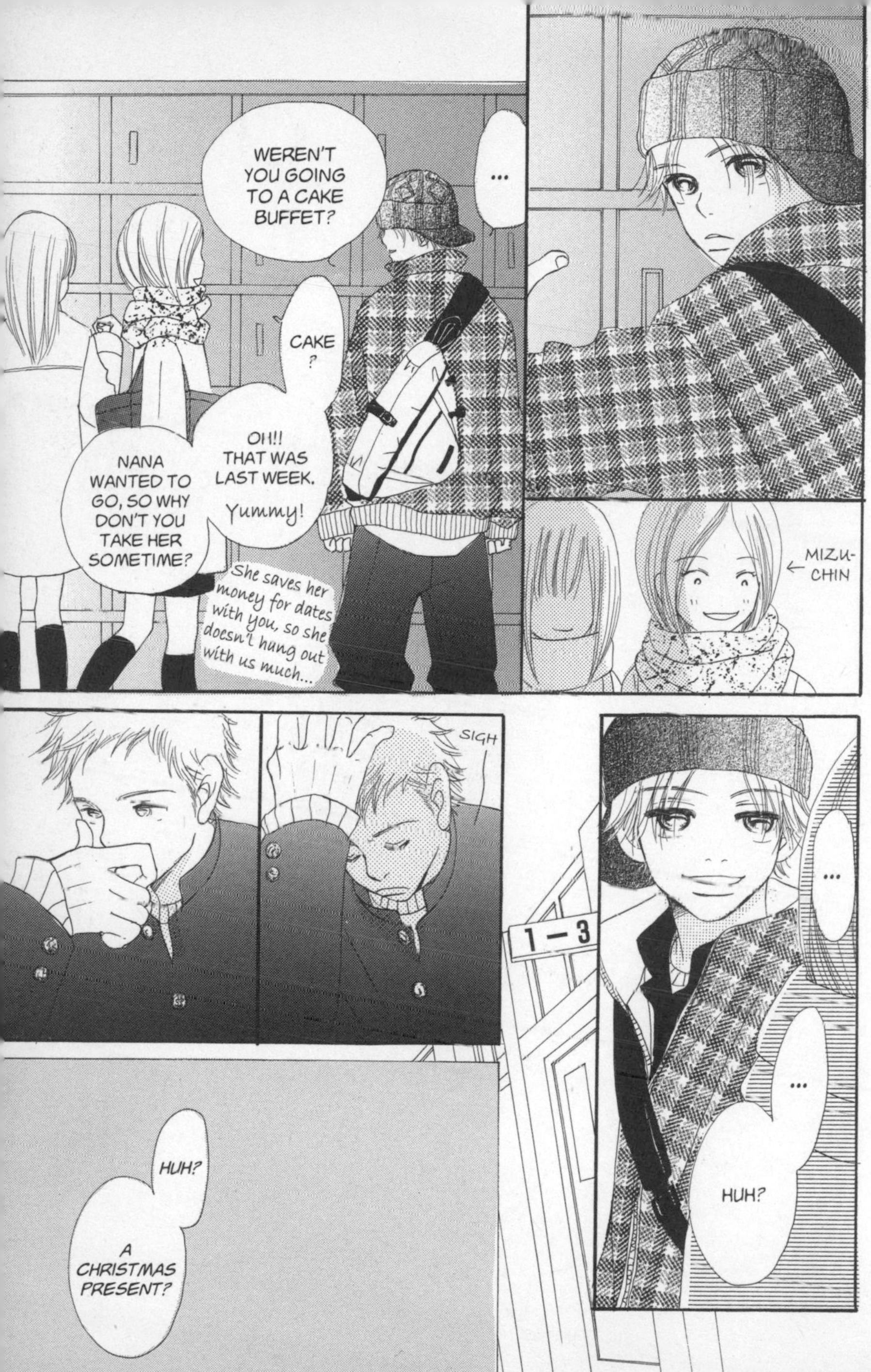

MIZU-CHIN
...
WEREN'T YOU GOING TO A CAKE BUFFET?
CAKE?
OH!! THAT WAS LAST WEEK.
Yummy!
NANA WANTED TO GO, SO WHY DON'T YOU TAKE HER SOMETIME?
She saves her money for dates with you, so she doesn't hang out with us much...
...
...
HUH?
1-3
SIGH
HUH?
A CHRISTMAS PRESENT?

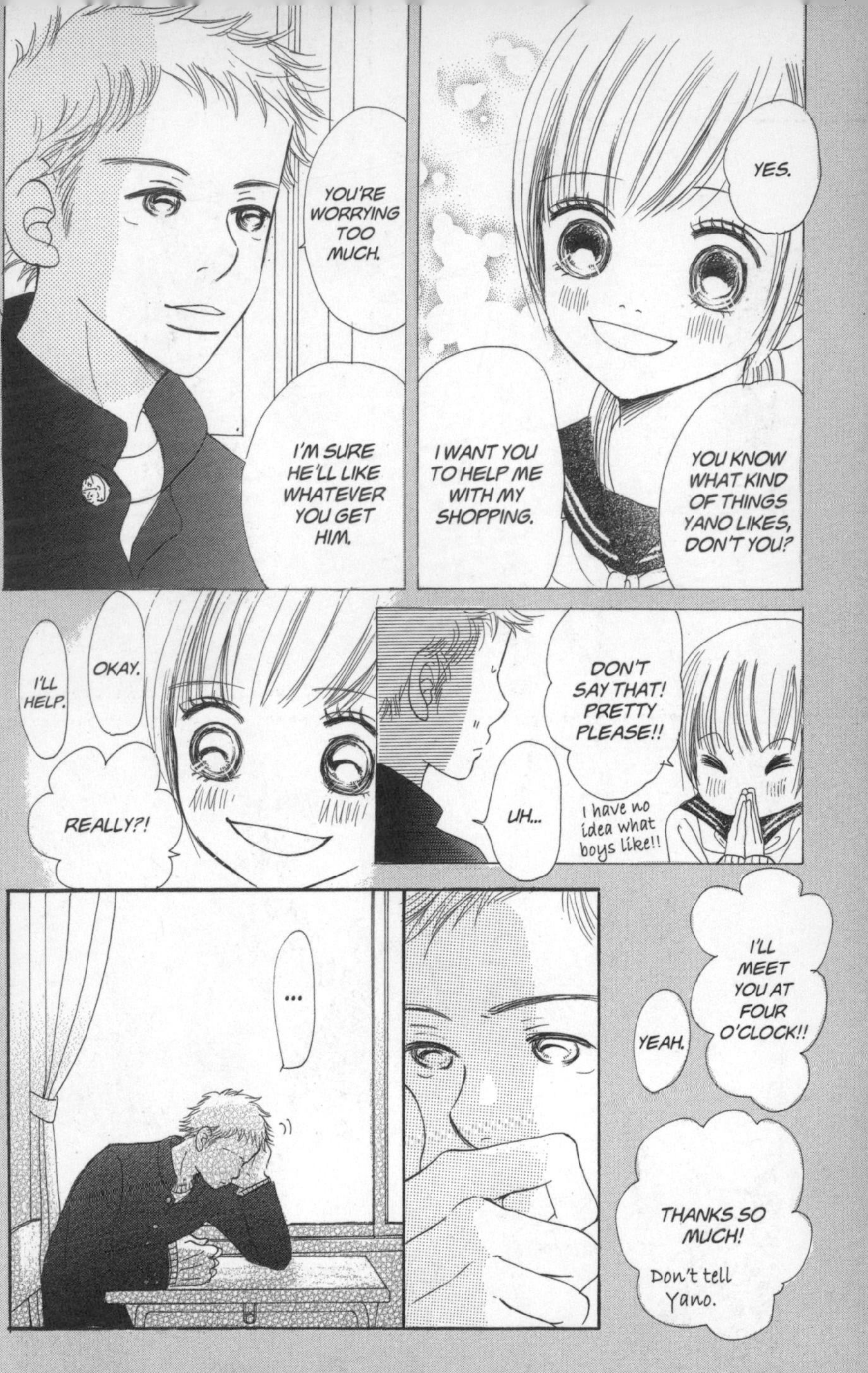
YES.
YOU KNOW WHAT KIND OF THINGS YANO LIKES, DON'T YOU?
I WANT YOU TO HELP ME WITH MY SHOPPING.
YOU'RE WORRYING TOO MUCH.
I'M SURE HE'LL LIKE WHATEVER YOU GET HIM.
DON'T SAY THAT! PRETTY PLEASE!!
I have no idea what boys like!!
UH...
OKAY.
I'LL HELP.
REALLY?!
I'LL MEET YOU AT FOUR O'CLOCK!!
YEAH.
THANKS SO MUCH!
Don't tell Yano.
...

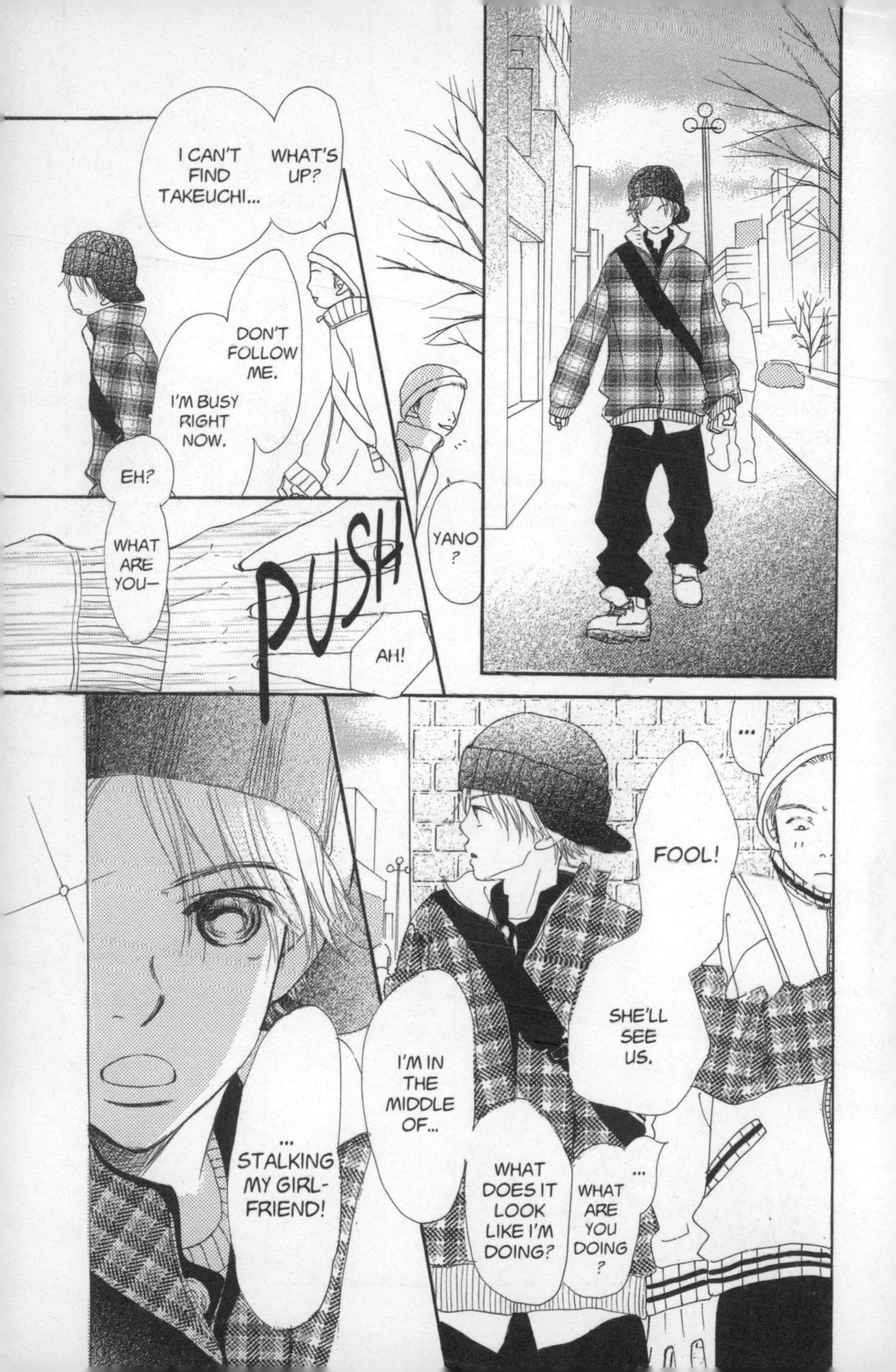
YANO ?
WHAT'S UP? I CAN'T FIND TAKEUCHI...
DON'T FOLLOW ME.
I'M BUSY RIGHT NOW.
EH?
WHAT ARE YOU—
PUSH
AH!
...
FOOL!
SHE'LL SEE US.
... WHAT ARE YOU DOING?
WHAT DOES IT LOOK LIKE I'M DOING?
I'M IN THE MIDDLE OF...
... STALKING MY GIRL-FRIEND!

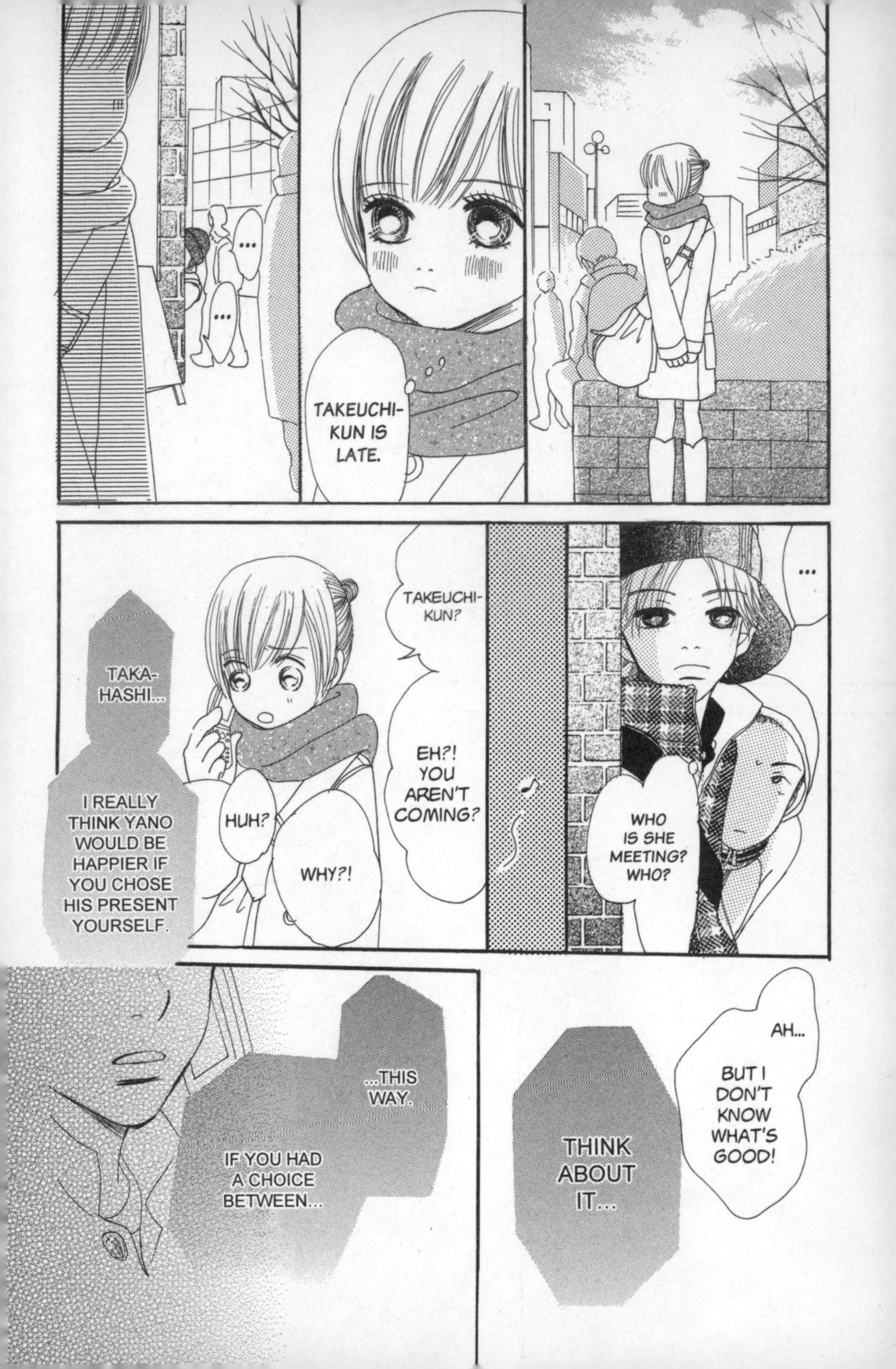
TAKEUCHI-KUN IS LATE.
...
...
...
WHO IS SHE MEETING? WHO?
TAKEUCHI-KUN?
EH?! YOU AREN'T COMING?
HUH?
WHY?!
TAKA-HASHI...
I REALLY THINK YANO WOULD BE HAPPIER IF YOU CHOSE HIS PRESENT YOURSELF.
AH...
BUT I DON'T KNOW WHAT'S GOOD!
THINK ABOUT IT...
...THIS WAY.
IF YOU HAD A CHOICE BETWEEN...

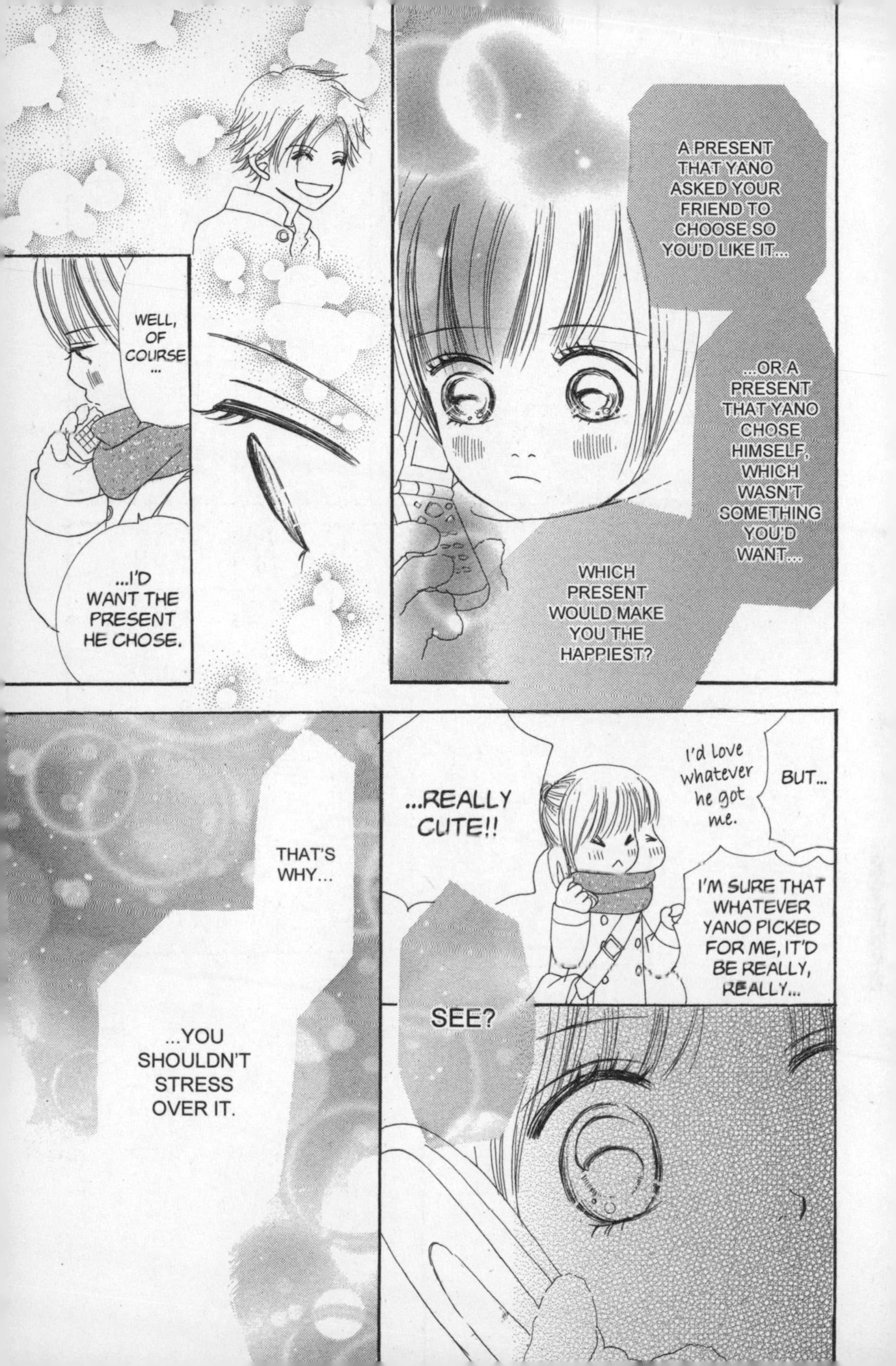
A PRESENT THAT YANO ASKED YOUR FRIEND TO CHOOSE SO YOU'D LIKE IT...
...OR A PRESENT THAT YANO CHOSE HIMSELF, WHICH WASN'T SOMETHING YOU'D WANT...
WHICH PRESENT WOULD MAKE YOU THE HAPPIEST?
WELL, OF COURSE ...
...I'D WANT THE PRESENT HE CHOSE.
BUT...
I'd love whatever he got me.
I'M SURE THAT WHATEVER YANO PICKED FOR ME, IT'D BE REALLY, REALLY...
...REALLY CUTE!!
SEE?
THAT'S WHY...
...YOU SHOULDN'T STRESS OVER IT.

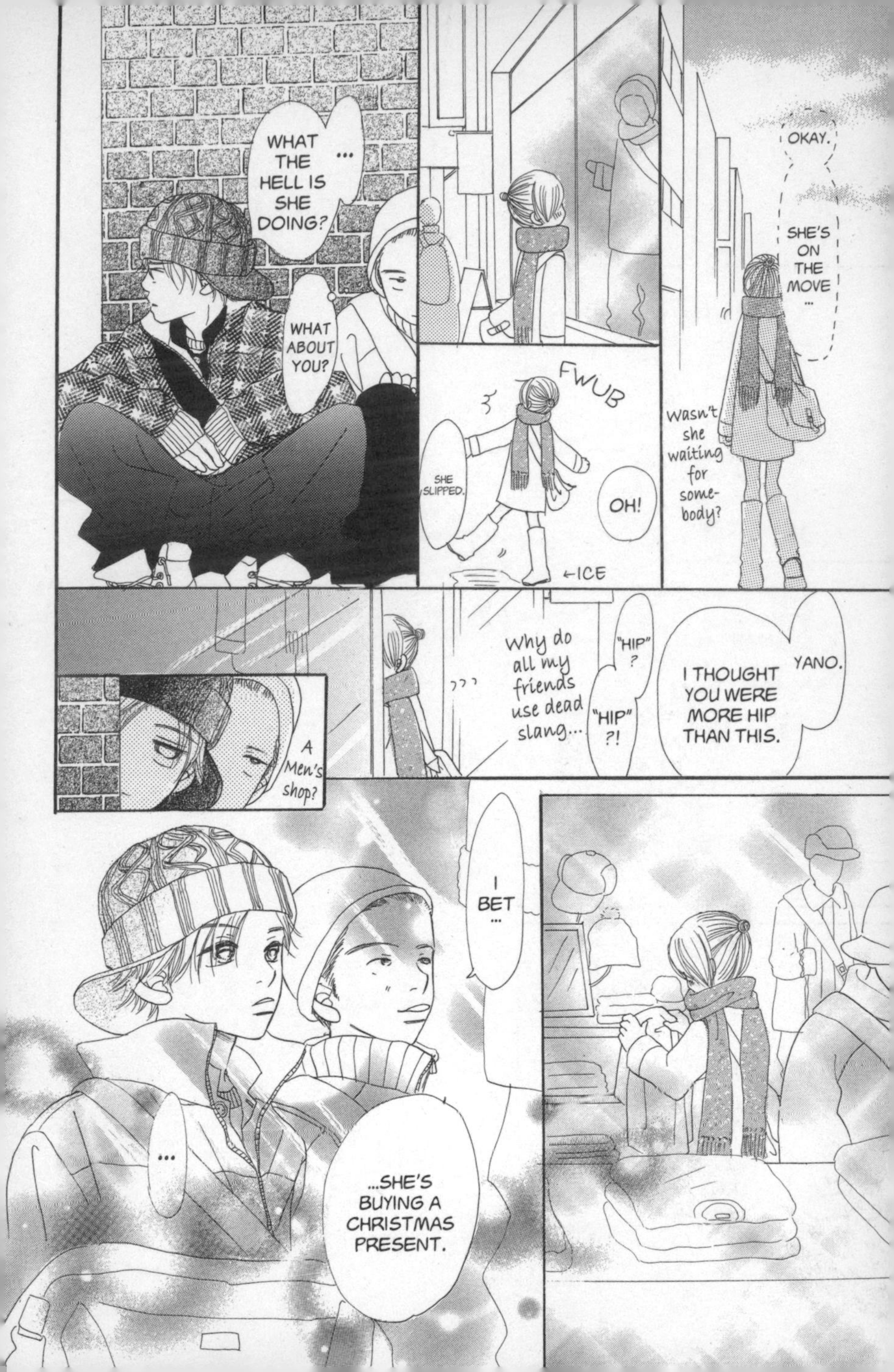
OKAY.
SHE'S ON THE MOVE...
Wasn't she waiting for somebody?
FWUB
OH!
SHE SLIPPED.
←ICE
WHAT THE HELL IS SHE DOING?
...
WHAT ABOUT YOU?
YANO.
I THOUGHT YOU WERE MORE HIP THAN THIS.
"HIP"?
"HIP"?!
Why do all my friends use dead slang...
A Men's shop?
I BET...
...SHE'S BUYING A CHRISTMAS PRESENT.
...

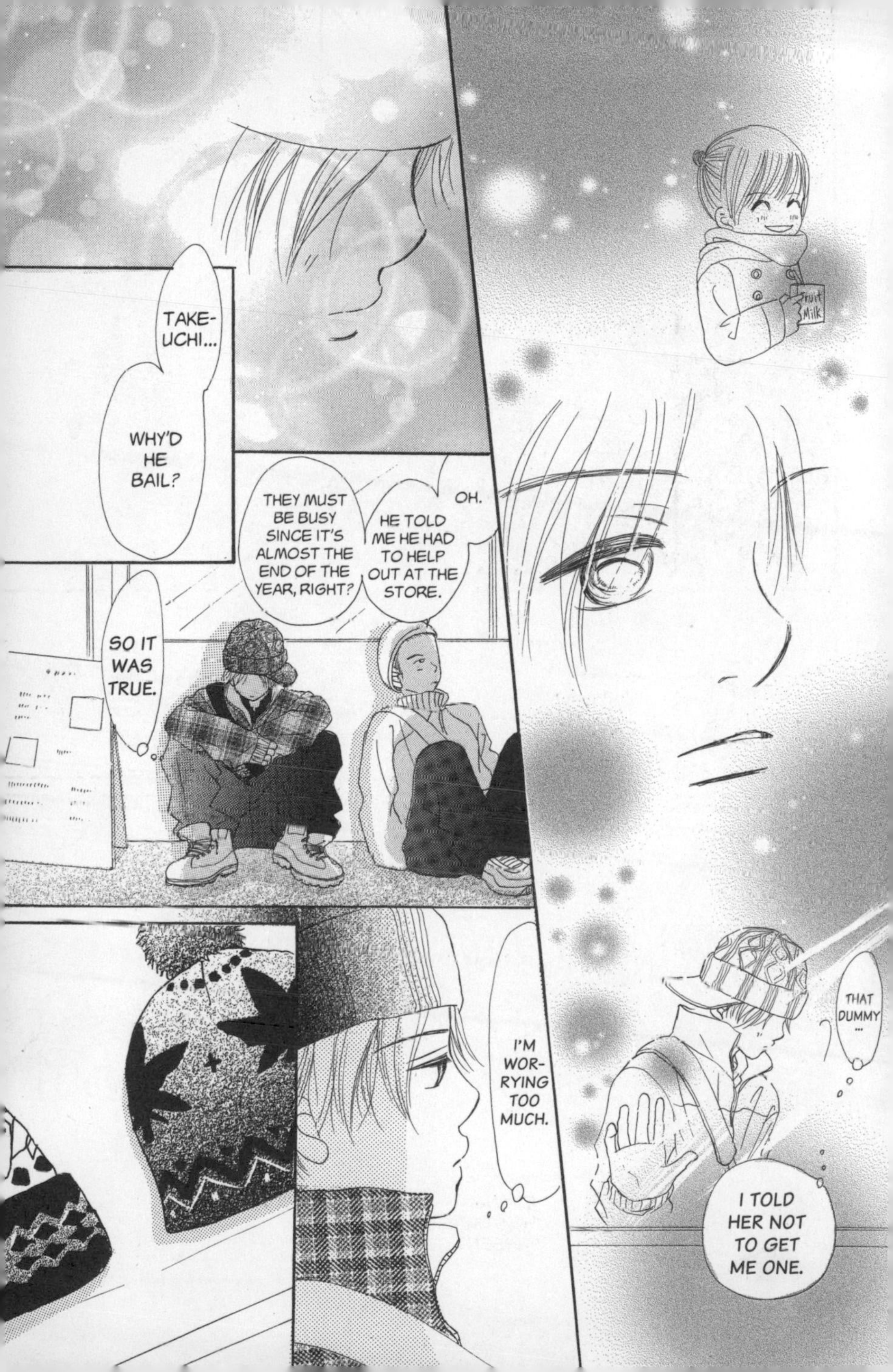
Fruit Milk
THAT DUMMY...
I TOLD HER NOT TO GET ME ONE.
TAKE-UCHI...
WHY'D HE BAIL?
OH.
HE TOLD ME HE HAD TO HELP OUT AT THE STORE.
THEY MUST BE BUSY SINCE IT'S ALMOST THE END OF THE YEAR, RIGHT?
SO IT WAS TRUE.
I'M WOR-RYING TOO MUCH.

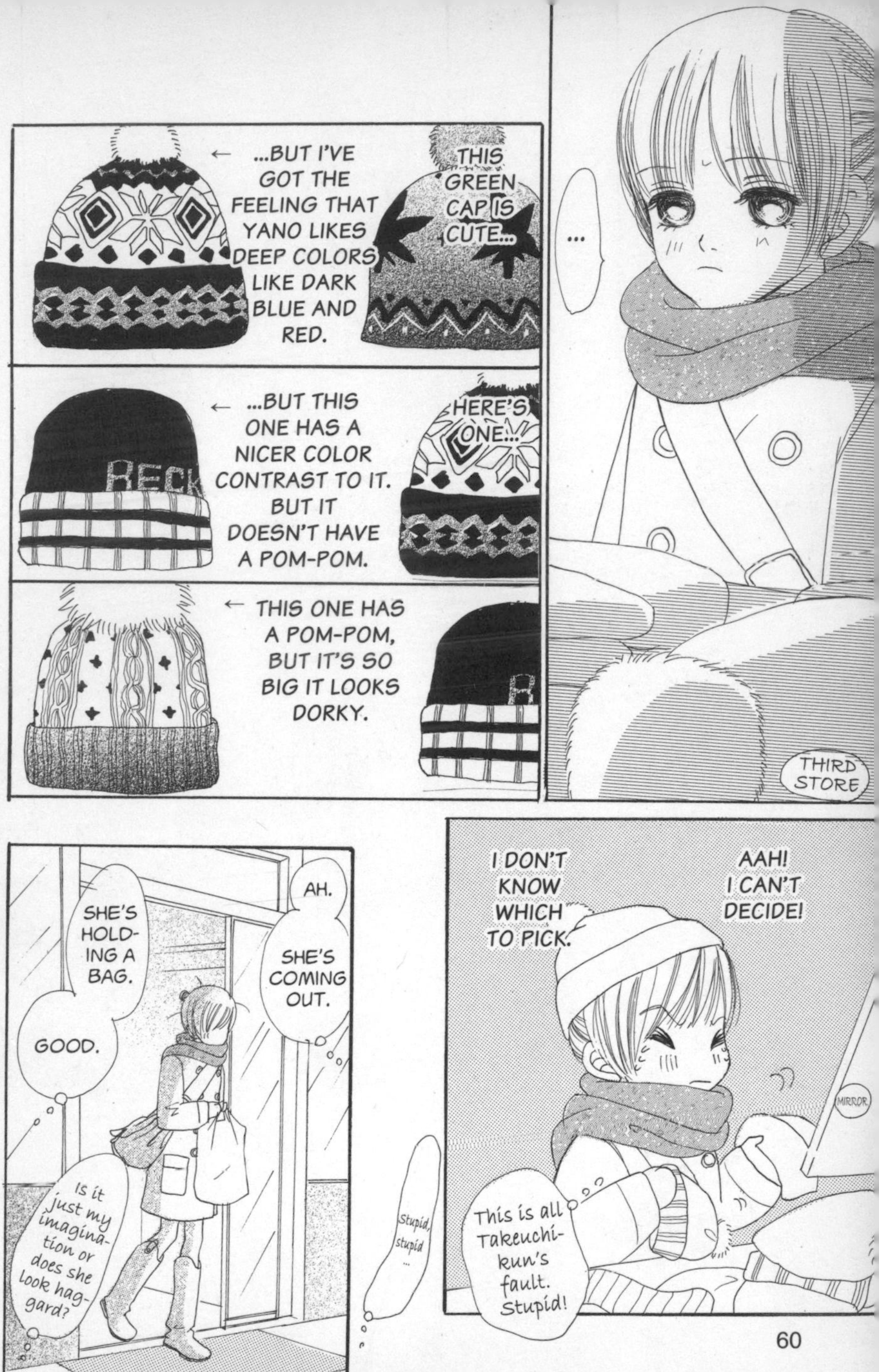
...
THIRD STORE
THIS GREEN CAP IS CUTE...
...BUT I'VE GOT THE FEELING THAT YANO LIKES DEEP COLORS LIKE DARK BLUE AND RED.
HERE'S ONE...
...BUT THIS ONE HAS A NICER COLOR CONTRAST TO IT. BUT IT DOESN'T HAVE A POM-POM.
THIS ONE HAS A POM-POM, BUT IT'S SO BIG IT LOOKS DORKY.
AAH! I CAN'T DECIDE!
I DON'T KNOW WHICH TO PICK.
MIRROR
This is all Takeuchi-kun's fault. Stupid!
Stupid, stupid...
AH.
SHE'S COMING OUT.
SHE'S HOLDING A BAG.
GOOD.
Is it just my imagination or does she look haggard?

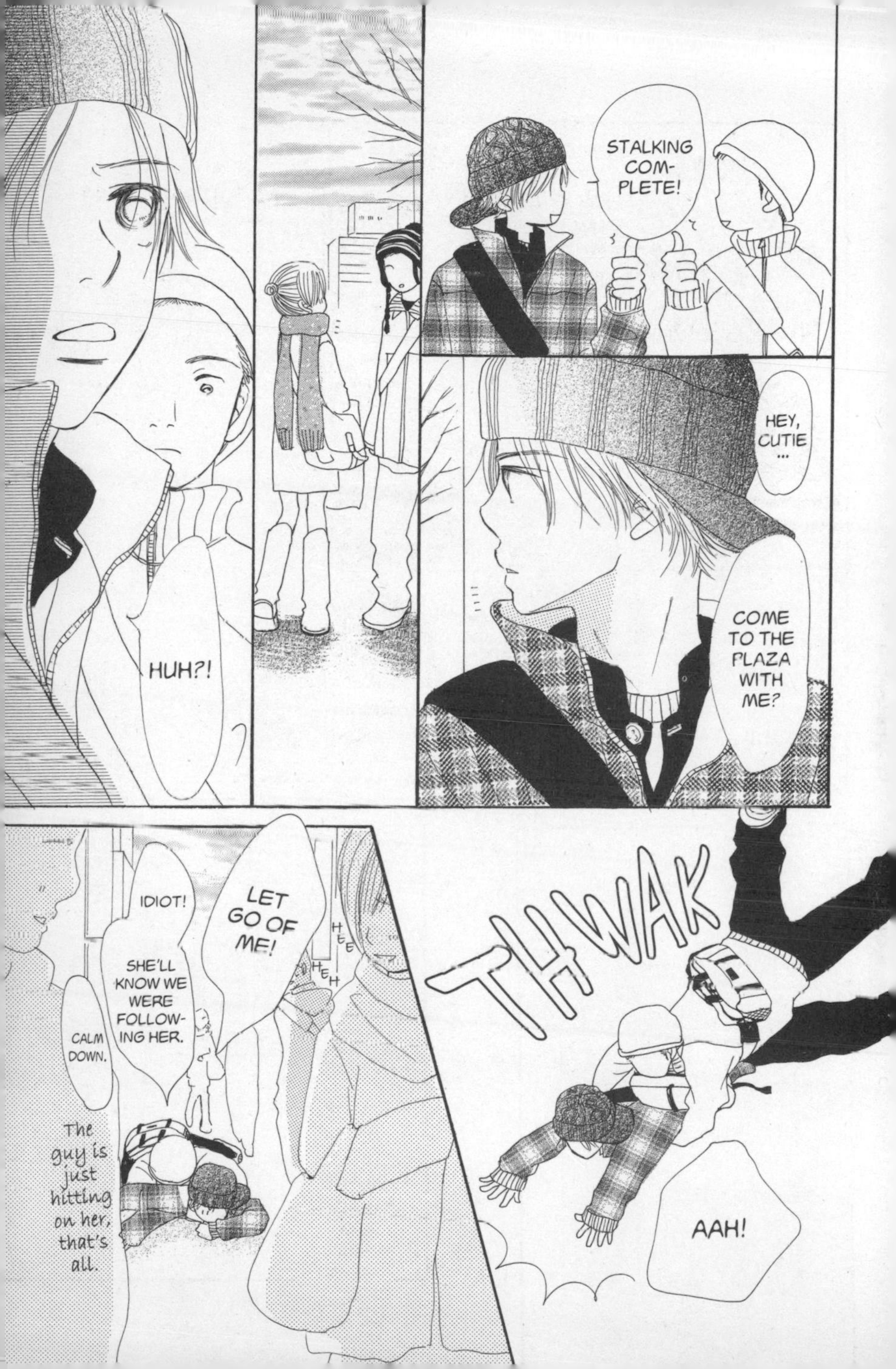
STALKING COM-PLETE!
HEY, CUTIE ...
COME TO THE PLAZA WITH ME?
HUH?!
THWAK
AAH!
LET GO OF ME!
HEH HEH
IDIOT!
SHE'LL KNOW WE WERE FOLLOW-ING HER.
CALM DOWN.
The guy is just hitting on her, that's all.

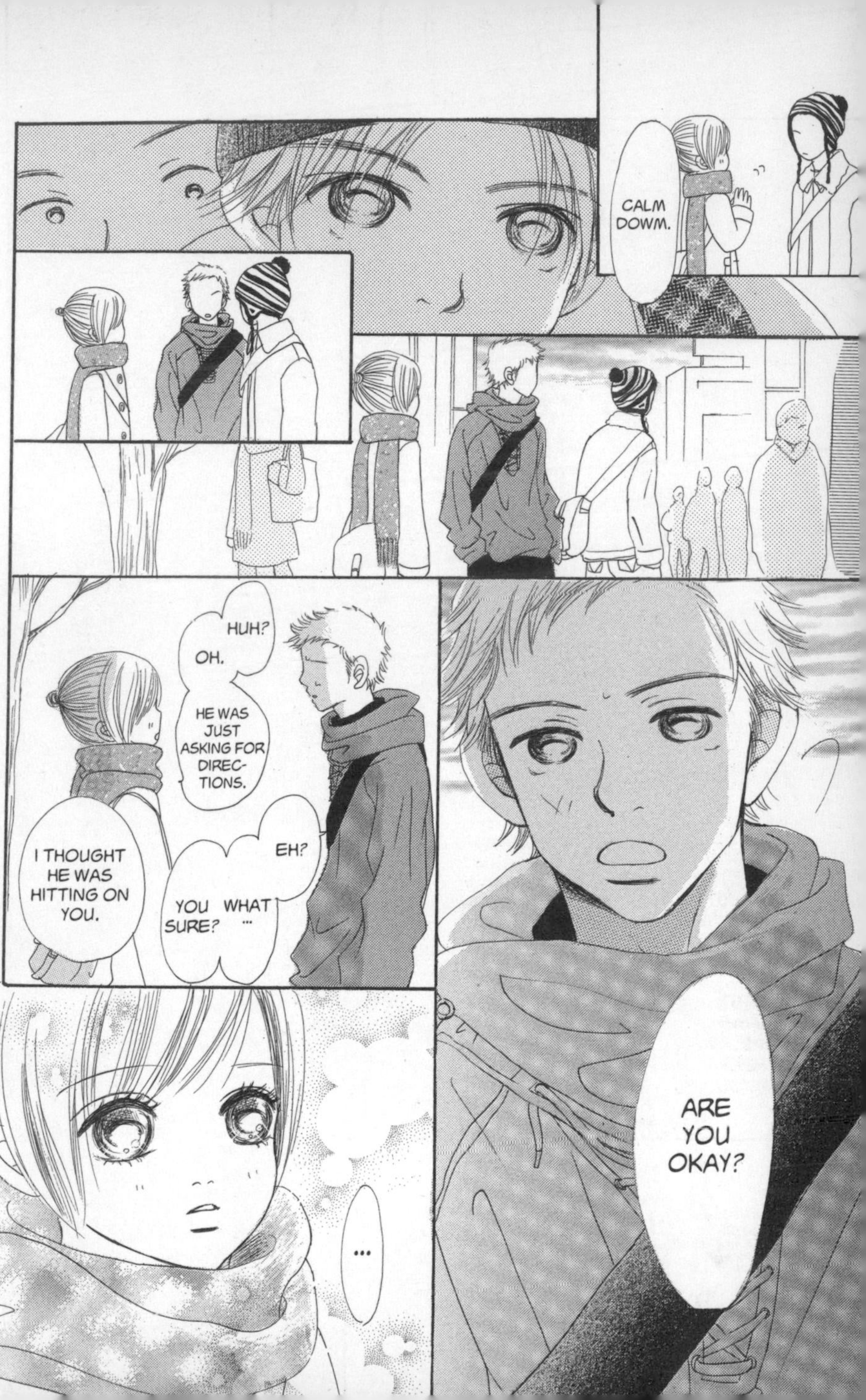
CALM DOWM.
ARE YOU OKAY?
HUH?
OH.
HE WAS JUST ASKING FOR DIRECTIONS.
EH?
WHAT ...
YOU SURE?
I THOUGHT HE WAS HITTING ON YOU.
...

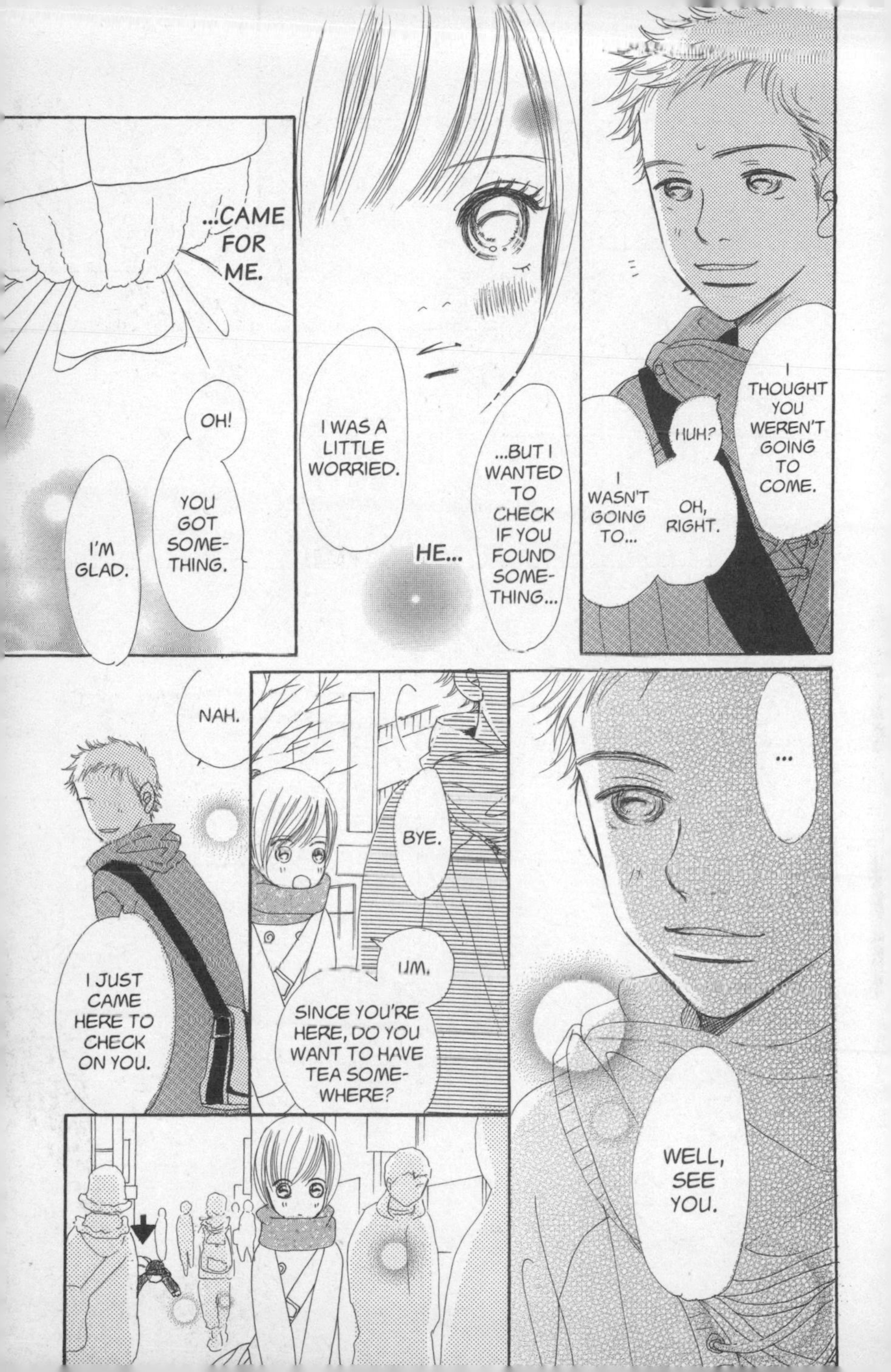
I THOUGHT YOU WEREN'T GOING TO COME.
HUH?
OH, RIGHT.
I WASN'T GOING TO...
I WAS A LITTLE WORRIED.
...BUT I WANTED TO CHECK IF YOU FOUND SOMETHING...
HE...
...CAME FOR ME.
OH!
YOU GOT SOMETHING.
I'M GLAD.
...
WELL, SEE YOU.
BYE.
UM.
SINCE YOU'RE HERE, DO YOU WANT TO HAVE TEA SOMEWHERE?
NAH.
I JUST CAME HERE TO CHECK ON YOU.

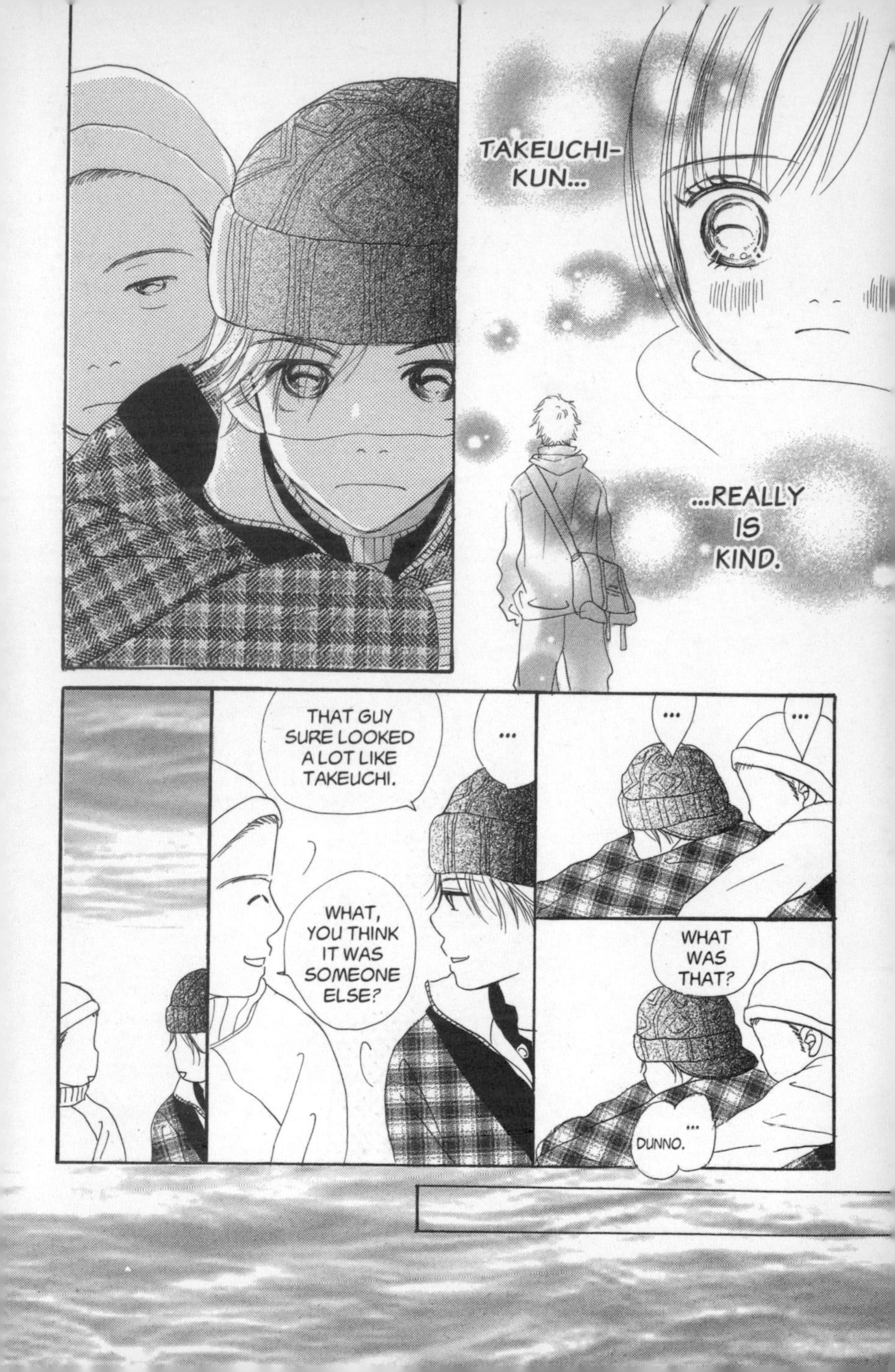
TAKEUCHI-KUN...
...REALLY IS KIND.
...
...
WHAT WAS THAT?
...DUNNO.
THAT GUY SURE LOOKED A LOT LIKE TAKEUCHI.
...
WHAT, YOU THINK IT WAS SOMEONE ELSE?

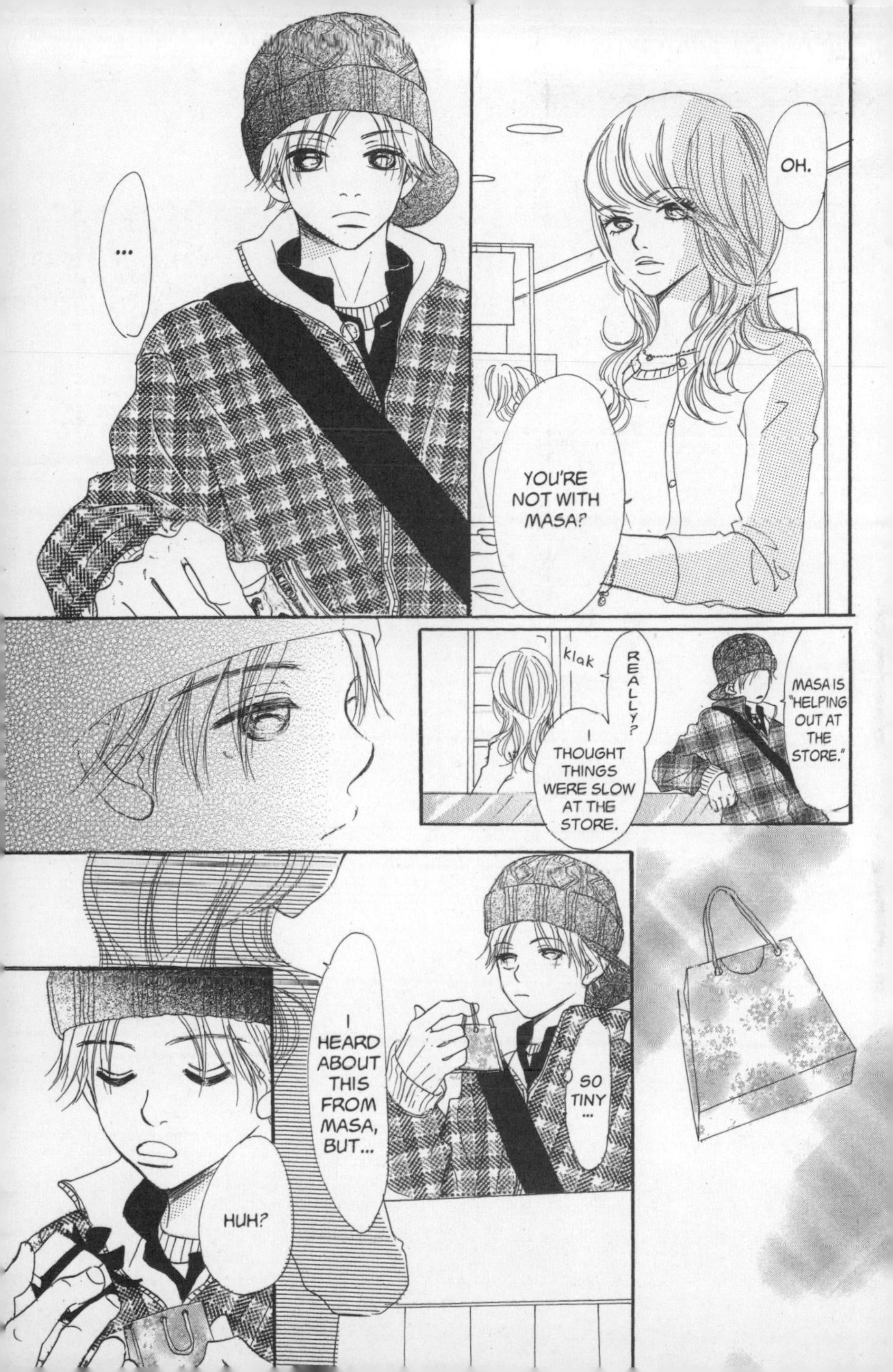
OH.
YOU'RE NOT WITH MASA?
...
MASA IS "HELPING OUT AT THE STORE."
REALLY?
klak
I THOUGHT THINGS WERE SLOW AT THE STORE.
SO TINY ...
I HEARD ABOUT THIS FROM MASA, BUT...
HUH?

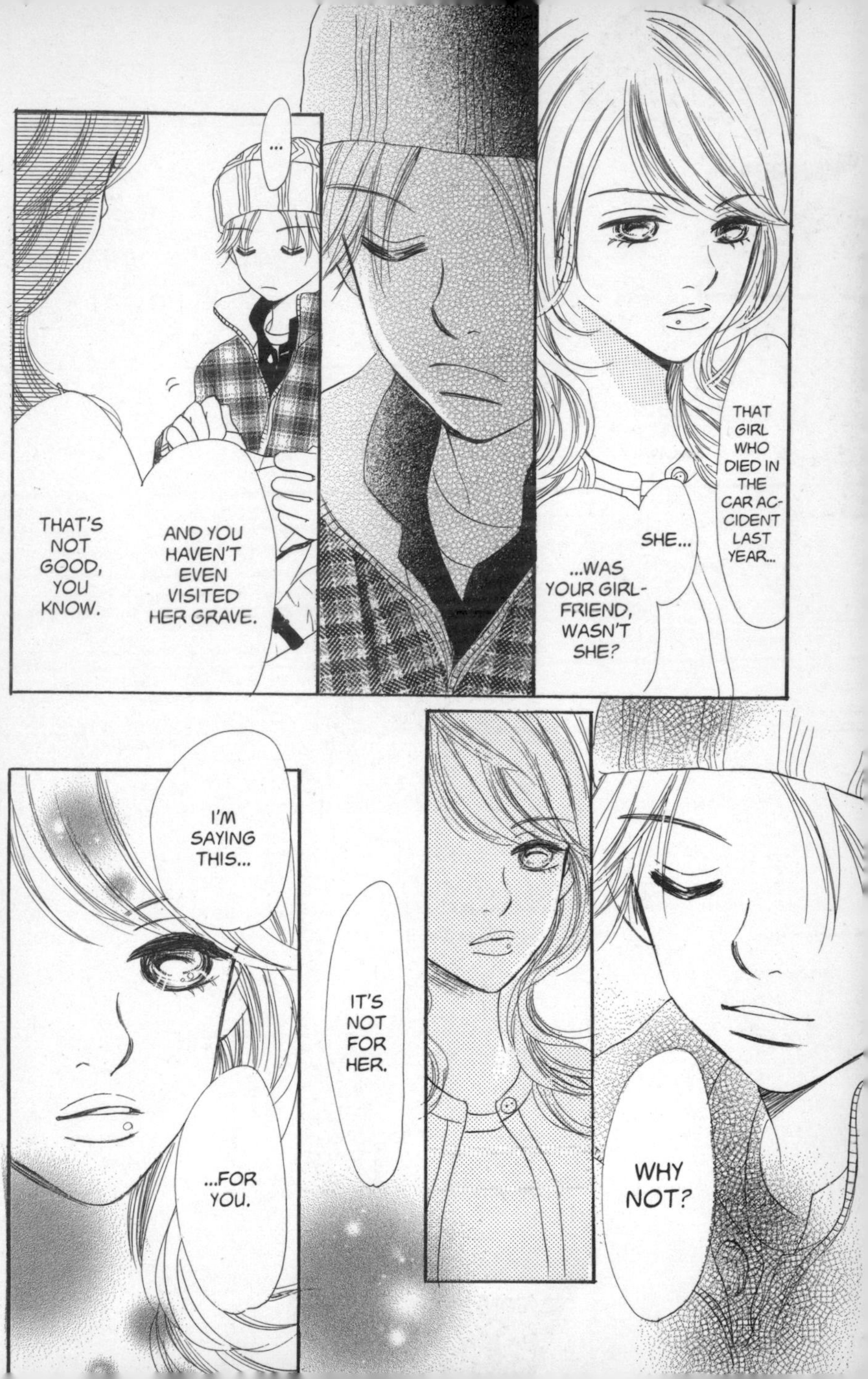
THAT GIRL WHO DIED IN THE CAR ACCIDENT LAST YEAR...
SHE...
...WAS YOUR GIRLFRIEND, WASN'T SHE?
...
AND YOU HAVEN'T EVEN VISITED HER GRAVE.
THAT'S NOT GOOD, YOU KNOW.
WHY NOT?
IT'S NOT FOR HER.
I'M SAYING THIS...
...FOR YOU.

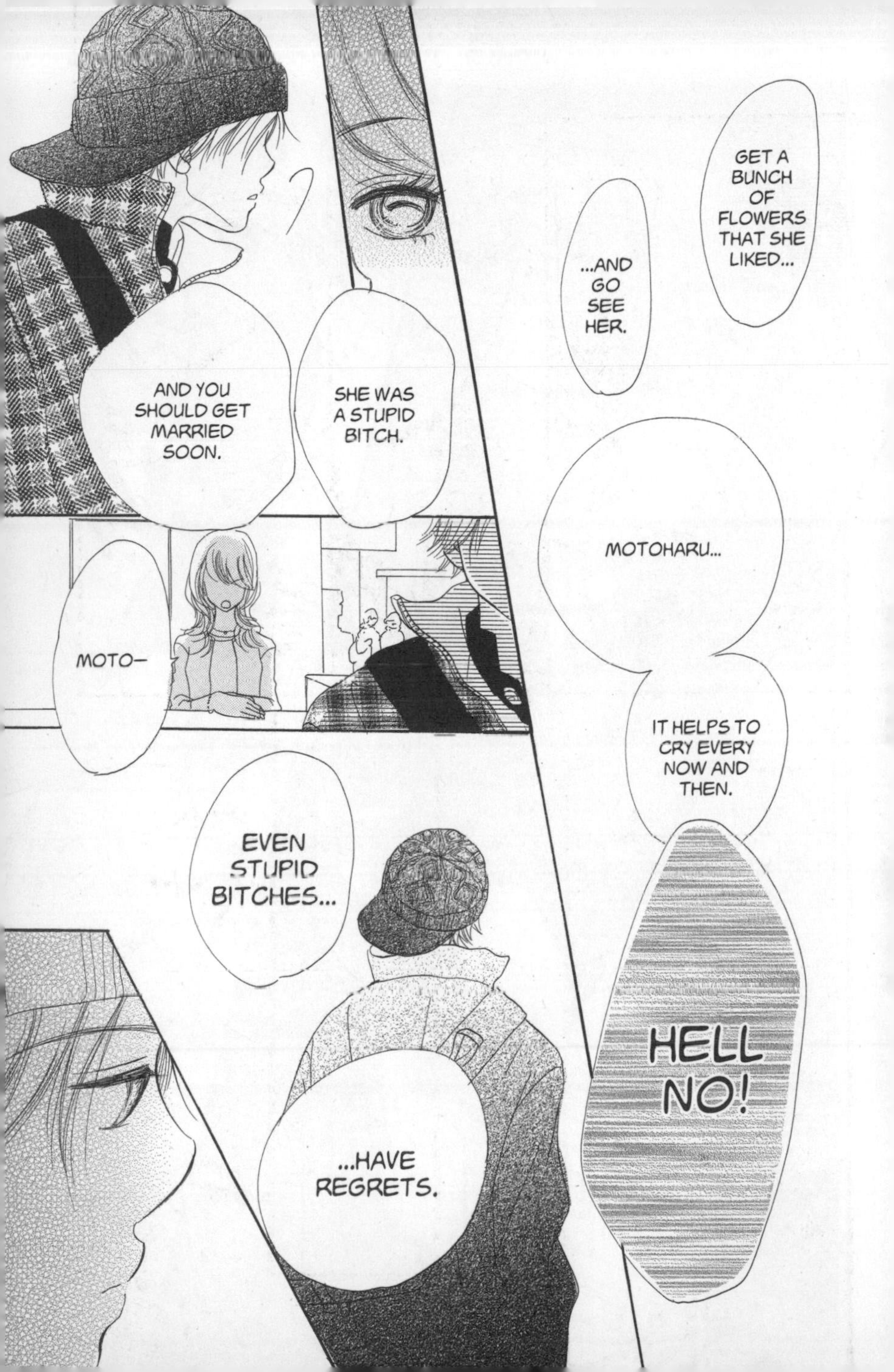
GET A BUNCH OF FLOWERS THAT SHE LIKED...
...AND GO SEE HER.
MOTOHARU...
IT HELPS TO CRY EVERY NOW AND THEN.
HELL NO!
SHE WAS A STUPID BITCH.
AND YOU SHOULD GET MARRIED SOON.
MOTO—
EVEN STUPID BITCHES...
...HAVE REGRETS.

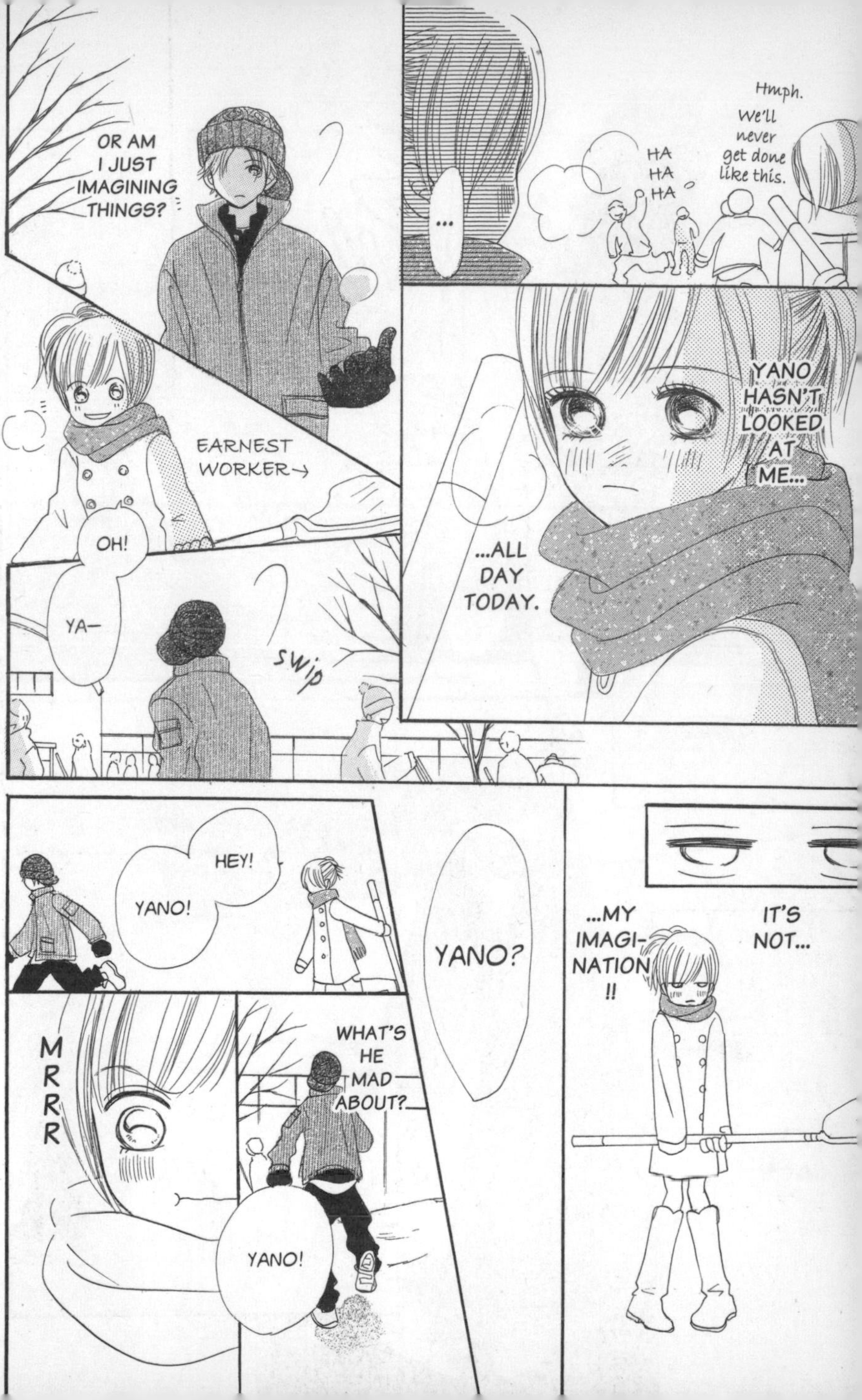
Hmph. We'll never get done like this.
HA HA HA
...
YANO HASN'T LOOKED AT ME...
...ALL DAY TODAY.
OR AM I JUST IMAGINING THINGS?
EARNEST WORKER→
OH!
YA—
SWIP
IT'S NOT...
...MY IMAGINATION!!
YANO?
HEY!
YANO!
WHAT'S HE MAD ABOUT?
YANO!
MRRR

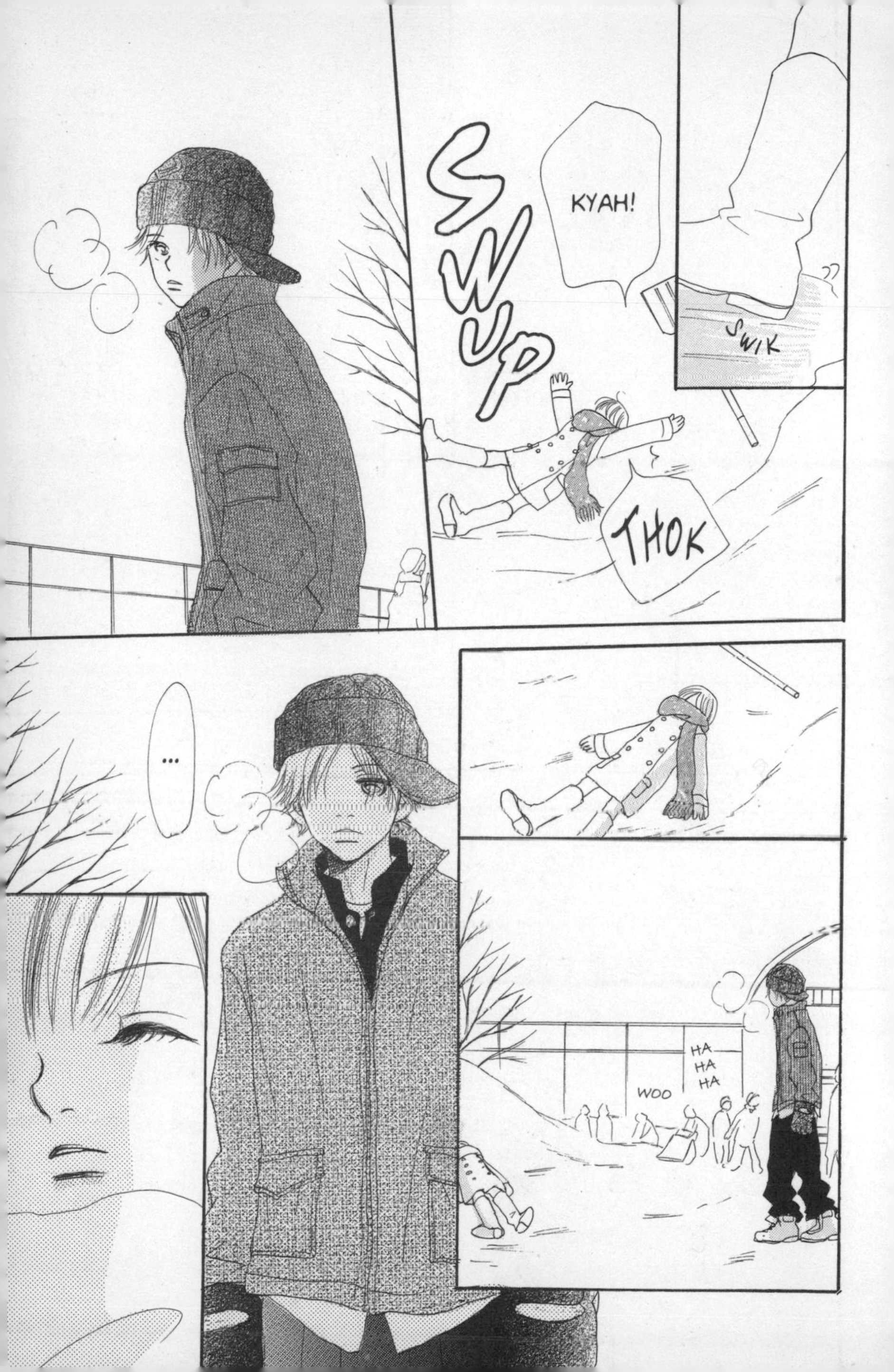
SWIK
KYAH!
SWUP
THOK
HA HA HA
WOO
...

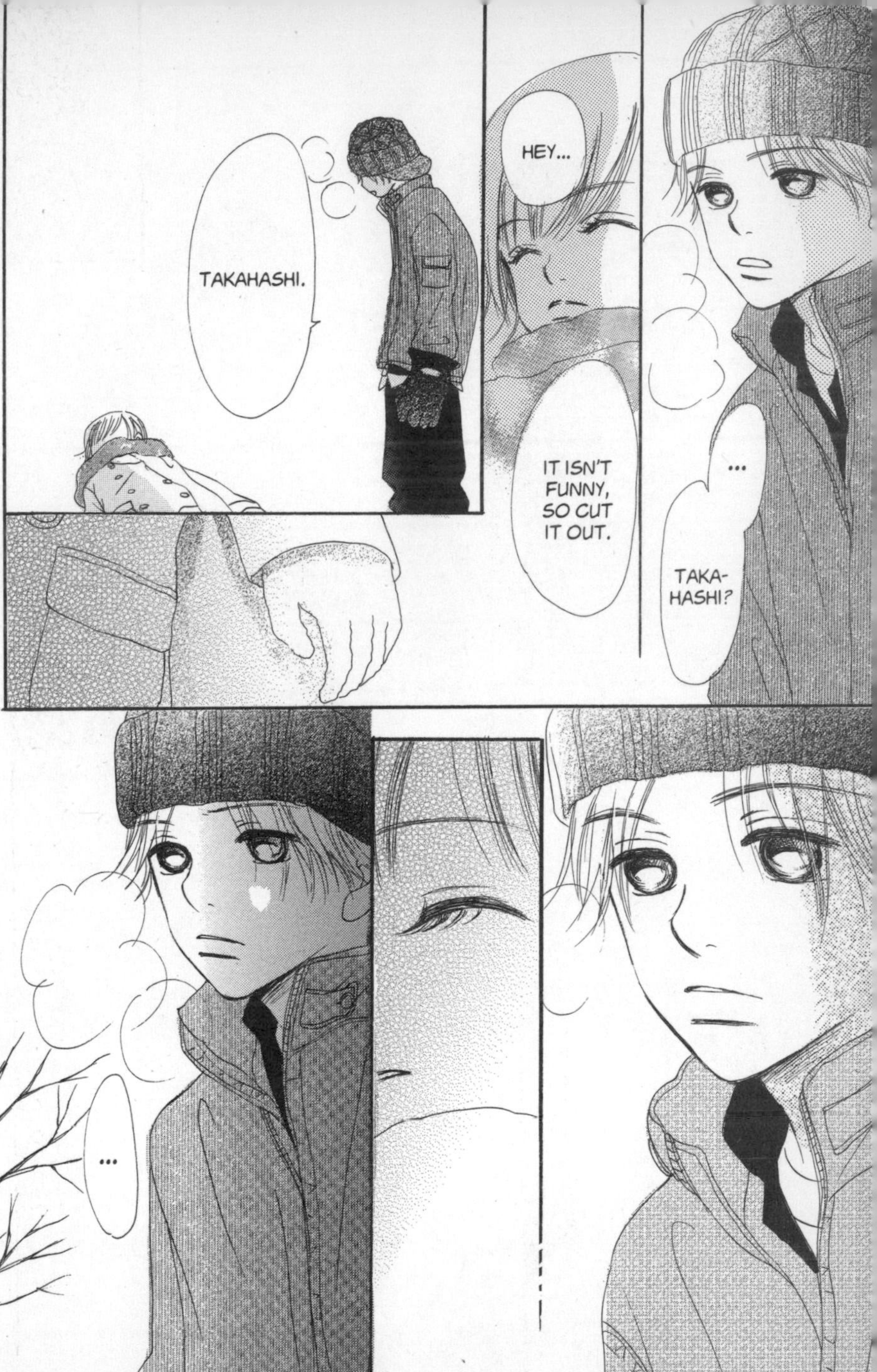
...
TAKA-HASHI?
HEY...
IT ISN'T FUNNY, SO CUT IT OUT.
TAKAHASHI.
...

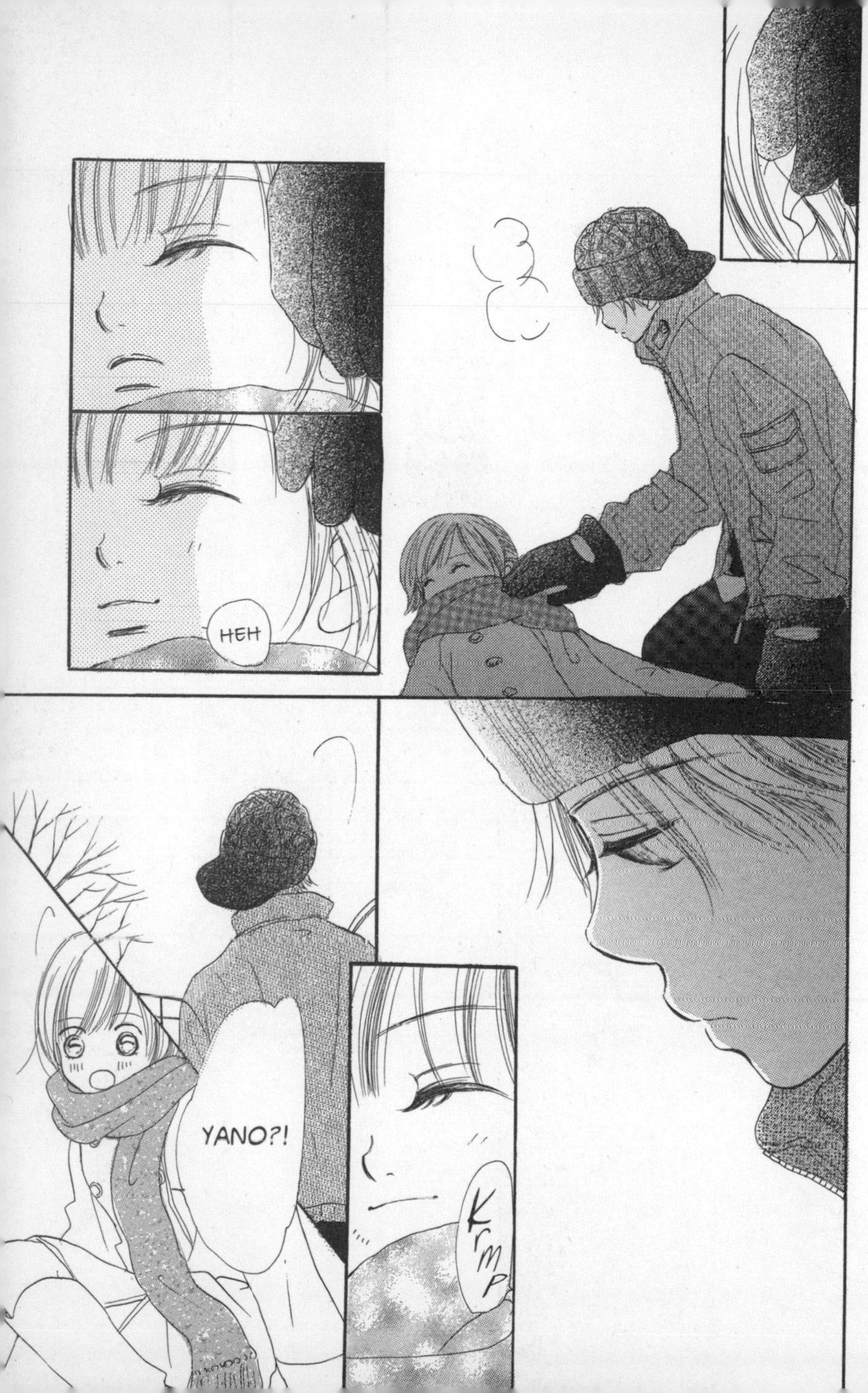
HEH
Krmp
YANO?!

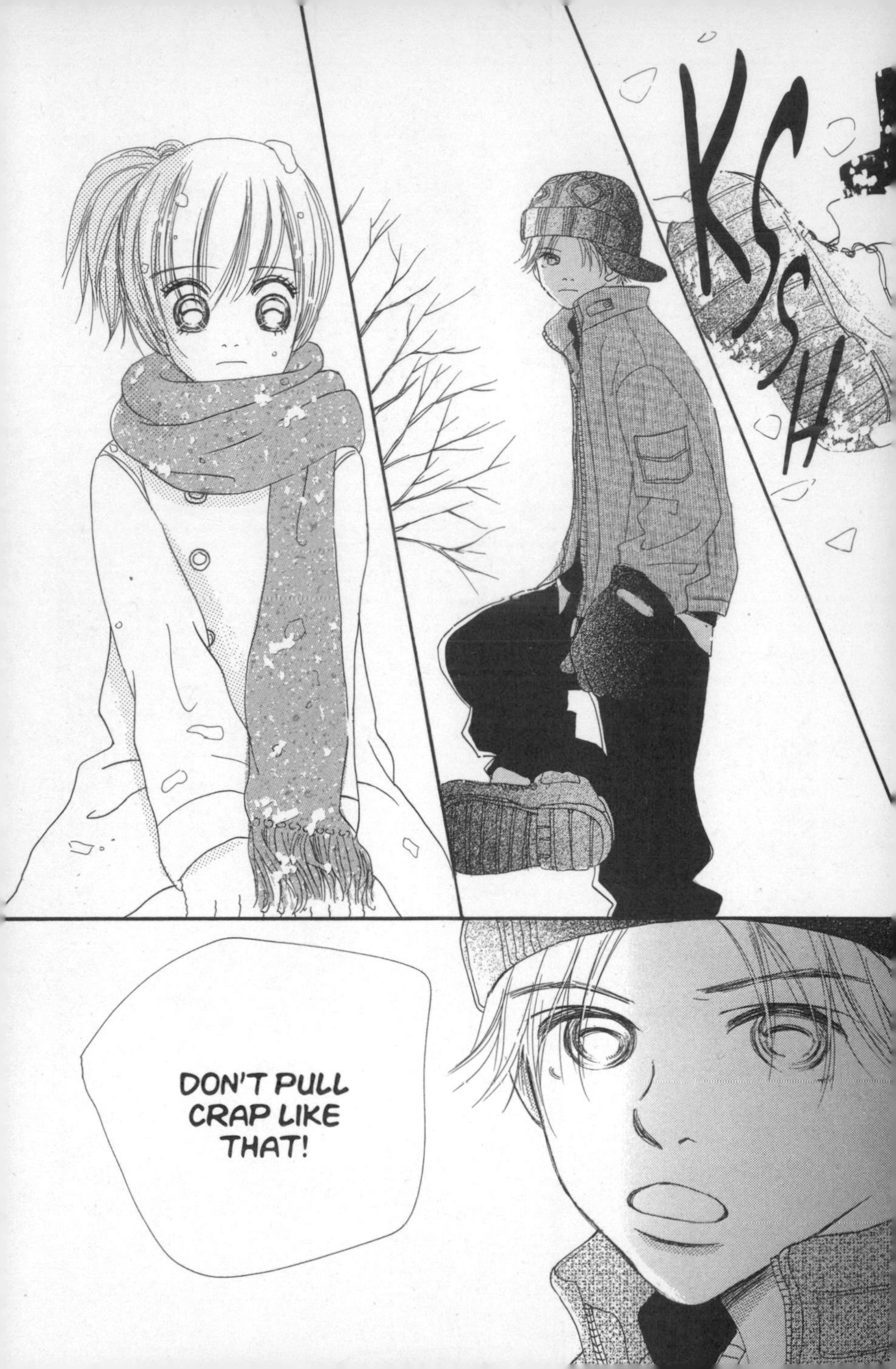
KSSH
DON'T PULL CRAP LIKE THAT!

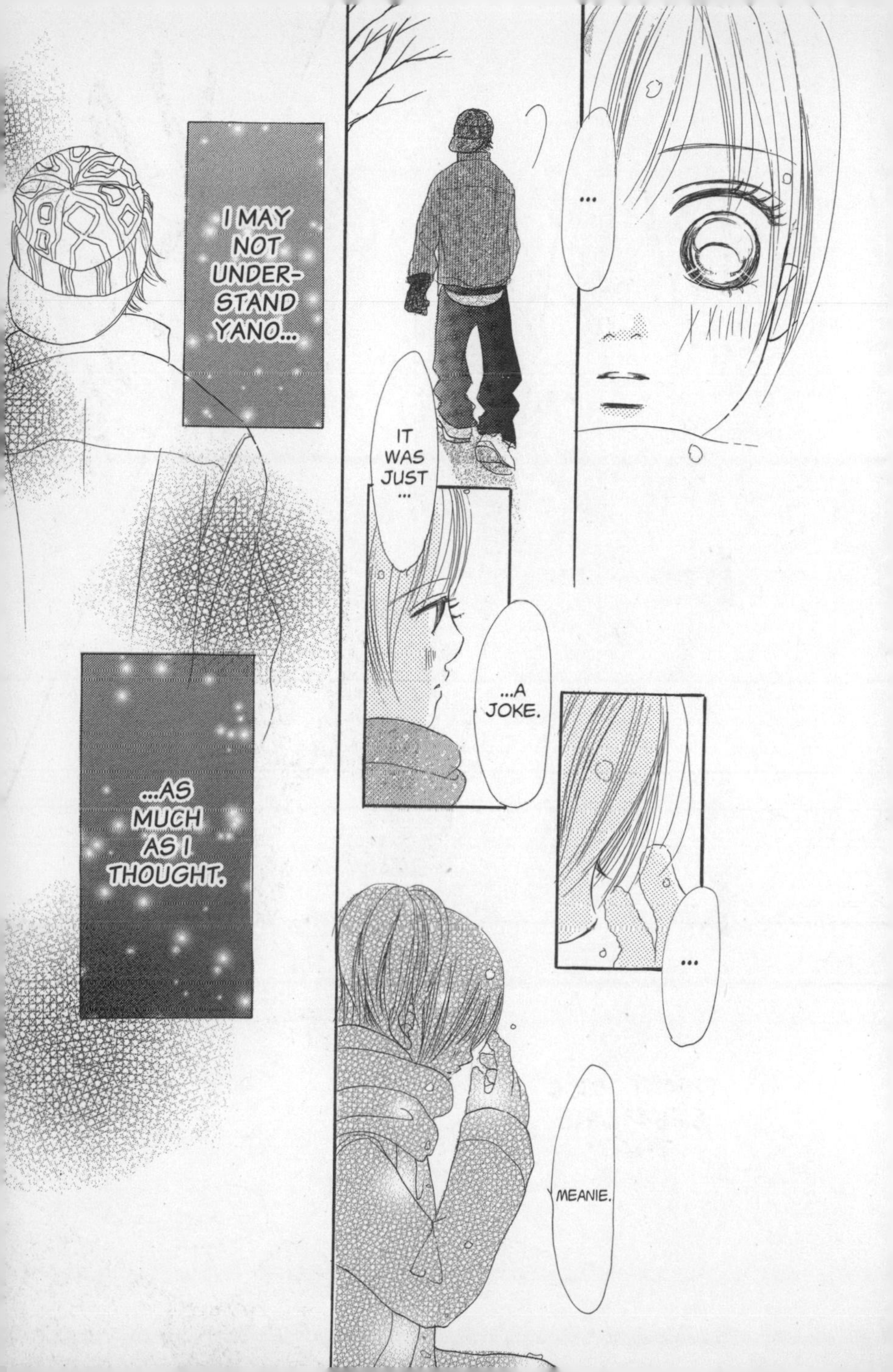
...
IT WAS JUST...
...A JOKE.
...
MEANIE.
I MAY NOT UNDER-STAND YANO...
...AS MUCH AS I THOUGHT.

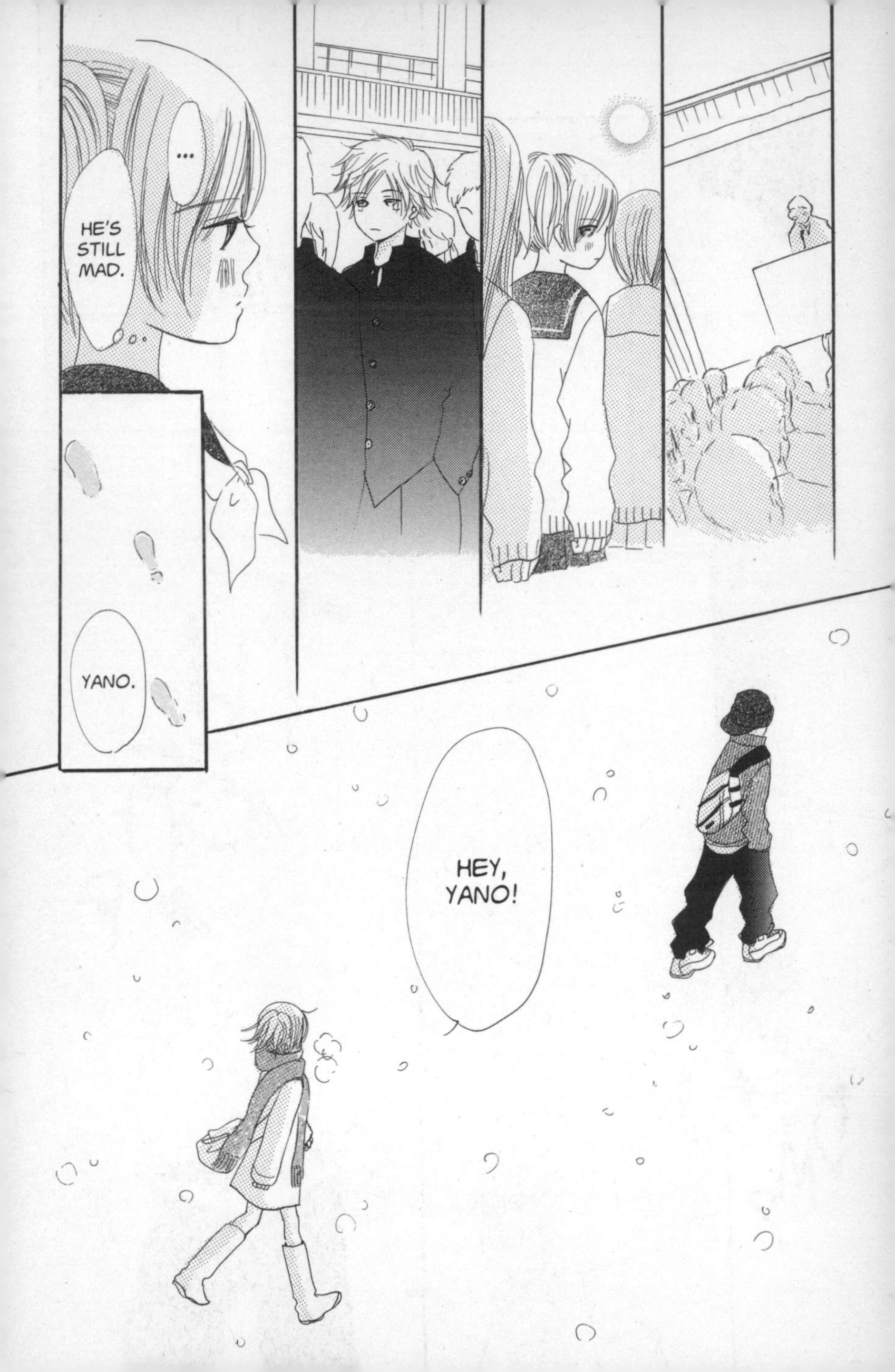
...
HE'S STILL MAD.
YANO.
HEY, YANO!

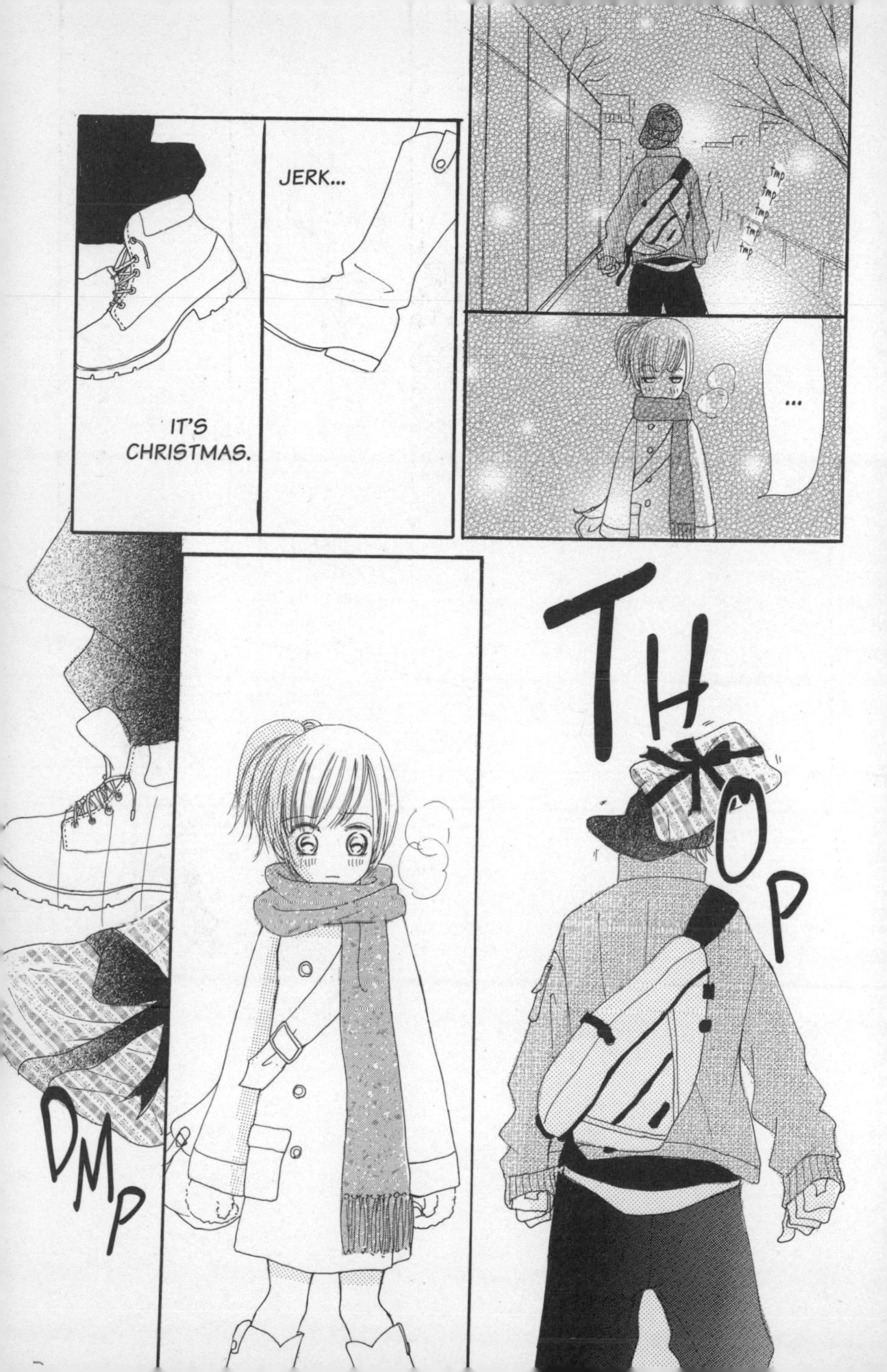

tmp tmp tmp tmp tmp
...
JERK...
IT'S CHRISTMAS.
THOP
DMP

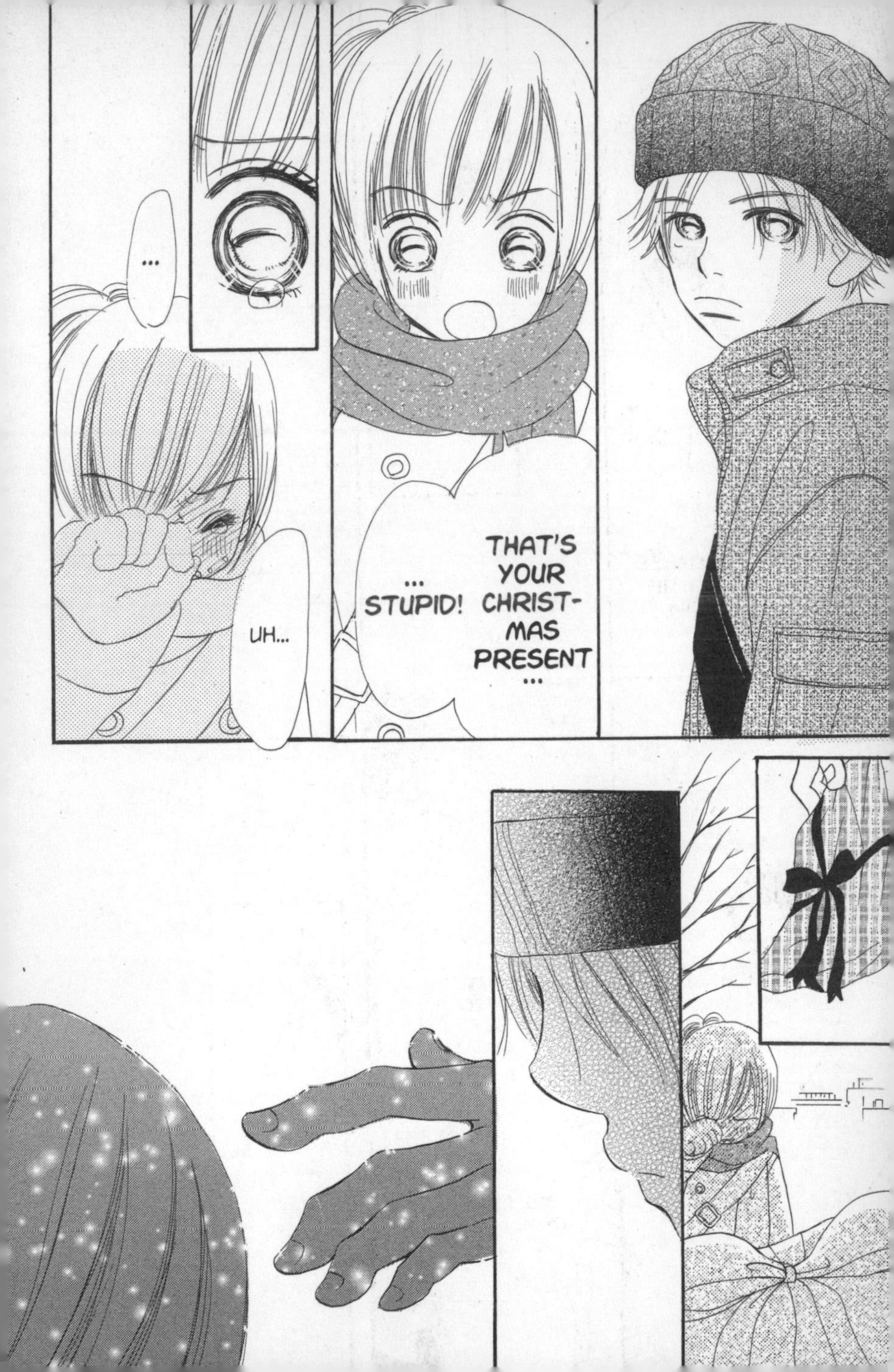
THAT'S YOUR CHRIST-MAS PRESENT ...
... STUPID!
...
UH...

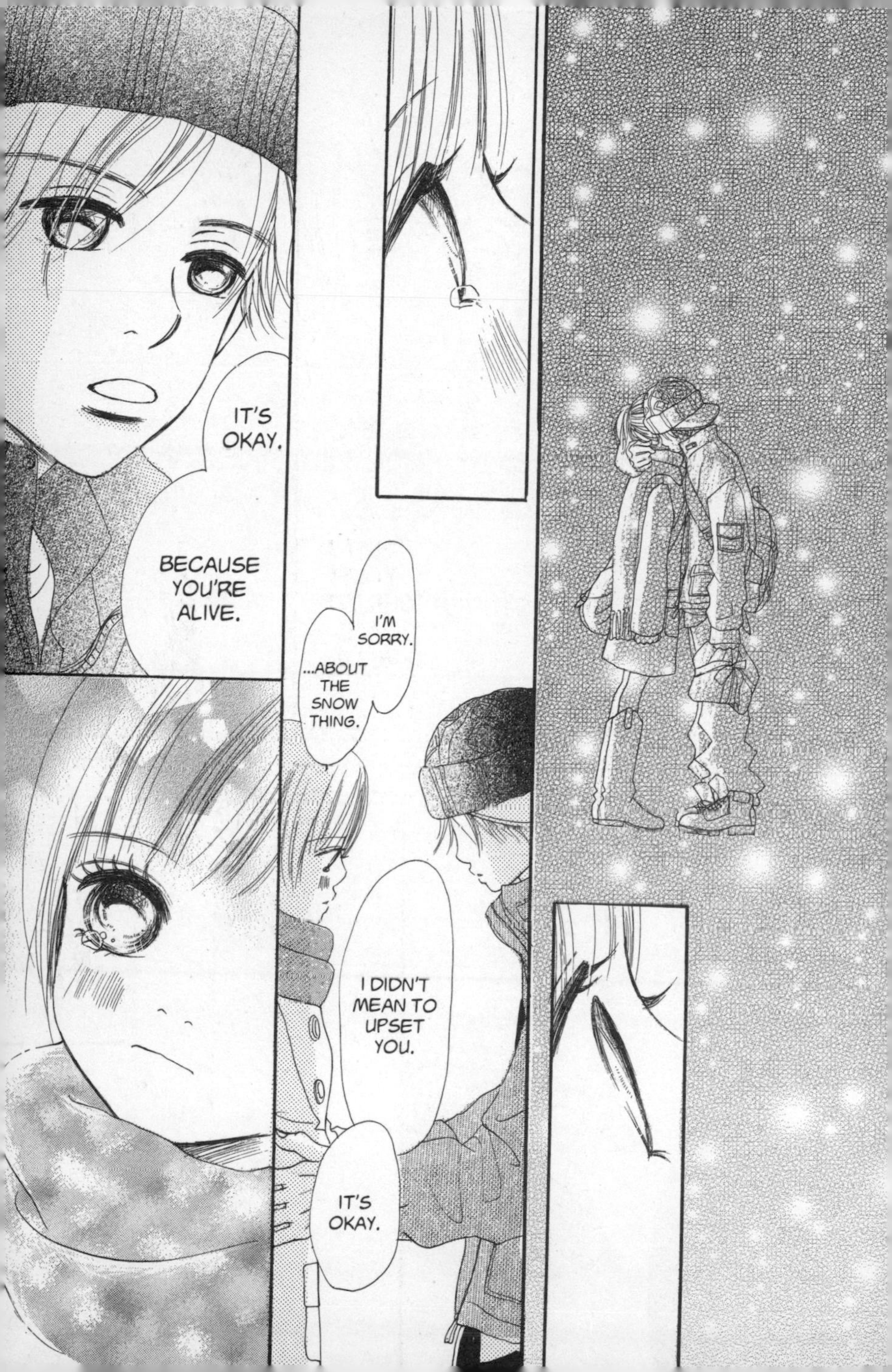
I'M SORRY.
...ABOUT THE SNOW THING.
I DIDN'T MEAN TO UPSET YOU.
IT'S OKAY.
IT'S OKAY.
BECAUSE YOU'RE ALIVE.

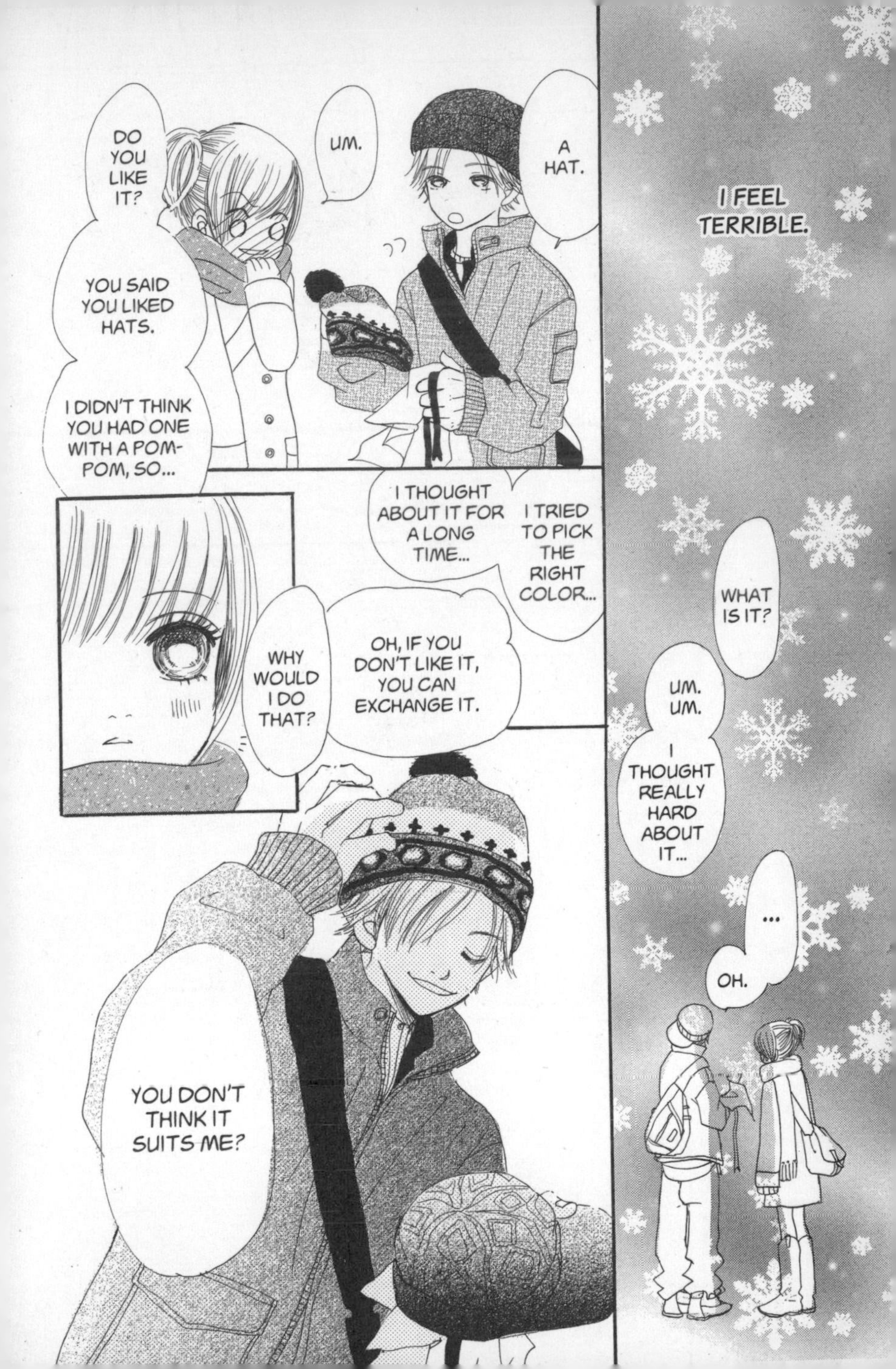
I FEEL TERRIBLE.
WHAT IS IT?
UM. UM.
I THOUGHT REALLY HARD ABOUT IT...
...
OH.
A HAT.
UM.
DO YOU LIKE IT?
YOU SAID YOU LIKED HATS.
I DIDN'T THINK YOU HAD ONE WITH A POM-POM, SO...
I TRIED TO PICK THE RIGHT COLOR...
I THOUGHT ABOUT IT FOR A LONG TIME...
OH, IF YOU DON'T LIKE IT, YOU CAN EXCHANGE IT.
WHY WOULD I DO THAT?
YOU DON'T THINK IT SUITS ME?

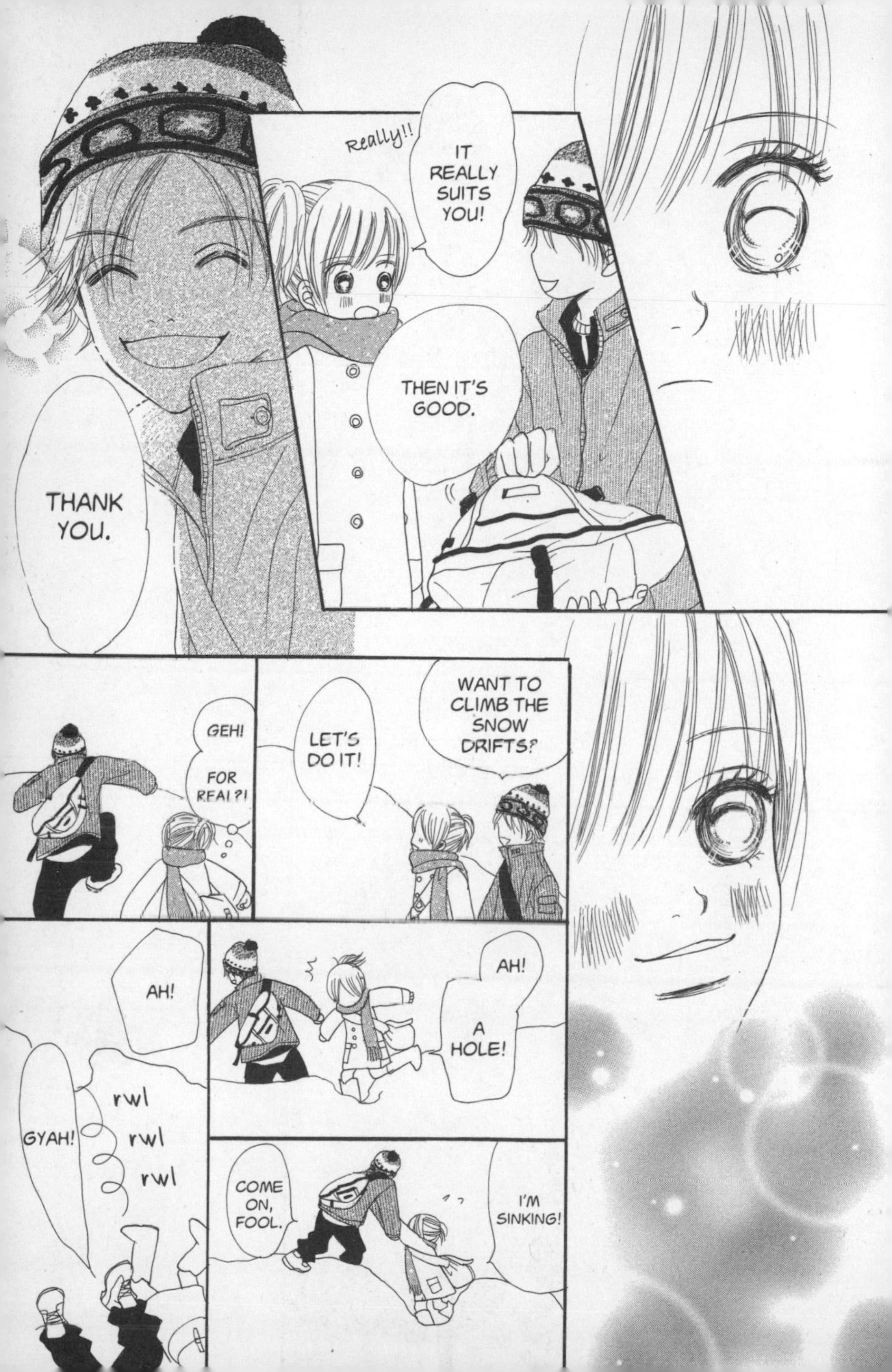
IT REALLY SUITS YOU!
Really!!
THEN IT'S GOOD.
THANK YOU.
WANT TO CLIMB THE SNOW DRIFTS?
LET'S DO IT!
GEH! FOR REAL?!
AH! A HOLE!
AH!
GYAH!
rwl rwl rwl
I'M SINKING!
COME ON, FOOL.

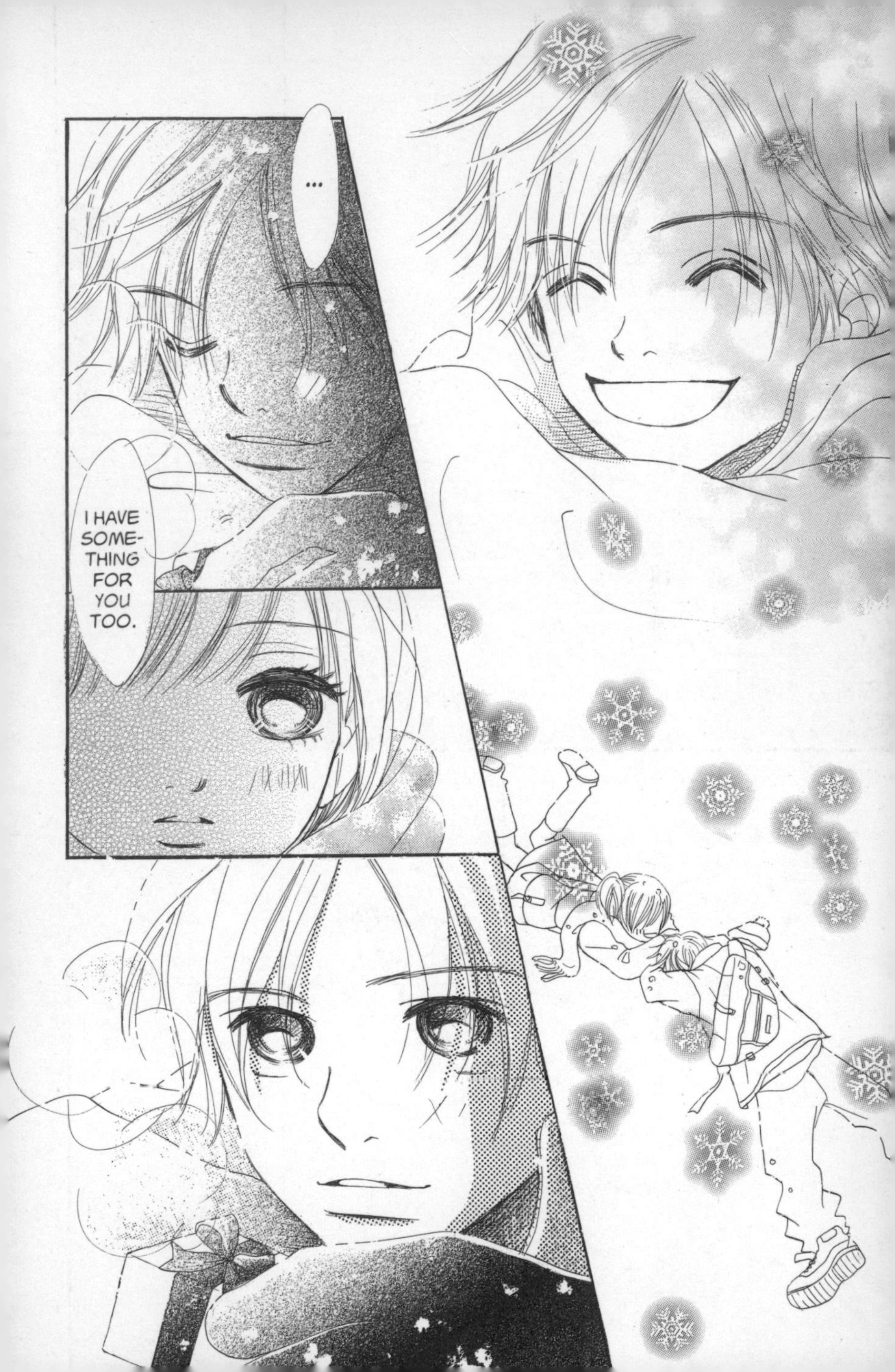
...
I HAVE SOME-THING FOR YOU TOO.

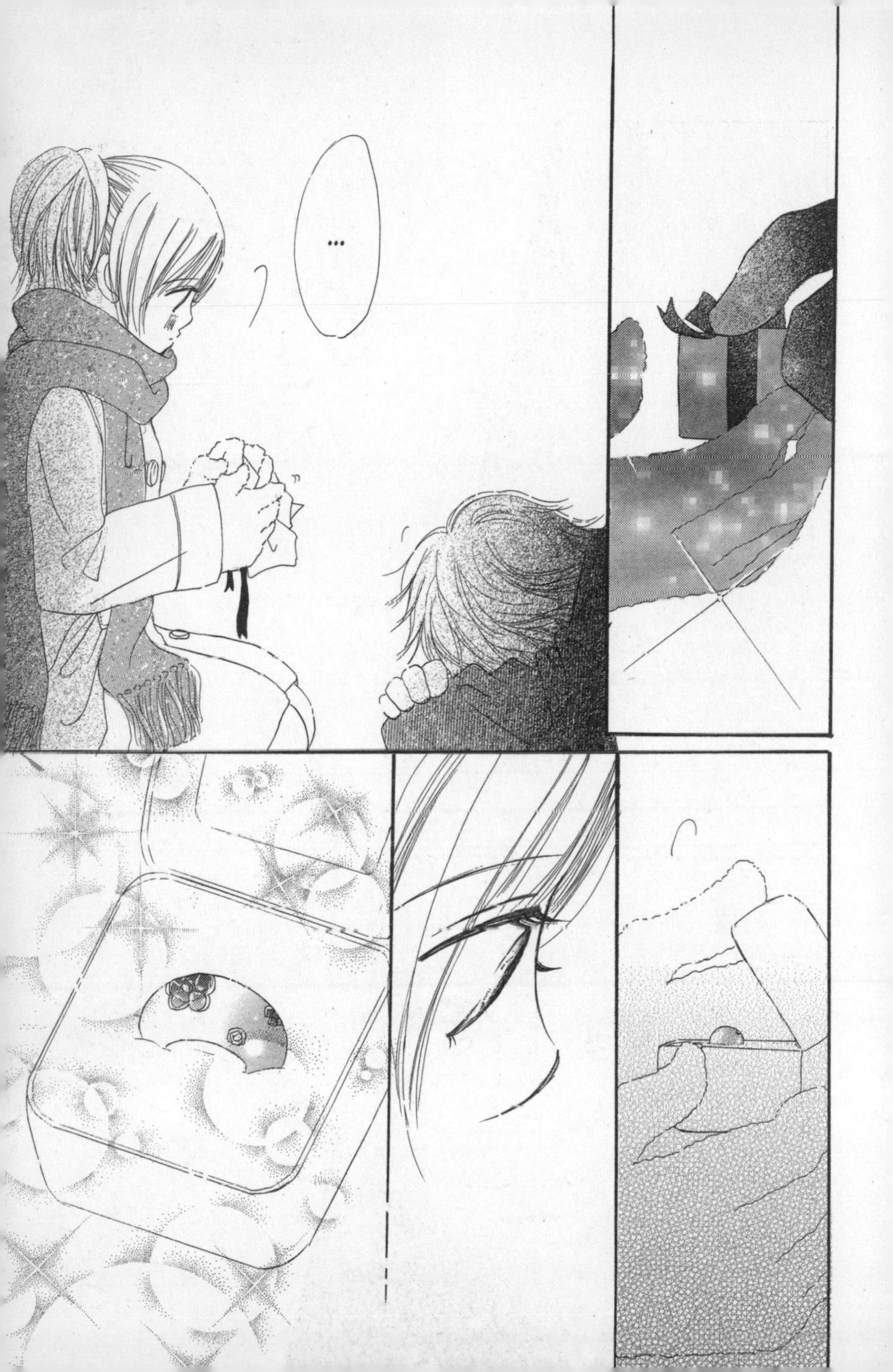
...

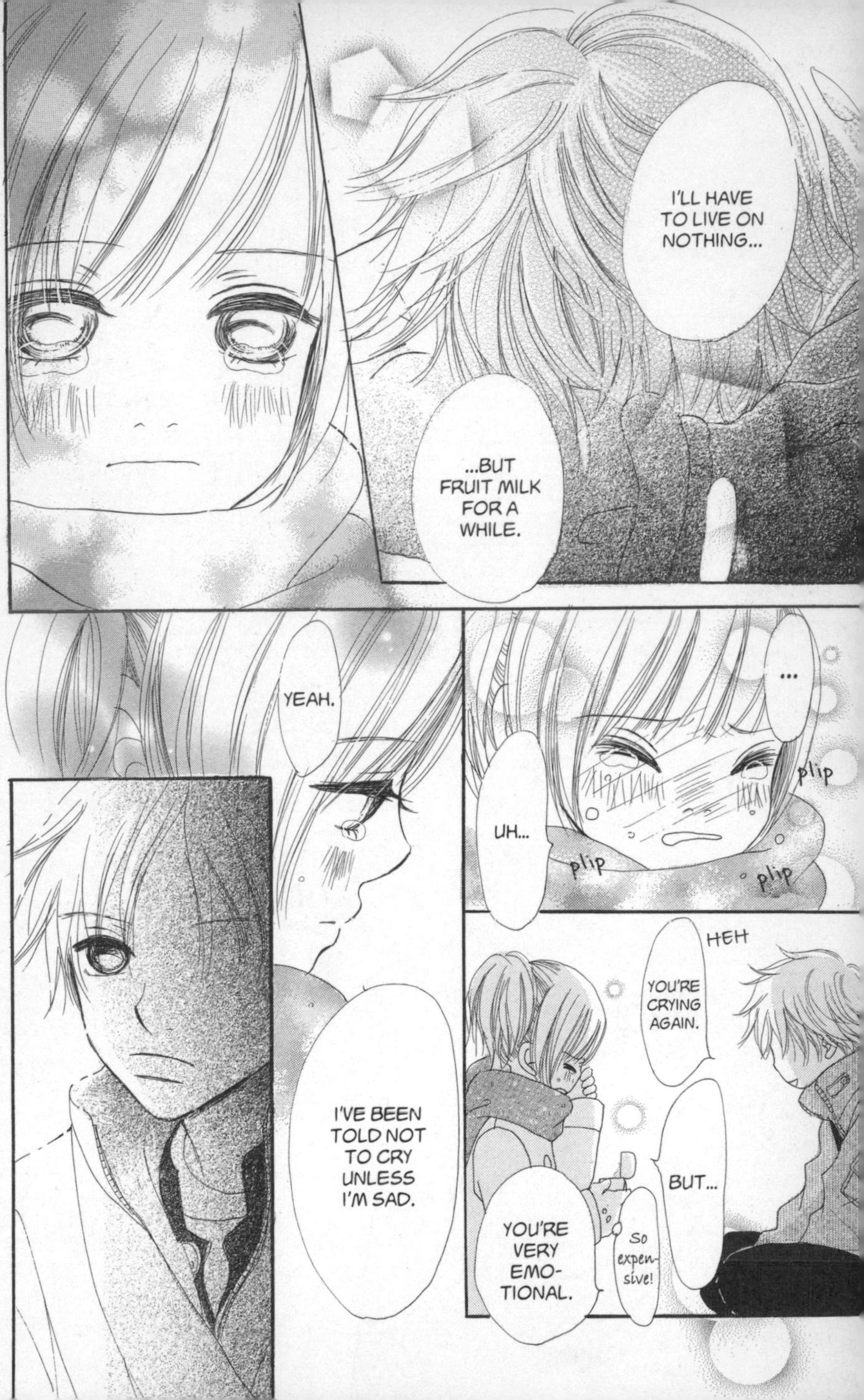
I'LL HAVE TO LIVE ON NOTHING...
...BUT FRUIT MILK FOR A WHILE.
...
UH...
plip
plip
plip
HEH
YOU'RE CRYING AGAIN.
BUT...
So expensive!
YOU'RE VERY EMO-TIONAL.
YEAH.
I'VE BEEN TOLD NOT TO CRY UNLESS I'M SAD.

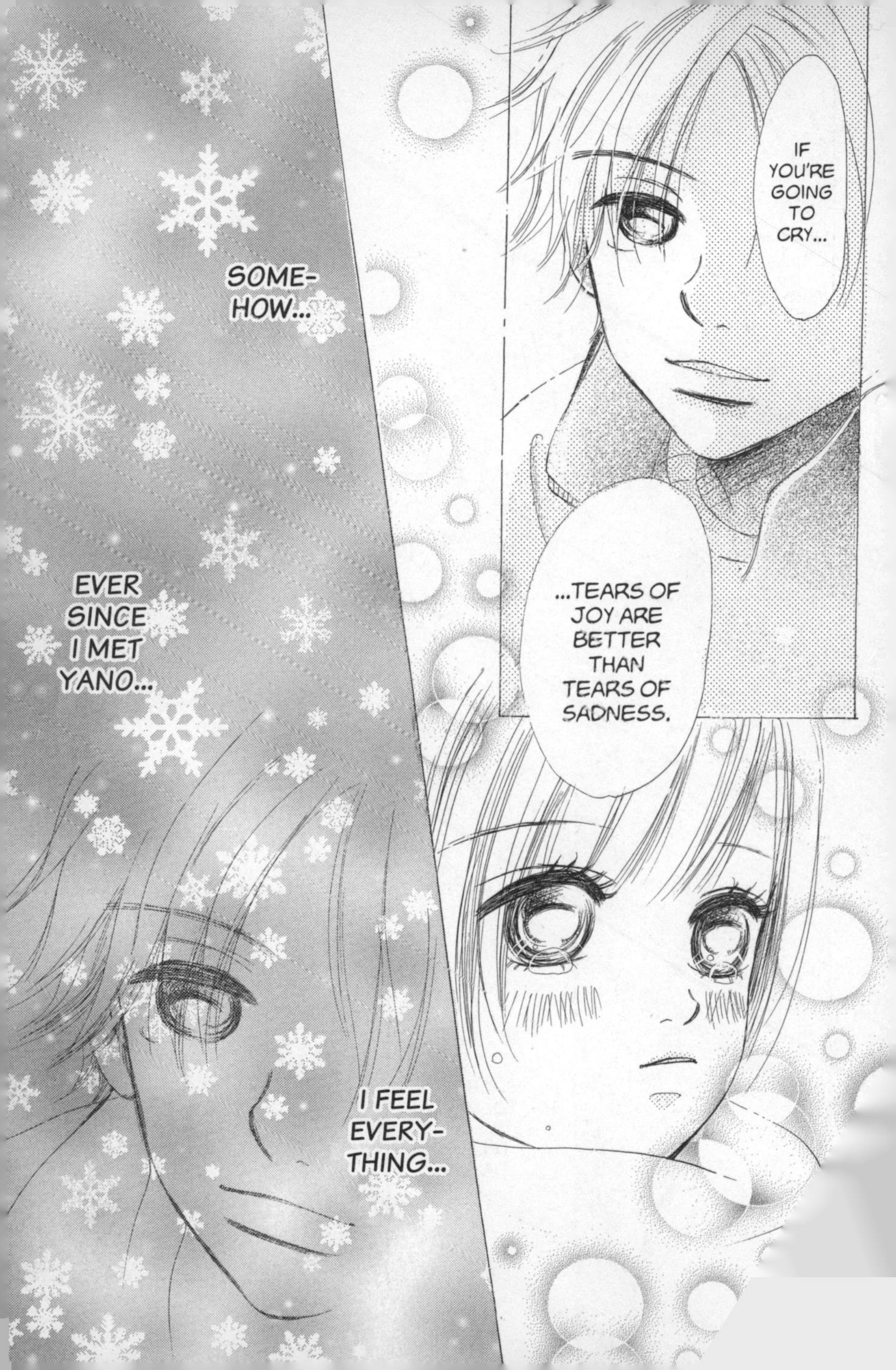
IF YOU'RE GOING TO CRY...
...TEARS OF JOY ARE BETTER THAN TEARS OF SADNESS.
SOME-HOW...
EVER SINCE I MET YANO...
I FEEL EVERY-THING...

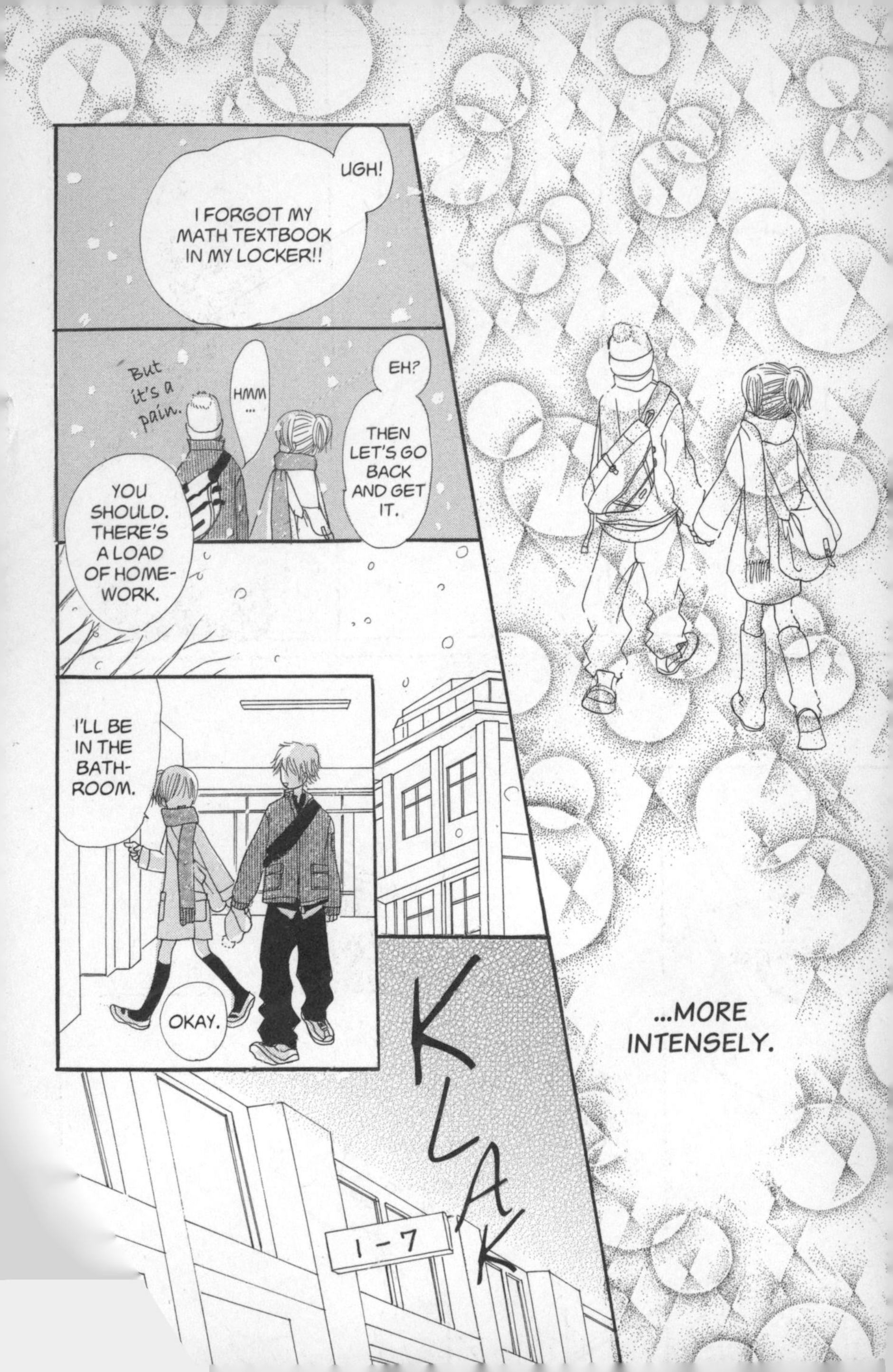
...MORE INTENSELY.
UGH!
I FORGOT MY MATH TEXTBOOK IN MY LOCKER!!
EH?
THEN LET'S GO BACK AND GET IT.
HMM ...
But it's a pain.
YOU SHOULD. THERE'S A LOAD OF HOME-WORK.
I'LL BE IN THE BATH-ROOM.
OKAY.
KLAK
1-7

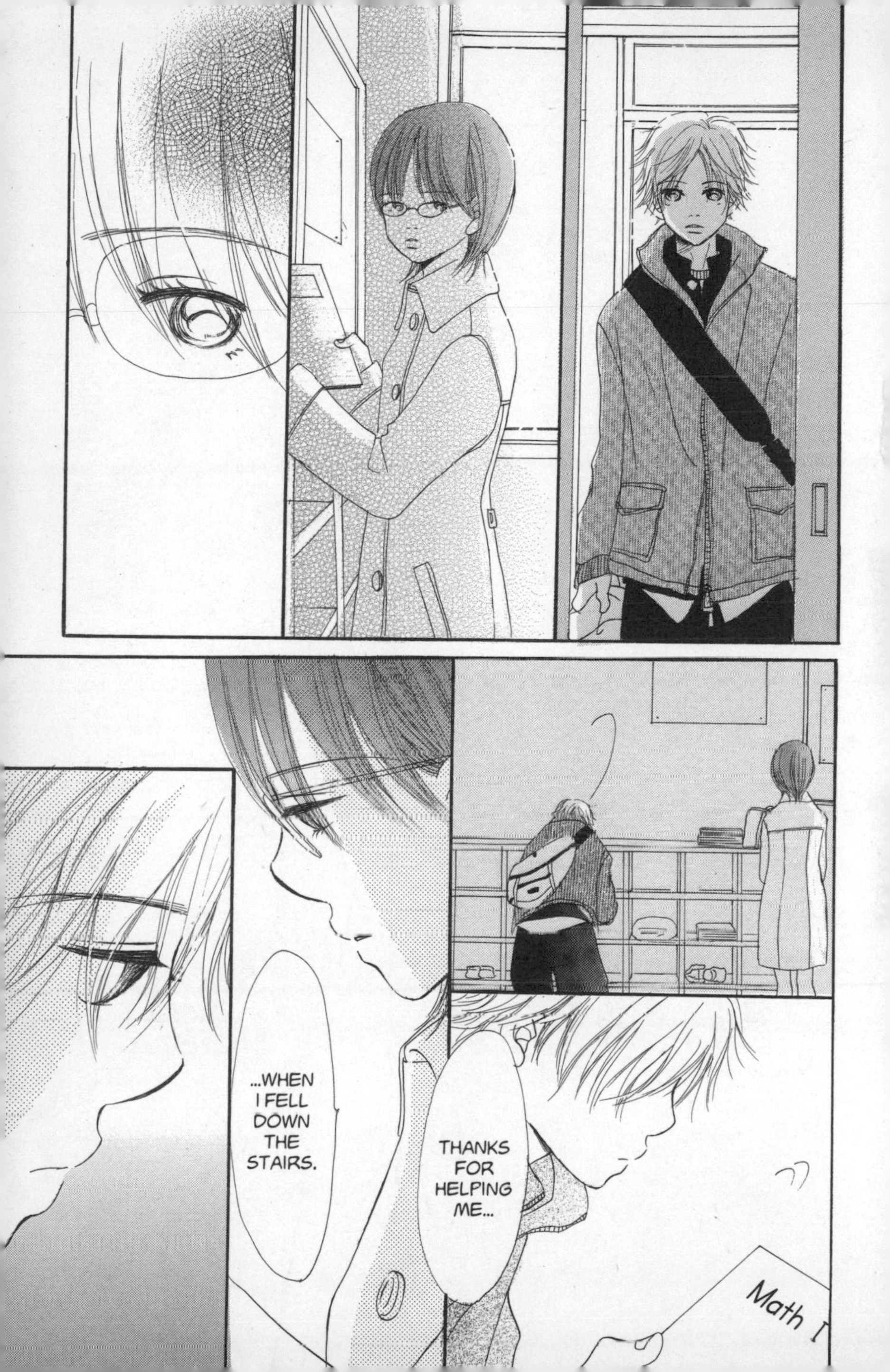
THANKS FOR HELPING ME...
Math I
...WHEN I FELL DOWN THE STAIRS.

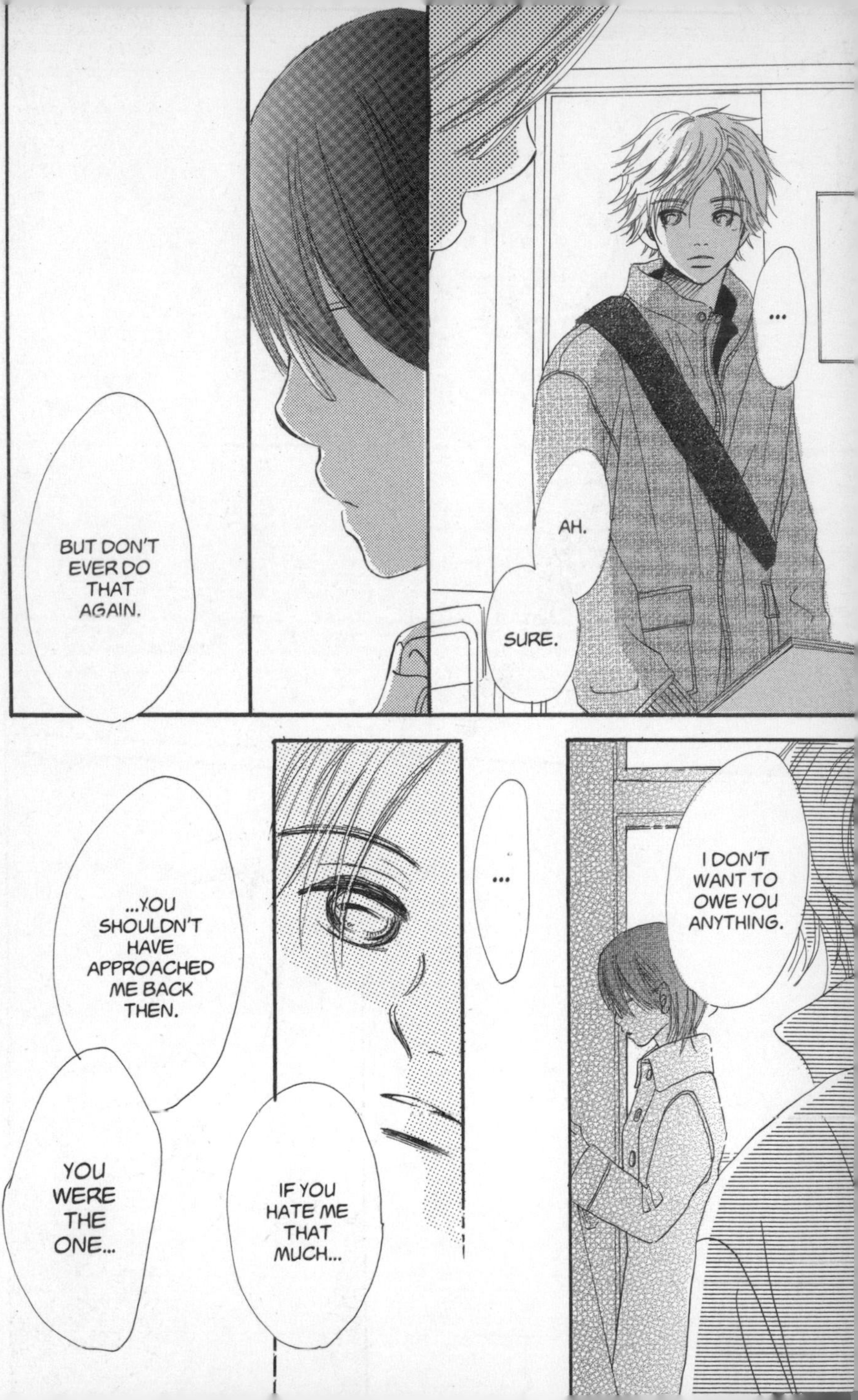
...
AH.
SURE.
BUT DON'T EVER DO THAT AGAIN.
I DON'T WANT TO OWE YOU ANYTHING.
...
IF YOU HATE ME THAT MUCH...
...YOU SHOULDN'T HAVE APPROACHED ME BACK THEN.
YOU WERE THE ONE...

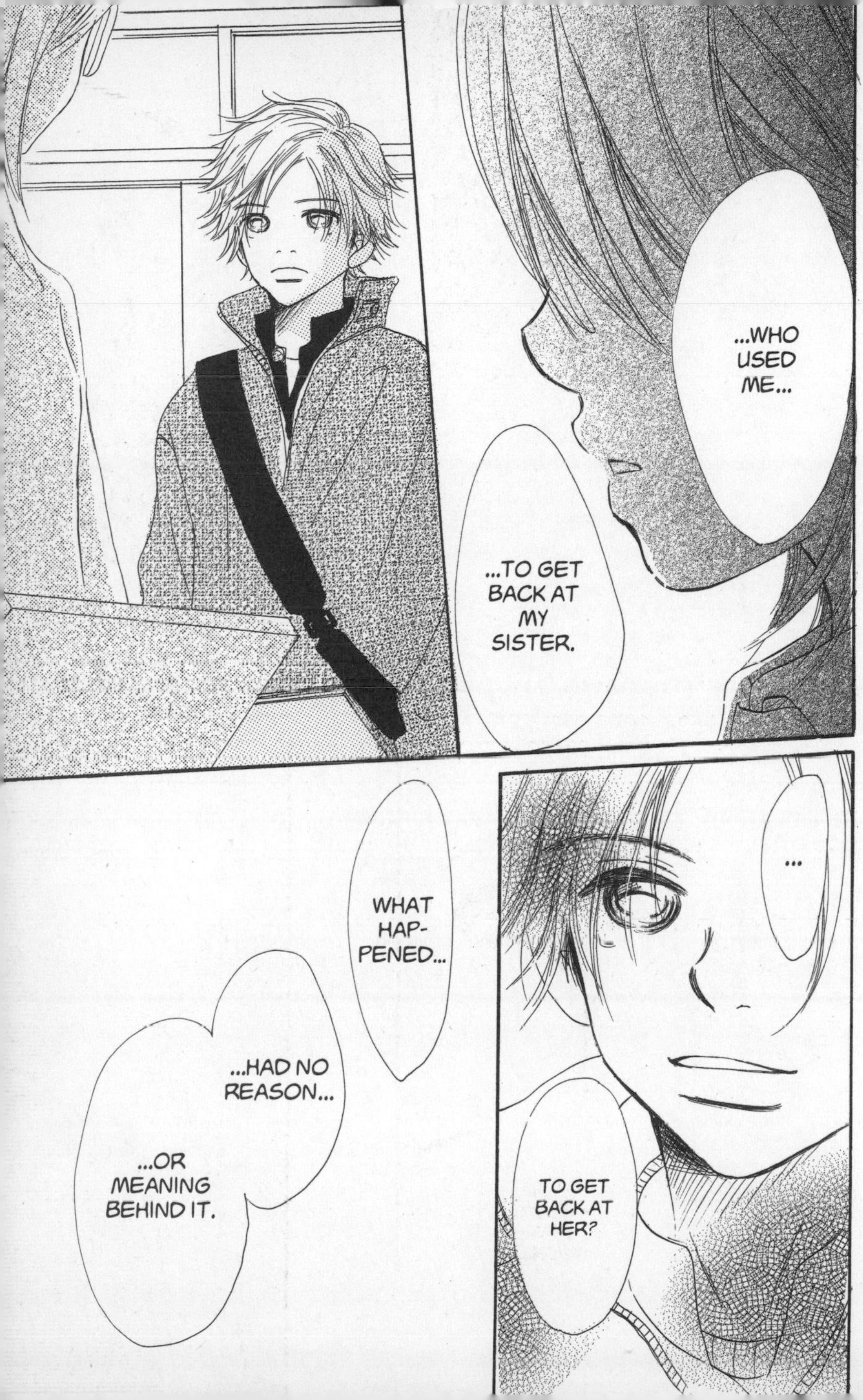
...WHO USED ME...
...TO GET BACK AT MY SISTER.
...
TO GET BACK AT HER?
WHAT HAP-PENED...
...HAD NO REASON...
...OR MEANING BEHIND IT.

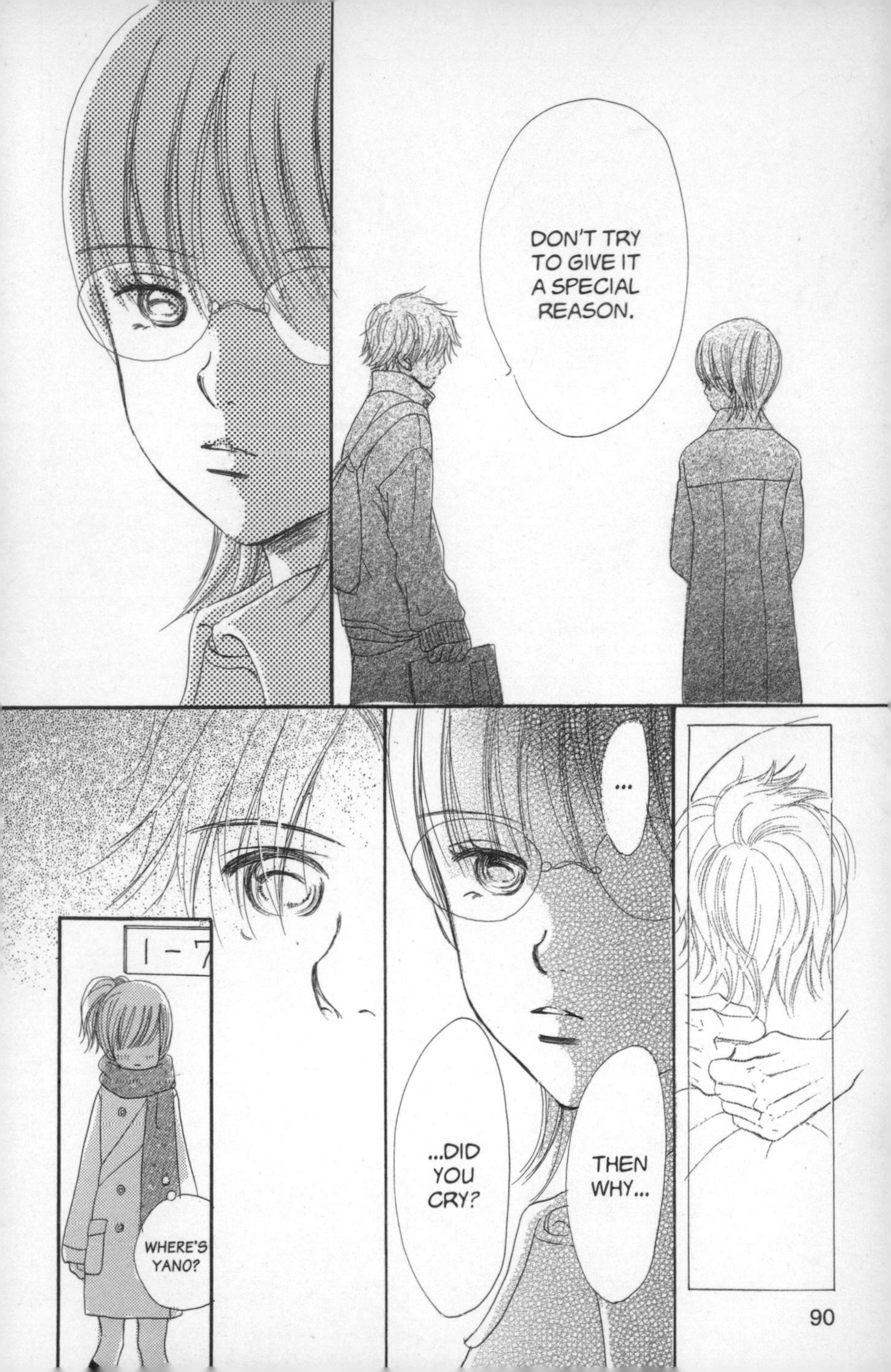
DON'T TRY TO GIVE IT A SPECIAL REASON.
...
THEN WHY...
...DID YOU CRY?
WHERE'S YANO?

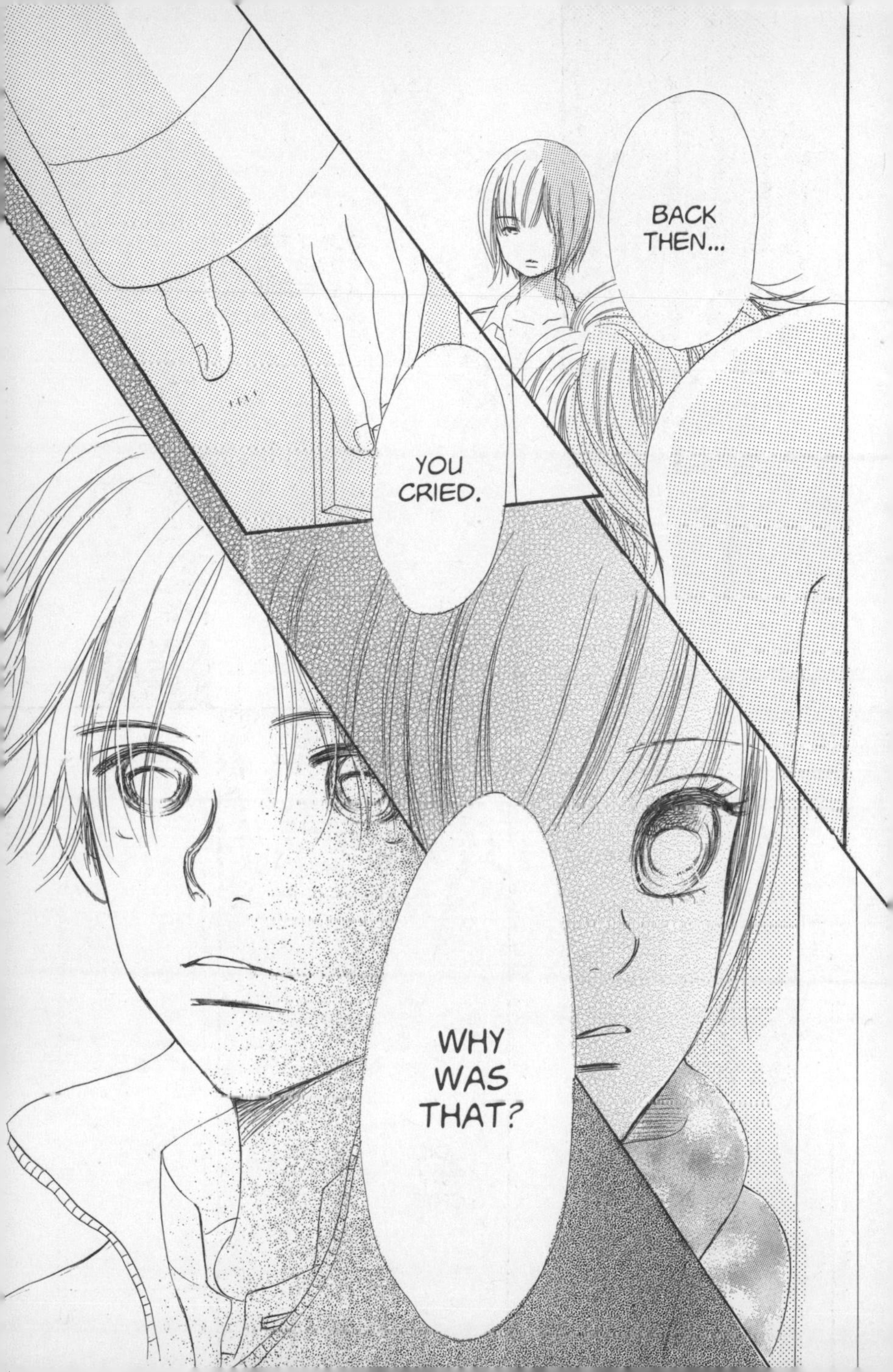
BACK THEN...
YOU CRIED.
WHY WAS THAT?

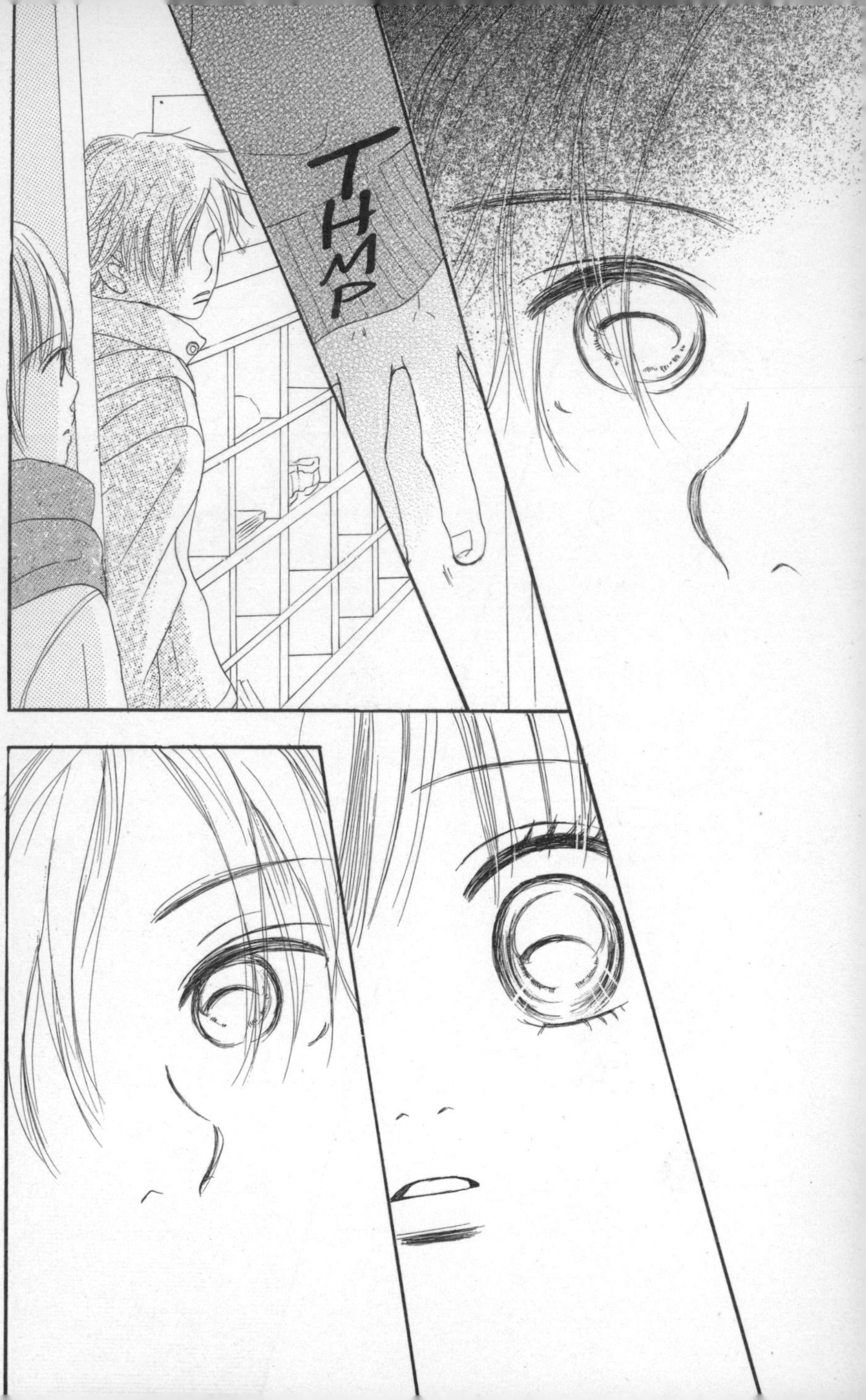
THMP

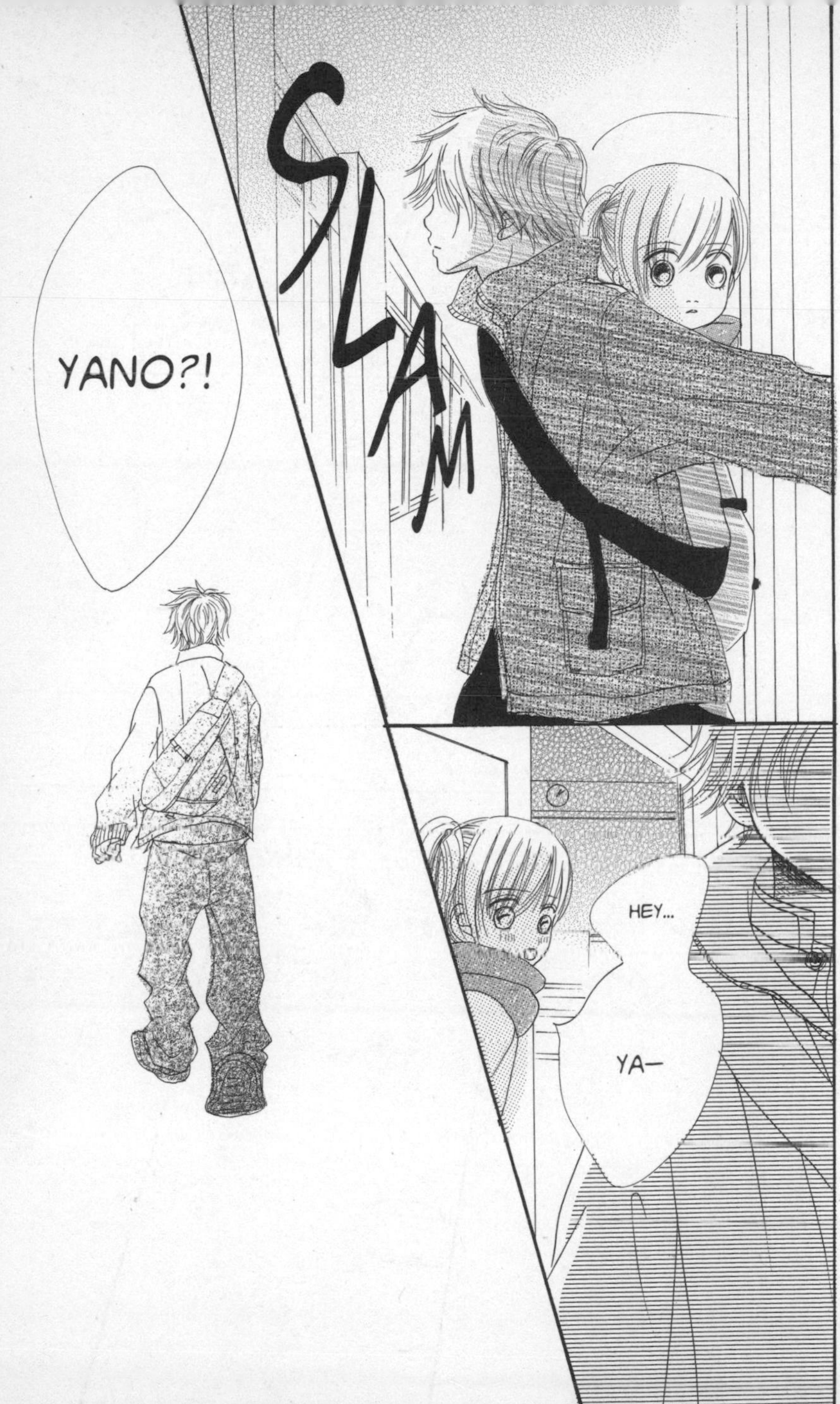
SLAM
HEY...
YA—
YANO?!

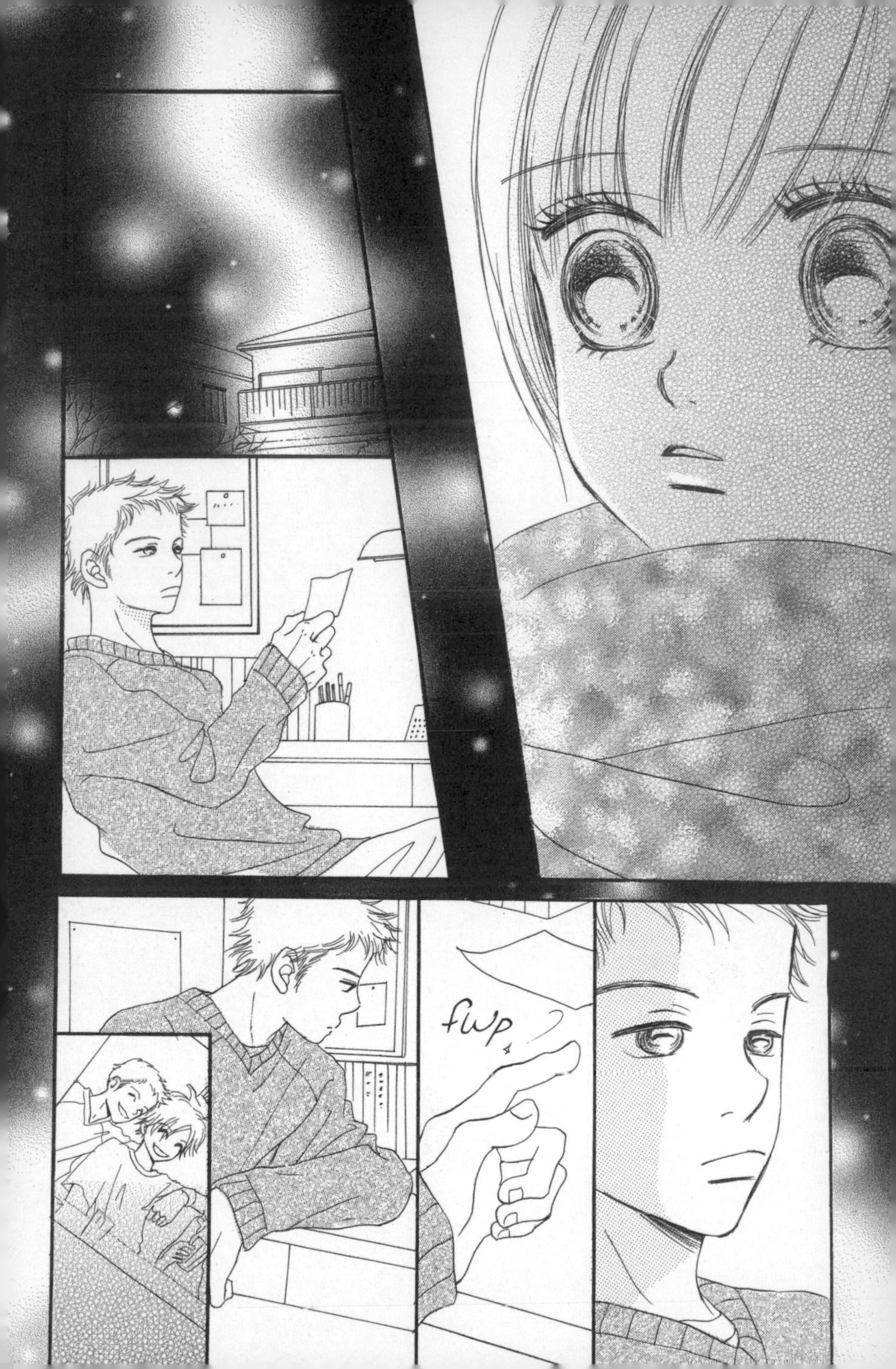
fwp

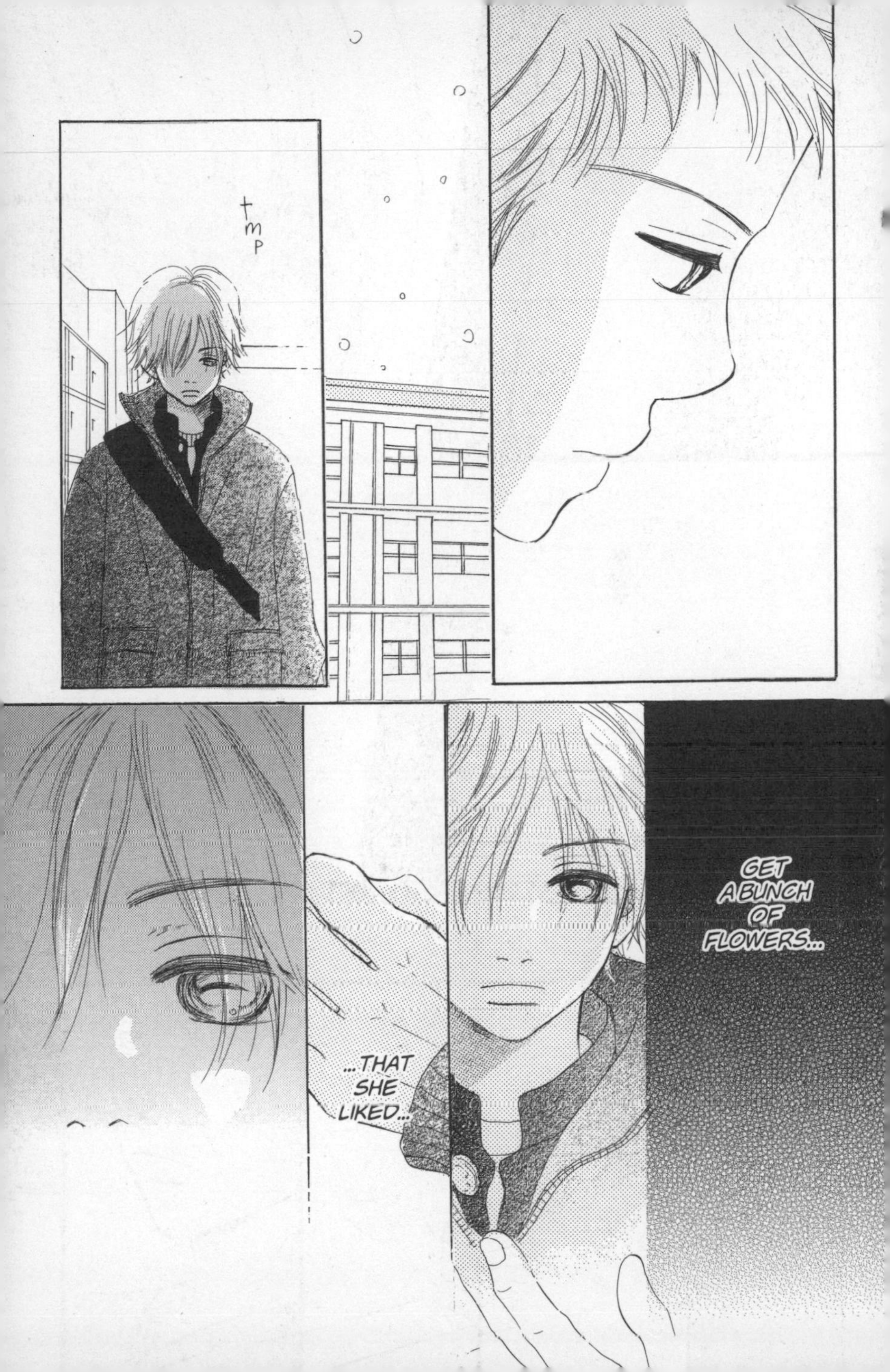
TMP
GET A BUNCH OF FLOWERS...
...THAT SHE LIKED...

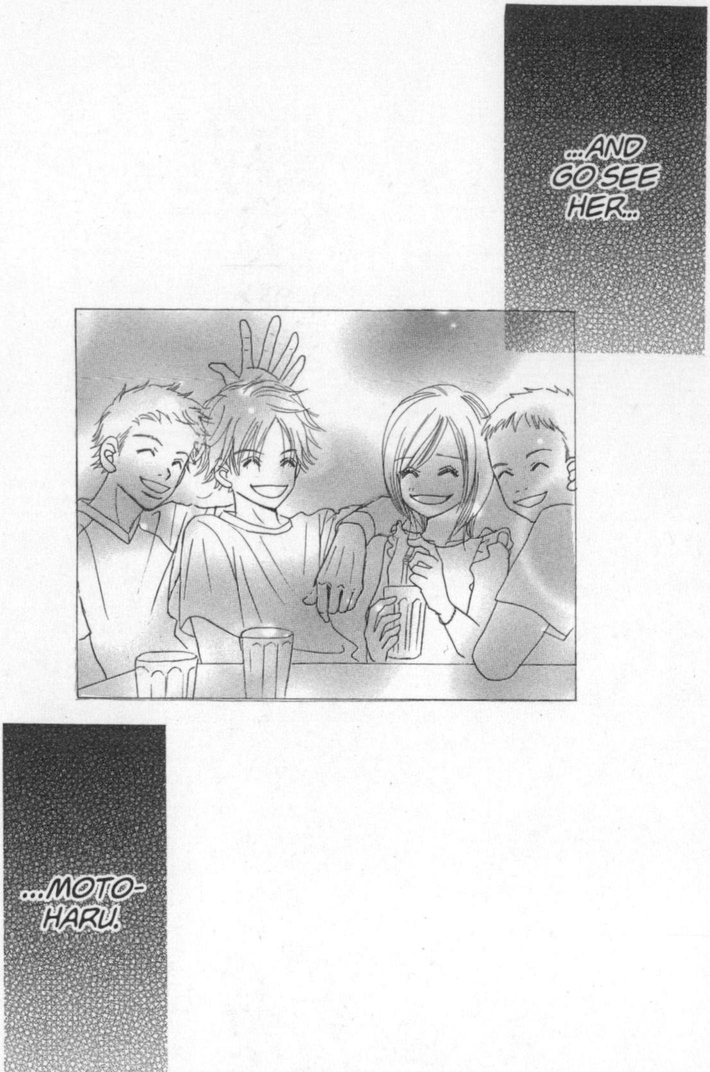
...AND GO SEE HER...
...MOTO-HARU.

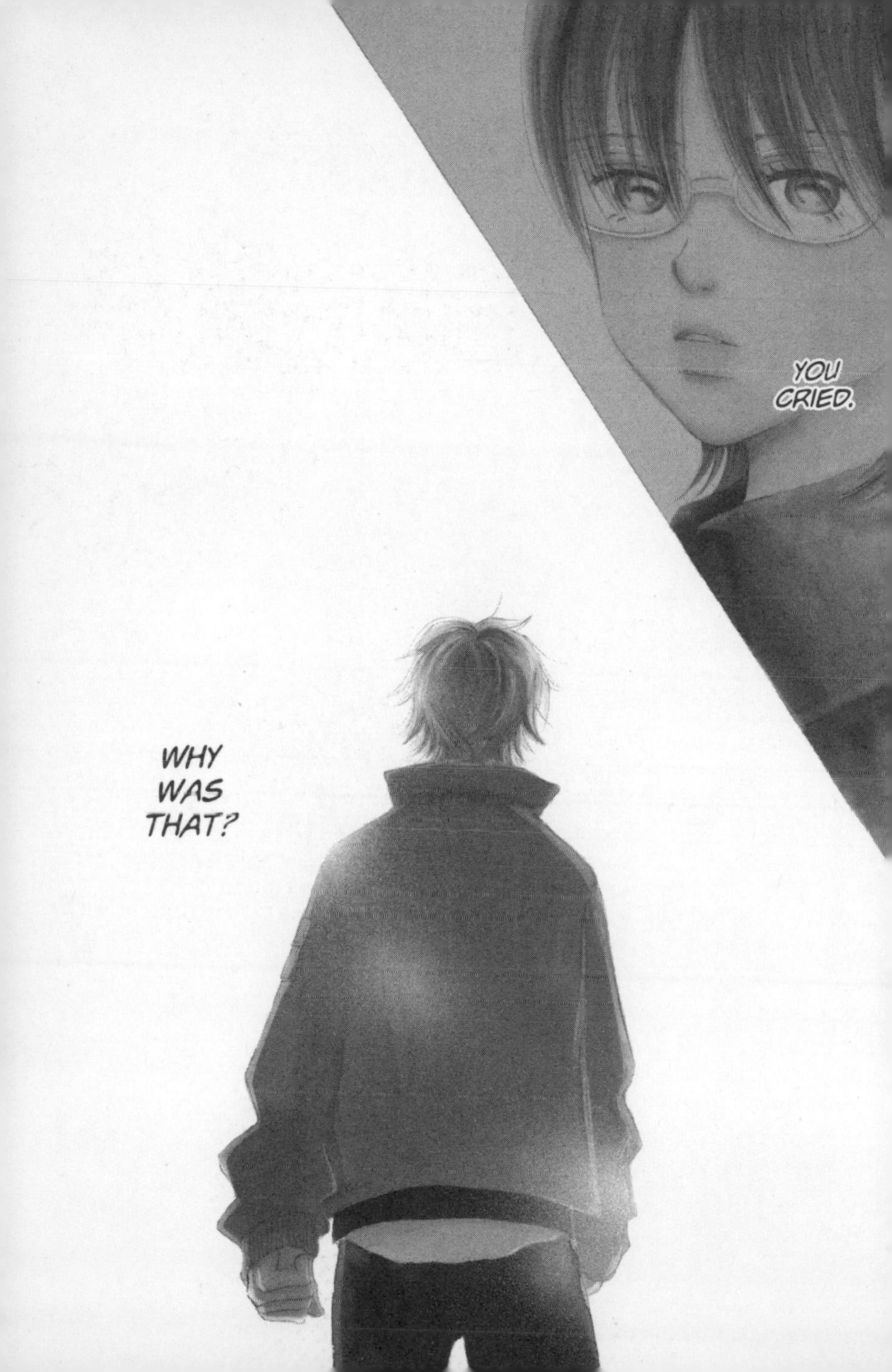
YOU CRIED.
WHY WAS THAT?

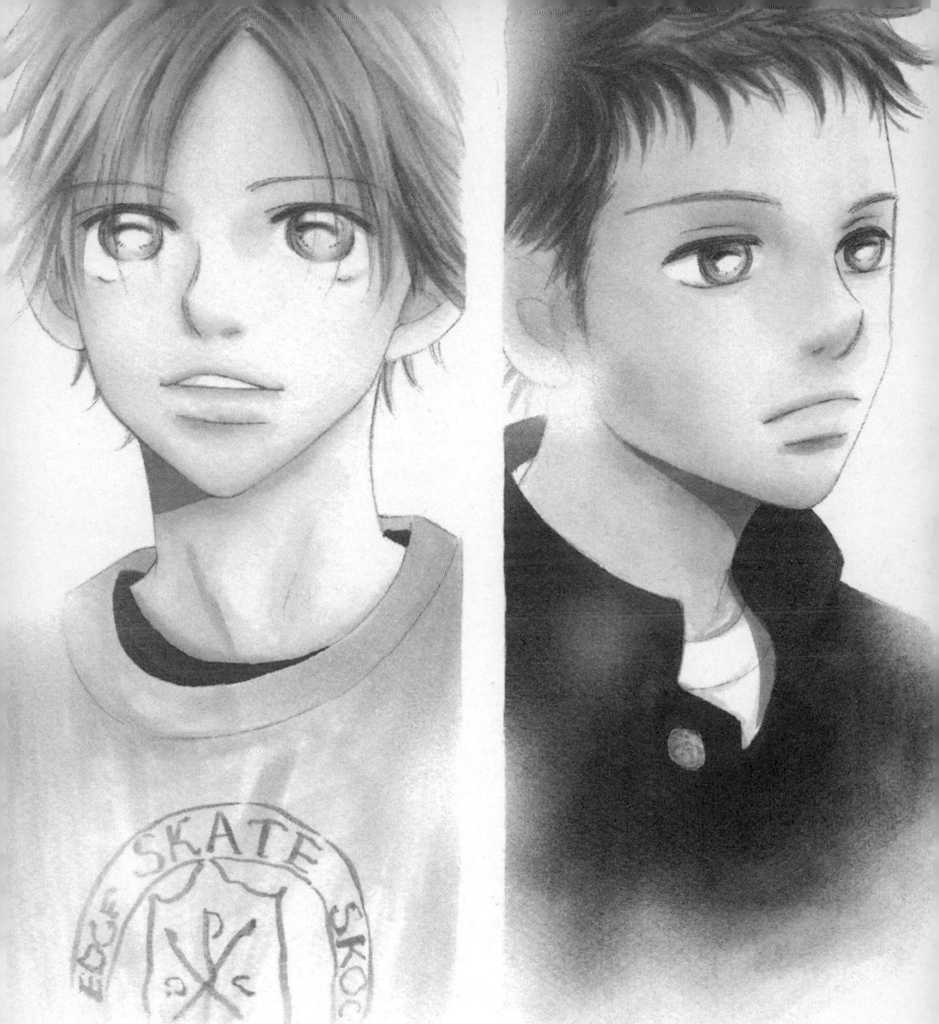
SKATE

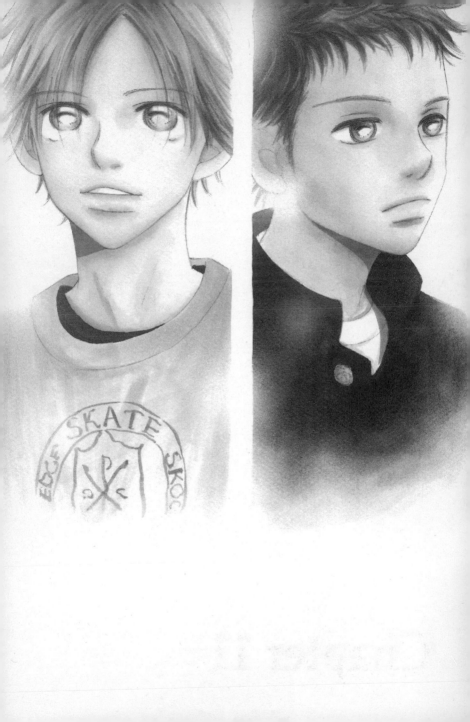

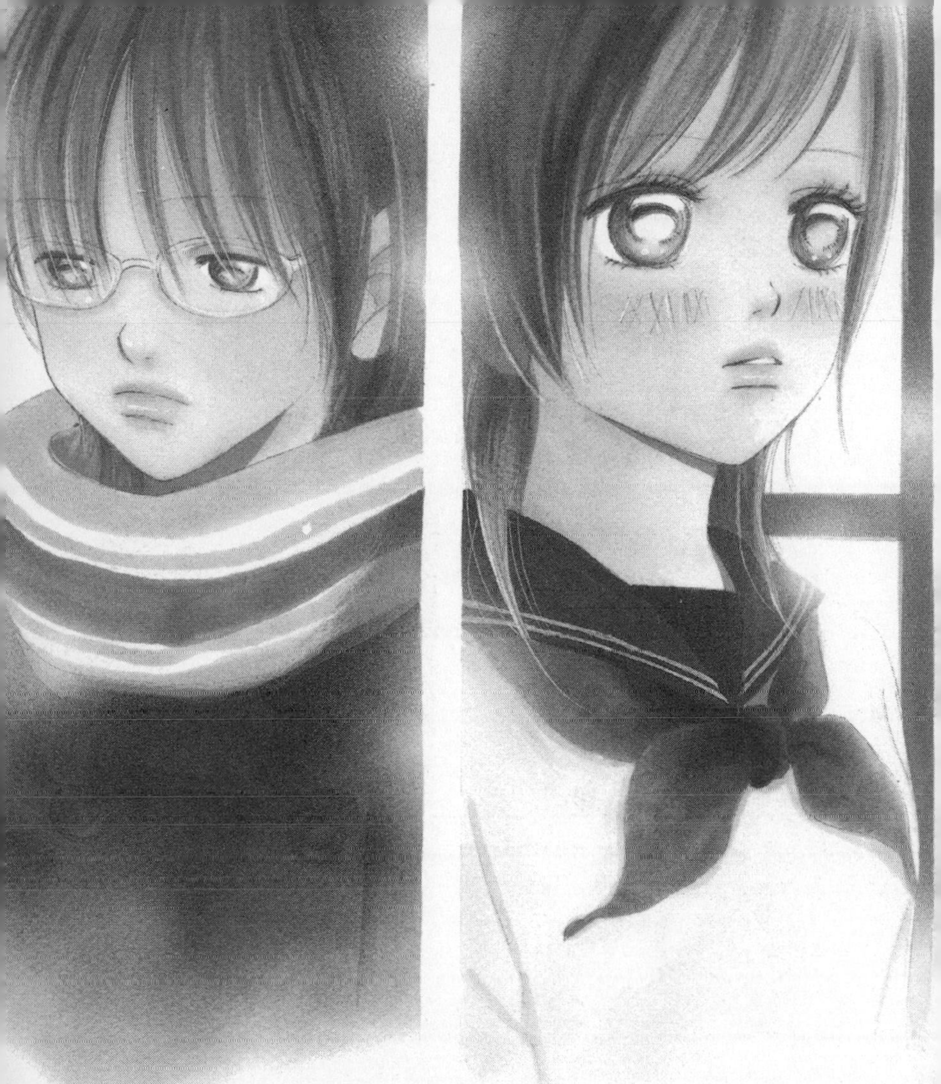

Chapter 11

"CRIED."

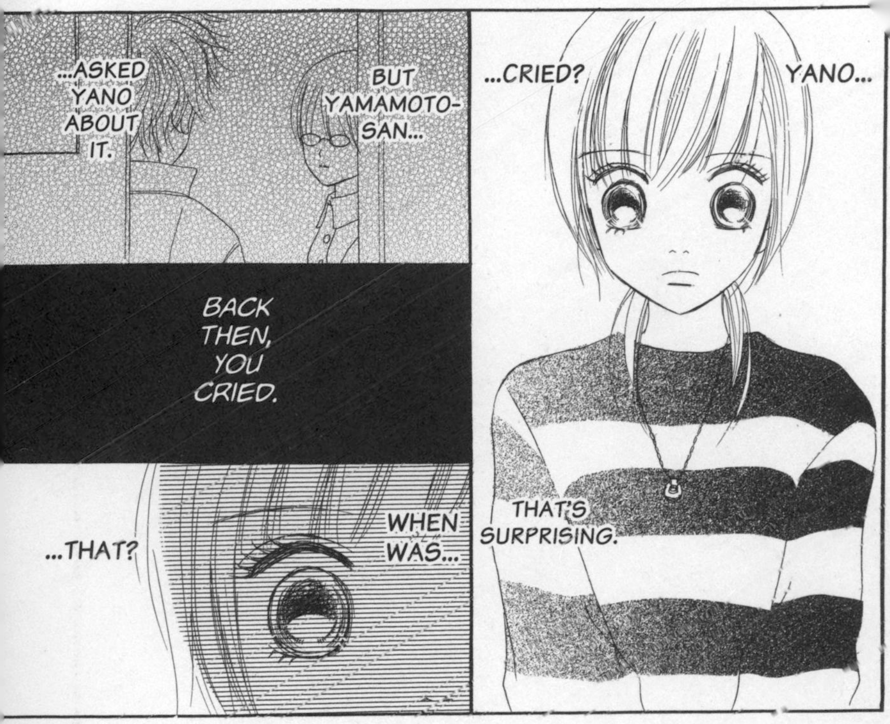
YANO...
...CRIED?
THAT'S SURPRISING.
BUT YAMAMOTO-SAN...
...ASKED YANO ABOUT IT.
BACK THEN, YOU CRIED.
WHEN WAS...
...THAT?

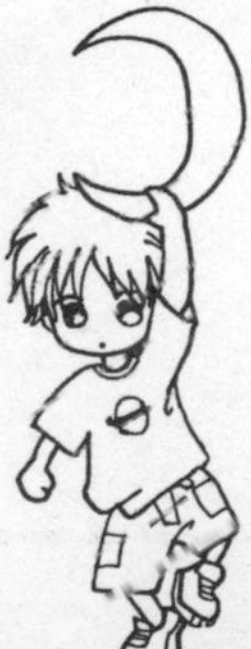

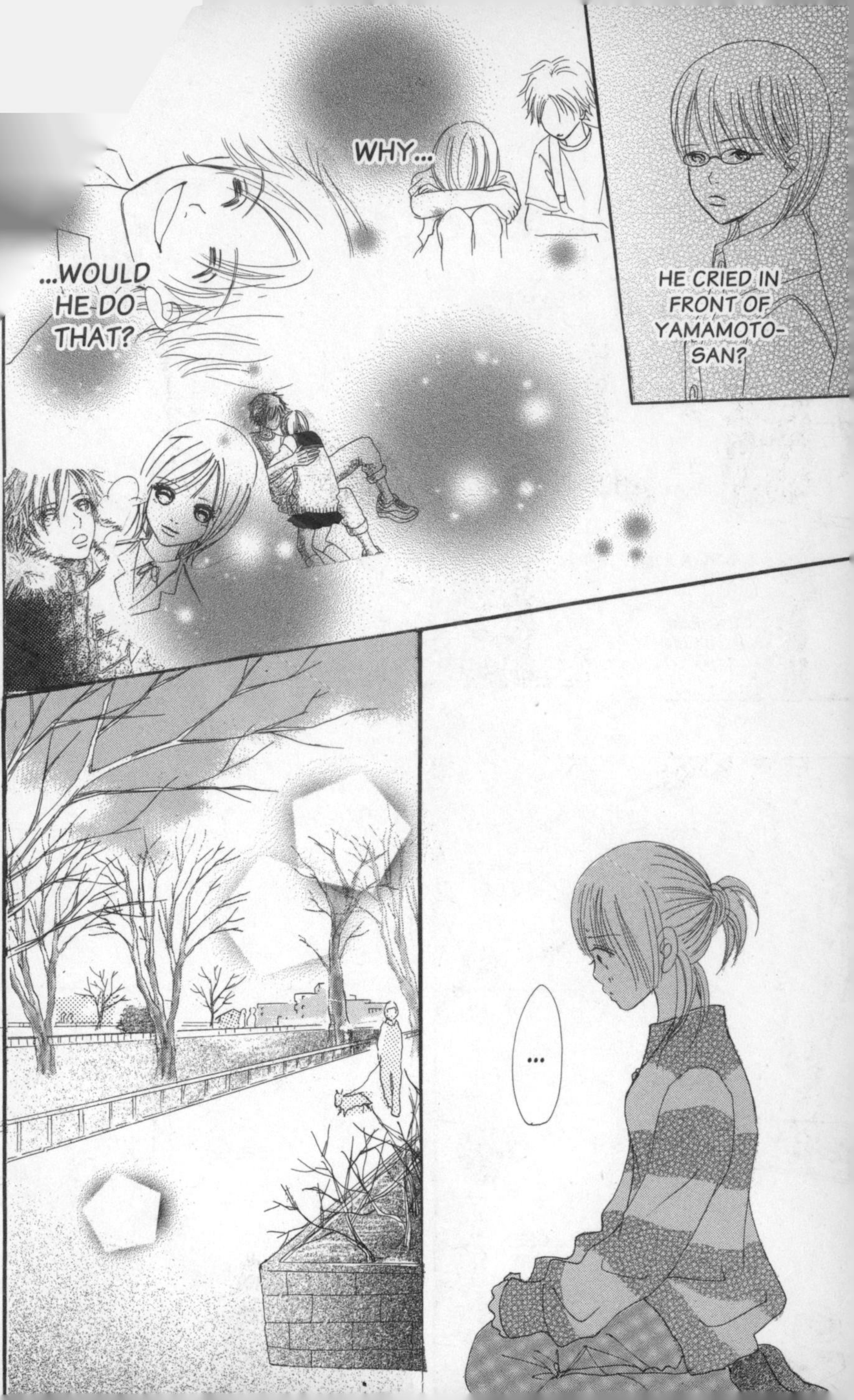
HE CRIED IN FRONT OF YAMAMOTO-SAN?
WHY...
...WOULD HE DO THAT?
...

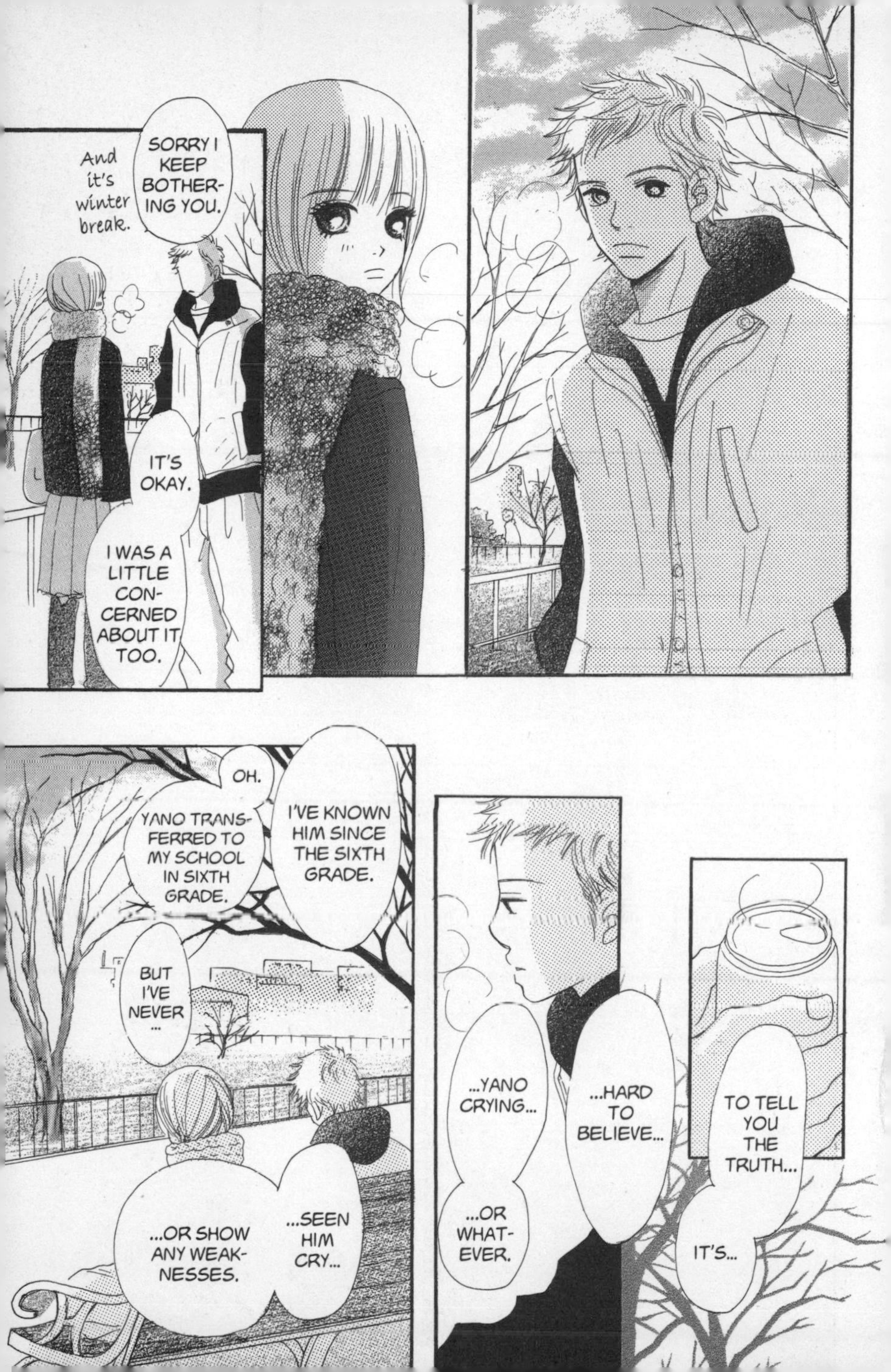
SORRY I KEEP BOTHERING YOU.
And it's winter break.
IT'S OKAY.
I WAS A LITTLE CONCERNED ABOUT IT TOO.
TO TELL YOU THE TRUTH...
IT'S...
...HARD TO BELIEVE...
...YANO CRYING...
...OR WHATEVER.
I'VE KNOWN HIM SINCE THE SIXTH GRADE.
OH.
YANO TRANSFERRED TO MY SCHOOL IN SIXTH GRADE.
BUT I'VE NEVER...
...SEEN HIM CRY...
...OR SHOW ANY WEAKNESSES.

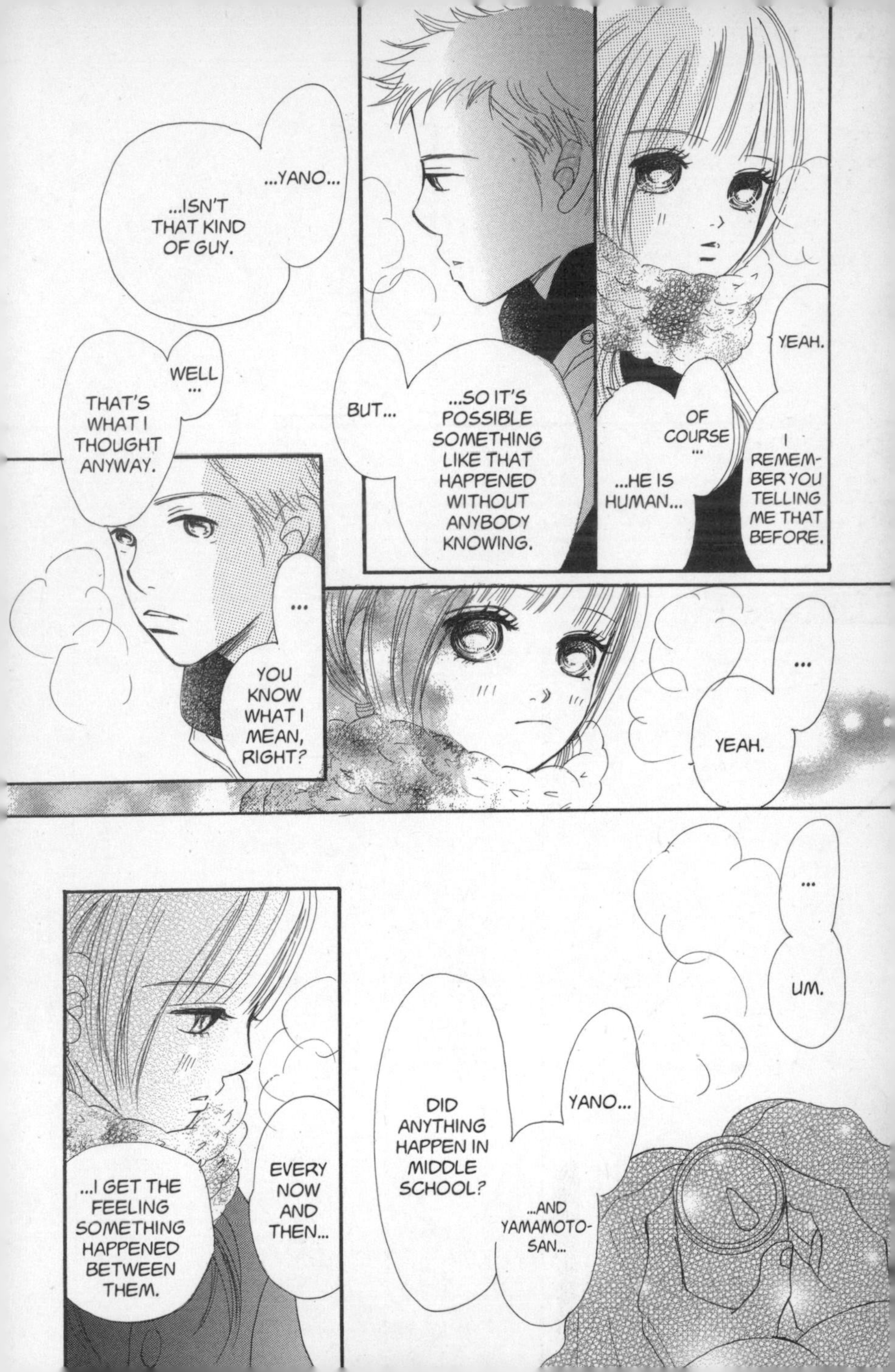
...YANO...
...ISN'T THAT KIND OF GUY.
YEAH.
I REMEMBER YOU TELLING ME THAT BEFORE.
OF COURSE...
...HE IS HUMAN...
...SO IT'S POSSIBLE SOMETHING LIKE THAT HAPPENED WITHOUT ANYBODY KNOWING.
BUT...
WELL...
THAT'S WHAT I THOUGHT ANYWAY.
...
YEAH.
...
YOU KNOW WHAT I MEAN, RIGHT?
...
UM.
YANO...
DID ANYTHING HAPPEN IN MIDDLE SCHOOL?
...AND YAMAMOTO-SAN...
EVERY NOW AND THEN...
...I GET THE FEELING SOMETHING HAPPENED BETWEEN THEM.

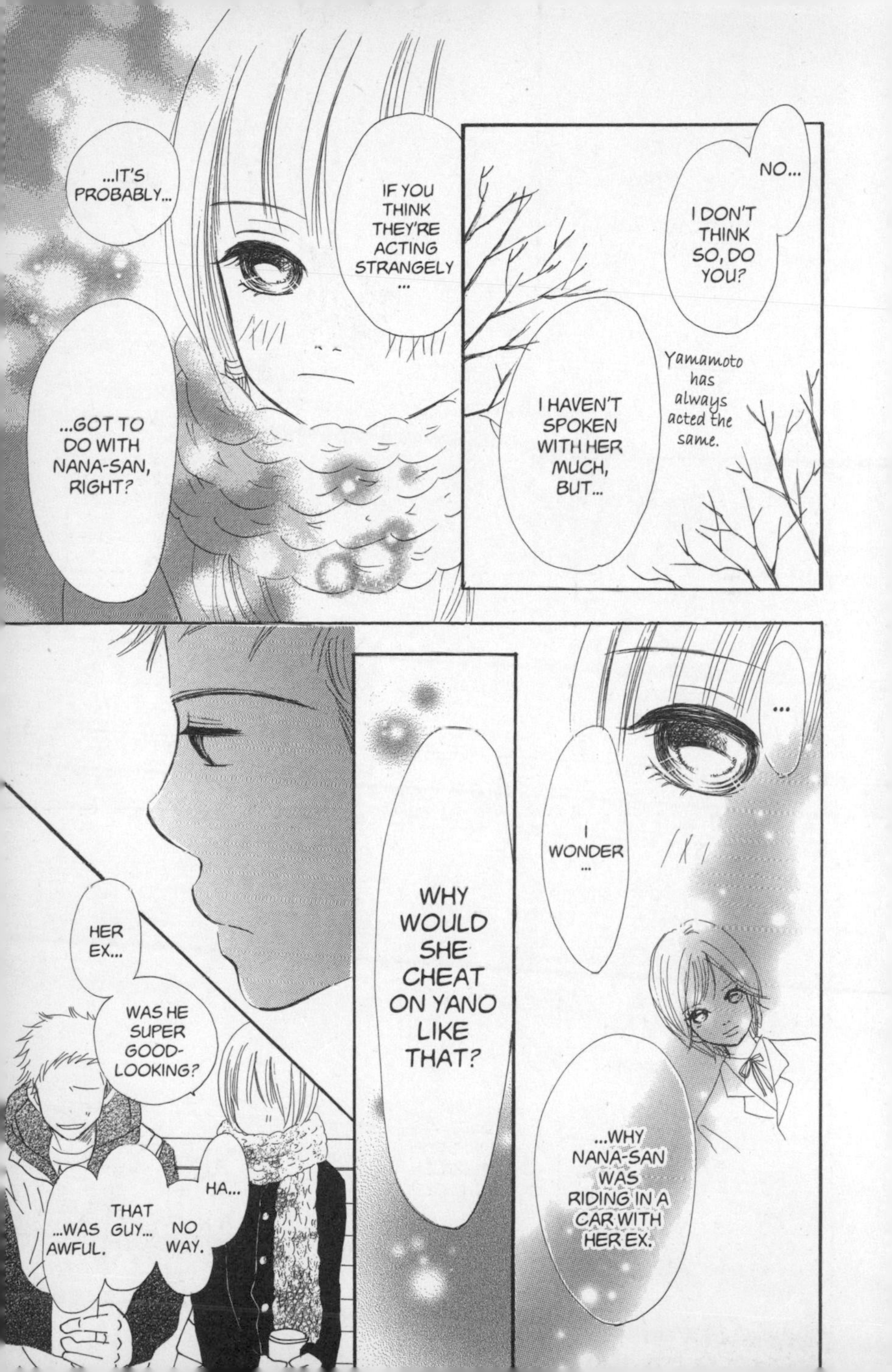
NO...
I DON'T THINK SO, DO YOU?
Yamamoto has always acted the same.
I HAVEN'T SPOKEN WITH HER MUCH, BUT...
IF YOU THINK THEY'RE ACTING STRANGELY ...
...IT'S PROBABLY...
...GOT TO DO WITH NANA-SAN, RIGHT?
...
I WONDER ...
...WHY NANA-SAN WAS RIDING IN A CAR WITH HER EX.
WHY WOULD SHE CHEAT ON YANO LIKE THAT?
HER EX...
WAS HE SUPER GOOD-LOOKING?
HA... NO WAY.
THAT GUY... ...WAS AWFUL.

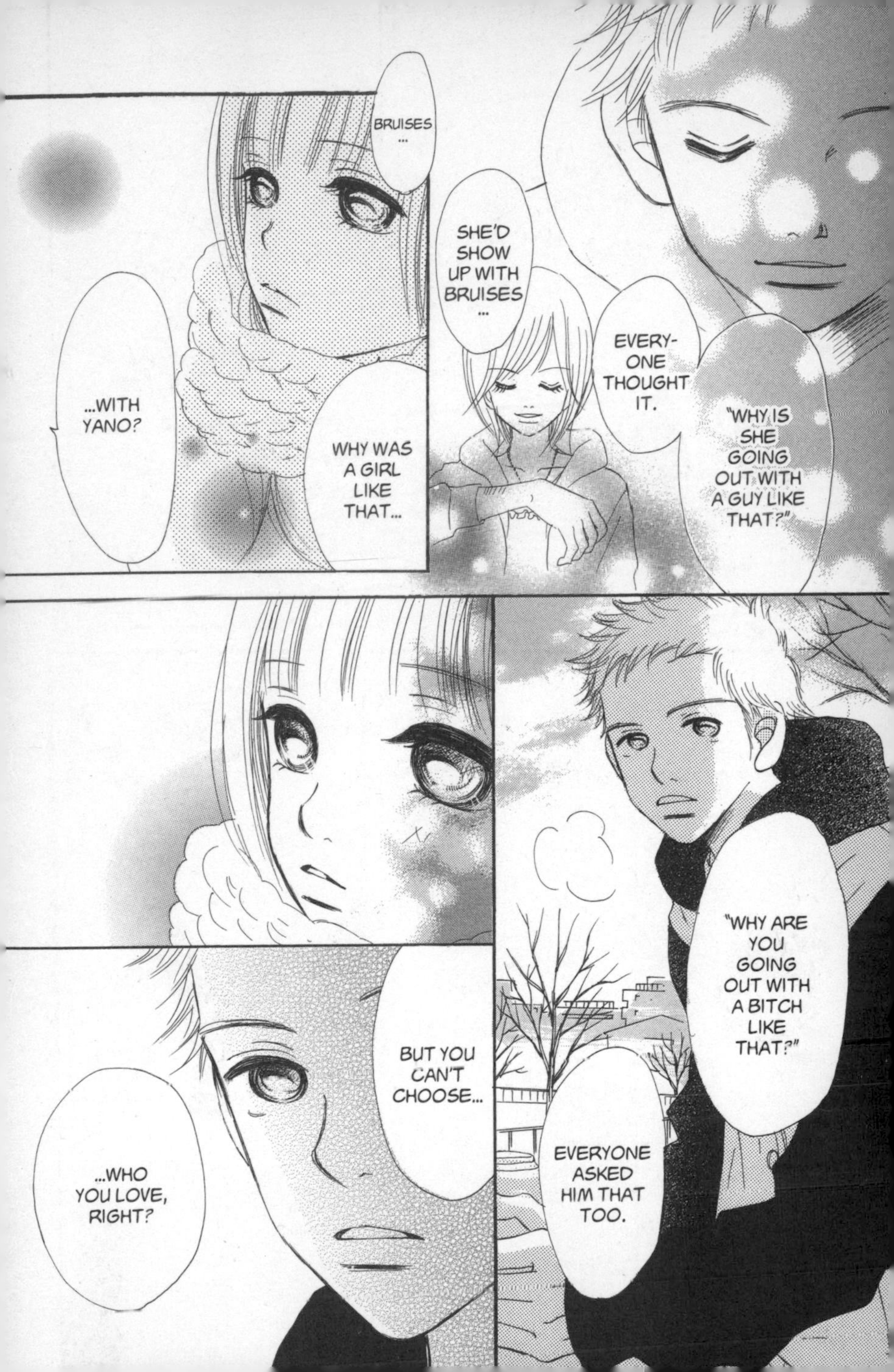
BRUISES...
SHE'D SHOW UP WITH BRUISES...
EVERYONE THOUGHT IT.
"WHY IS SHE GOING OUT WITH A GUY LIKE THAT?"
WHY WAS A GIRL LIKE THAT...
...WITH YANO?
"WHY ARE YOU GOING OUT WITH A BITCH LIKE THAT?"
EVERYONE ASKED HIM THAT TOO.
BUT YOU CAN'T CHOOSE...
...WHO YOU LOVE, RIGHT?

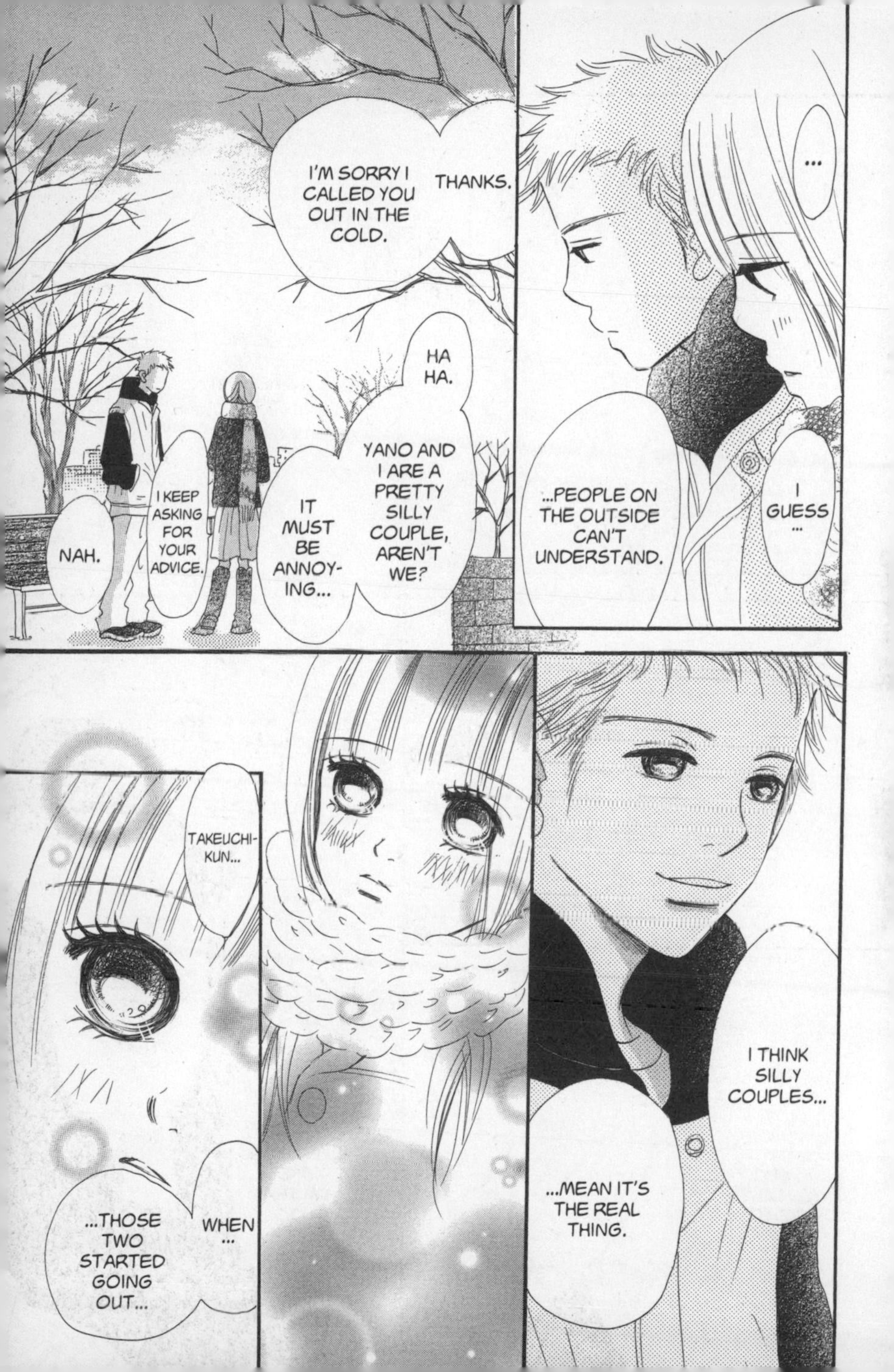
...
I GUESS...
...PEOPLE ON THE OUTSIDE CAN'T UNDERSTAND.
THANKS.
I'M SORRY I CALLED YOU OUT IN THE COLD.
HA HA.
YANO AND I ARE A PRETTY SILLY COUPLE, AREN'T WE?
IT MUST BE ANNOYING...
I KEEP ASKING FOR YOUR ADVICE.
NAH.
I THINK SILLY COUPLES...
...MEAN IT'S THE REAL THING.
TAKEUCHI-KUN...
WHEN...
...THOSE TWO STARTED GOING OUT...

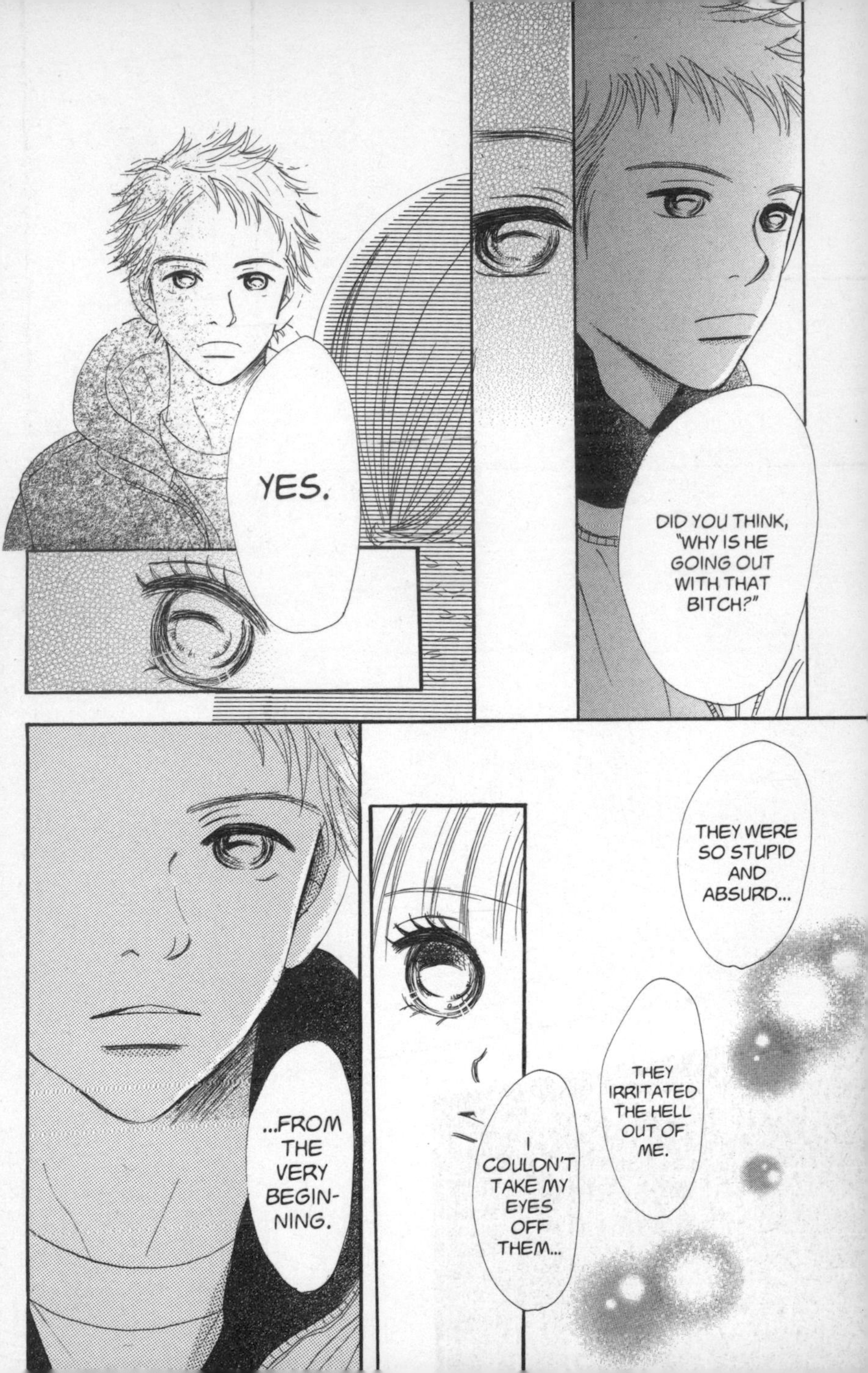
DID YOU THINK, "WHY IS HE GOING OUT WITH THAT BITCH?"
YES.
THEY WERE SO STUPID AND ABSURD...
THEY IRRITATED THE HELL OUT OF ME.
I COULDN'T TAKE MY EYES OFF THEM...
...FROM THE VERY BEGIN-NING.

BYE.

Third Trimester Seating

rai	Hashiba		Otsuki	Narita		Taka-hashi
wara	Mori		Nakao	Shira-kawa		Sugi-yama
aki	Aihara		Meguro	Kawa-guchi		Higash

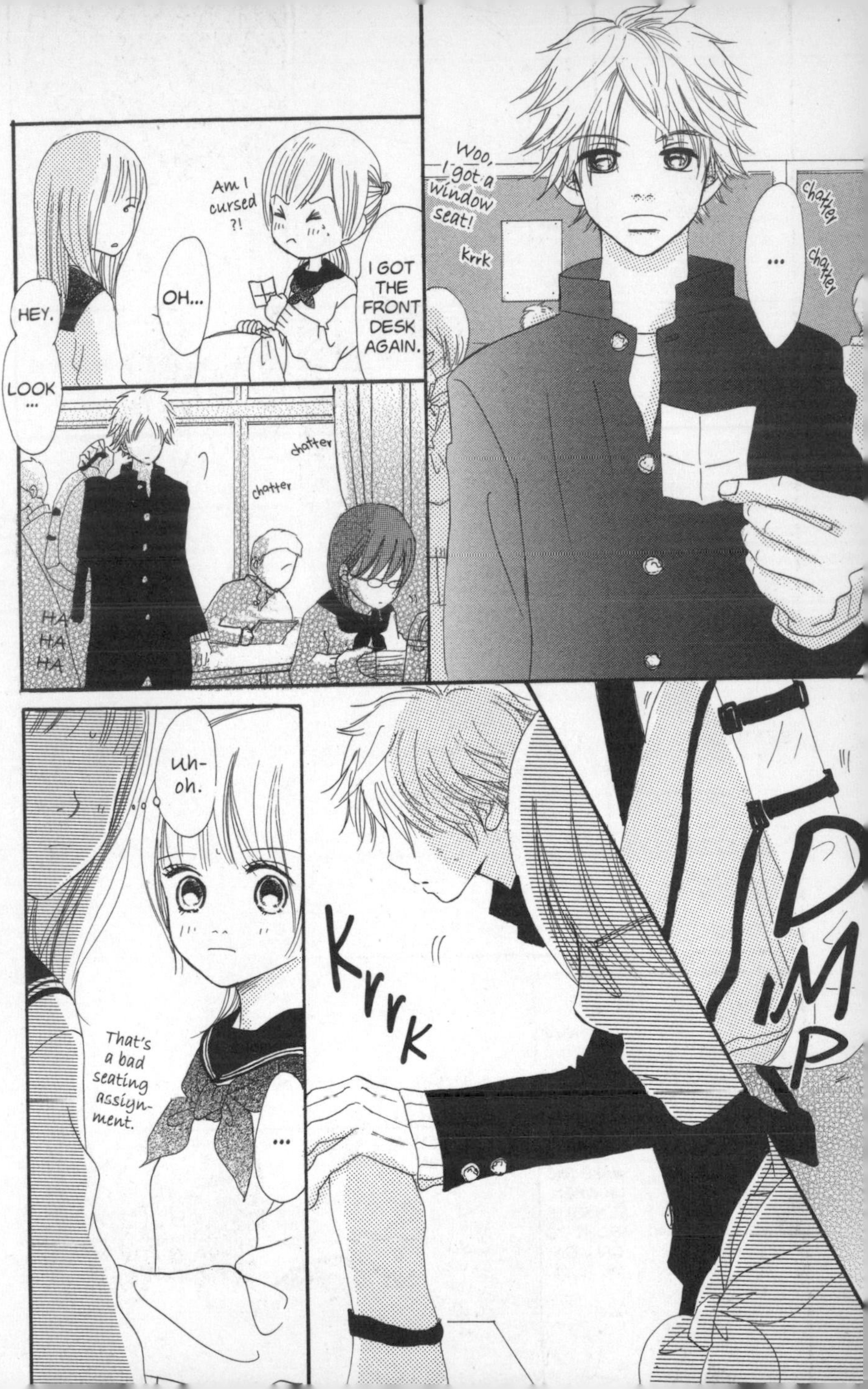
Woo, I got a window seat!
krrk
chatter
chatter
...
I GOT THE FRONT DESK AGAIN.
Am I cursed ?!
OH...
HEY.
LOOK...
chatter
chatter
HA HA HA
DIMP
Krrk
uh-oh.
...
That's a bad seating assignment.

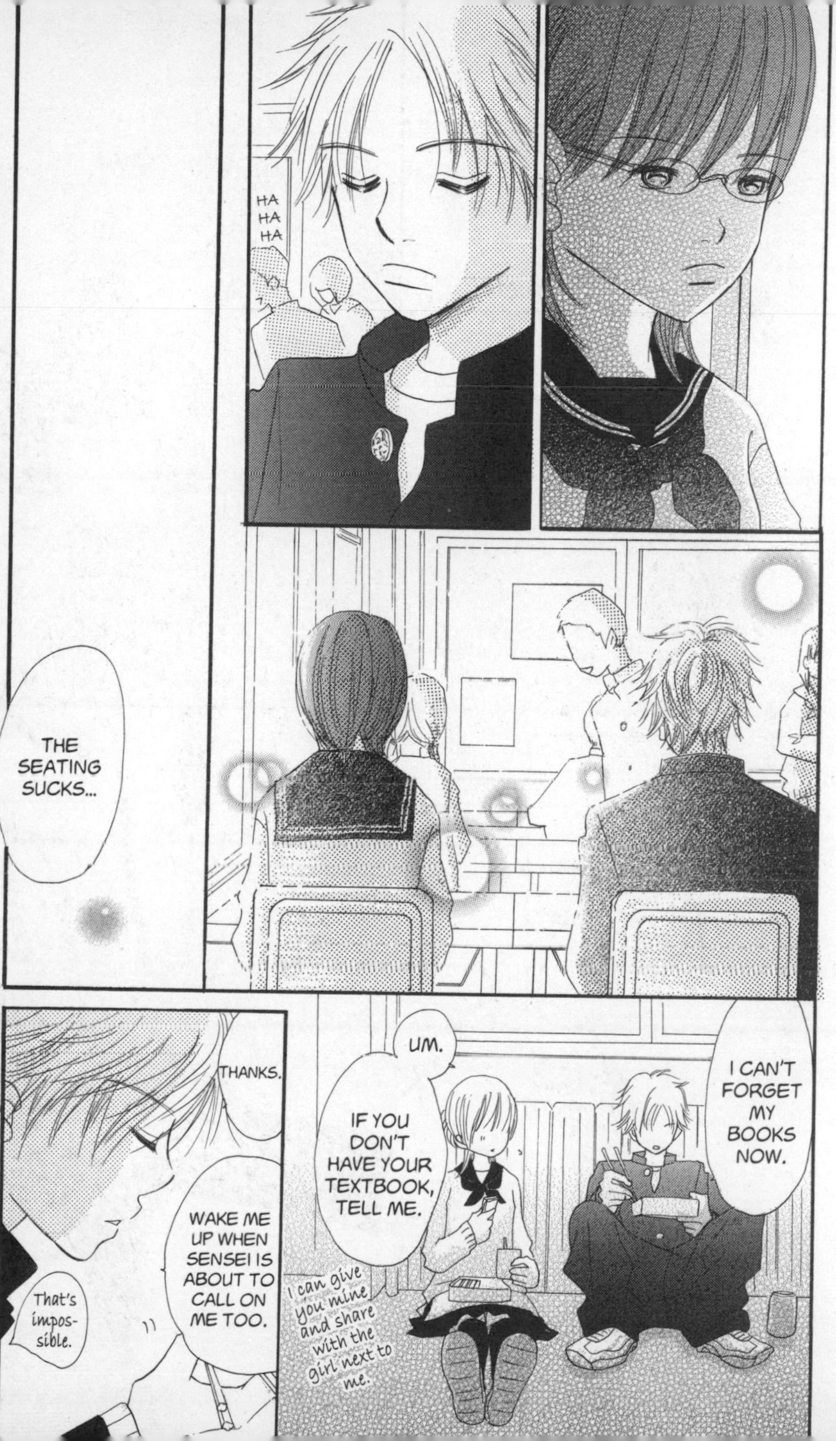
HA HA HA
THE SEATING SUCKS...
I CAN'T FORGET MY BOOKS NOW.
UM.
IF YOU DON'T HAVE YOUR TEXTBOOK, TELL ME.
I can give you mine and share with the girl next to me.
THANKS.
WAKE ME UP WHEN SENSEI IS ABOUT TO CALL ON ME TOO.
That's impos-sible.

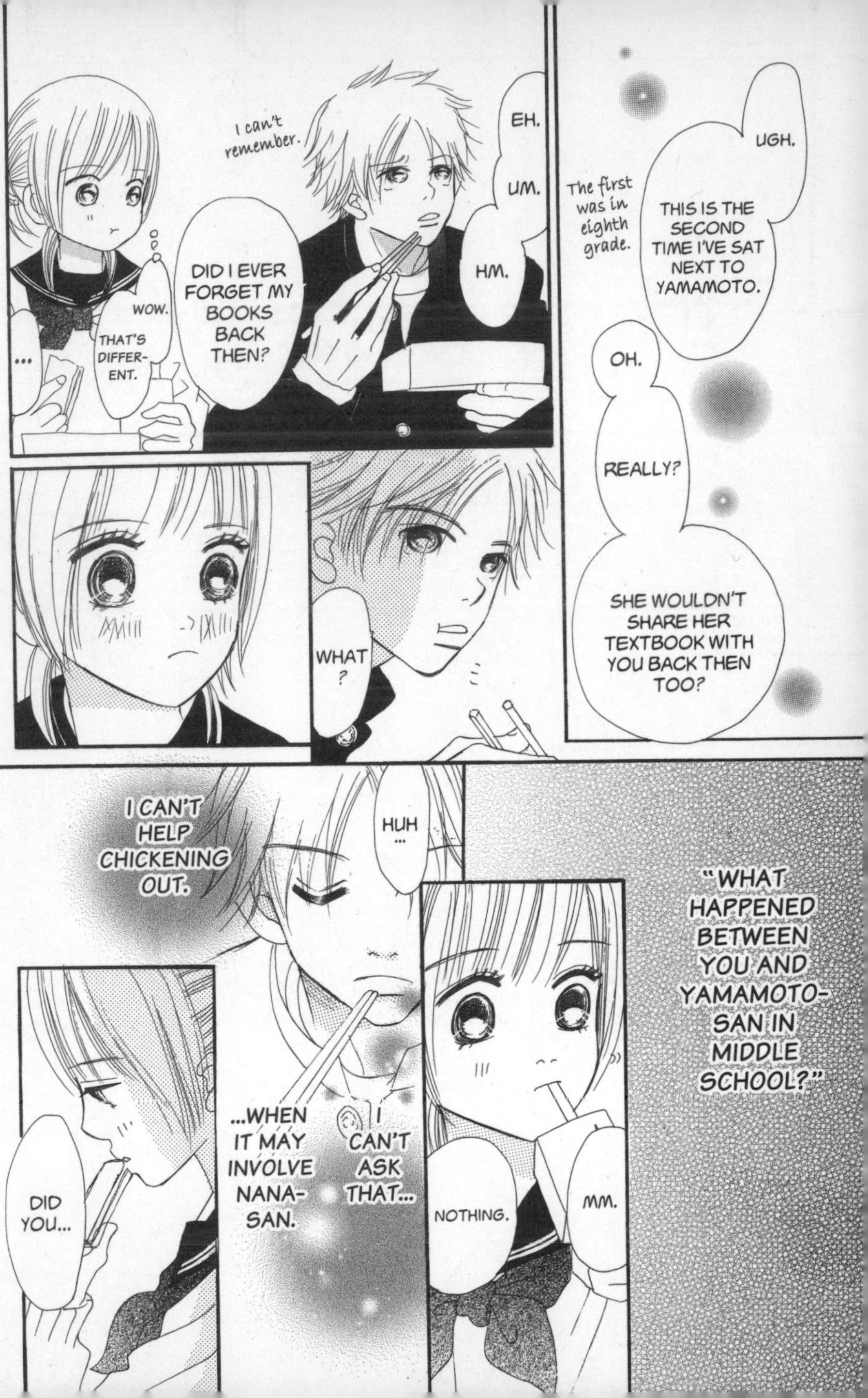
UGH.
THIS IS THE SECOND TIME I'VE SAT NEXT TO YAMAMOTO.
The first was in eighth grade.
OH.
REALLY?
SHE WOULDN'T SHARE HER TEXTBOOK WITH YOU BACK THEN TOO?
EH.
UM.
HM.
I can't remember.
DID I EVER FORGET MY BOOKS BACK THEN?
WOW.
THAT'S DIFFER-ENT.
...
WHAT?
"WHAT HAPPENED BETWEEN YOU AND YAMAMOTO-SAN IN MIDDLE SCHOOL?"
HUH...
I CAN'T HELP CHICKENING OUT.
MM.
NOTHING.
I CAN'T ASK THAT...
...WHEN IT MAY INVOLVE NANA-SAN.
DID YOU...

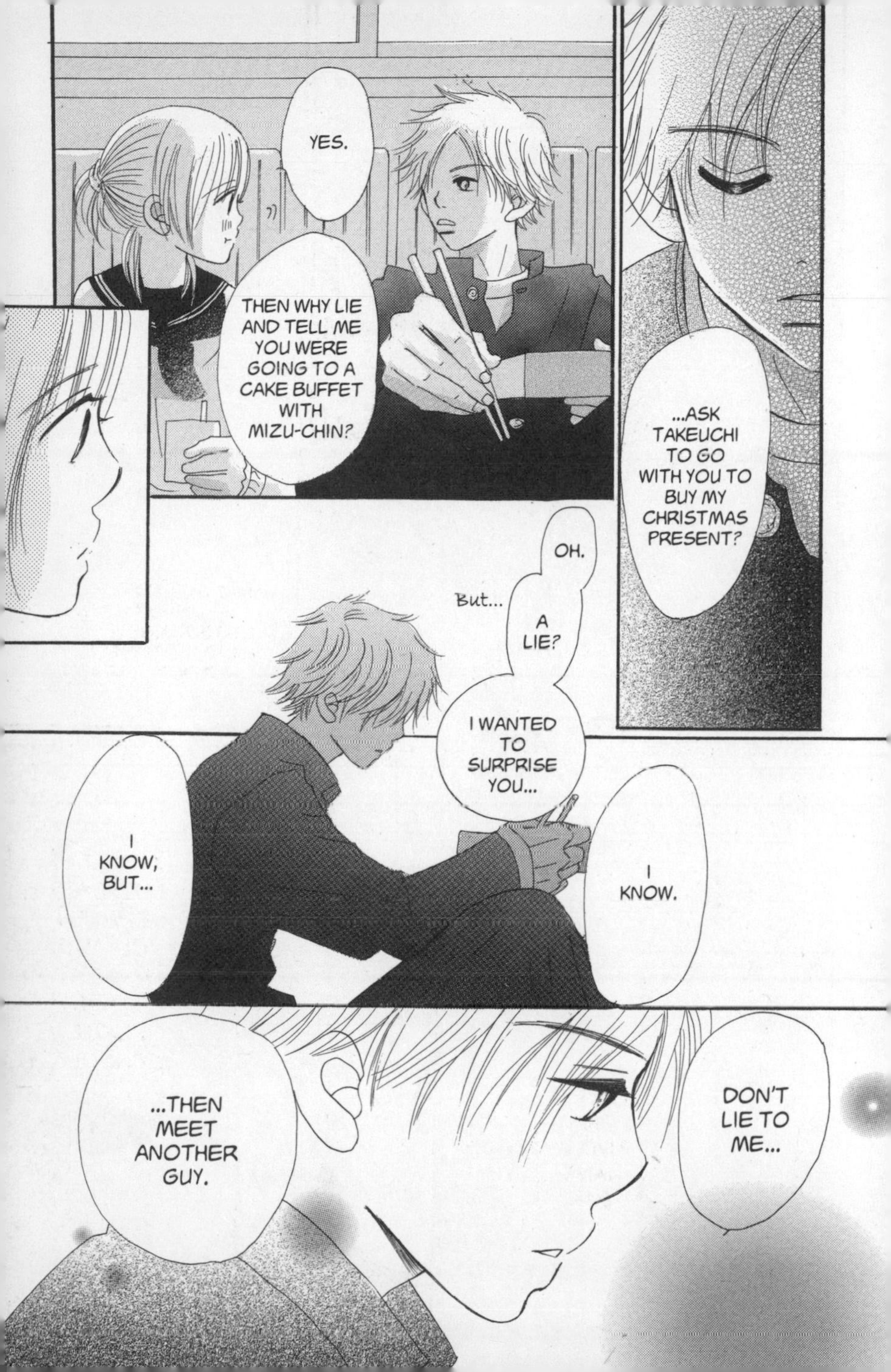

...ASK TAKEUCHI TO GO WITH YOU TO BUY MY CHRISTMAS PRESENT?
YES.
THEN WHY LIE AND TELL ME YOU WERE GOING TO A CAKE BUFFET WITH MIZU-CHIN?
OH.
But...
A LIE?
I WANTED TO SURPRISE YOU...
I KNOW.
I KNOW, BUT...
DON'T LIE TO ME...
...THEN MEET ANOTHER GUY.

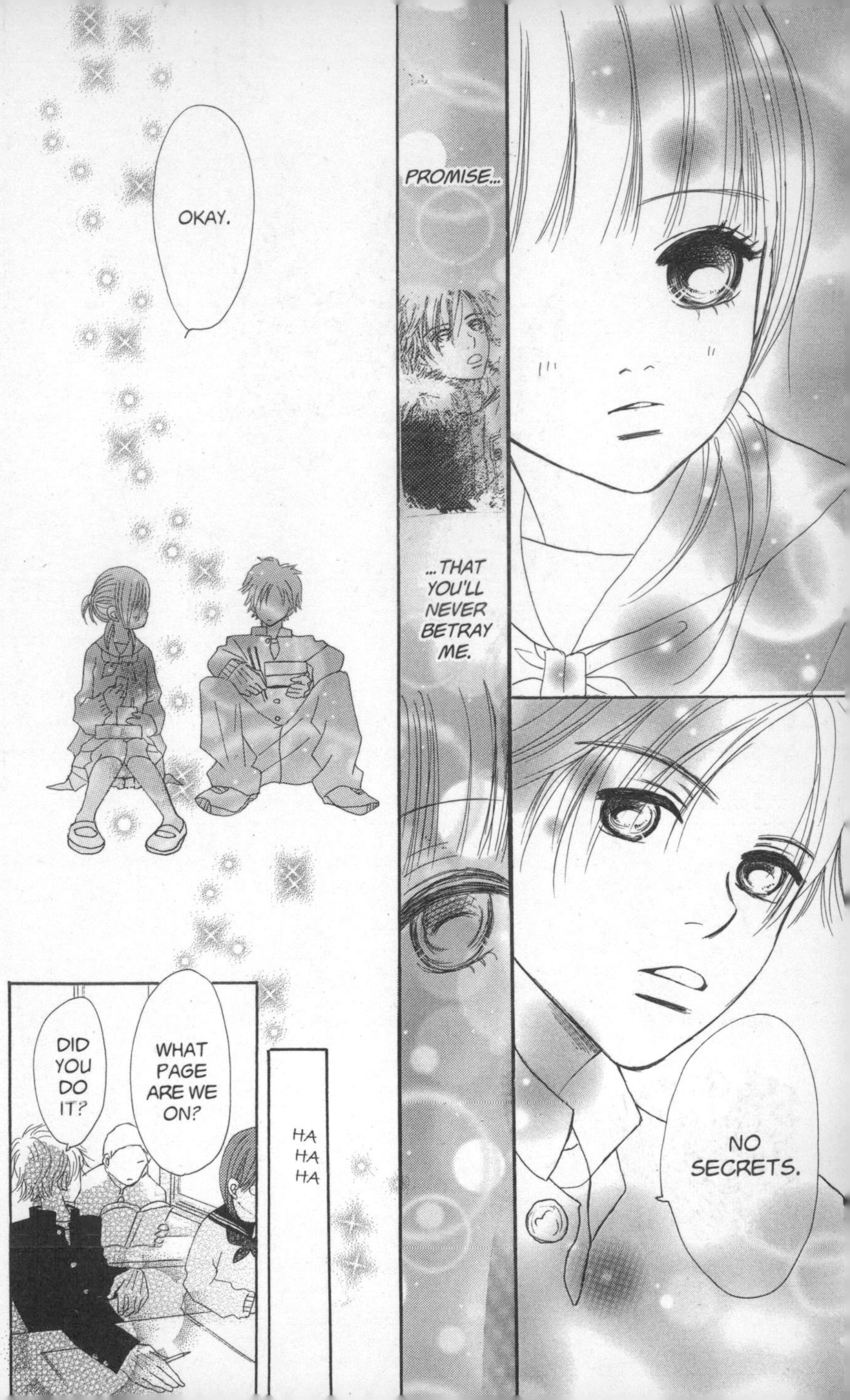
PROMISE...
...THAT YOU'LL NEVER BETRAY ME.
NO SECRETS.
OKAY.
HA HA HA
WHAT PAGE ARE WE ON?
DID YOU DO IT?

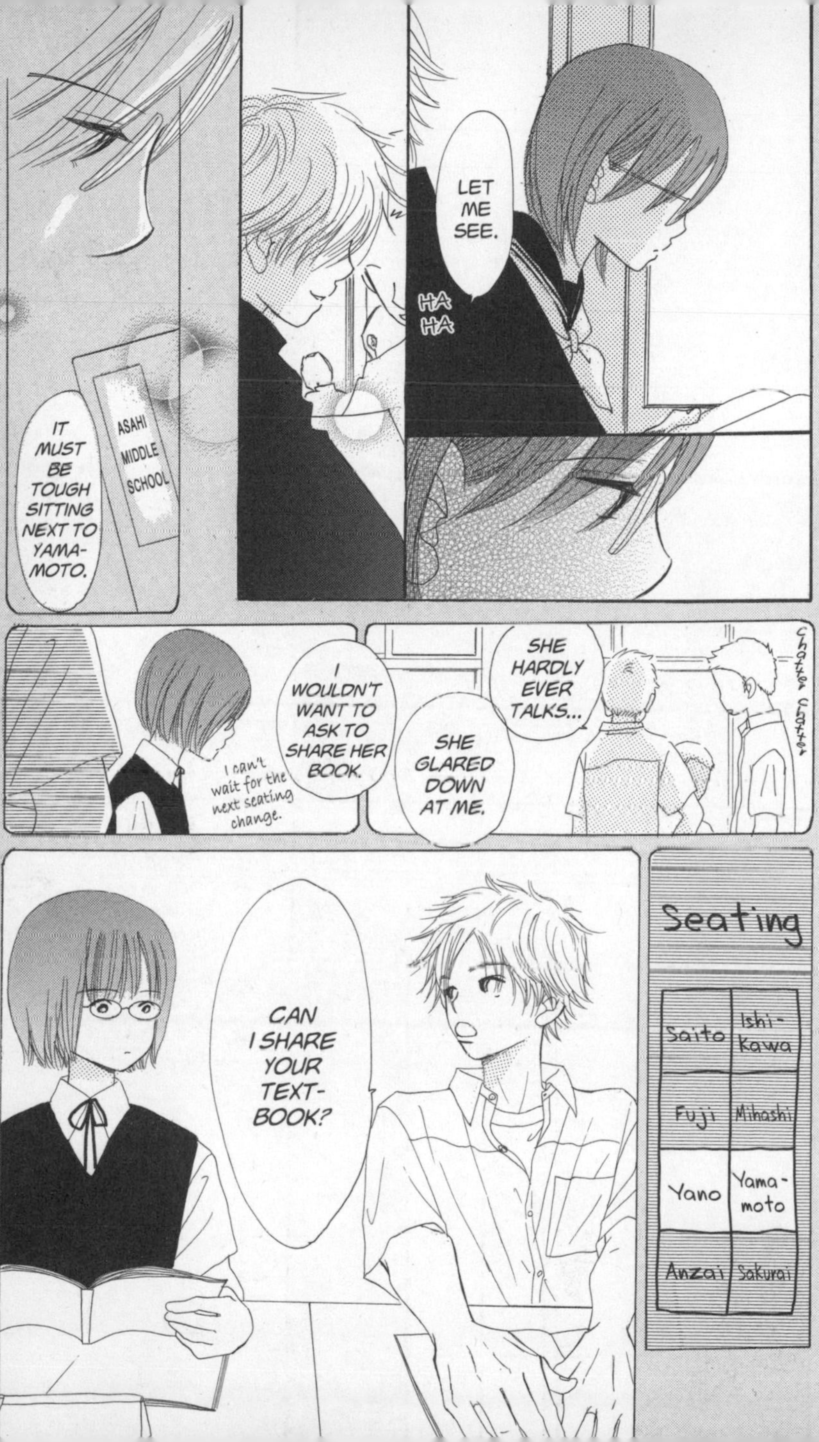
LET ME SEE.
HA HA
ASAHI MIDDLE SCHOOL
IT MUST BE TOUGH SITTING NEXT TO YAMAMOTO.
Chatter Chatter
SHE HARDLY EVER TALKS...
SHE GLARED DOWN AT ME.
I WOULDN'T WANT TO ASK TO SHARE HER BOOK.
I can't wait for the next seating change.
Seating
Saito Ishi-kawa
Fuji Mihashi
Yano Yama-moto
Anzai Sakurai
CAN I SHARE YOUR TEXT-BOOK?

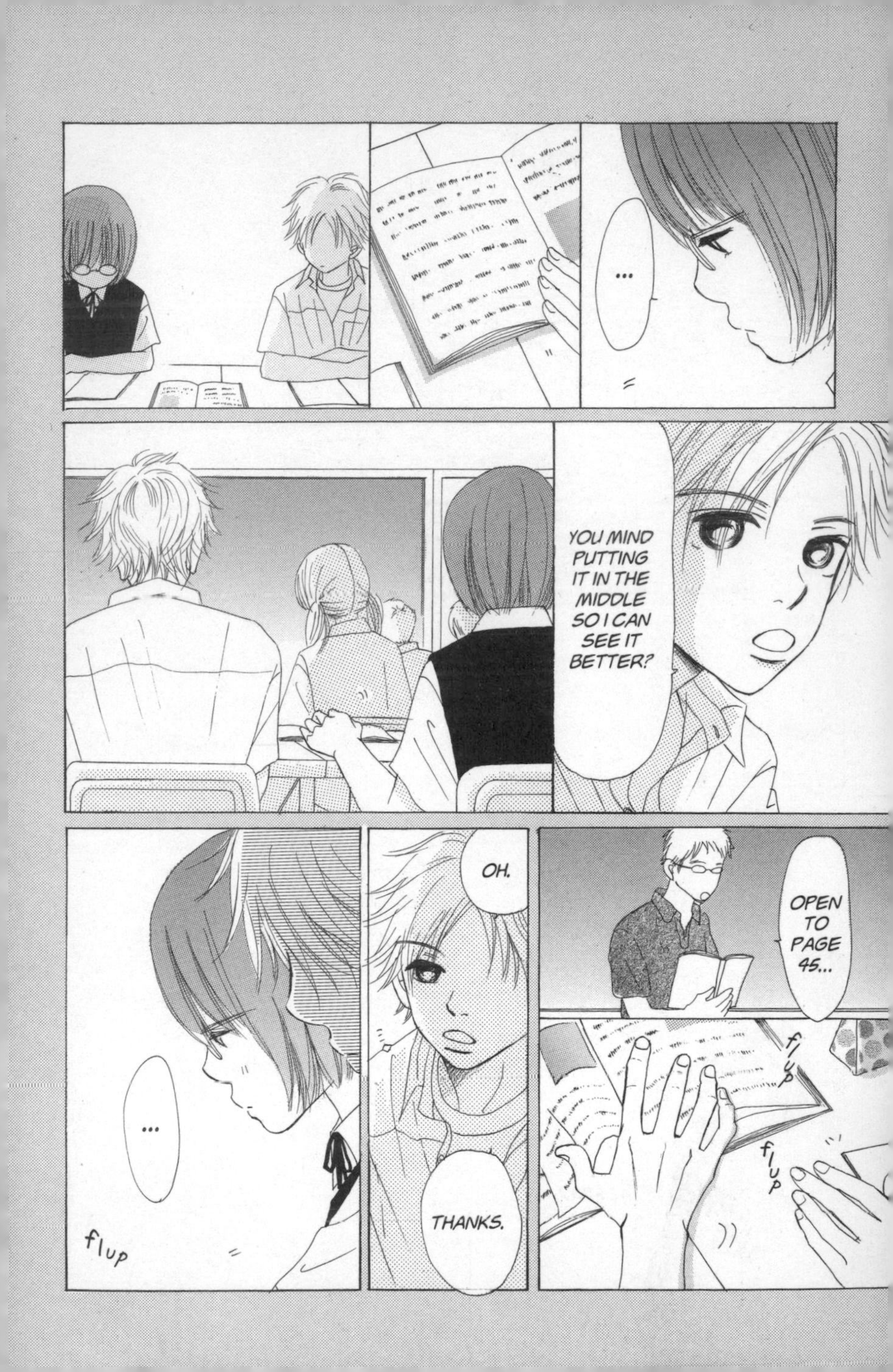
...
YOU MIND PUTTING IT IN THE MIDDLE SO I CAN SEE IT BETTER?
OPEN TO PAGE 45...
flup
flup
OH.
THANKS.
...
flup

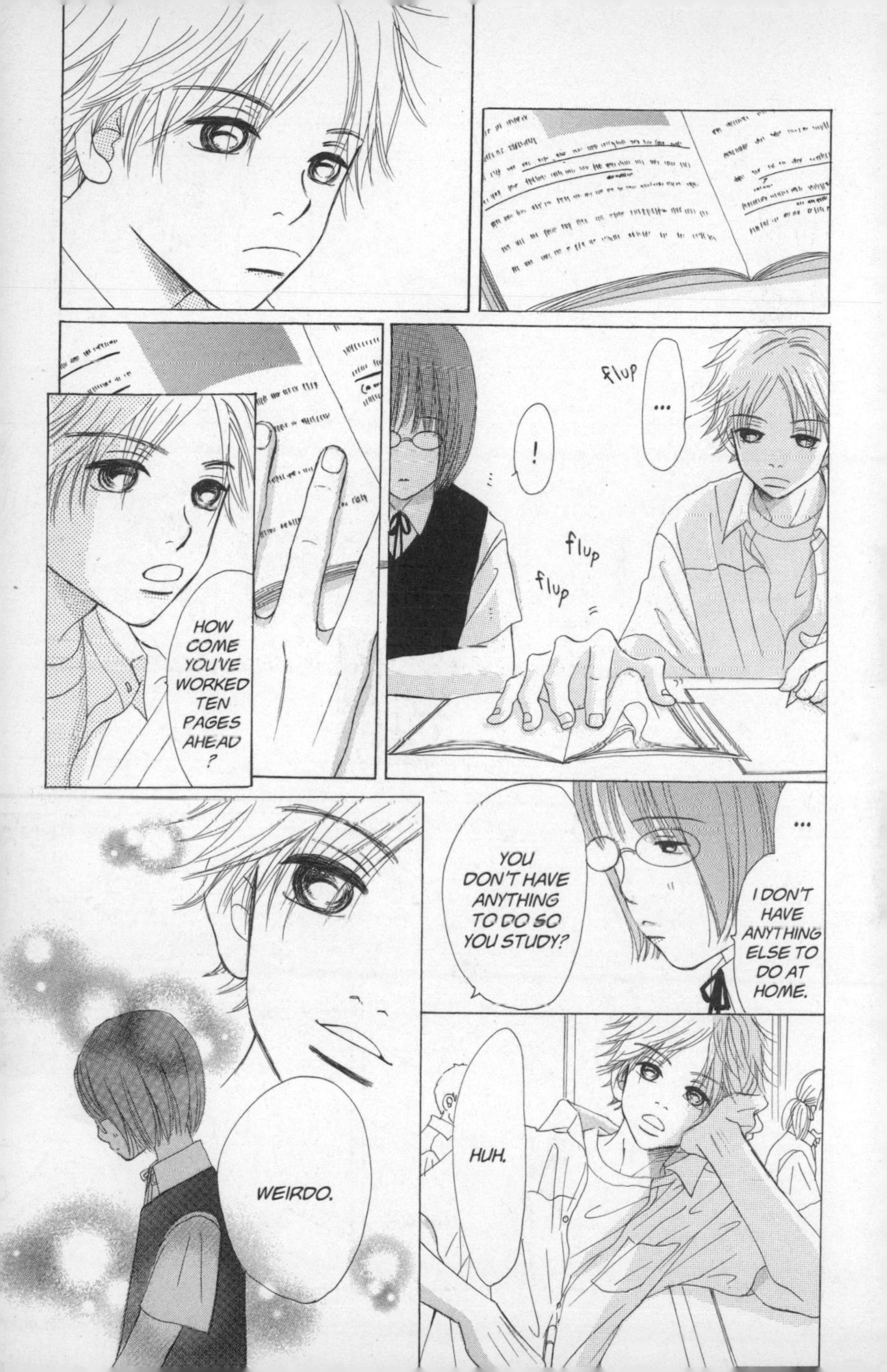
...
flup
!
flup
flup
HOW COME YOU'VE WORKED TEN PAGES AHEAD?
...
I DON'T HAVE ANYTHING ELSE TO DO AT HOME.
YOU DON'T HAVE ANYTHING TO DO SO YOU STUDY?
HUH.
WEIRDO.

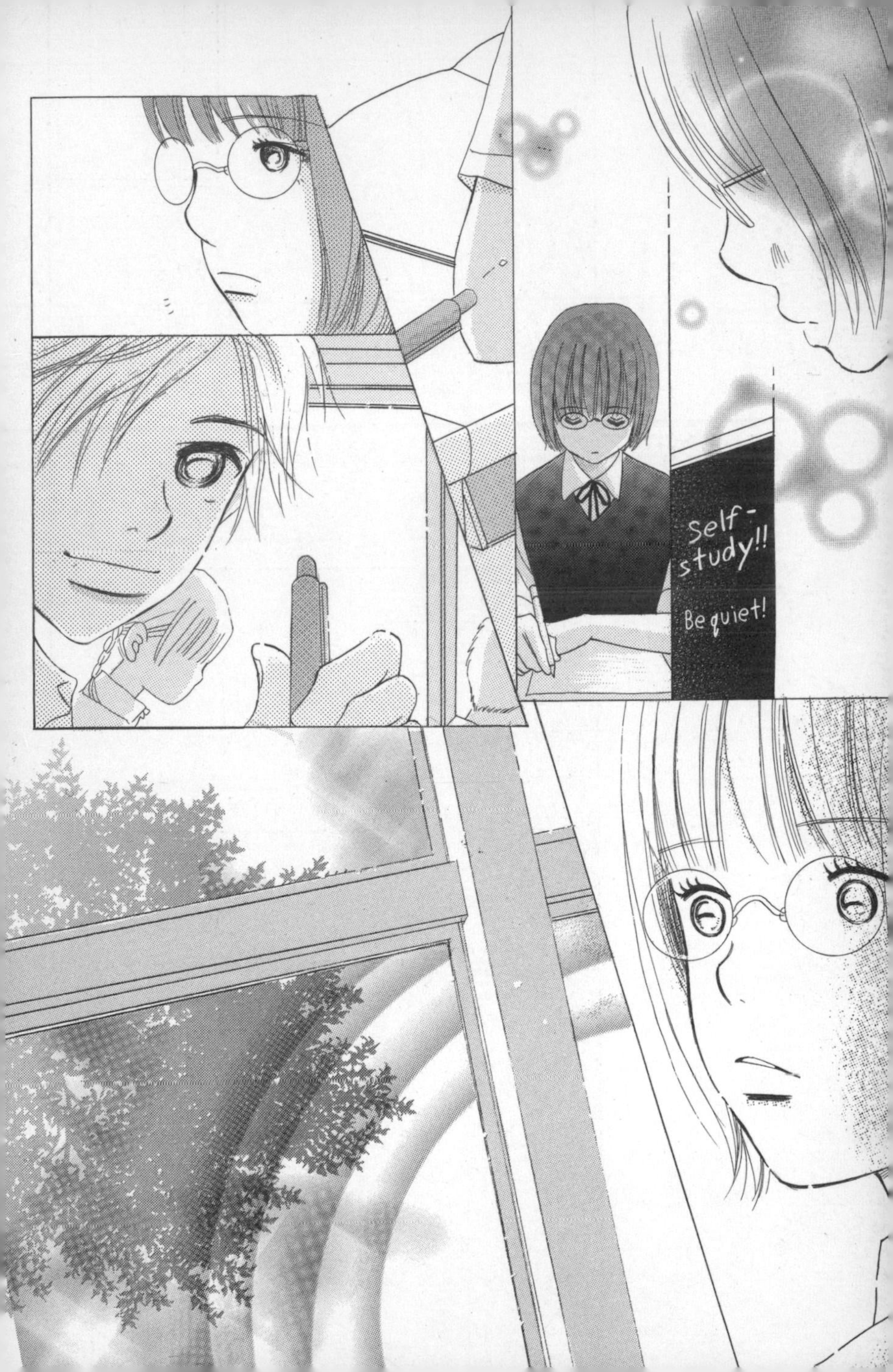
Self-study!!
Be quiet!

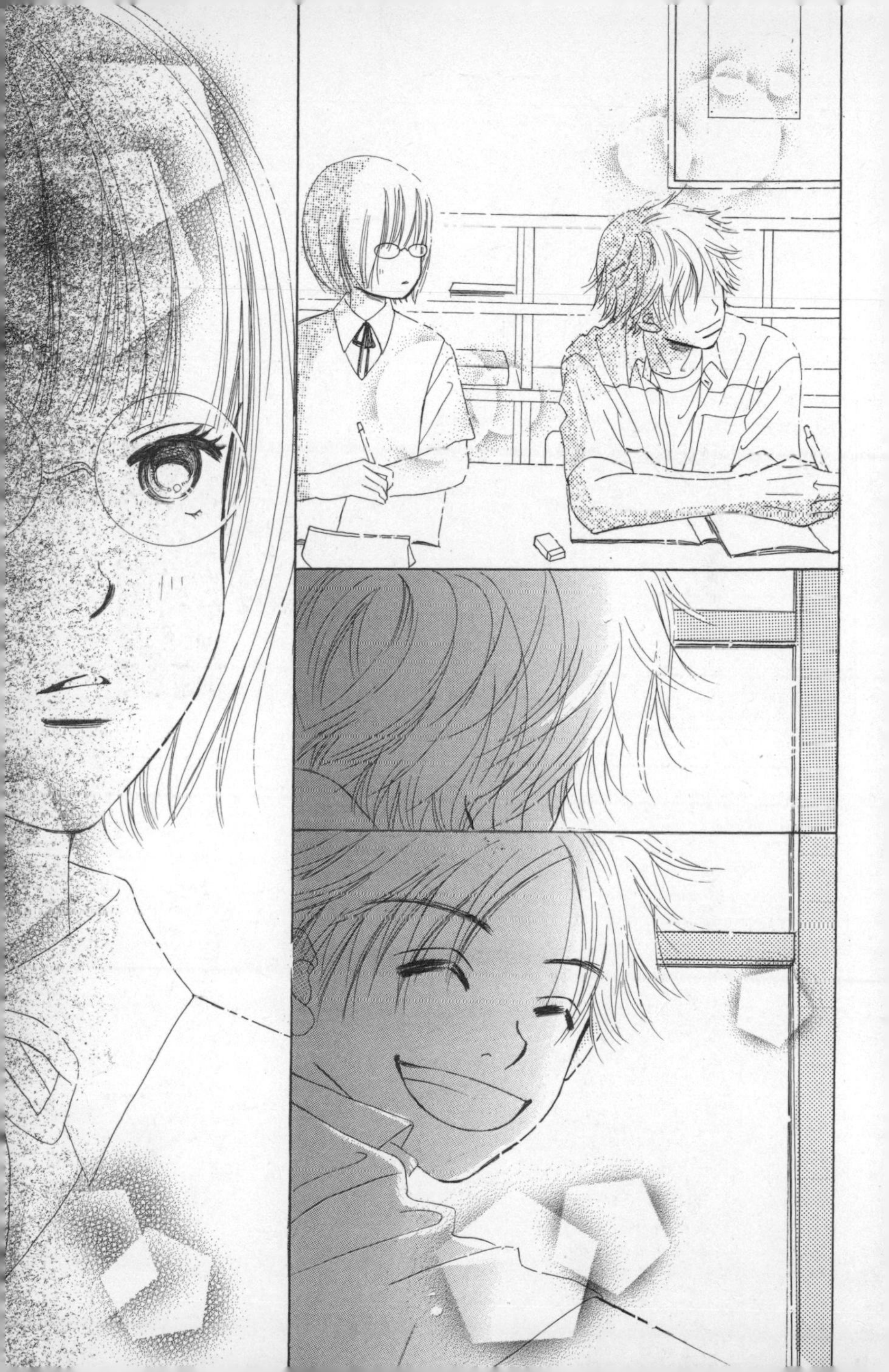

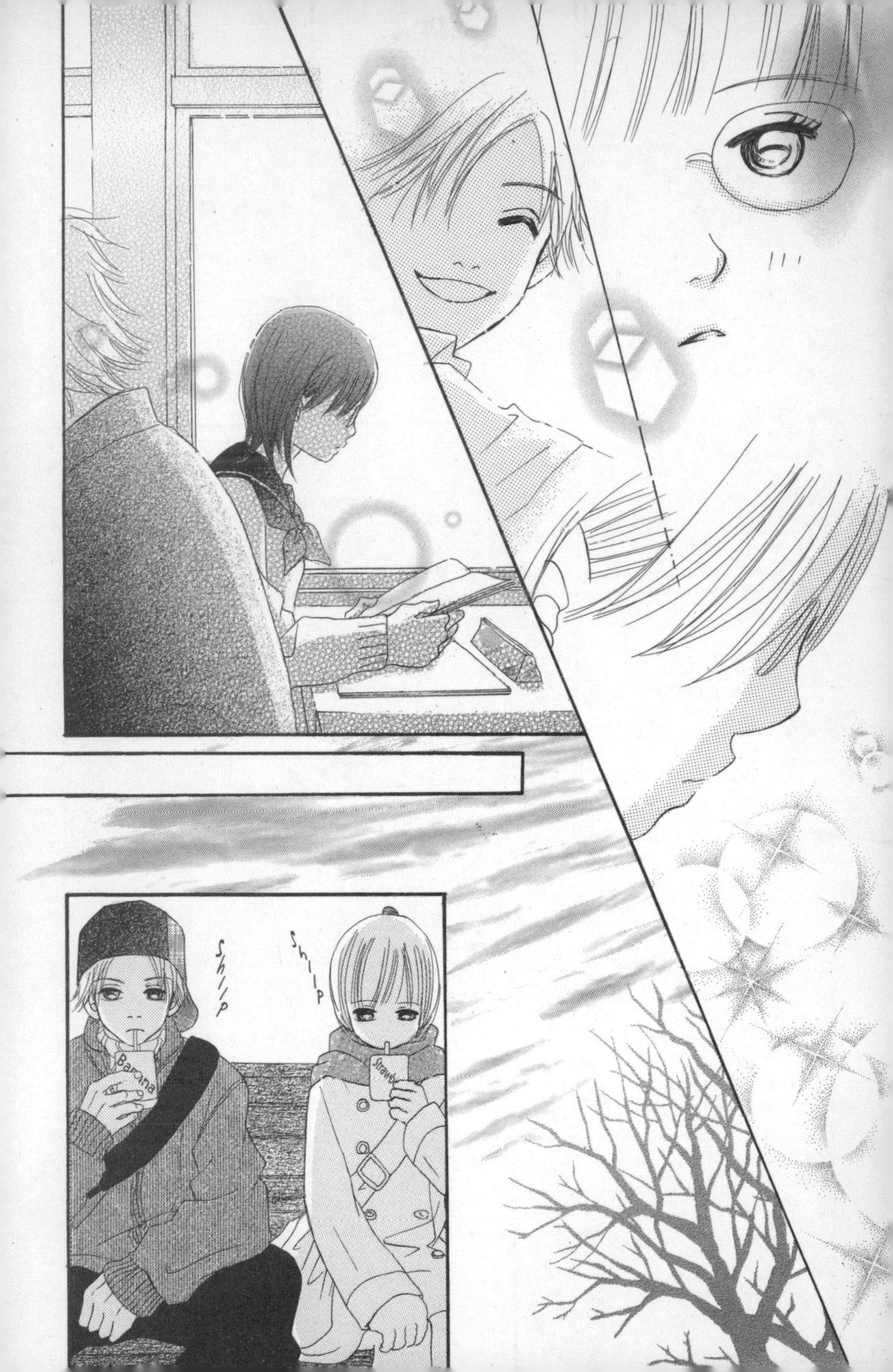
Shlip
Shlip
Banana

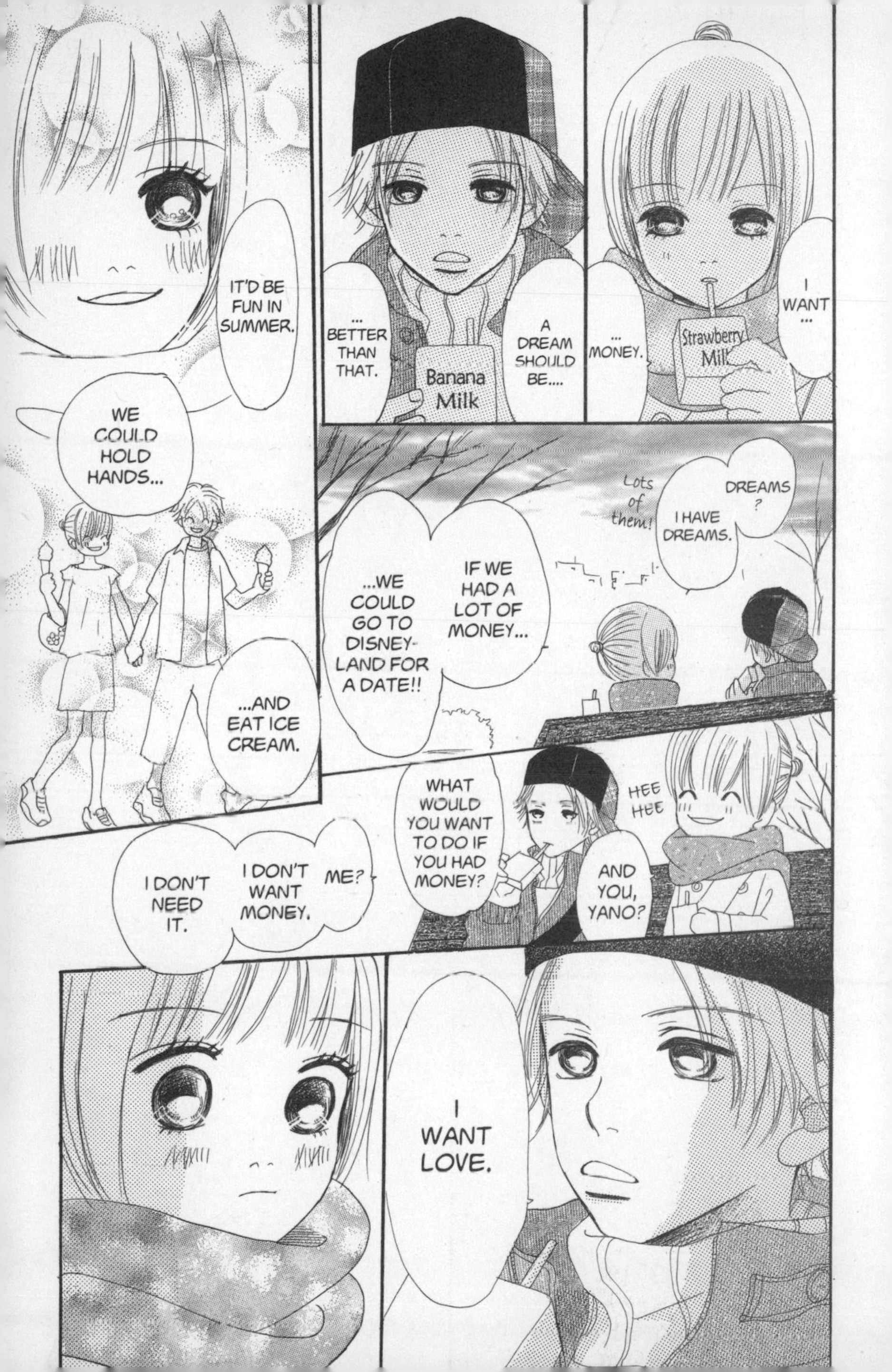
I WANT ...
... MONEY.
A DREAM SHOULD BE....
... BETTER THAN THAT.
Banana Milk
Strawberry Milk
DREAMS?
I HAVE DREAMS.
Lots of them!
IF WE HAD A LOT OF MONEY...
...WE COULD GO TO DISNEYLAND FOR A DATE!!
IT'D BE FUN IN SUMMER.
WE COULD HOLD HANDS...
...AND EAT ICE CREAM.
HEE HEE
AND YOU, YANO?
WHAT WOULD YOU WANT TO DO IF YOU HAD MONEY?
ME?
I DON'T WANT MONEY.
I DON'T NEED IT.
I WANT LOVE.

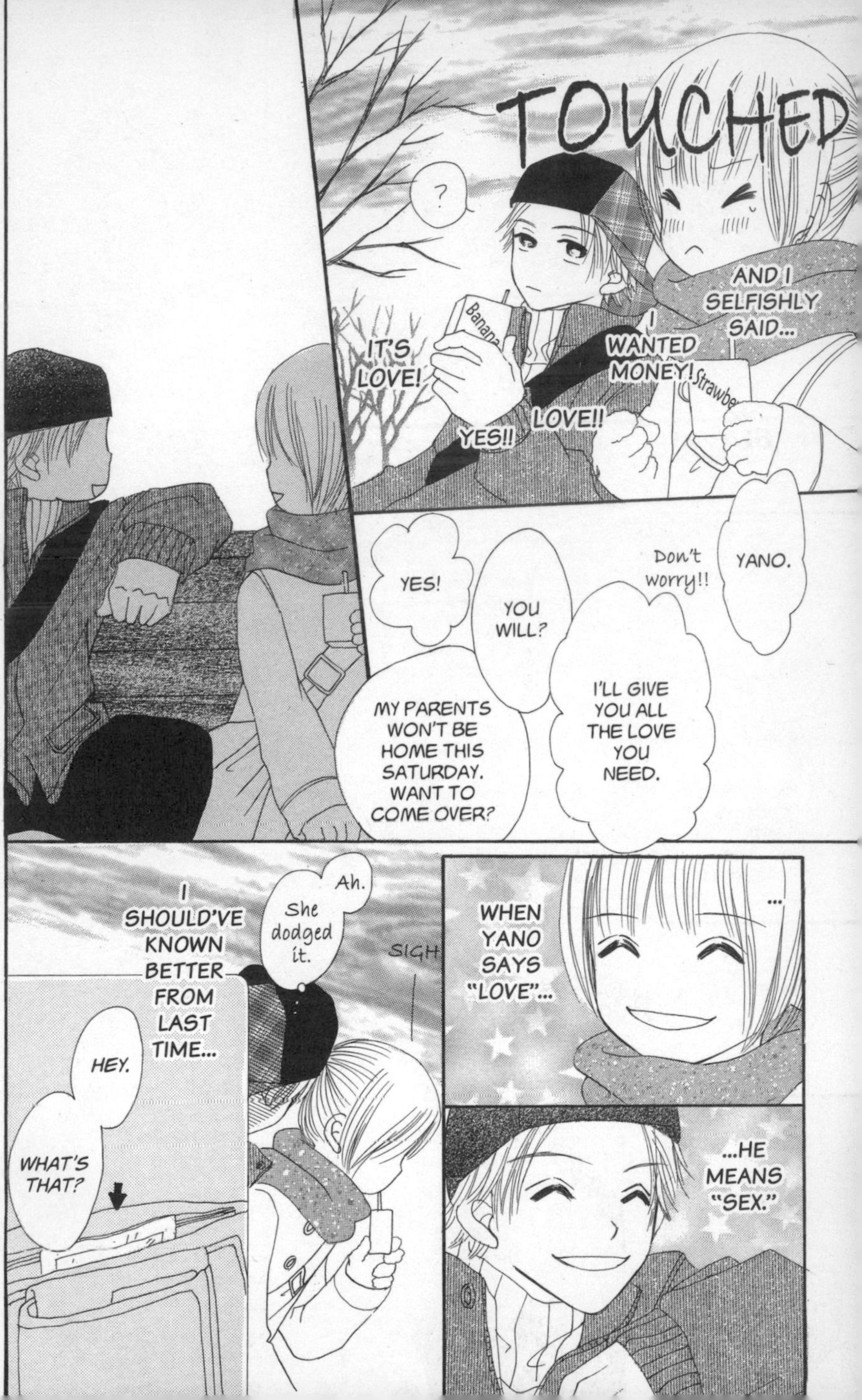
TOUCHED
AND I SELFISHLY SAID...
?
I WANTED MONEY!
Strawbe
Banana
IT'S LOVE!
LOVE!!
YES!!
YANO.
Don't worry!!
I'LL GIVE YOU ALL THE LOVE YOU NEED.
YOU WILL?
YES!
MY PARENTS WON'T BE HOME THIS SATURDAY. WANT TO COME OVER?
...
WHEN YANO SAYS "LOVE"...
...HE MEANS "SEX."
Ah.
She dodged it.
SIGH
I SHOULD'VE KNOWN BETTER FROM LAST TIME...
HEY.
WHAT'S THAT?

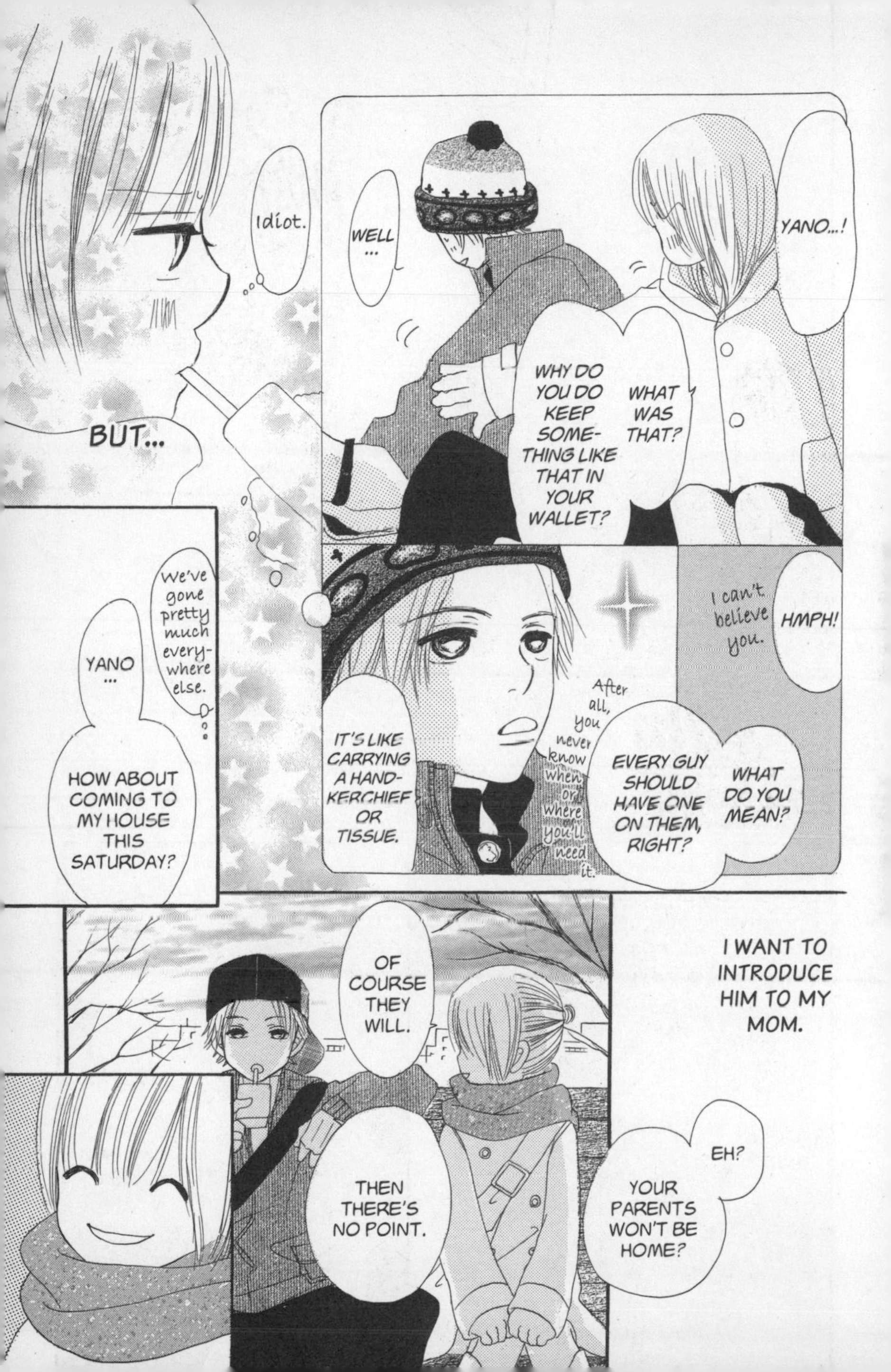
YANO...!
WHAT WAS THAT?
WHY DO YOU DO KEEP SOMETHING LIKE THAT IN YOUR WALLET?
WELL ...
HMPH!
I can't believe you.
WHAT DO YOU MEAN?
EVERY GUY SHOULD HAVE ONE ON THEM, RIGHT?
After all, you never know when or where you'll need it.
IT'S LIKE CARRYING A HANDKERCHIEF OR TISSUE.
Idiot.
BUT...
We've gone pretty much everywhere else.
YANO ...
HOW ABOUT COMING TO MY HOUSE THIS SATURDAY?
I WANT TO INTRODUCE HIM TO MY MOM.
EH?
YOUR PARENTS WON'T BE HOME?
OF COURSE THEY WILL.
THEN THERE'S NO POINT.

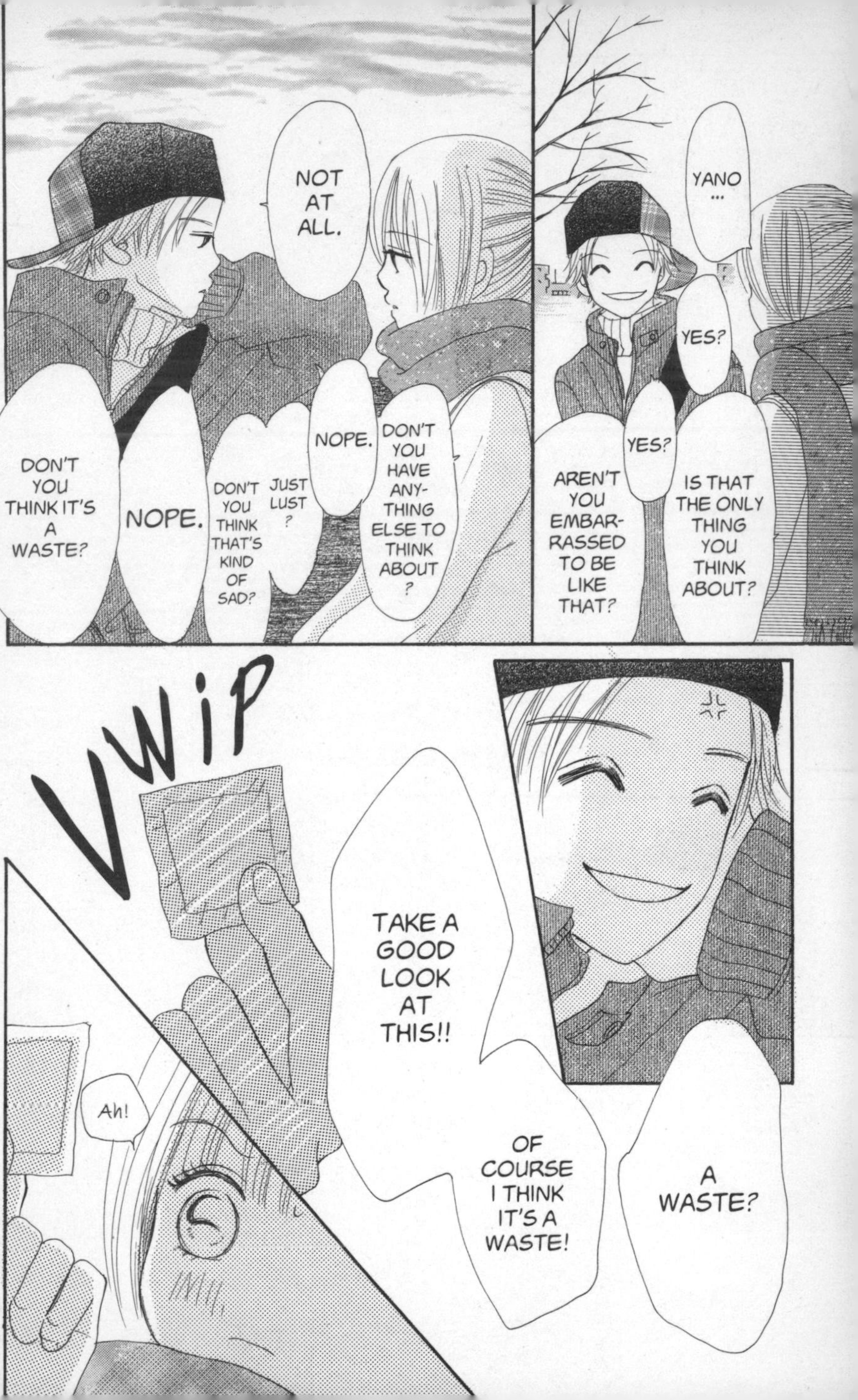
YANO ...
YES?
IS THAT THE ONLY THING YOU THINK ABOUT?
YES?
AREN'T YOU EMBARRASSED TO BE LIKE THAT?
NOT AT ALL.
DON'T YOU HAVE ANYTHING ELSE TO THINK ABOUT?
NOPE.
JUST LUST?
DON'T YOU THINK THAT'S KIND OF SAD?
NOPE.
DON'T YOU THINK IT'S A WASTE?
A WASTE?
OF COURSE I THINK IT'S A WASTE!
TAKE A GOOD LOOK AT THIS!!
VWIP
Ah!

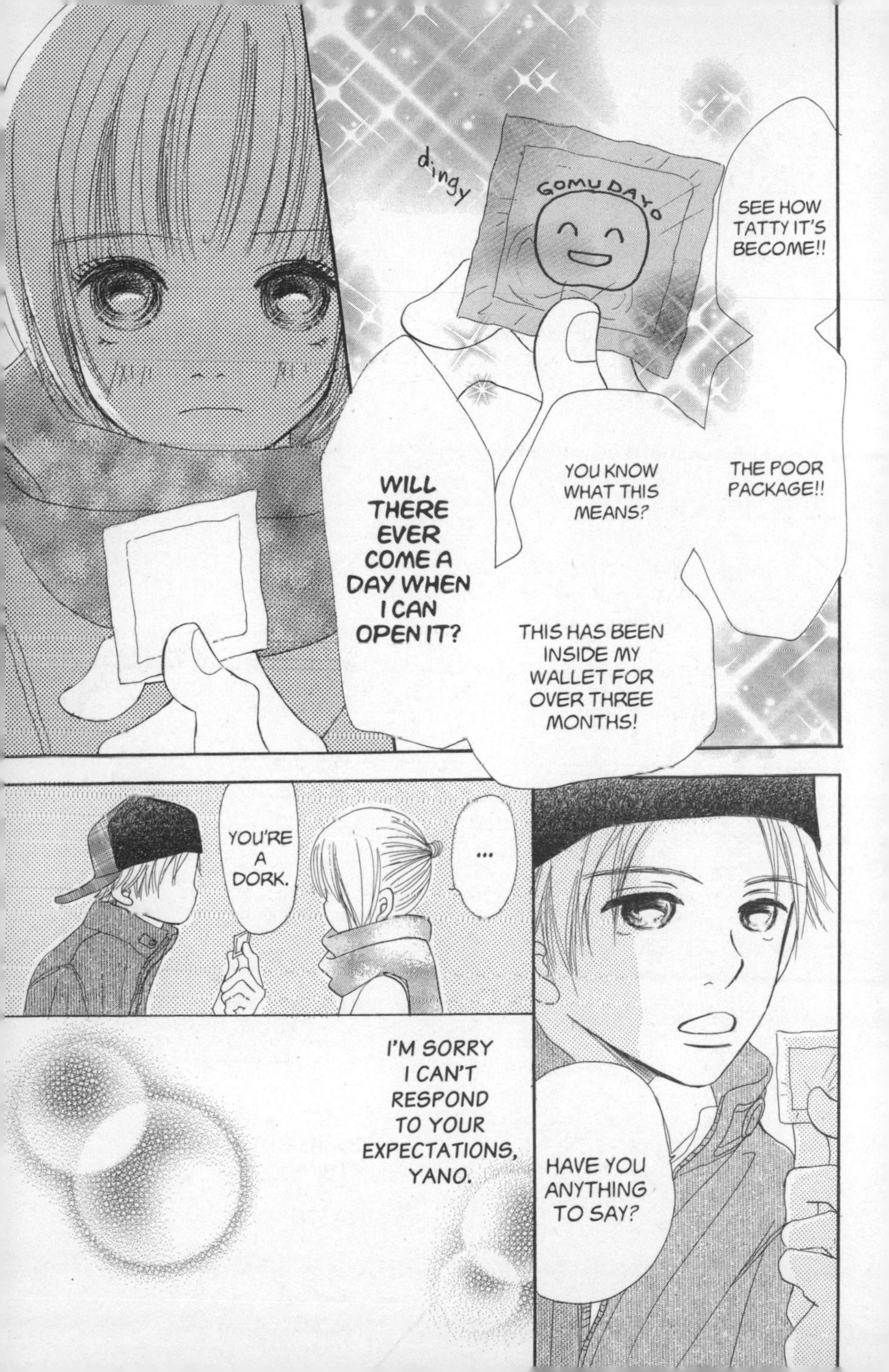
SEE HOW TATTY IT'S BECOME!!
THE POOR PACKAGE!!
GOMU DAYO
dingy
YOU KNOW WHAT THIS MEANS?
THIS HAS BEEN INSIDE MY WALLET FOR OVER THREE MONTHS!
WILL THERE EVER COME A DAY WHEN I CAN OPEN IT?
HAVE YOU ANYTHING TO SAY?
...
YOU'RE A DORK.
I'M SORRY I CAN'T RESPOND TO YOUR EXPECTATIONS, YANO.

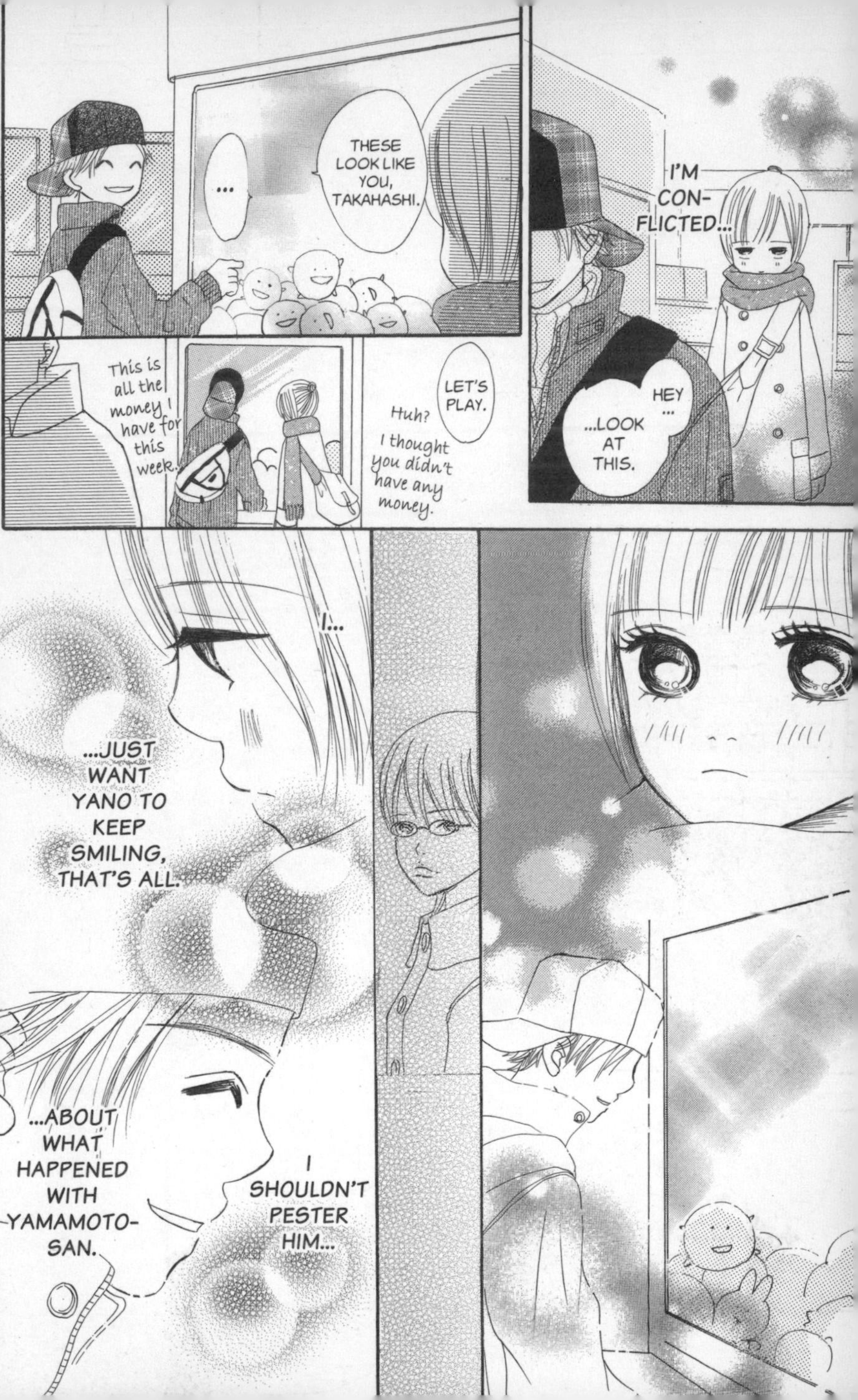
I'M CON-FLICTED...
HEY ...
...LOOK AT THIS.
THESE LOOK LIKE YOU, TAKAHASHI.
...
LET'S PLAY.
Huh? I thought you didn't have any money.
This is all the money I have for this week.
I...
...JUST WANT YANO TO KEEP SMILING, THAT'S ALL.
I SHOULDN'T PESTER HIM...
...ABOUT WHAT HAPPENED WITH YAMAMOTO-SAN.

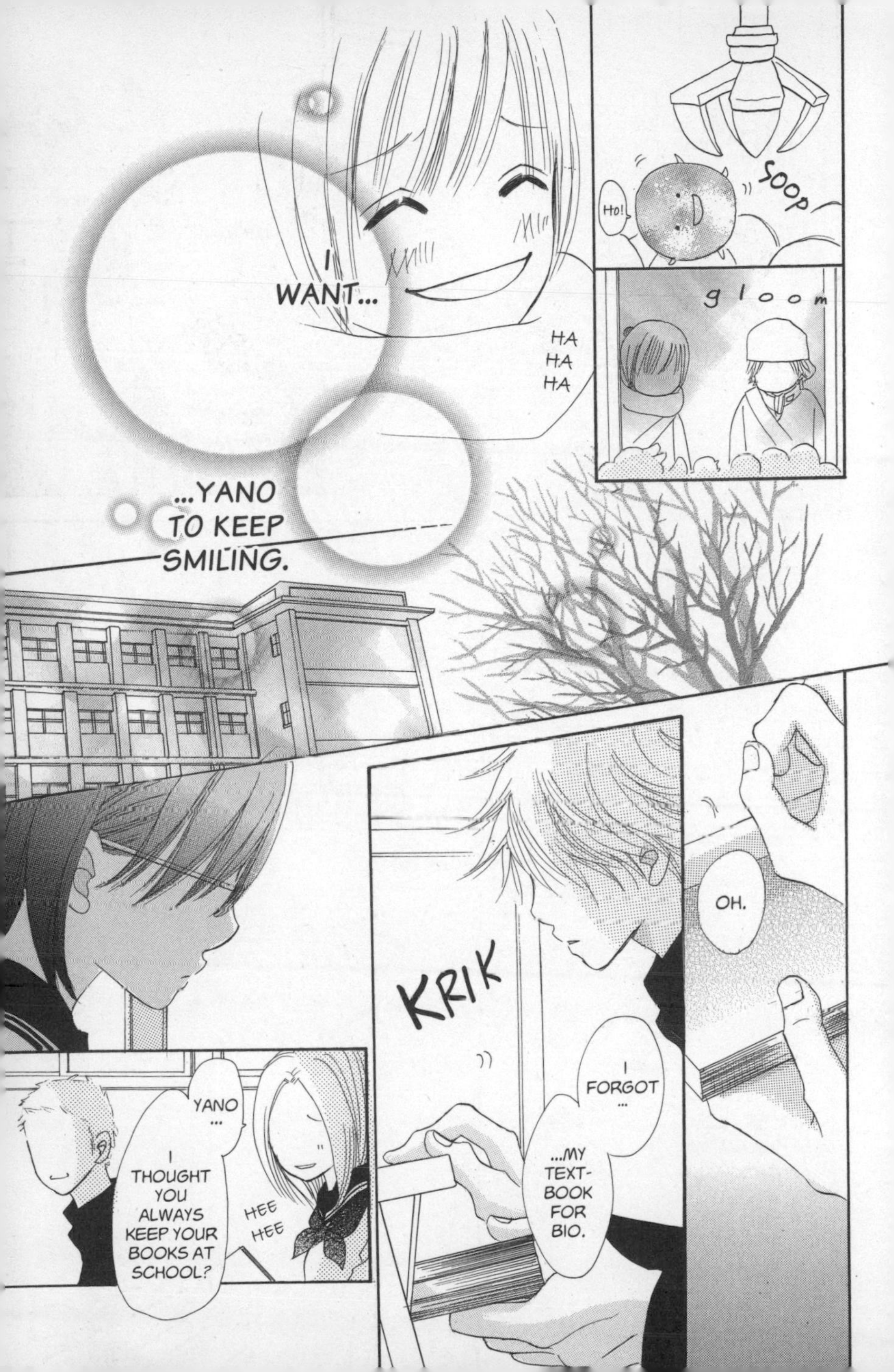
SOOP
Ho!
gloom
I WANT...
HA HA HA
...YANO TO KEEP SMILING.
OH.
KRIK
I FORGOT...
...MY TEXT-BOOK FOR BIO.
YANO...
I THOUGHT YOU ALWAYS KEEP YOUR BOOKS AT SCHOOL?
HEE HEE

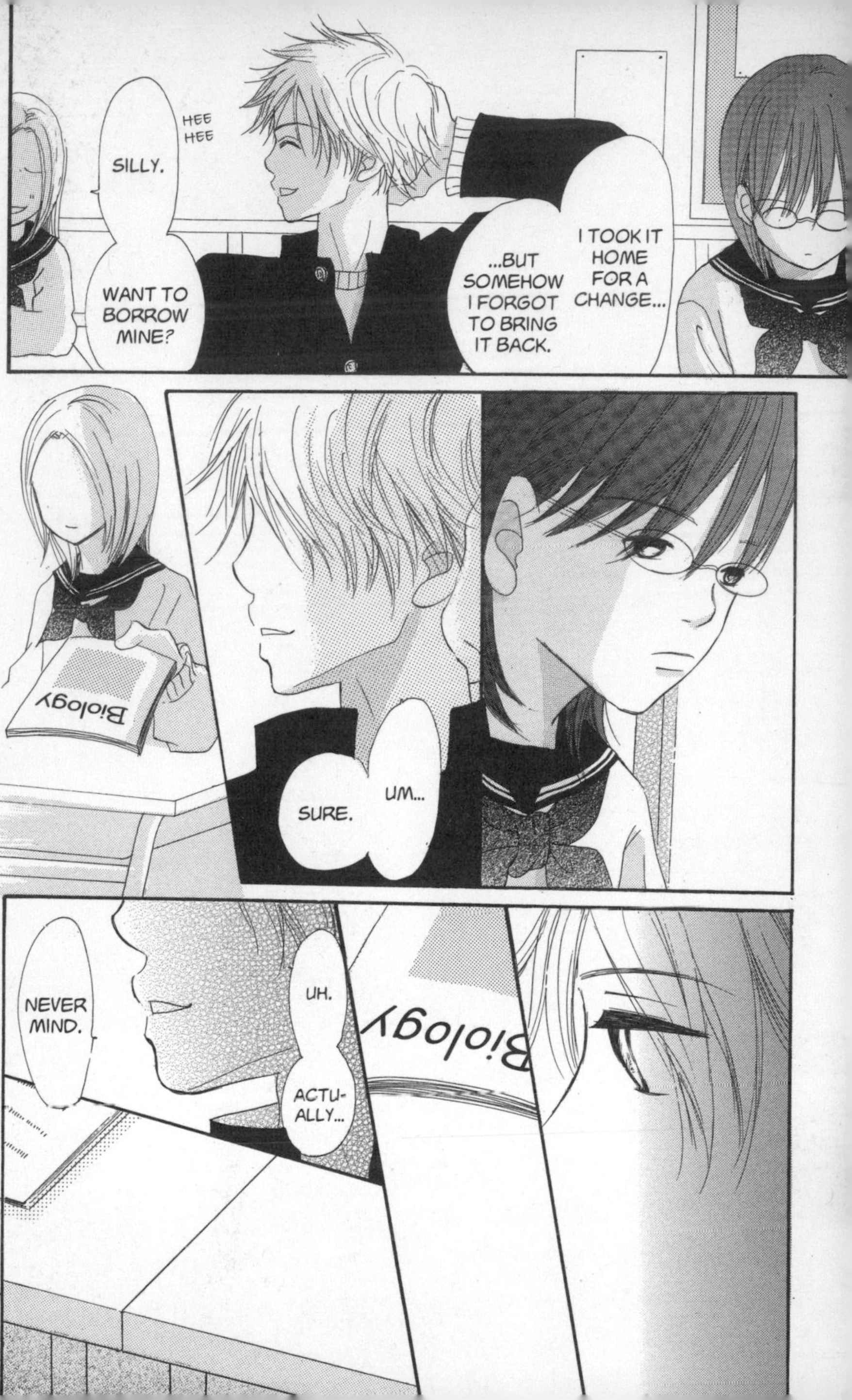

I TOOK IT HOME FOR A CHANGE...
...BUT SOMEHOW I FORGOT TO BRING IT BACK.
HEE HEE
SILLY.
WANT TO BORROW MINE?
UM...
SURE.
Biology
Biology
UH.
ACTU-ALLY...
NEVER MIND.

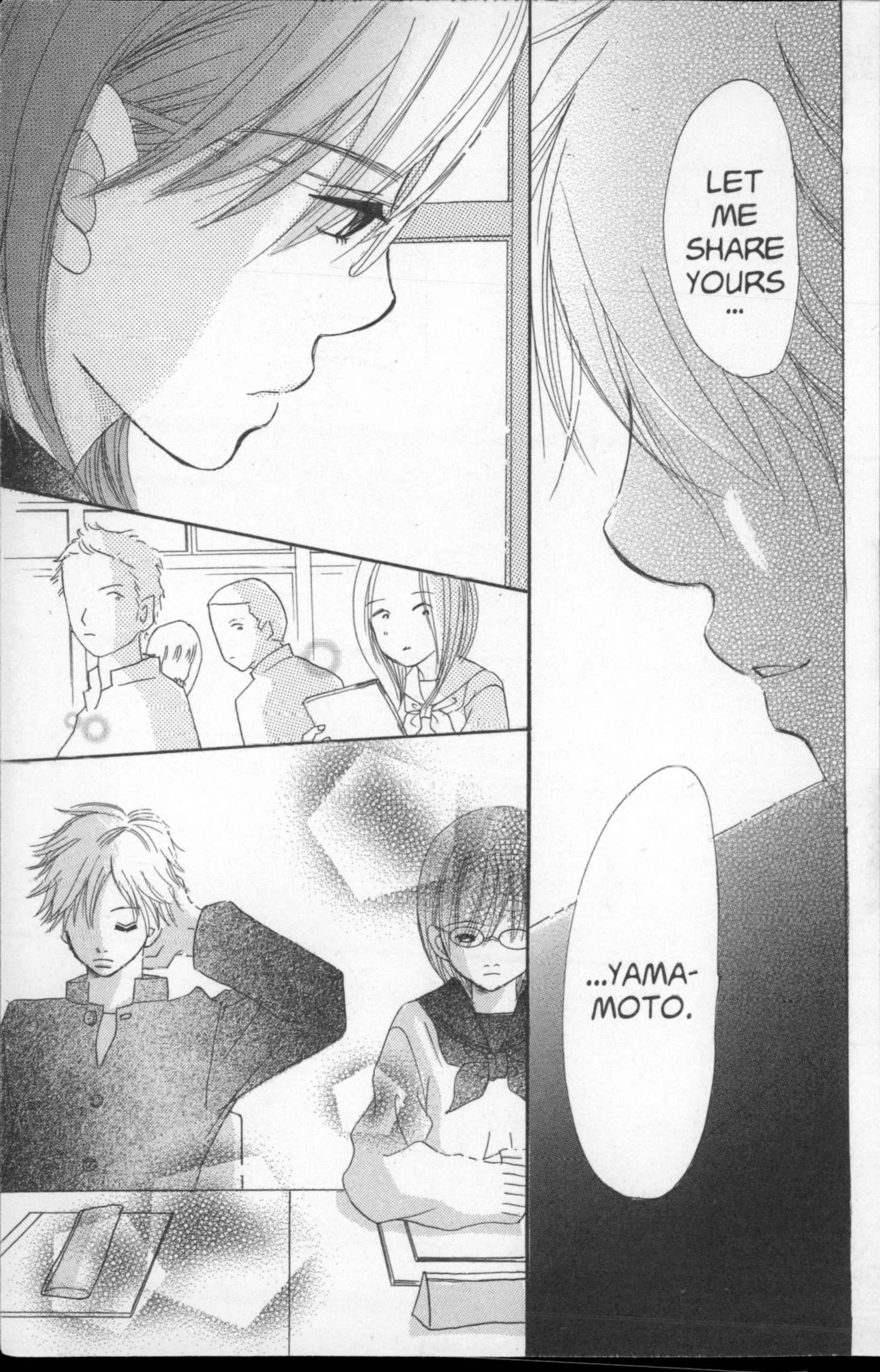
LET ME SHARE YOURS ...
...YAMA-MOTO.

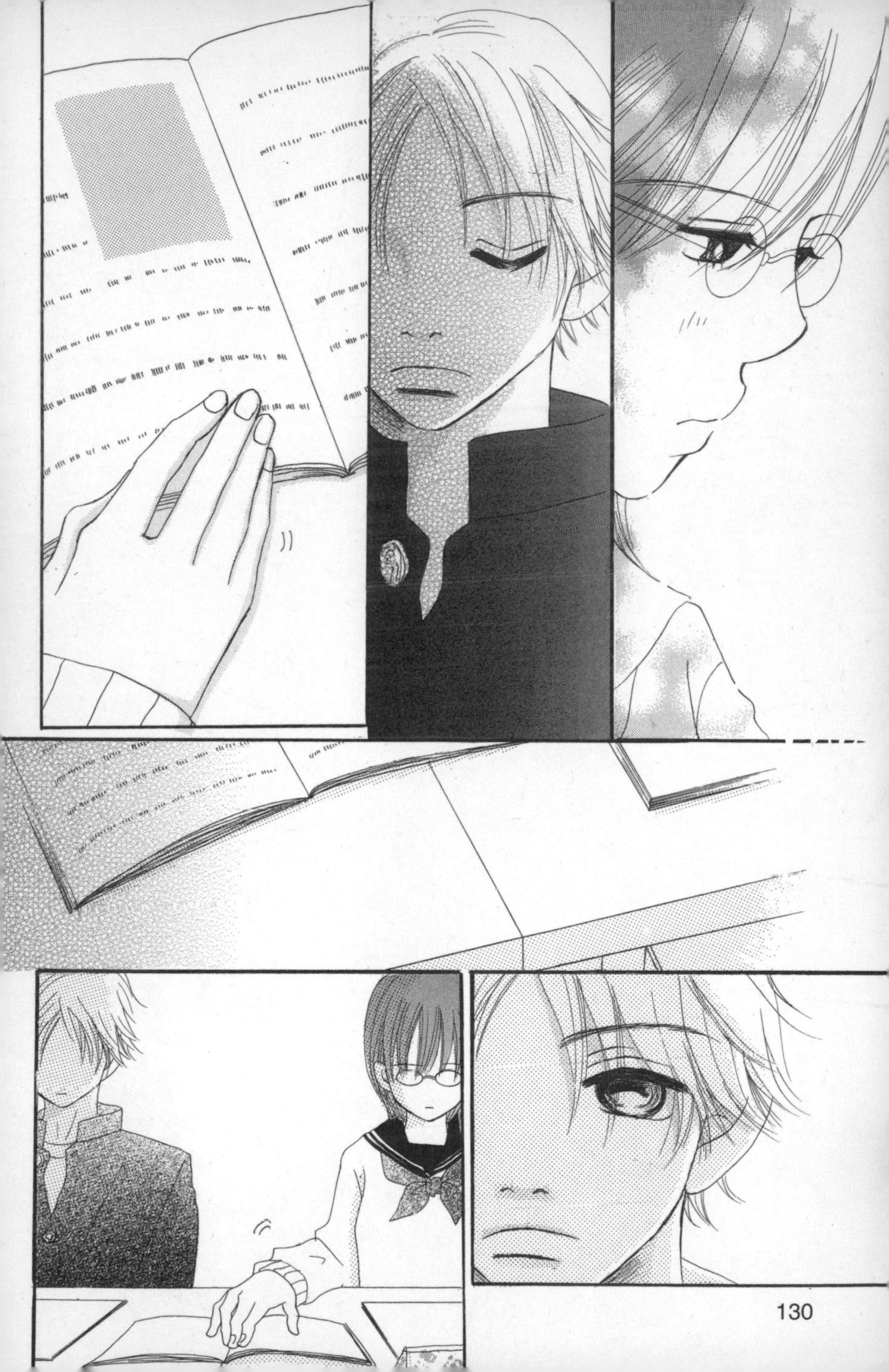

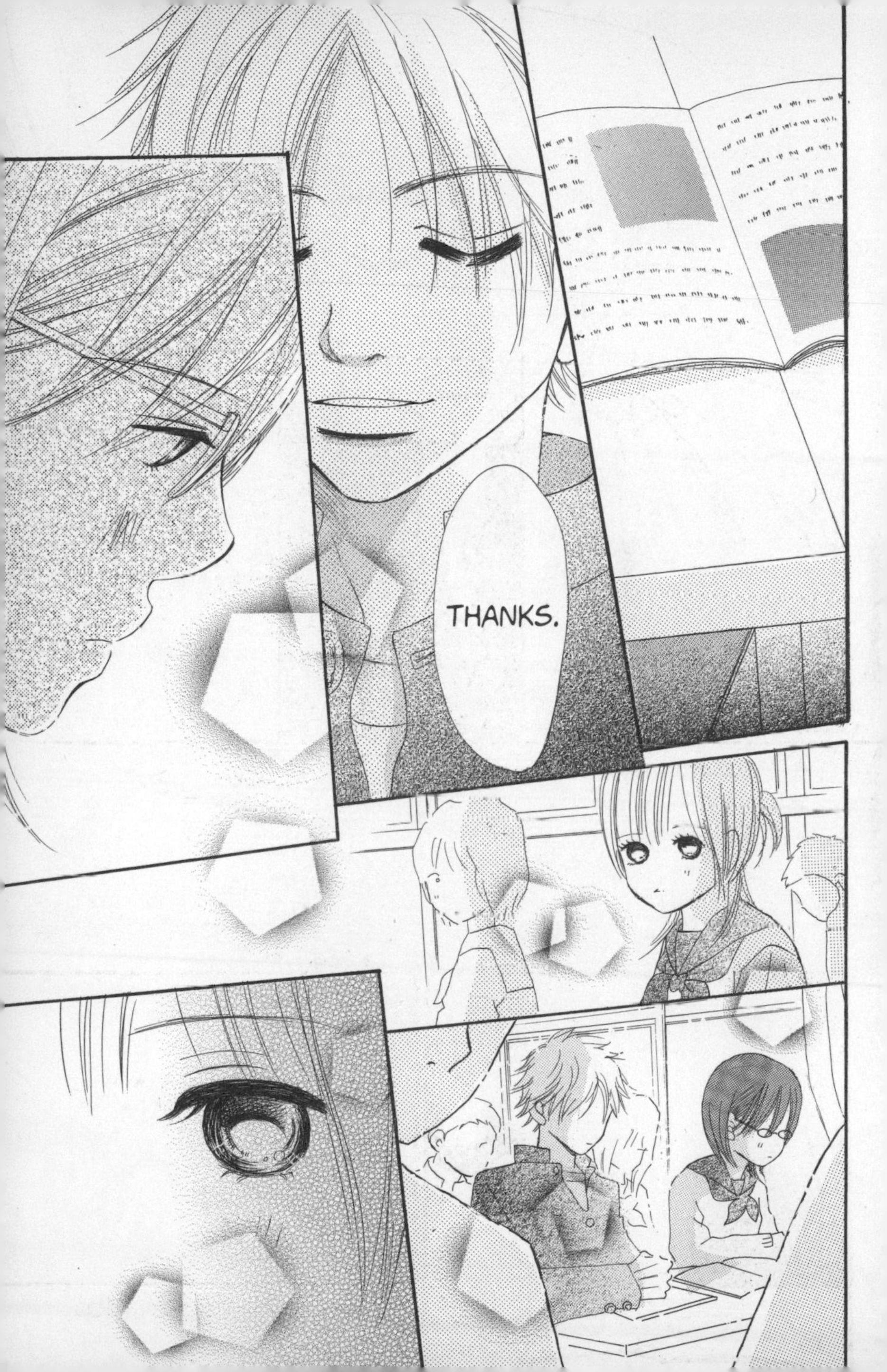
THANKS.

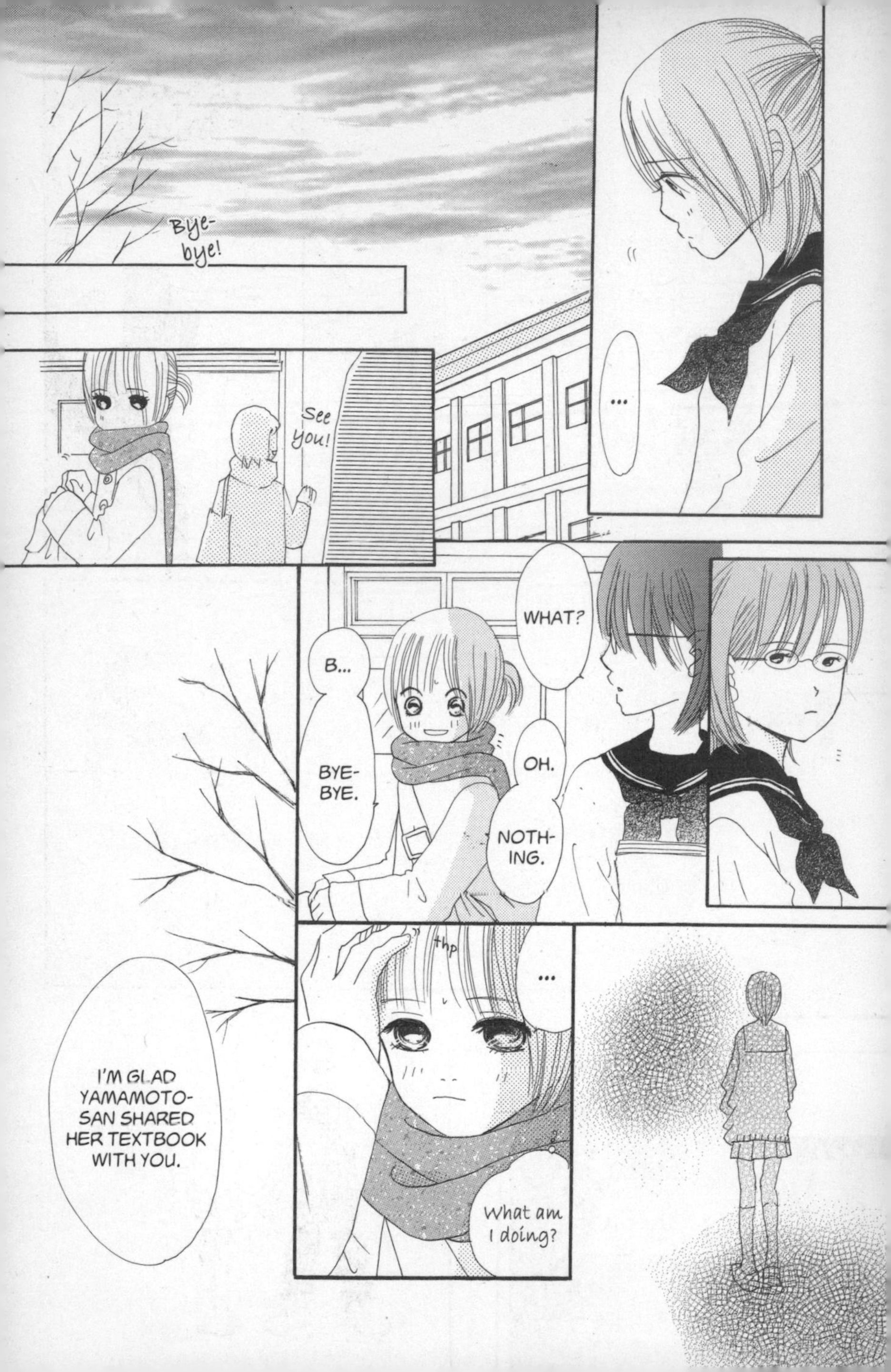
...
Bye-bye!
See you!
WHAT?
B... BYE-BYE.
OH. NOTHING.
thp
...
What am I doing?
I'M GLAD YAMAMOTO-SAN SHARED HER TEXTBOOK WITH YOU.

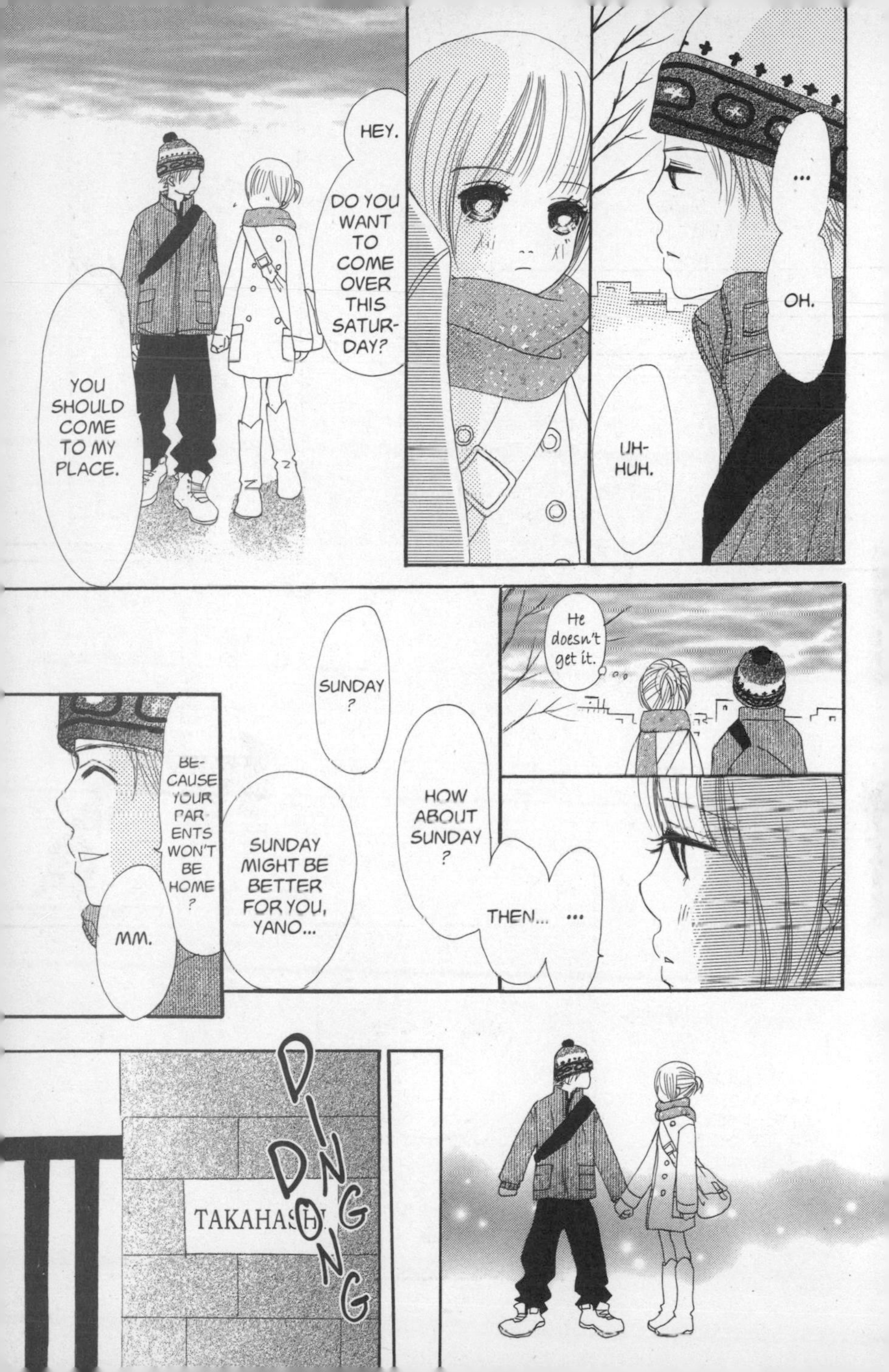
...
OH.
UH-HUH.
HEY.
DO YOU WANT TO COME OVER THIS SATURDAY?
YOU SHOULD COME TO MY PLACE.
He doesn't get it.
THEN... ...
HOW ABOUT SUNDAY?
SUNDAY?
SUNDAY MIGHT BE BETTER FOR YOU, YANO...
BE-CAUSE YOUR PAR-ENTS WON'T BE HOME?
MM.
TAKAHASHI
DING DONG

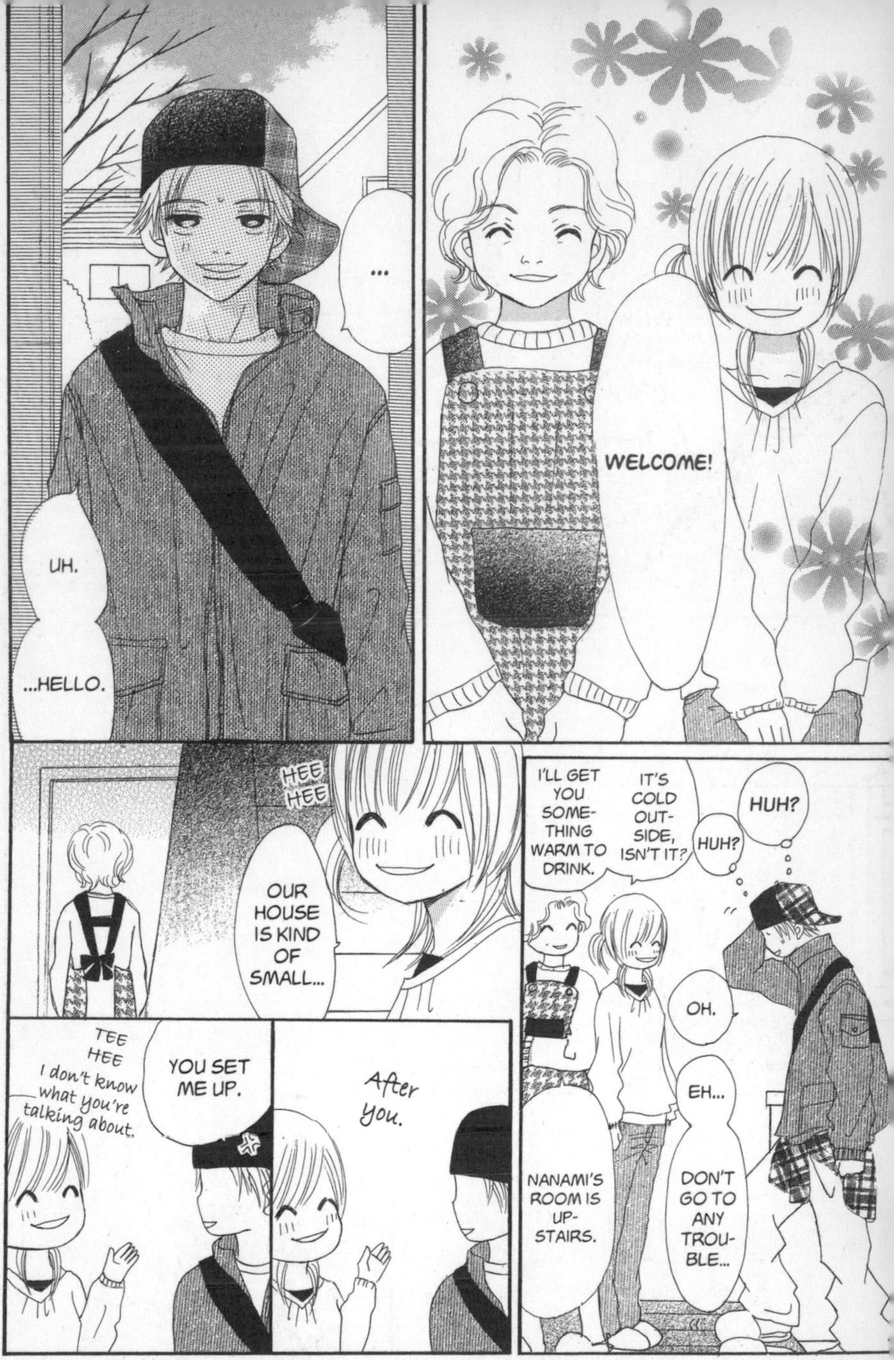
WELCOME!
...
UH.
...HELLO.
HUH?
HUH?
IT'S COLD OUTSIDE, ISN'T IT?
I'LL GET YOU SOMETHING WARM TO DRINK.
OH.
EH...
DON'T GO TO ANY TROUBLE...
NANAMI'S ROOM IS UPSTAIRS.
HEE HEE
OUR HOUSE IS KIND OF SMALL...
After you.
YOU SET ME UP.
TEE HEE
I don't know what you're talking about.

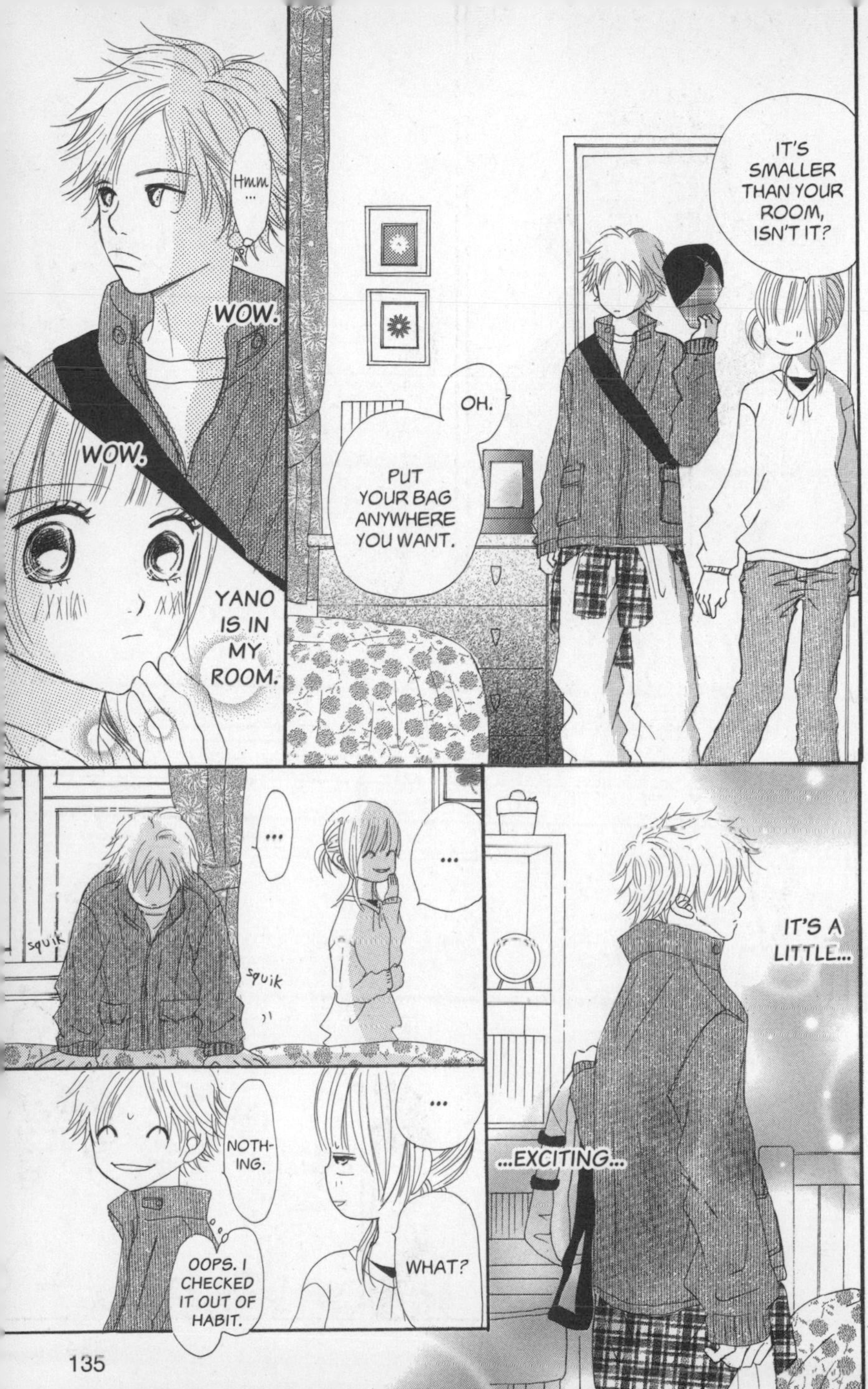
IT'S SMALLER THAN YOUR ROOM, ISN'T IT?
OH.
PUT YOUR BAG ANYWHERE YOU WANT.
Hmm...
WOW.
WOW.
YANO IS IN MY ROOM.
IT'S A LITTLE...
...EXCITING...
...
...
squik
squik
...
NOTH-ING.
WHAT?
OOPS. I CHECKED IT OUT OF HABIT.

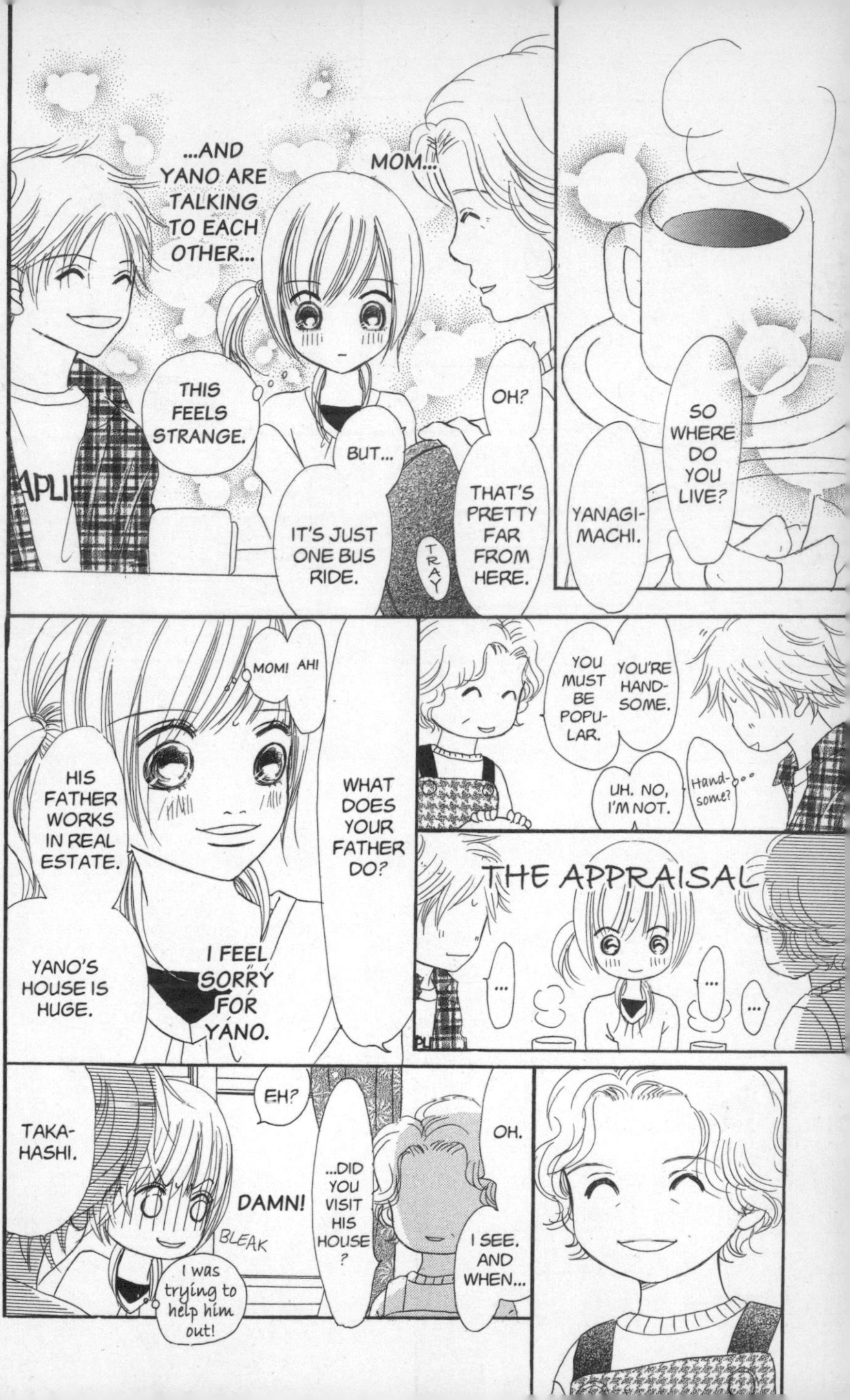
SO WHERE DO YOU LIVE?
YANAGI-MACHI.
OH?
THAT'S PRETTY FAR FROM HERE.
BUT...
IT'S JUST ONE BUS RIDE.
TRAY
MOM...
...AND YANO ARE TALKING TO EACH OTHER...
THIS FEELS STRANGE.
APLI
YOU'RE HAND-SOME.
YOU MUST BE POPU-LAR.
Hand-some?
UH. NO, I'M NOT.
THE APPRAISAL
...
...
...
PLI
WHAT DOES YOUR FATHER DO?
AH!
MOM!
HIS FATHER WORKS IN REAL ESTATE.
I FEEL SORRY FOR YANO.
YANO'S HOUSE IS HUGE.
OH.
I SEE. AND WHEN...
...DID YOU VISIT HIS HOUSE?
EH?
DAMN!
BLEAK
TAKA-HASHI.
I was trying to help him out!

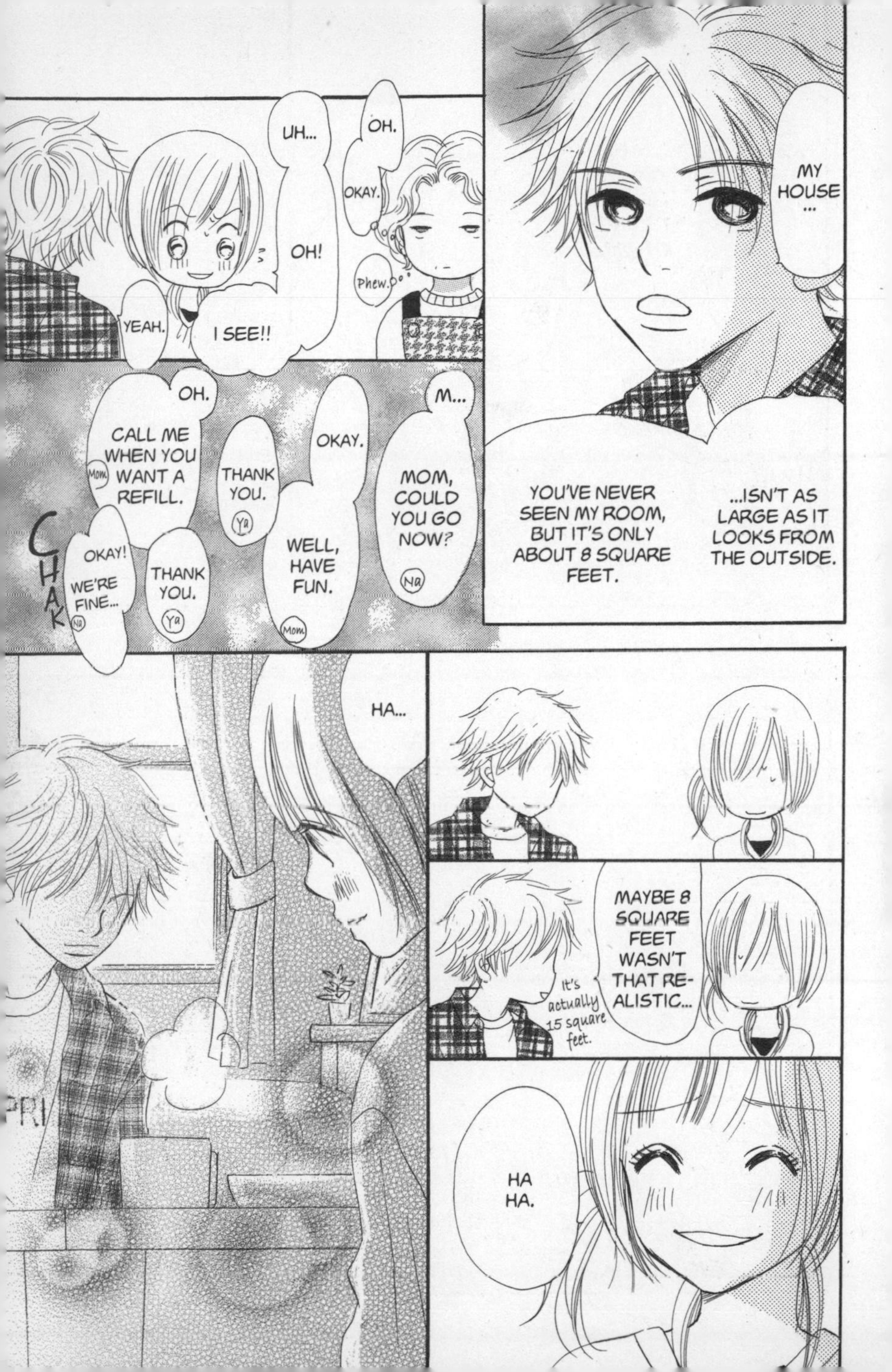
MY HOUSE ...
...ISN'T AS LARGE AS IT LOOKS FROM THE OUTSIDE.
YOU'VE NEVER SEEN MY ROOM, BUT IT'S ONLY ABOUT 8 SQUARE FEET.
OH.
OKAY.
UH...
OH!
Phew.
I SEE!!
YEAH.
M...
MOM, COULD YOU GO NOW?
OKAY.
WELL, HAVE FUN.
OH.
THANK YOU.
CALL ME WHEN YOU WANT A REFILL.
THANK YOU.
OKAY! WE'RE FINE...
CHAK
MAYBE 8 SQUARE FEET WASN'T THAT RE-ALISTIC...
It's actually 15 square feet.
HA HA.
HA...

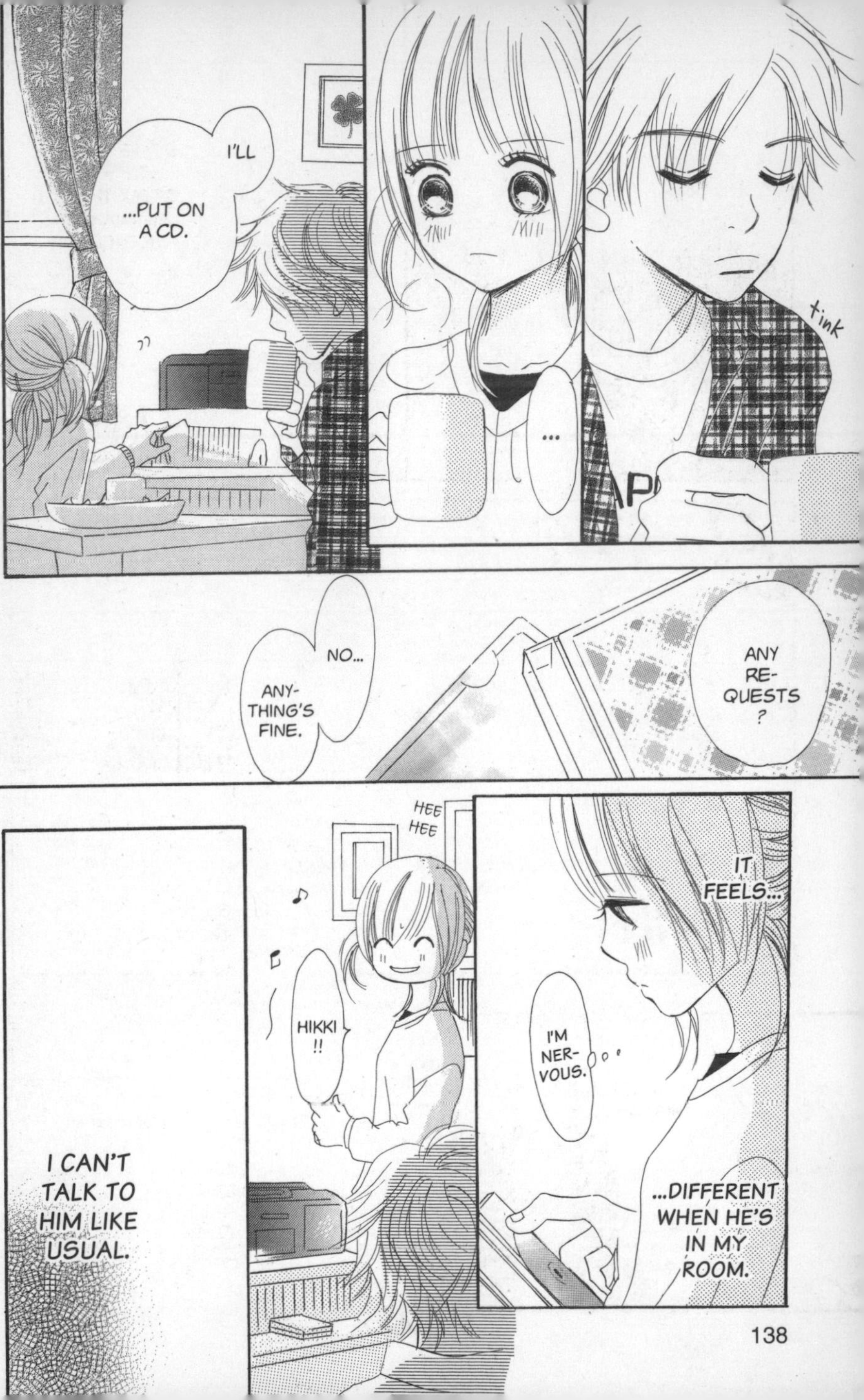
tink
...
I'LL
...PUT ON A CD.
ANY RE-QUESTS?
NO...
ANY-THING'S FINE.
IT FEELS...
I'M NER-VOUS.
...DIFFERENT WHEN HE'S IN MY ROOM.
HEE HEE
HIKKI!!
I CAN'T TALK TO HIM LIKE USUAL.

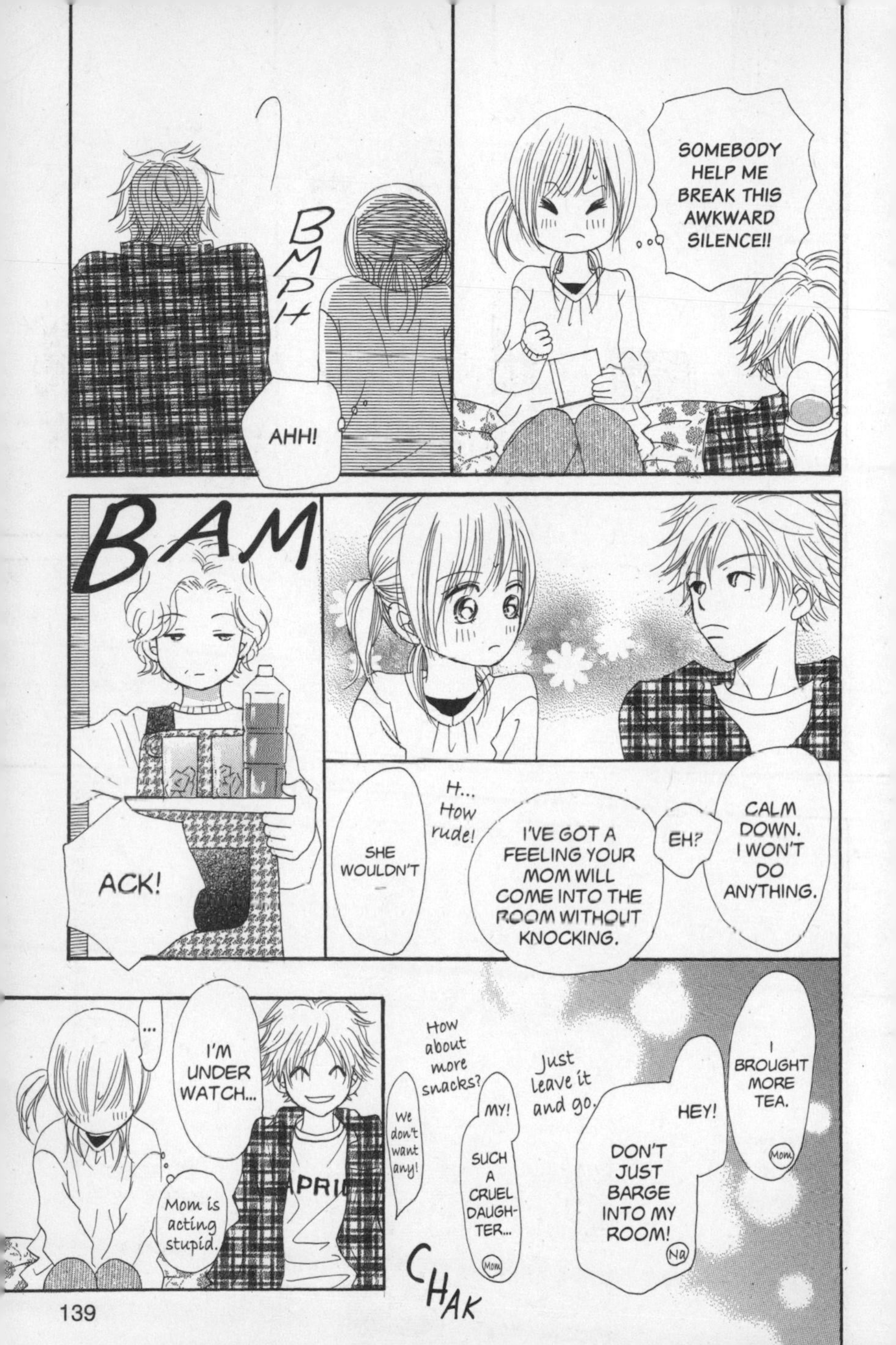
SOMEBODY HELP ME BREAK THIS AWKWARD SILENCE!!
BMPH
AHH!
CALM DOWN. I WON'T DO ANYTHING.
EH?
I'VE GOT A FEELING YOUR MOM WILL COME INTO THE ROOM WITHOUT KNOCKING.
H... How rude!
SHE WOULDN'T —
BAM
ACK!
I BROUGHT MORE TEA.
Mom
HEY!
DON'T JUST BARGE INTO MY ROOM!
Na
Just leave it and go.
MY!
SUCH A CRUEL DAUGHTER...
Mom
How about more snacks?
We don't want any!
CHAK
...
I'M UNDER WATCH...
Mom is acting stupid.

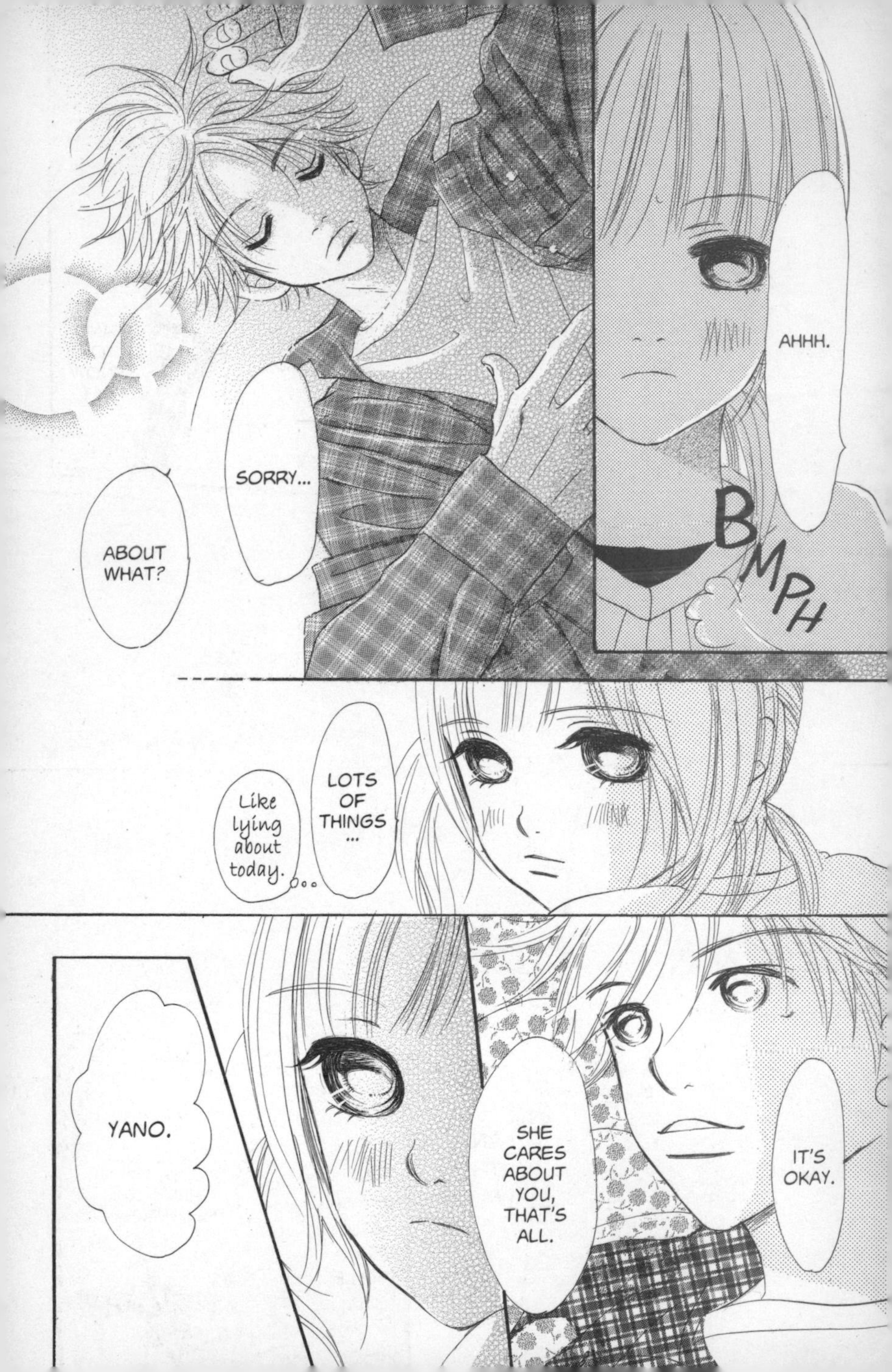
AHHH.
BMPH
SORRY...
ABOUT WHAT?
LOTS OF THINGS ...
Like lying about today.
IT'S OKAY.
SHE CARES ABOUT YOU, THAT'S ALL.
YANO.

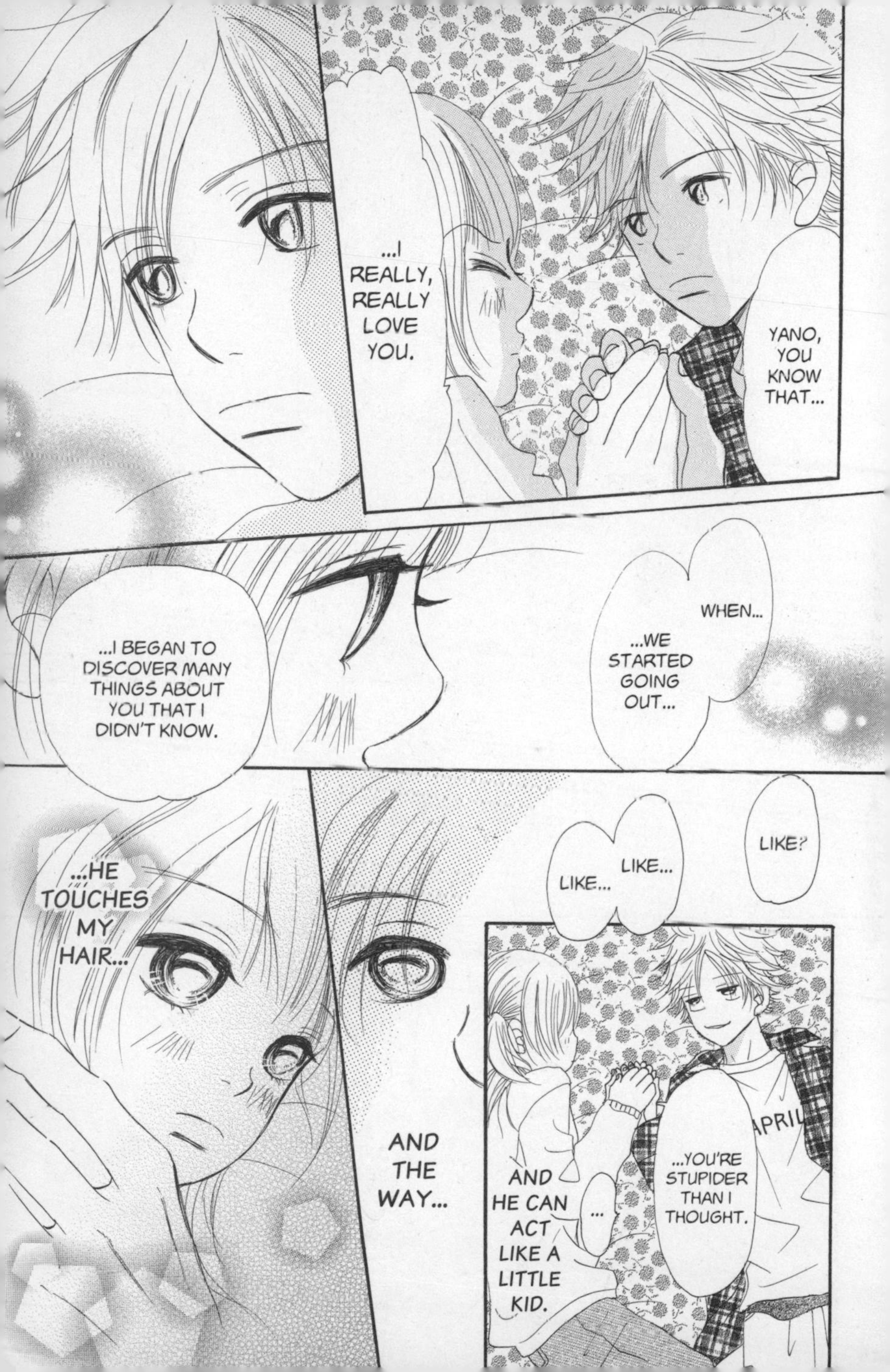
YANO, YOU KNOW THAT...
...I REALLY, REALLY LOVE YOU.
WHEN...
...WE STARTED GOING OUT...
...I BEGAN TO DISCOVER MANY THINGS ABOUT YOU THAT I DIDN'T KNOW.
LIKE?
LIKE...
LIKE...
...YOU'RE STUPIDER THAN I THOUGHT.
APRIL
...
AND HE CAN ACT LIKE A LITTLE KID.
AND THE WAY...
...HE TOUCHES MY HAIR...

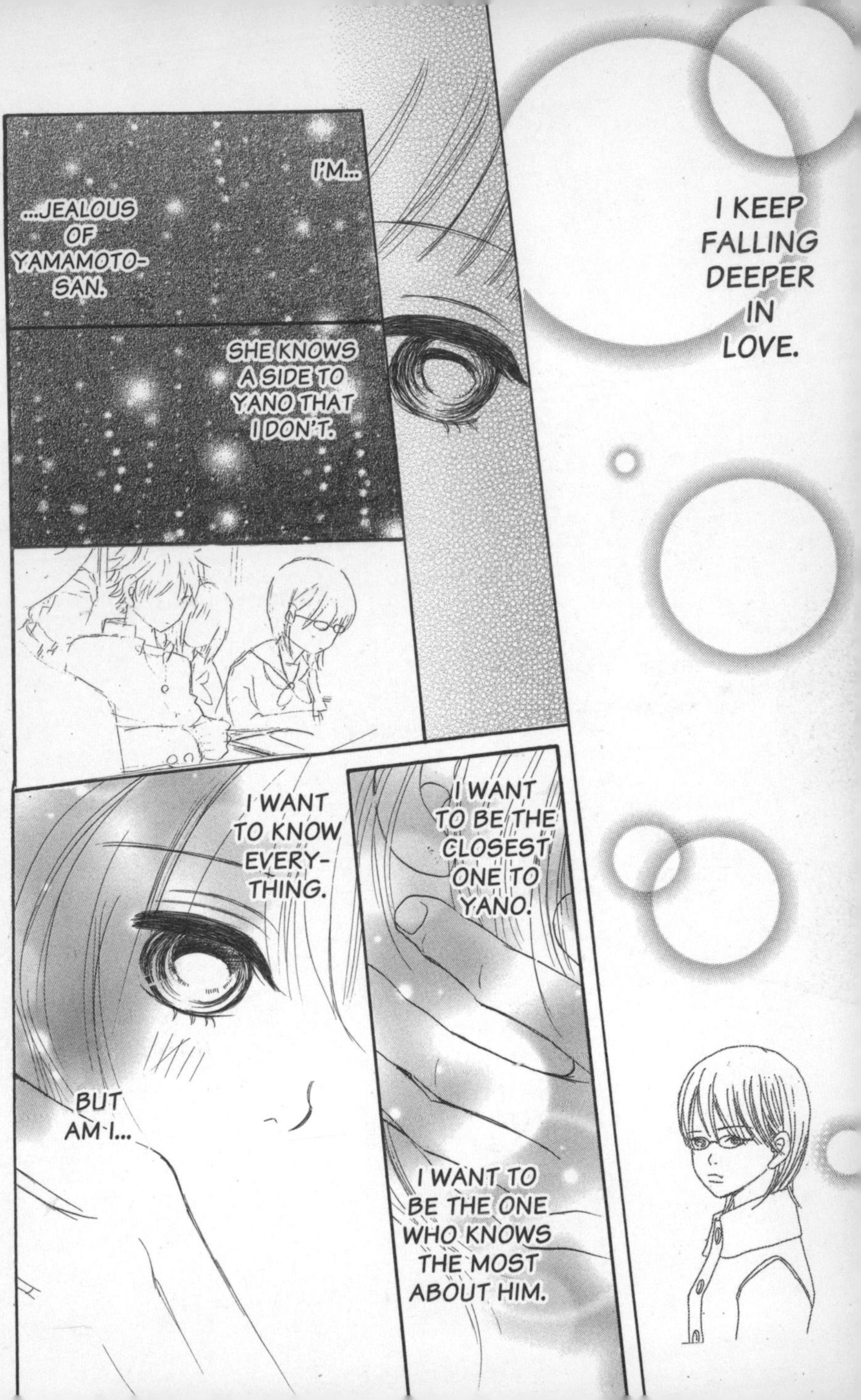
I KEEP FALLING DEEPER IN LOVE.
I'M...
...JEALOUS OF YAMAMOTO-SAN.
SHE KNOWS A SIDE TO YANO THAT I DON'T.
I WANT TO BE THE CLOSEST ONE TO YANO.
I WANT TO BE THE ONE WHO KNOWS THE MOST ABOUT HIM.
I WANT TO KNOW EVERYTHING.
BUT AM I...

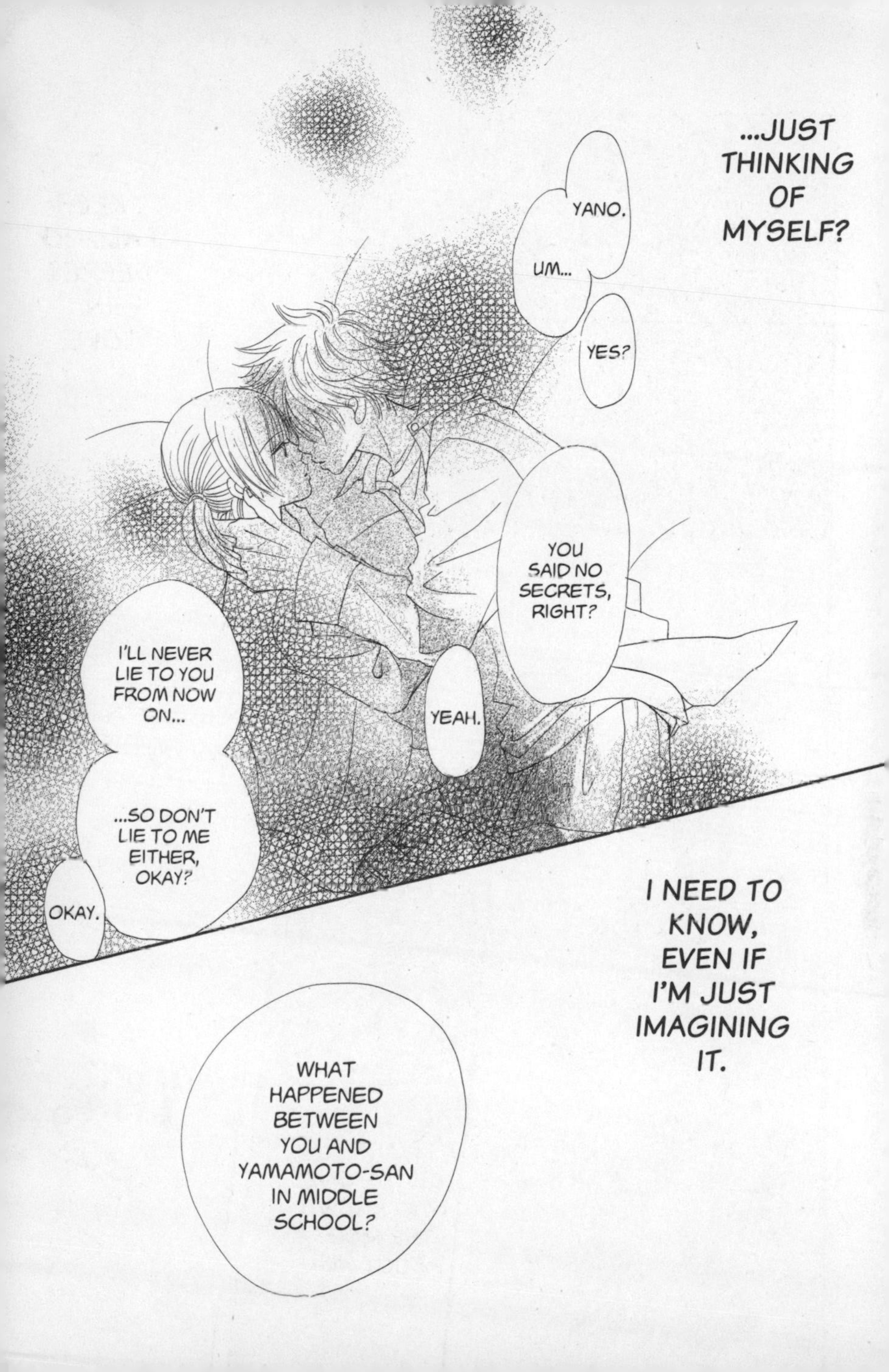
...JUST THINKING OF MYSELF?
YANO.
UM...
YES?
YOU SAID NO SECRETS, RIGHT?
YEAH.
I'LL NEVER LIE TO YOU FROM NOW ON...
...SO DON'T LIE TO ME EITHER, OKAY?
OKAY.
I NEED TO KNOW, EVEN IF I'M JUST IMAGINING IT.
WHAT HAPPENED BETWEEN YOU AND YAMAMOTO-SAN IN MIDDLE SCHOOL?

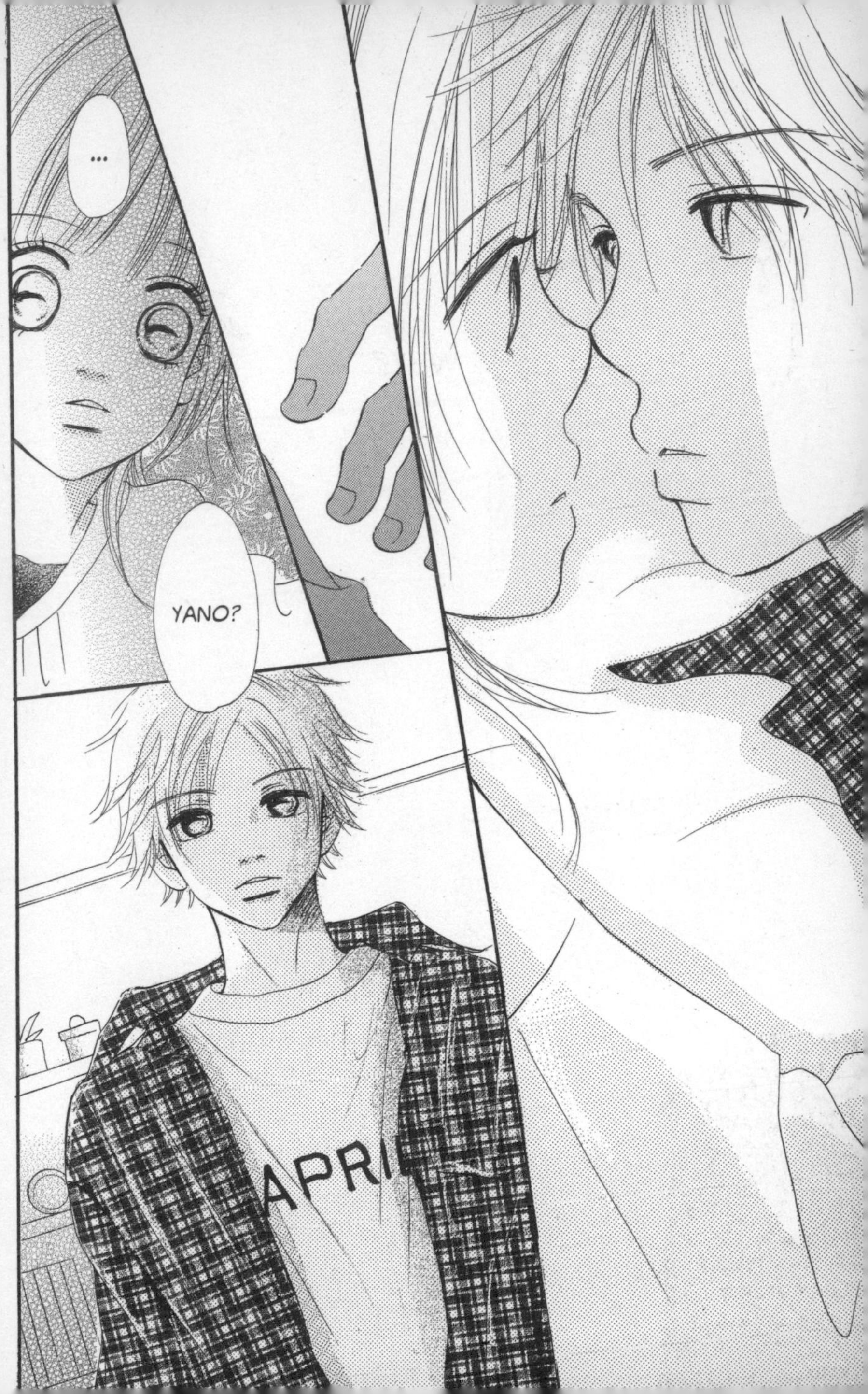
...
YANO?
APRI

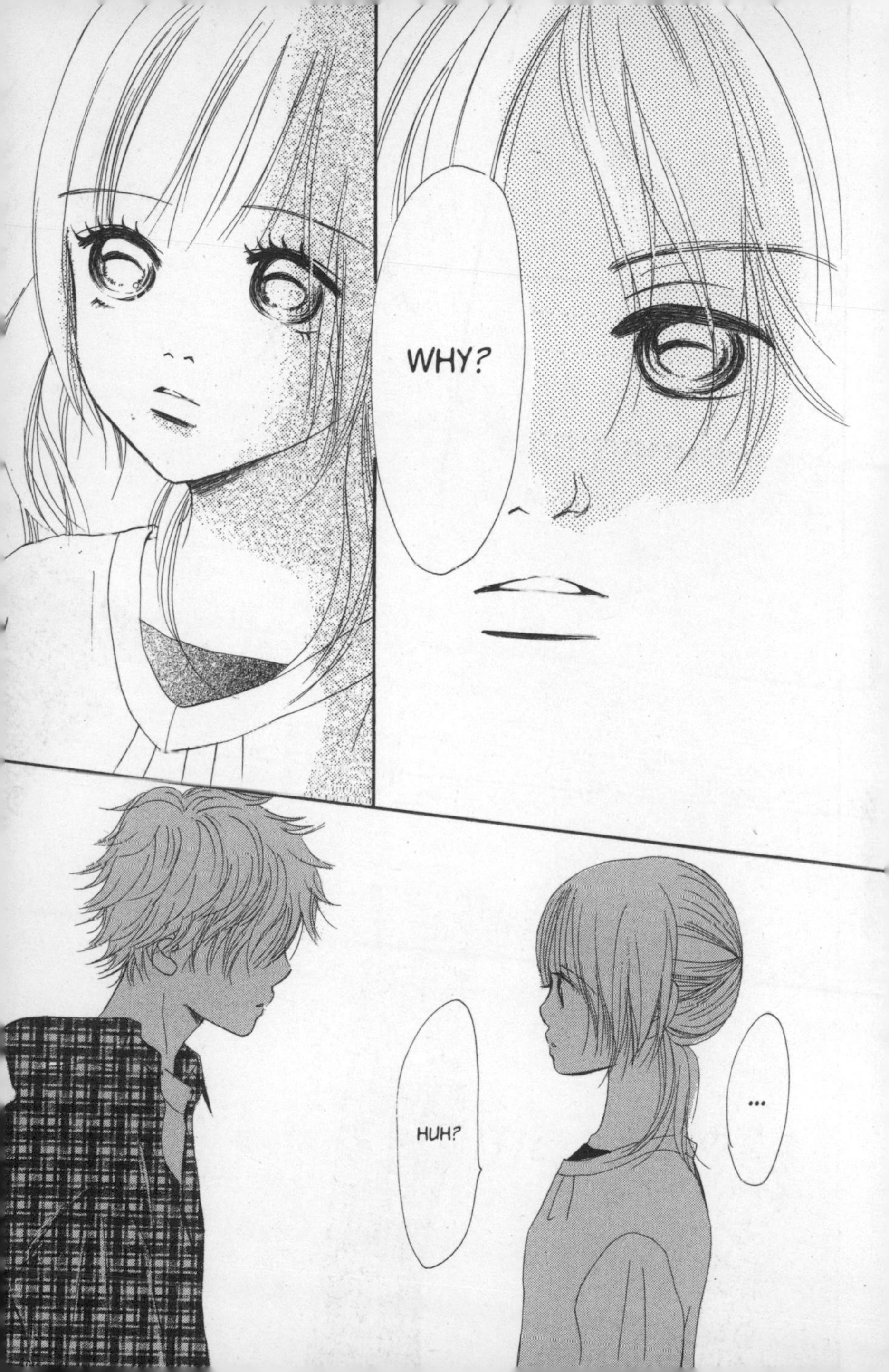
WHY?
...
HUH?

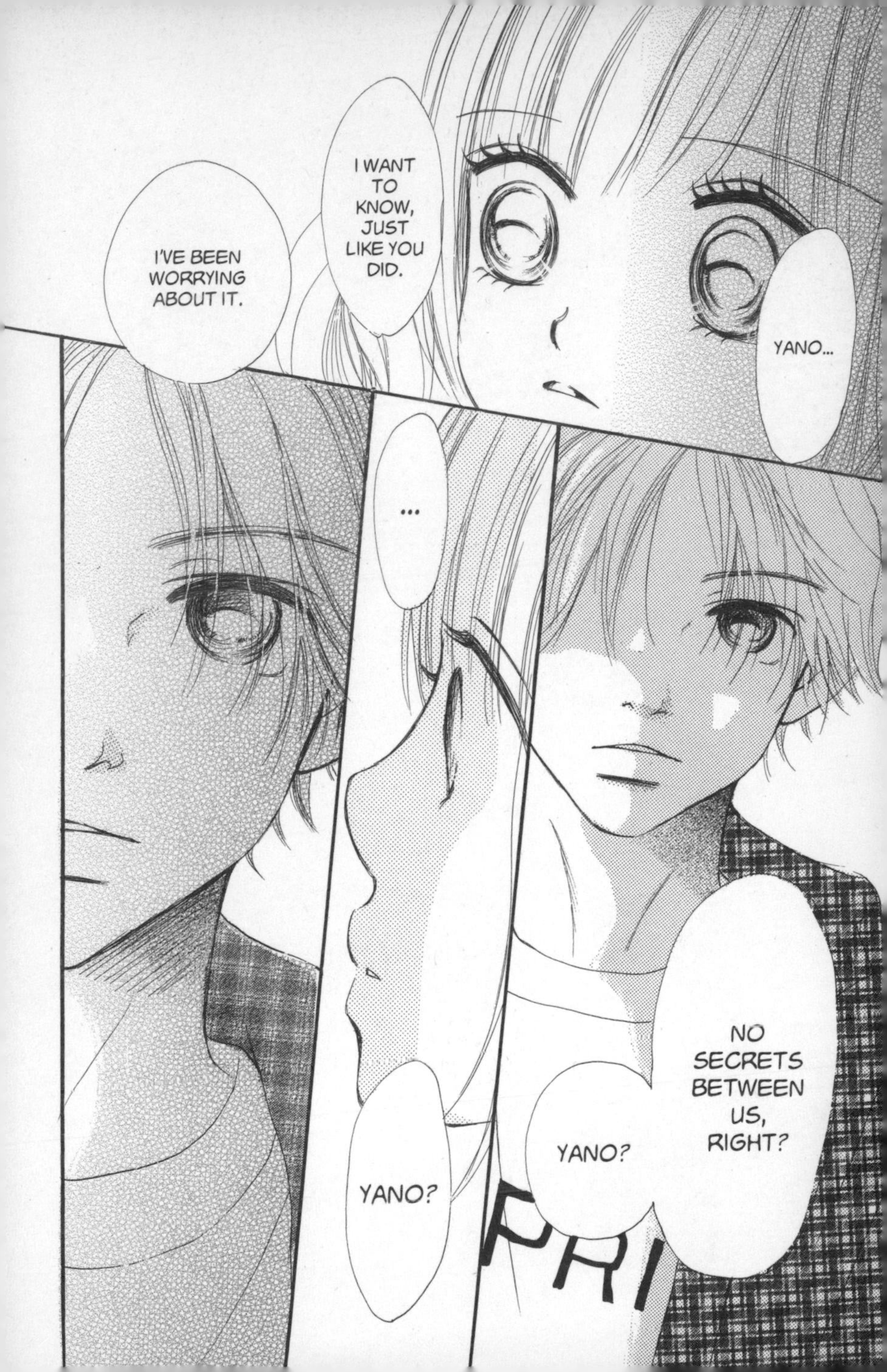
YANO...
I WANT TO KNOW, JUST LIKE YOU DID.
I'VE BEEN WORRYING ABOUT IT.
NO SECRETS BETWEEN US, RIGHT?
YANO?
PRI
...
YANO?

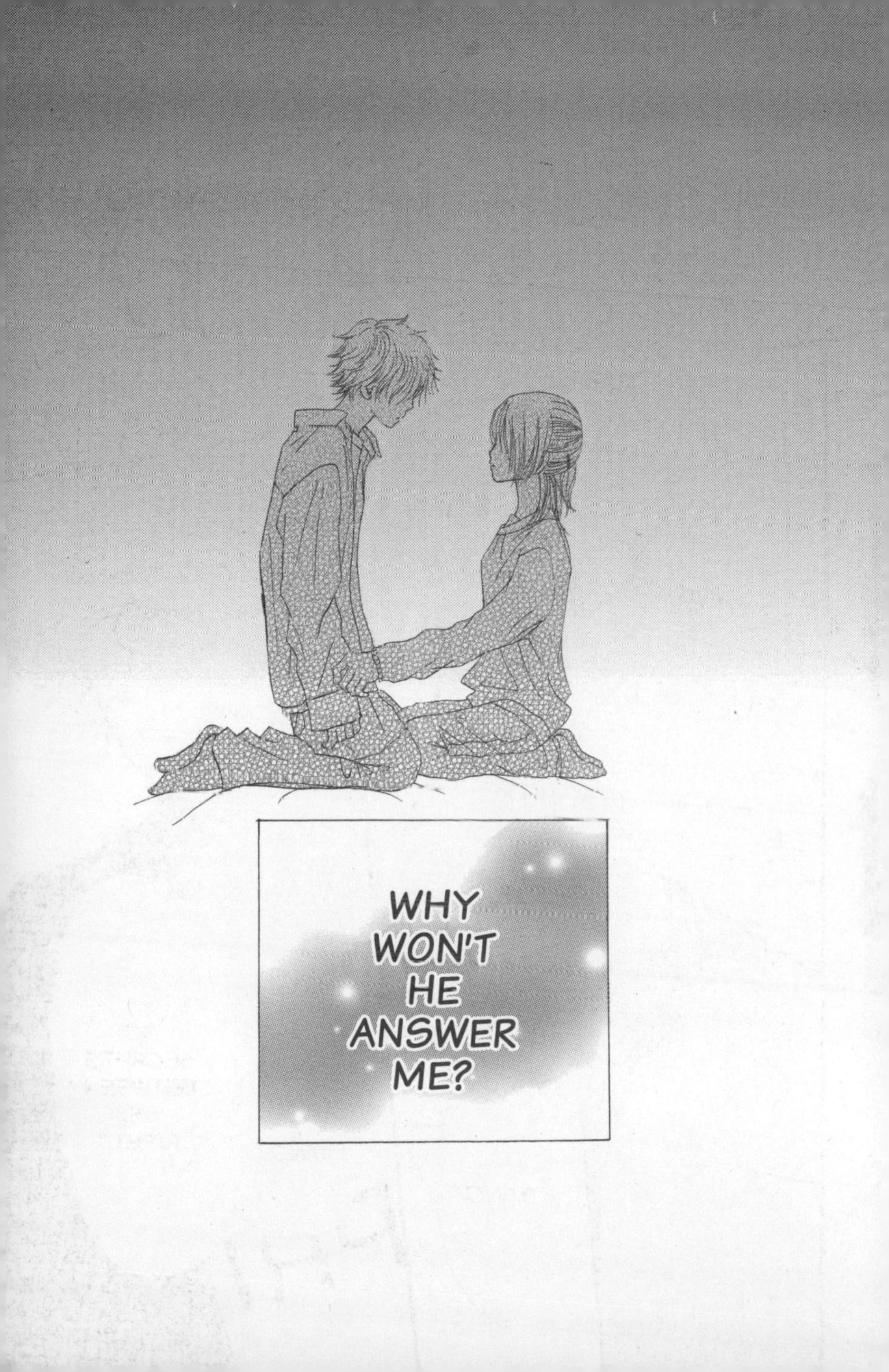
WHY WON'T HE ANSWER ME?

Chapter 12

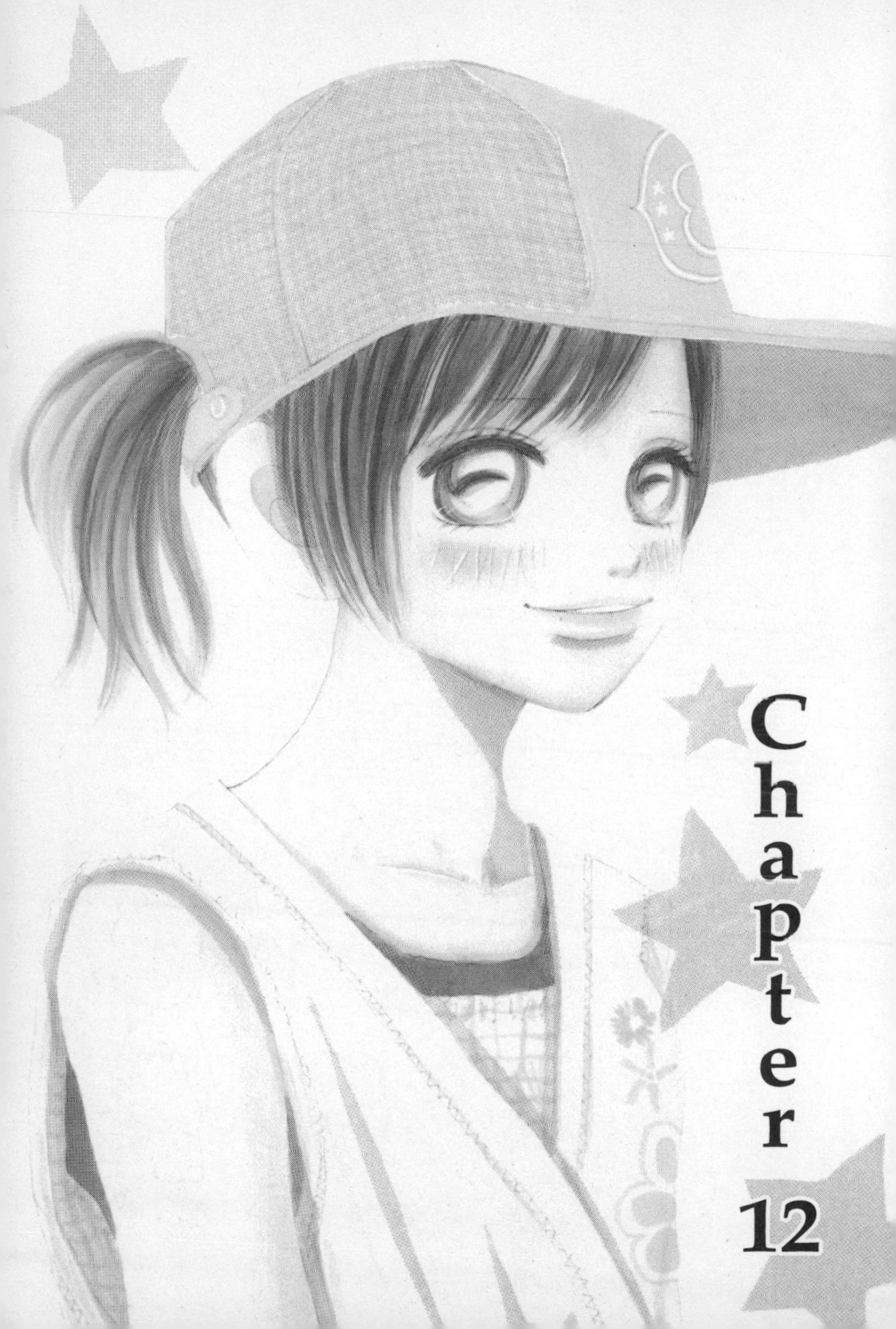

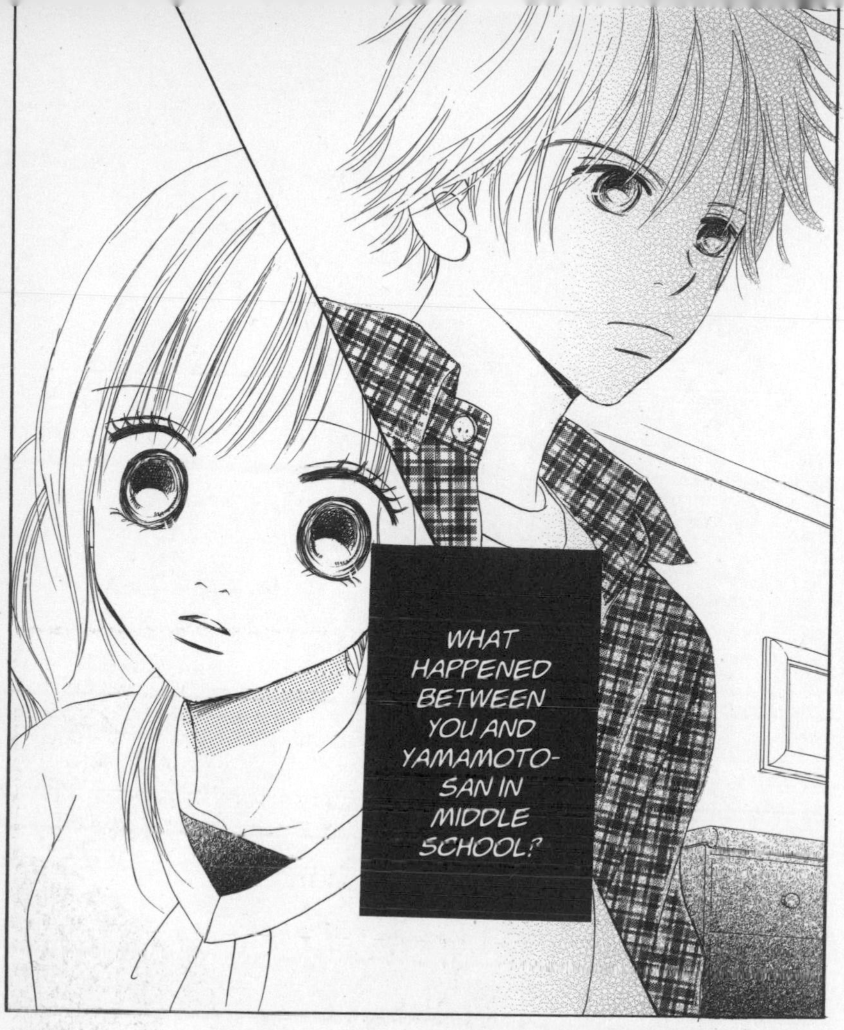
WHAT HAPPENED BETWEEN YOU AND YAMAMOTO-SAN IN MIDDLE SCHOOL?

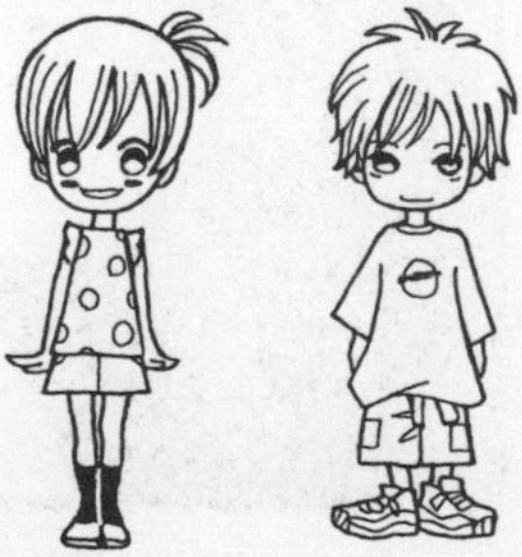

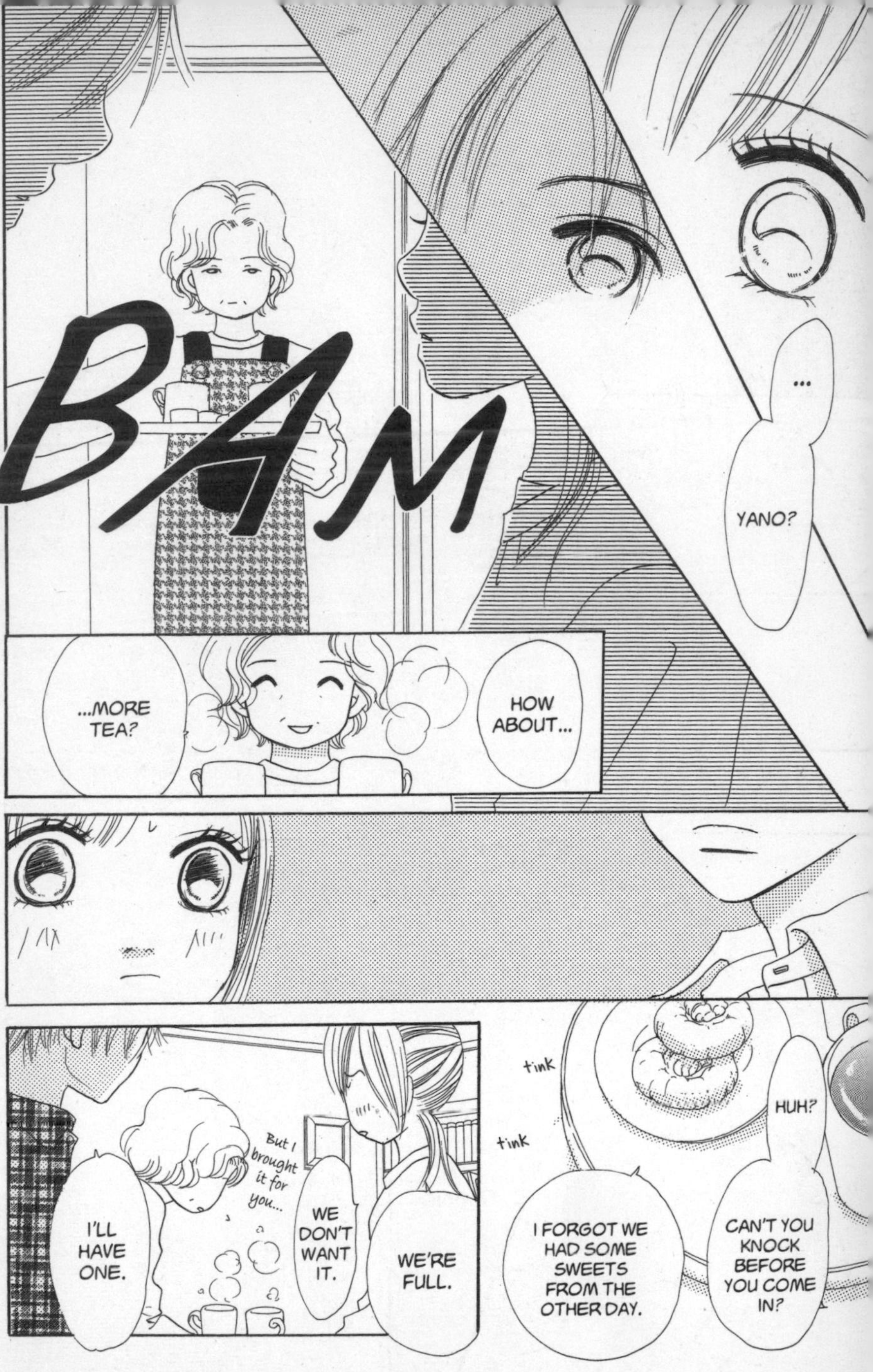
...
YANO?
BAM
HOW ABOUT...
...MORE TEA?
tink
tink
HUH?
CAN'T YOU KNOCK BEFORE YOU COME IN?
I FORGOT WE HAD SOME SWEETS FROM THE OTHER DAY.
WE'RE FULL.
WE DON'T WANT IT.
But I brought it for you...
I'LL HAVE ONE.

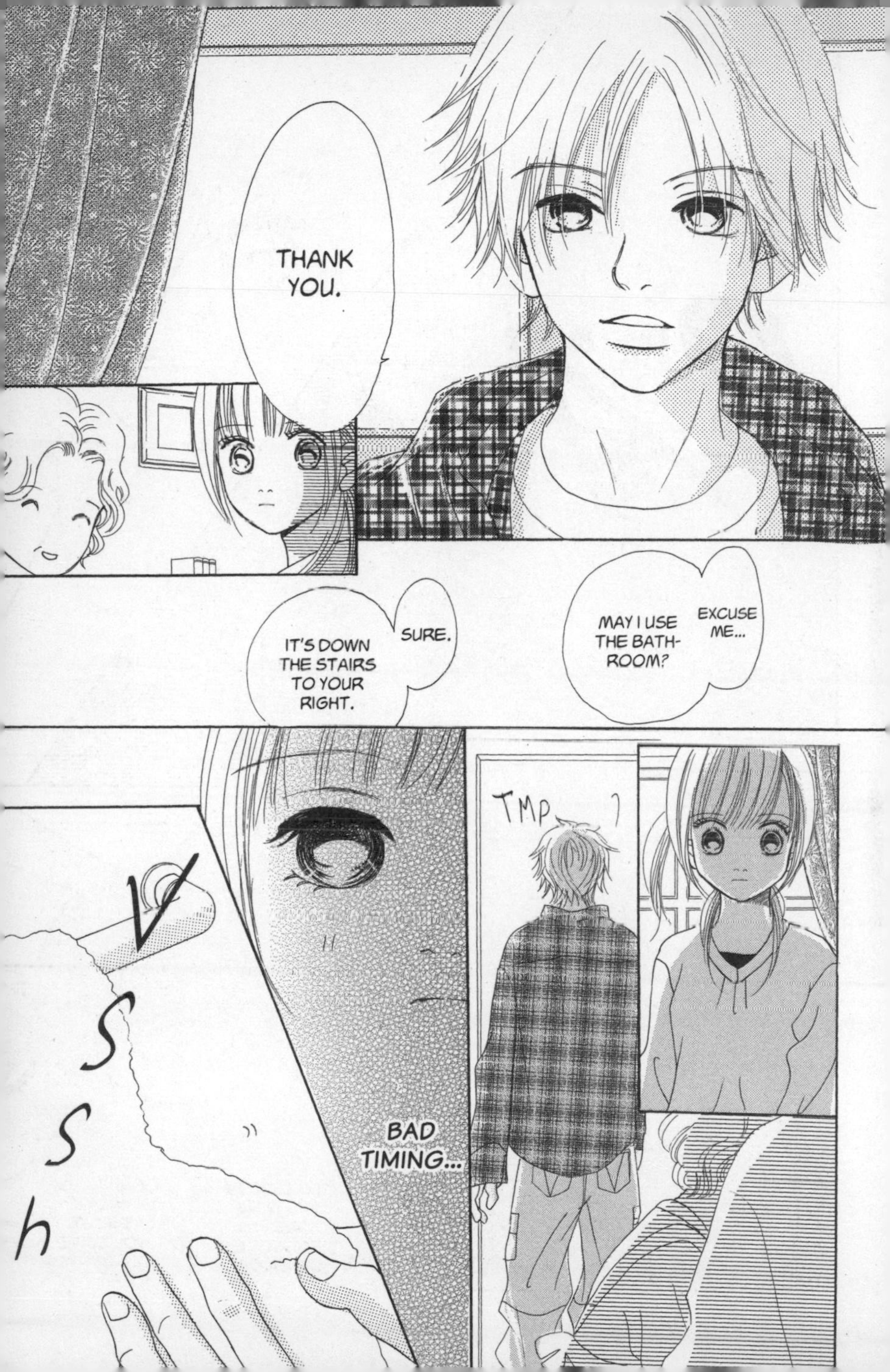

THANK YOU.
EXCUSE ME...
MAY I USE THE BATH-ROOM?
SURE.
IT'S DOWN THE STAIRS TO YOUR RIGHT.
TMP
BAD TIMING...

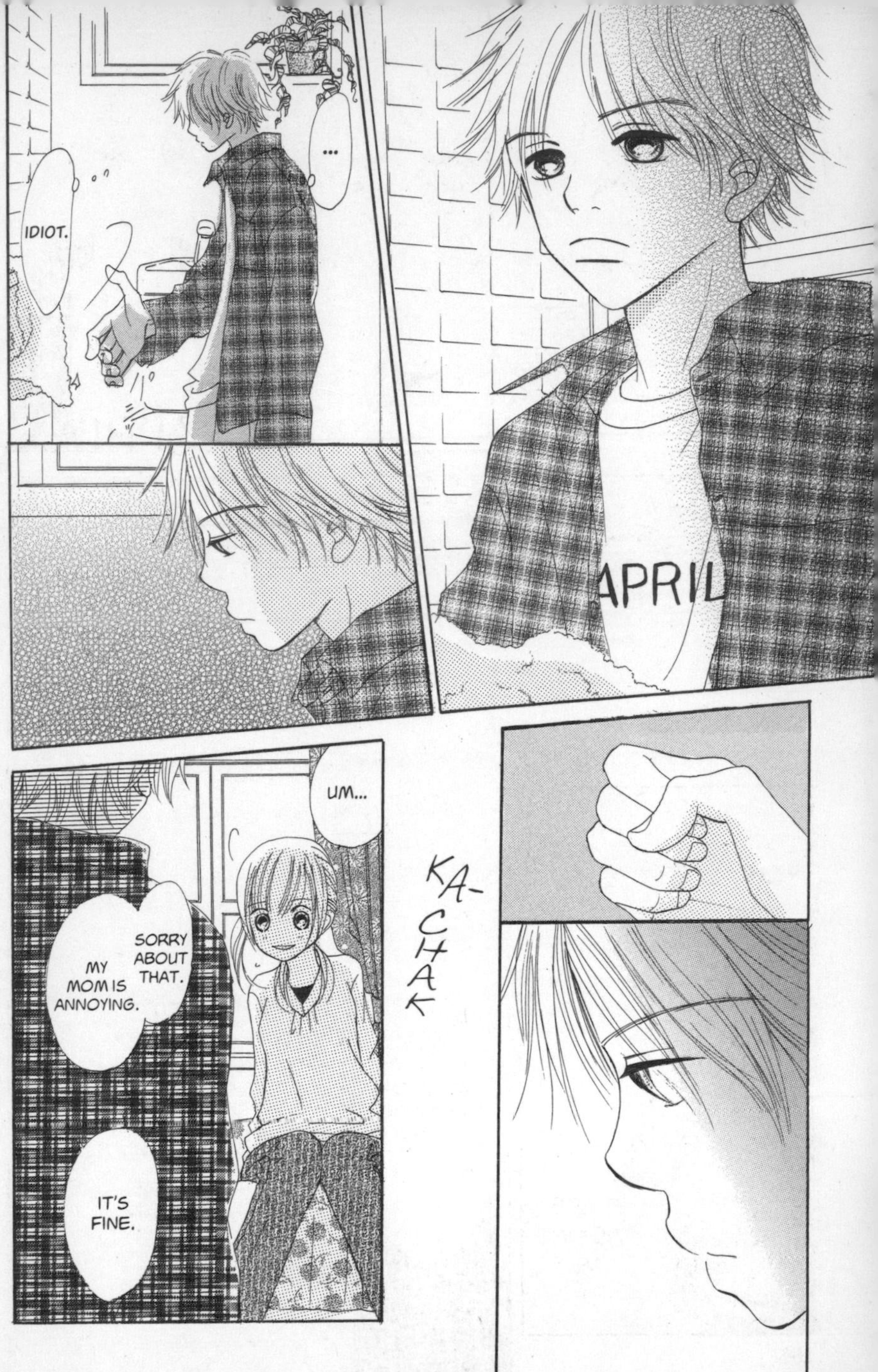
APRIL
...
IDIOT.
KA-CHAK
UM...
SORRY ABOUT THAT. MY MOM IS ANNOYING.
IT'S FINE.

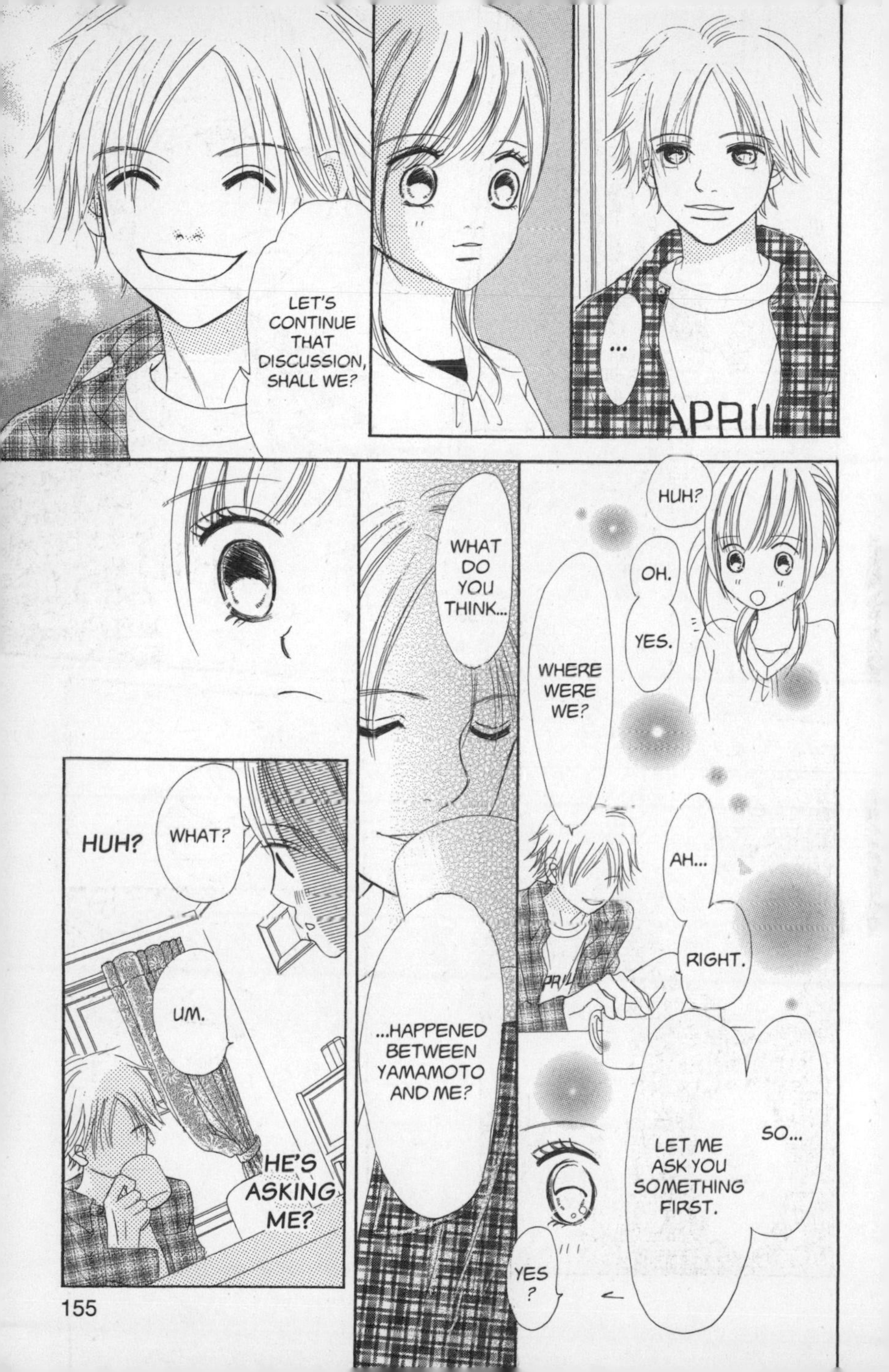
...
LET'S CONTINUE THAT DISCUSSION, SHALL WE?
HUH?
OH.
YES.
WHERE WERE WE?
AH...
RIGHT.
SO...
LET ME ASK YOU SOMETHING FIRST.
YES?
WHAT DO YOU THINK...
...HAPPENED BETWEEN YAMAMOTO AND ME?
WHAT?
HUH?
UM.
HE'S ASKING ME?

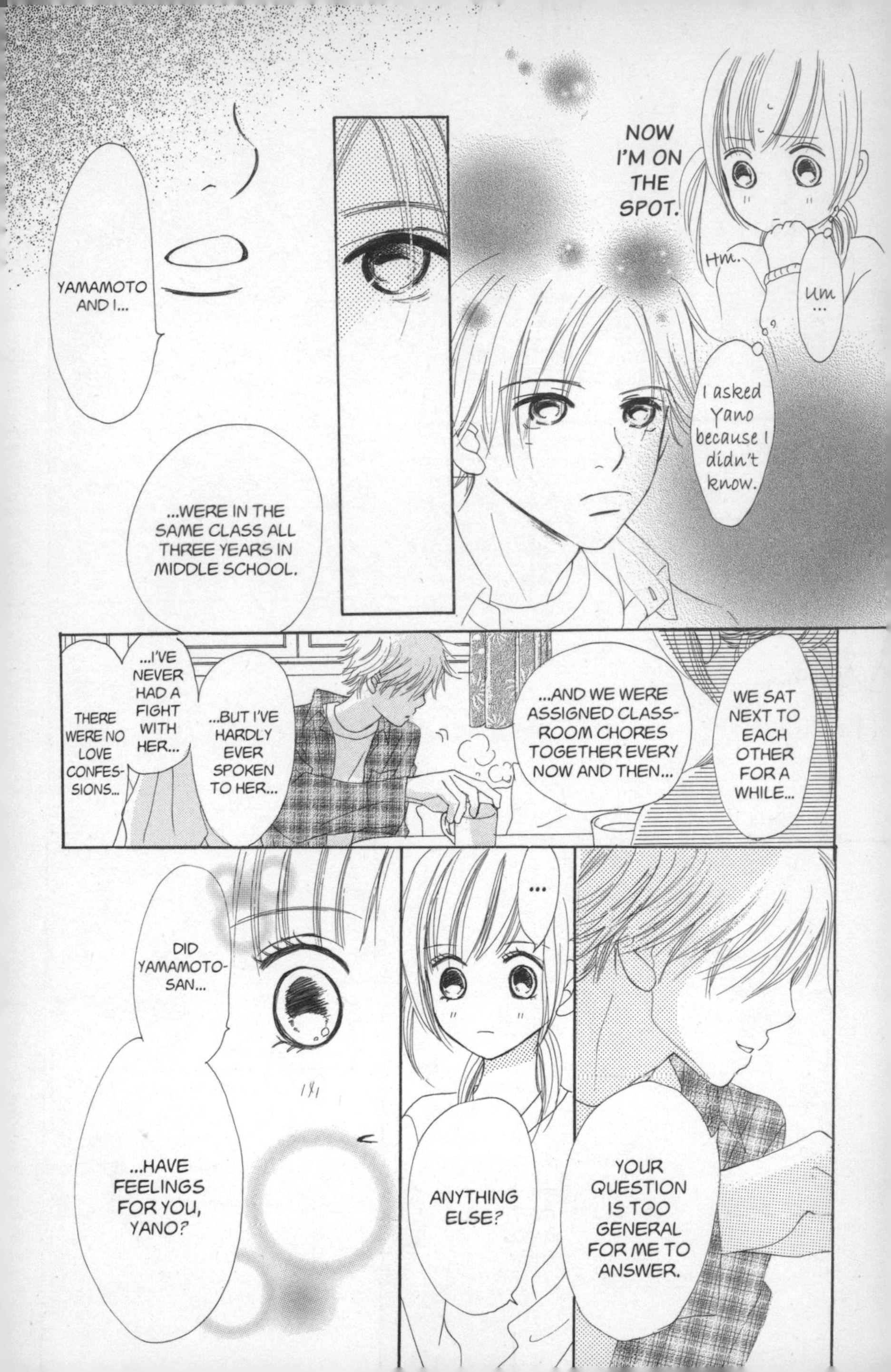
NOW I'M ON THE SPOT.
Hm.
Um...
I asked Yano because I didn't know.
YAMAMOTO AND I...
...WERE IN THE SAME CLASS ALL THREE YEARS IN MIDDLE SCHOOL.
WE SAT NEXT TO EACH OTHER FOR A WHILE...
...AND WE WERE ASSIGNED CLASSROOM CHORES TOGETHER EVERY NOW AND THEN...
...BUT I'VE HARDLY EVER SPOKEN TO HER...
...I'VE NEVER HAD A FIGHT WITH HER...
THERE WERE NO LOVE CONFESSIONS...
YOUR QUESTION IS TOO GENERAL FOR ME TO ANSWER.
...
ANYTHING ELSE?
DID YAMAMOTO-SAN...
...HAVE FEELINGS FOR YOU, YANO?

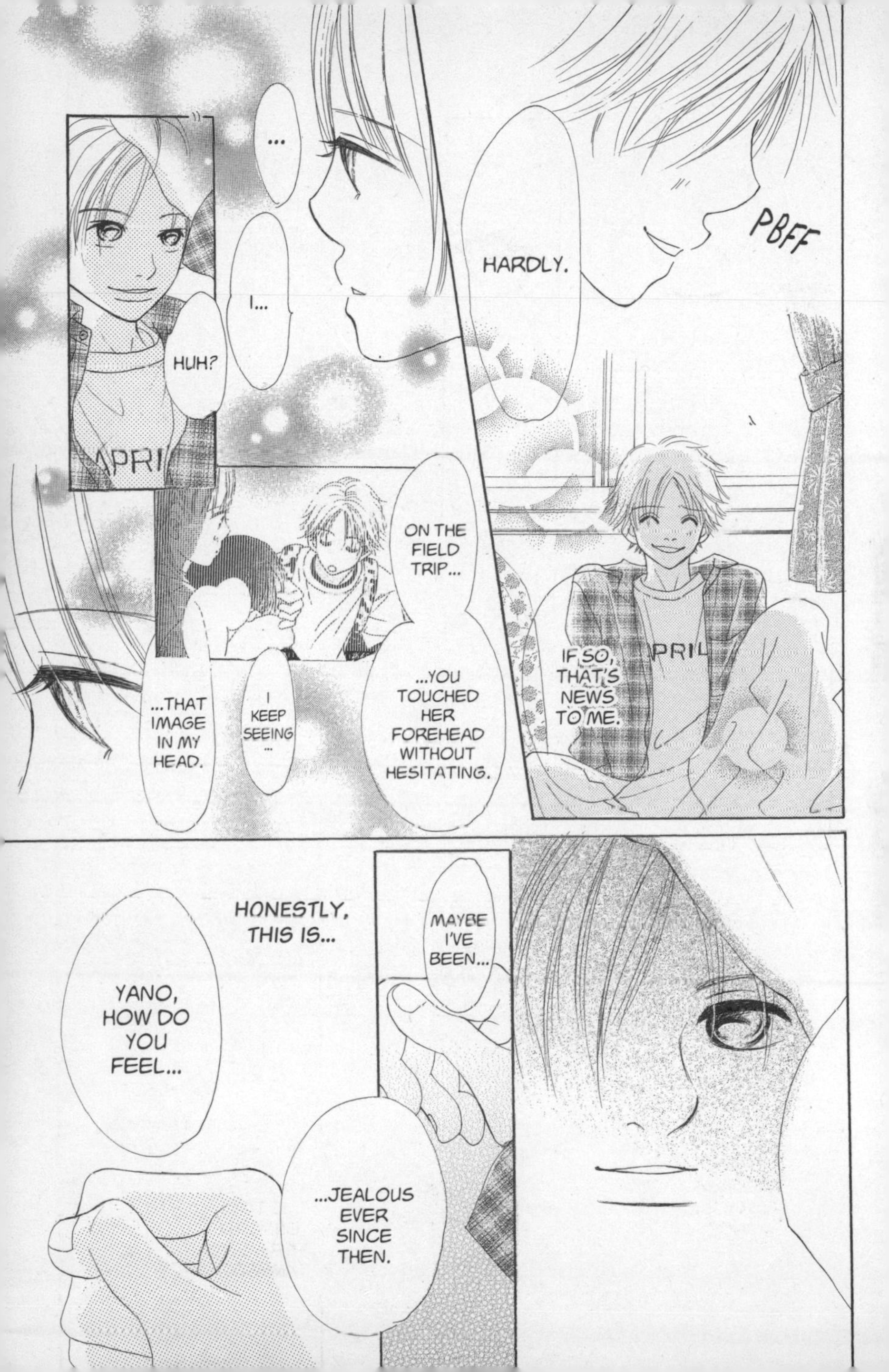

PBFF
HARDLY.
IF SO, THAT'S NEWS TO ME.
...
I...
HUH?
ON THE FIELD TRIP...
...YOU TOUCHED HER FOREHEAD WITHOUT HESITATING.
I KEEP SEEING...
...THAT IMAGE IN MY HEAD.
MAYBE I'VE BEEN...
...JEALOUS EVER SINCE THEN.
HONESTLY, THIS IS...
YANO, HOW DO YOU FEEL...

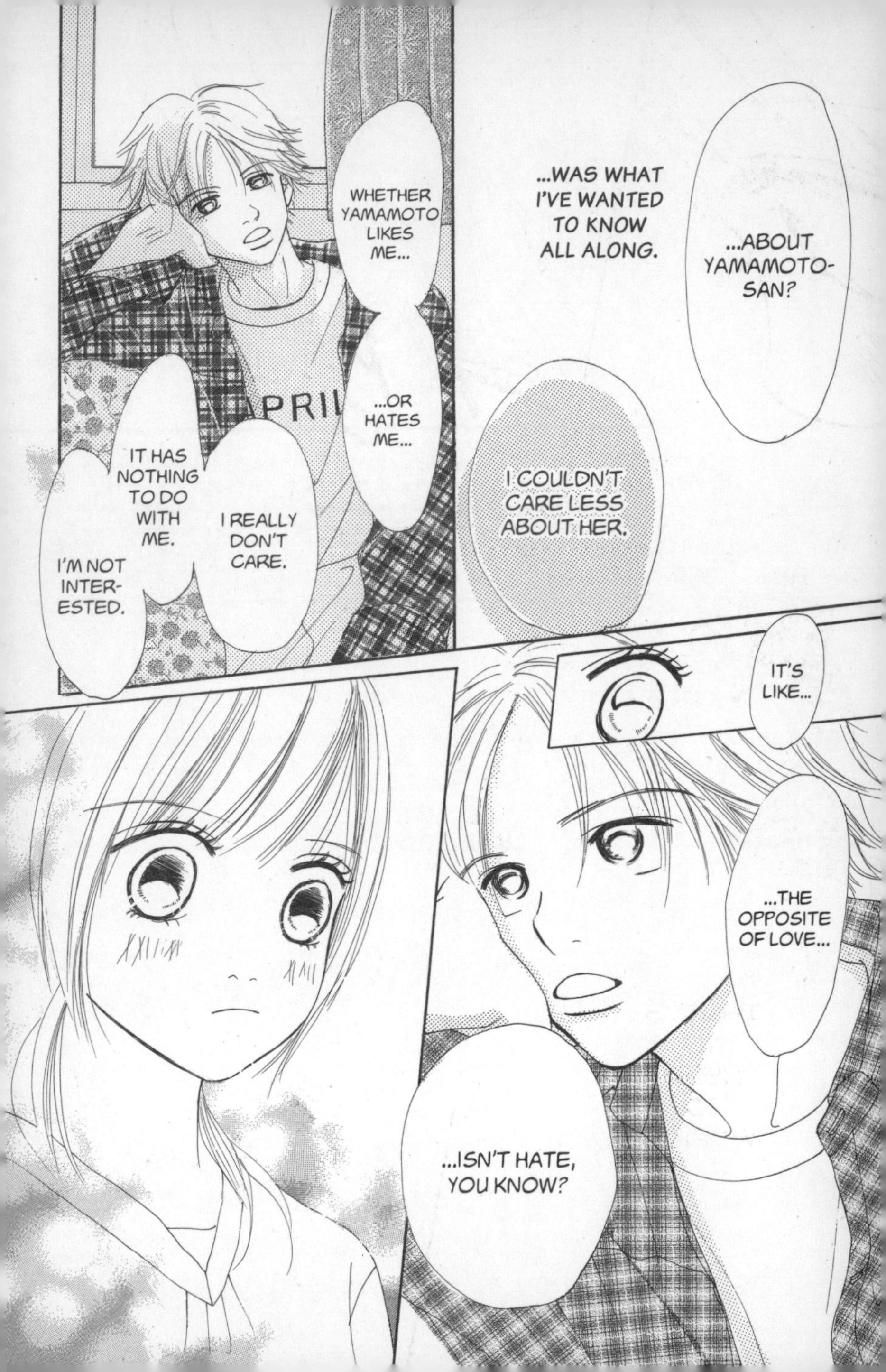

...ABOUT YAMAMOTO-SAN?
...WAS WHAT I'VE WANTED TO KNOW ALL ALONG.
I COULDN'T CARE LESS ABOUT HER.
WHETHER YAMAMOTO LIKES ME...
...OR HATES ME...
I REALLY DON'T CARE.
IT HAS NOTHING TO DO WITH ME.
I'M NOT INTER-ESTED.
APRIL
IT'S LIKE...
...THE OPPOSITE OF LOVE...
...ISN'T HATE, YOU KNOW?

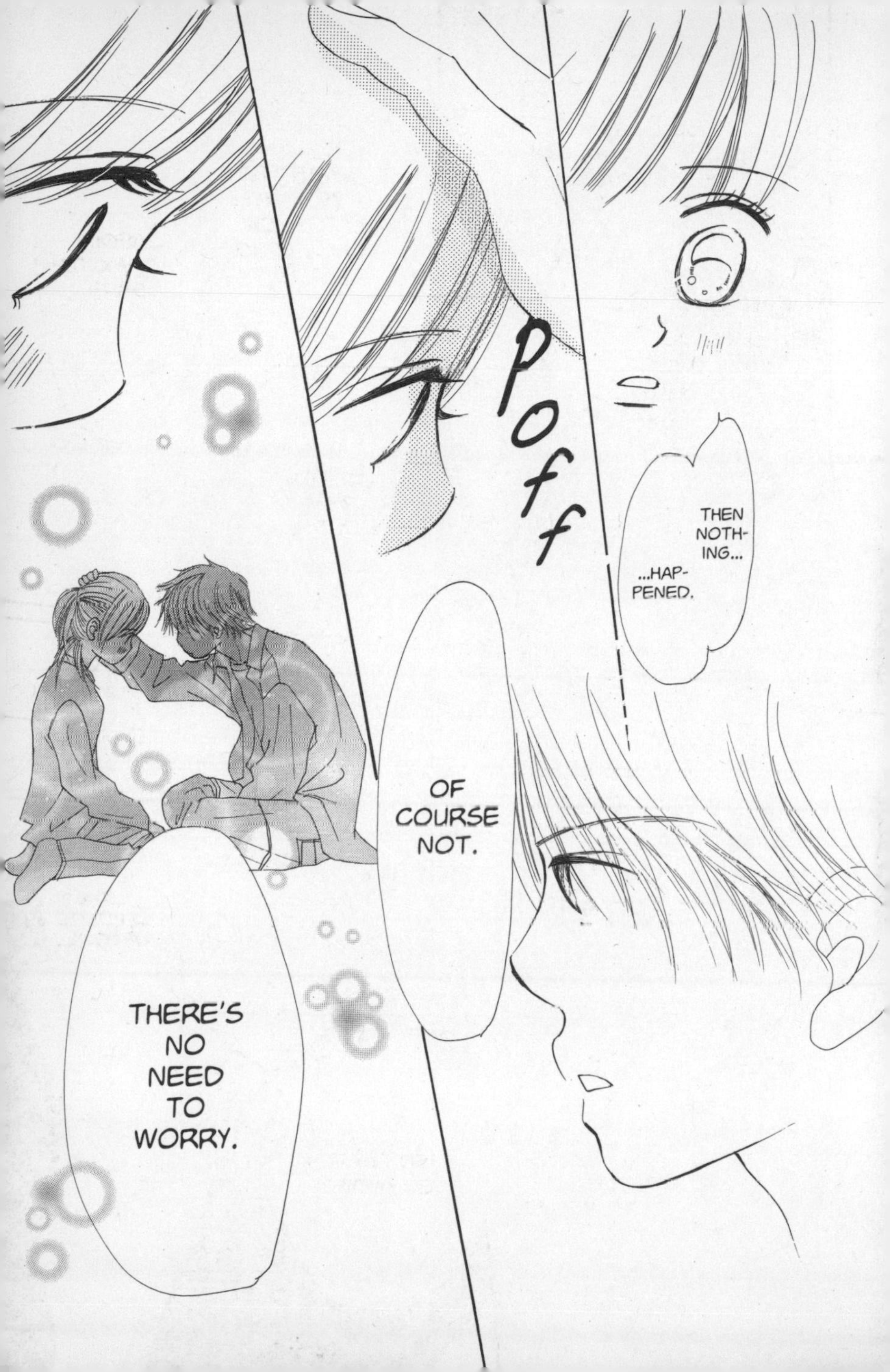
POFF
THEN NOTHING... ...HAPPENED.
OF COURSE NOT.
THERE'S NO NEED TO WORRY.

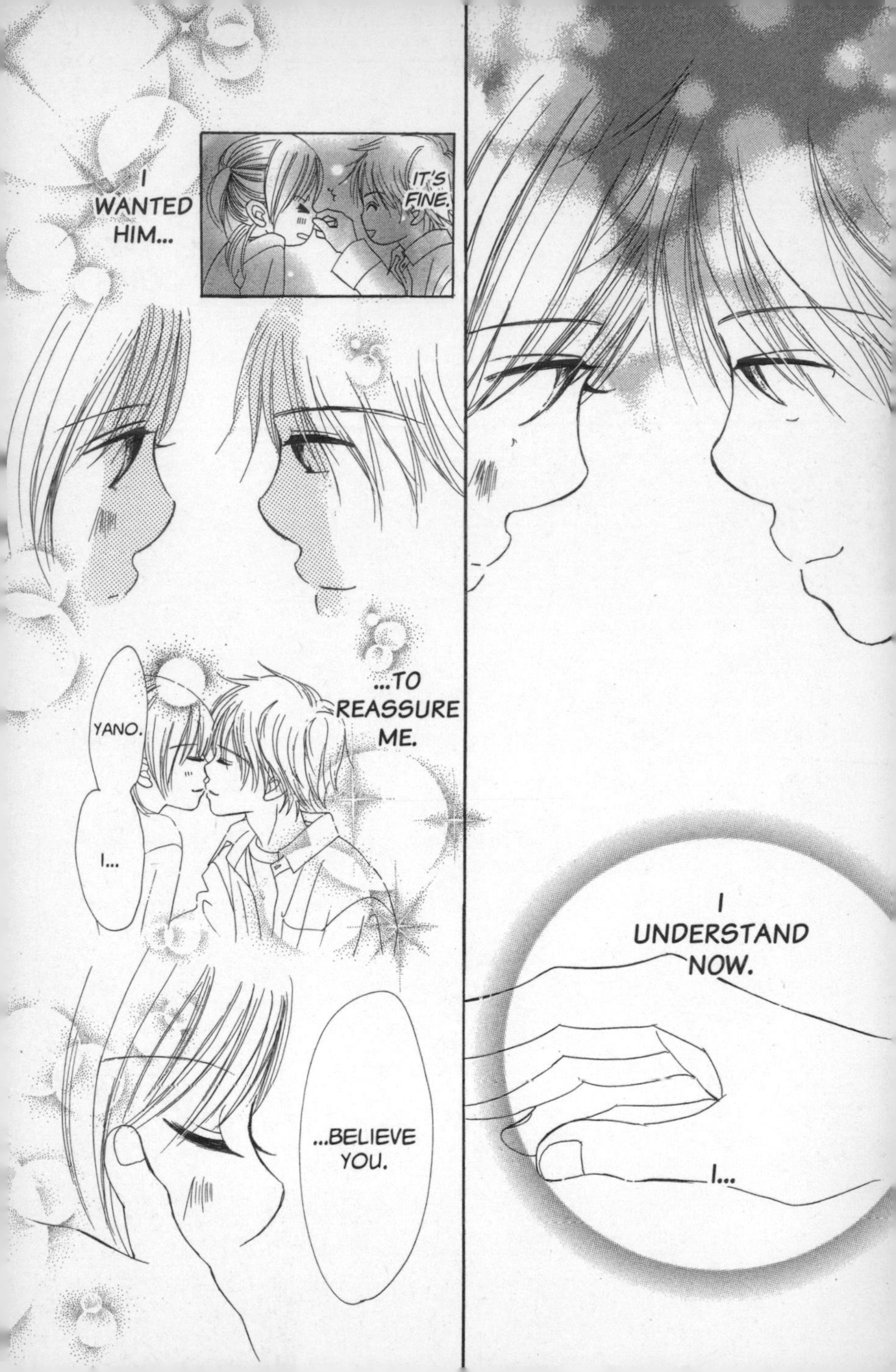
I UNDERSTAND NOW.
I...
IT'S FINE.
I WANTED HIM...
...TO REASSURE ME.
YANO.
I...
...BELIEVE YOU.

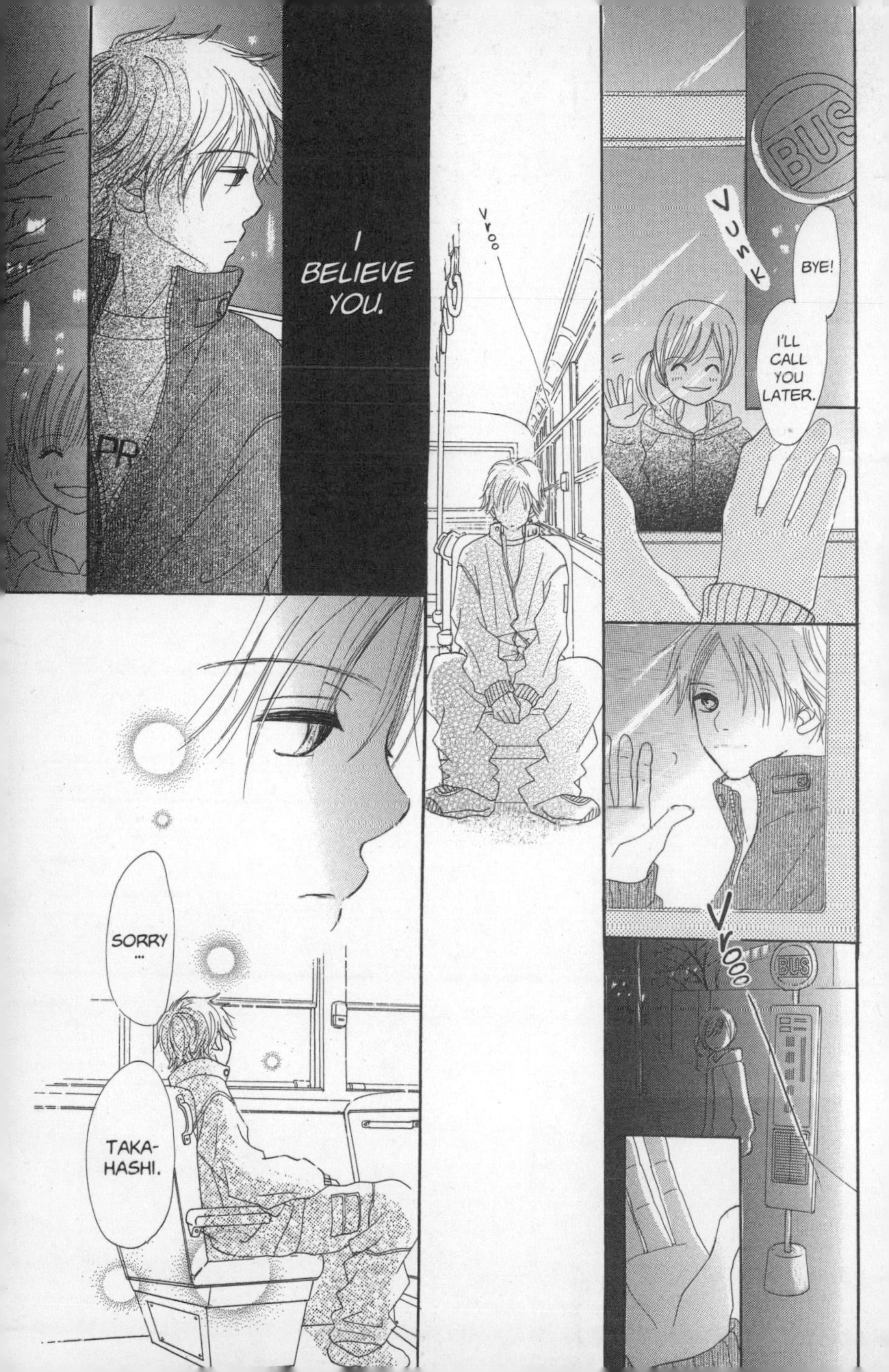
BUS
VUSK
BYE!
I'LL CALL YOU LATER.
VROOO
BUS
VROO
I BELIEVE YOU.
PR
SORRY ...
TAKA-HASHI.

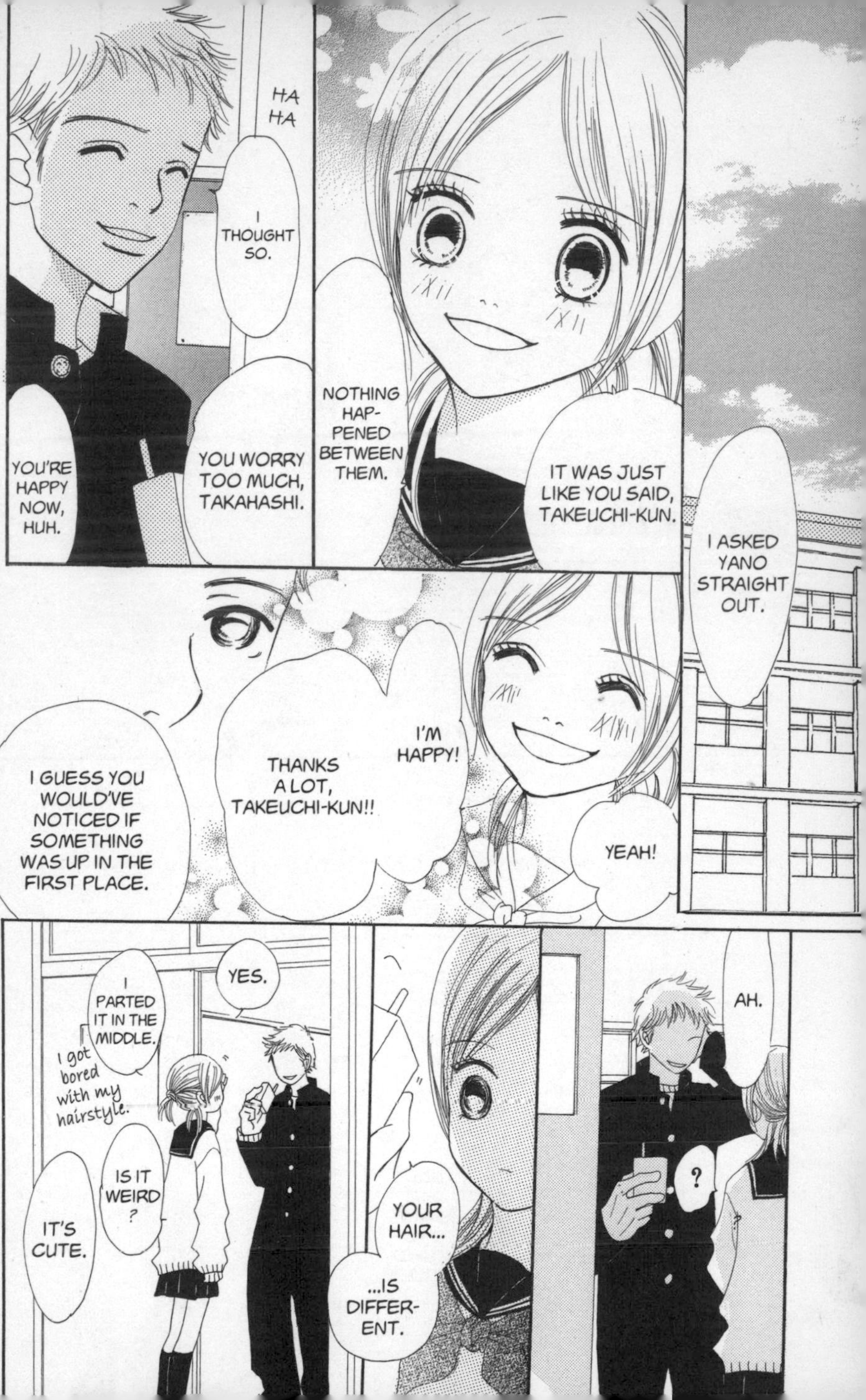
I ASKED YANO STRAIGHT OUT.
IT WAS JUST LIKE YOU SAID, TAKEUCHI-KUN.
NOTHING HAP-PENED BETWEEN THEM.
HA HA
I THOUGHT SO.
YOU WORRY TOO MUCH, TAKAHASHI.
YOU'RE HAPPY NOW, HUH.
YEAH!
I'M HAPPY!
THANKS A LOT, TAKEUCHI-KUN!!
I GUESS YOU WOULD'VE NOTICED IF SOMETHING WAS UP IN THE FIRST PLACE.
AH.
?
YOUR HAIR...
...IS DIFFER-ENT.
YES.
I PARTED IT IN THE MIDDLE.
I got bored with my hairstyle.
IS IT WEIRD?
IT'S CUTE.

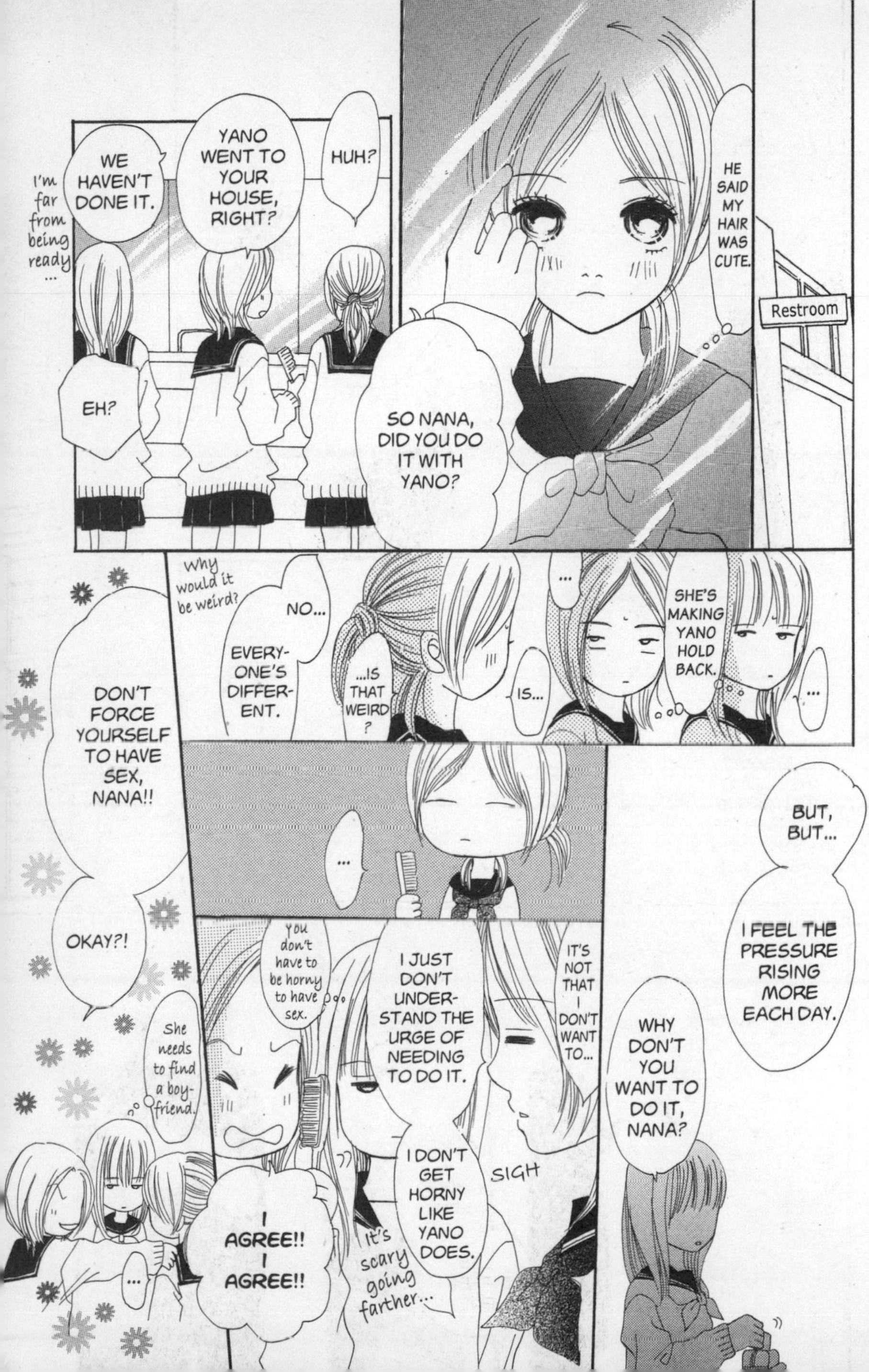
HE SAID MY HAIR WAS CUTE.
Restroom
SO NANA, DID YOU DO IT WITH YANO?
HUH?
YANO WENT TO YOUR HOUSE, RIGHT?
WE HAVEN'T DONE IT.
I'm far from being ready...
EH?
...
SHE'S MAKING YANO HOLD BACK.
...
IS...
...IS THAT WEIRD?
NO...
Why would it be weird?
EVERYONE'S DIFFERENT.
DON'T FORCE YOURSELF TO HAVE SEX, NANA!!
OKAY?!
BUT, BUT...
I FEEL THE PRESSURE RISING MORE EACH DAY.
...
WHY DON'T YOU WANT TO DO IT, NANA?
IT'S NOT THAT I DON'T WANT TO...
I JUST DON'T UNDERSTAND THE URGE OF NEEDING TO DO IT.
You don't have to be horny to have sex.
SIGH
I DON'T GET HORNY LIKE YANO DOES.
It's scary going farther...
I AGREE!! I AGREE!!
She needs to find a boyfriend.
...

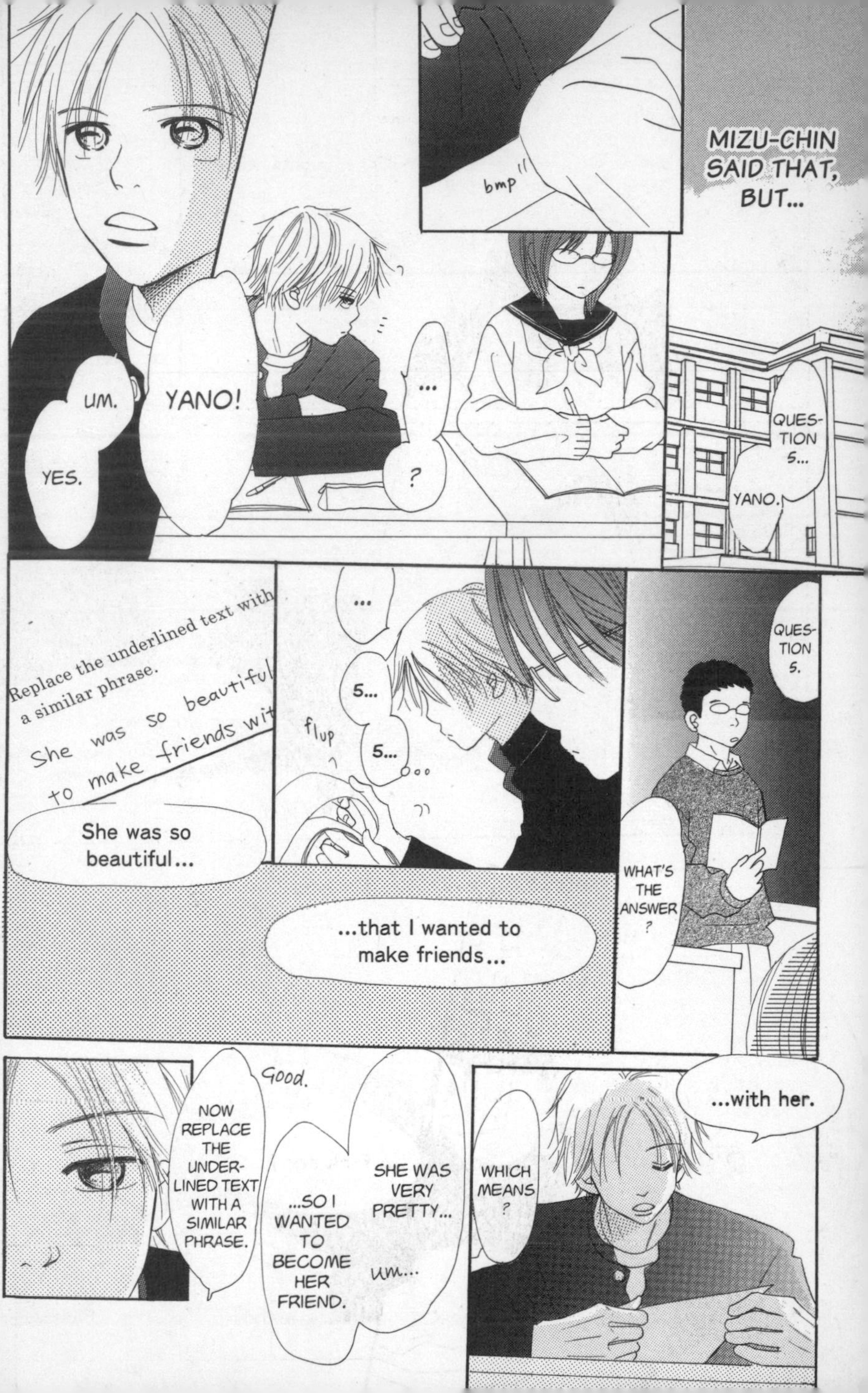
MIZU-CHIN SAID THAT, BUT...
QUESTION 5...
YANO.
bmp
...
?
YANO!
UM.
YES.
QUESTION 5.
WHAT'S THE ANSWER?
...
5...
flup
5...
Replace the underlined text with a similar phrase.
She was so beautiful to make friends wit
She was so beautiful...
...that I wanted to make friends...
...with her.
WHICH MEANS?
Good.
NOW REPLACE THE UNDERLINED TEXT WITH A SIMILAR PHRASE.
SHE WAS VERY PRETTY...
um...
...SO I WANTED TO BECOME HER FRIEND.

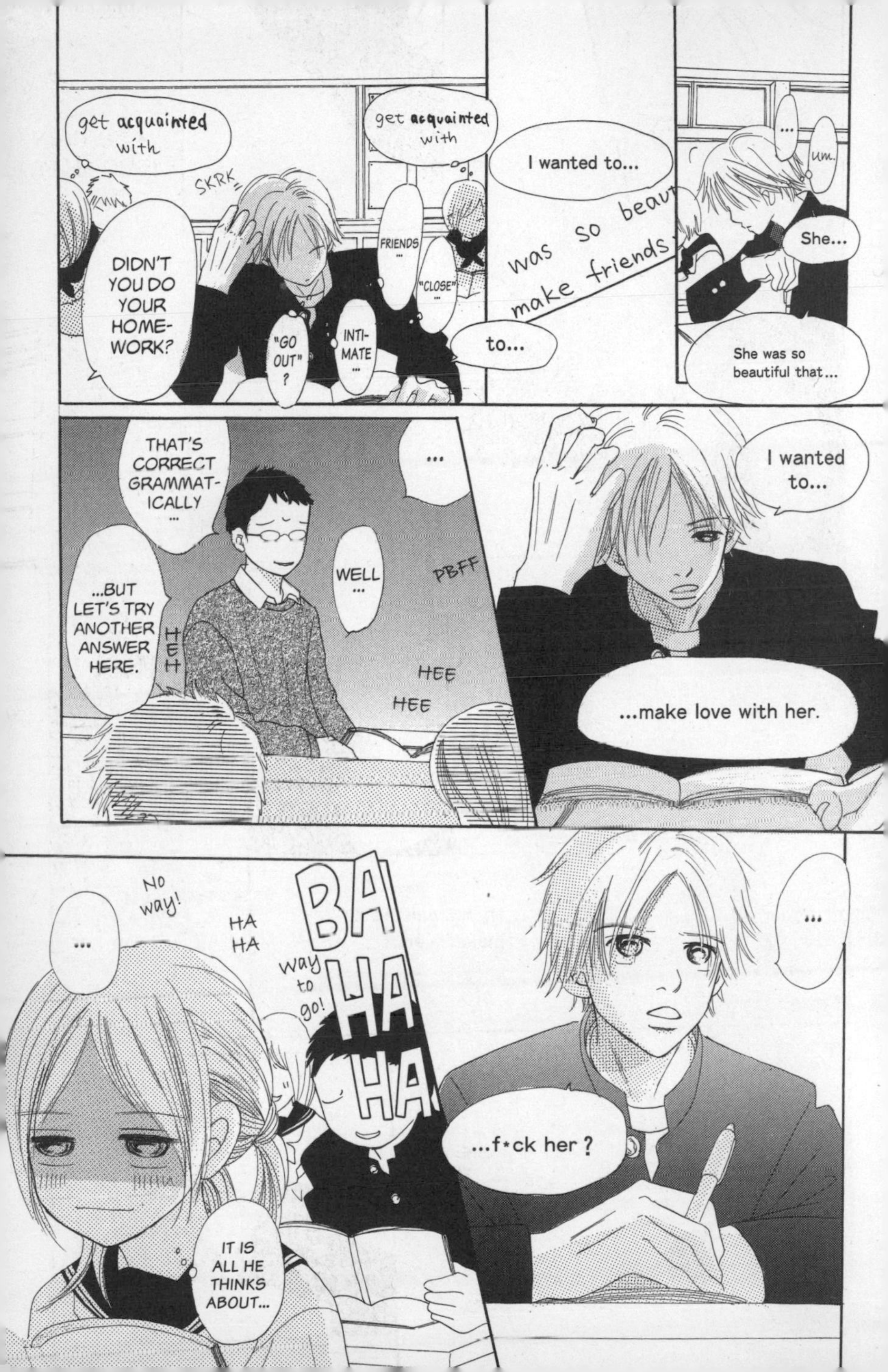
...
um.
She...
She was so beautiful that...
I wanted to...
was so beaut
make friends
to...
get acquainted with
FRIENDS...
"CLOSE"...
get acquainted with
SKRK
INTI-MATE...
"GO OUT"?
DIDN'T YOU DO YOUR HOME-WORK?
I wanted to...
...make love with her.
...
WELL...
PBFF
THAT'S CORRECT GRAMMAT-ICALLY...
HEE
HEE
...BUT LET'S TRY ANOTHER ANSWER HERE.
HEH
...
...f*ck her?
BAHAHAHA
way to go!
HA HA
No way!
...
IT IS ALL HE THINKS ABOUT...

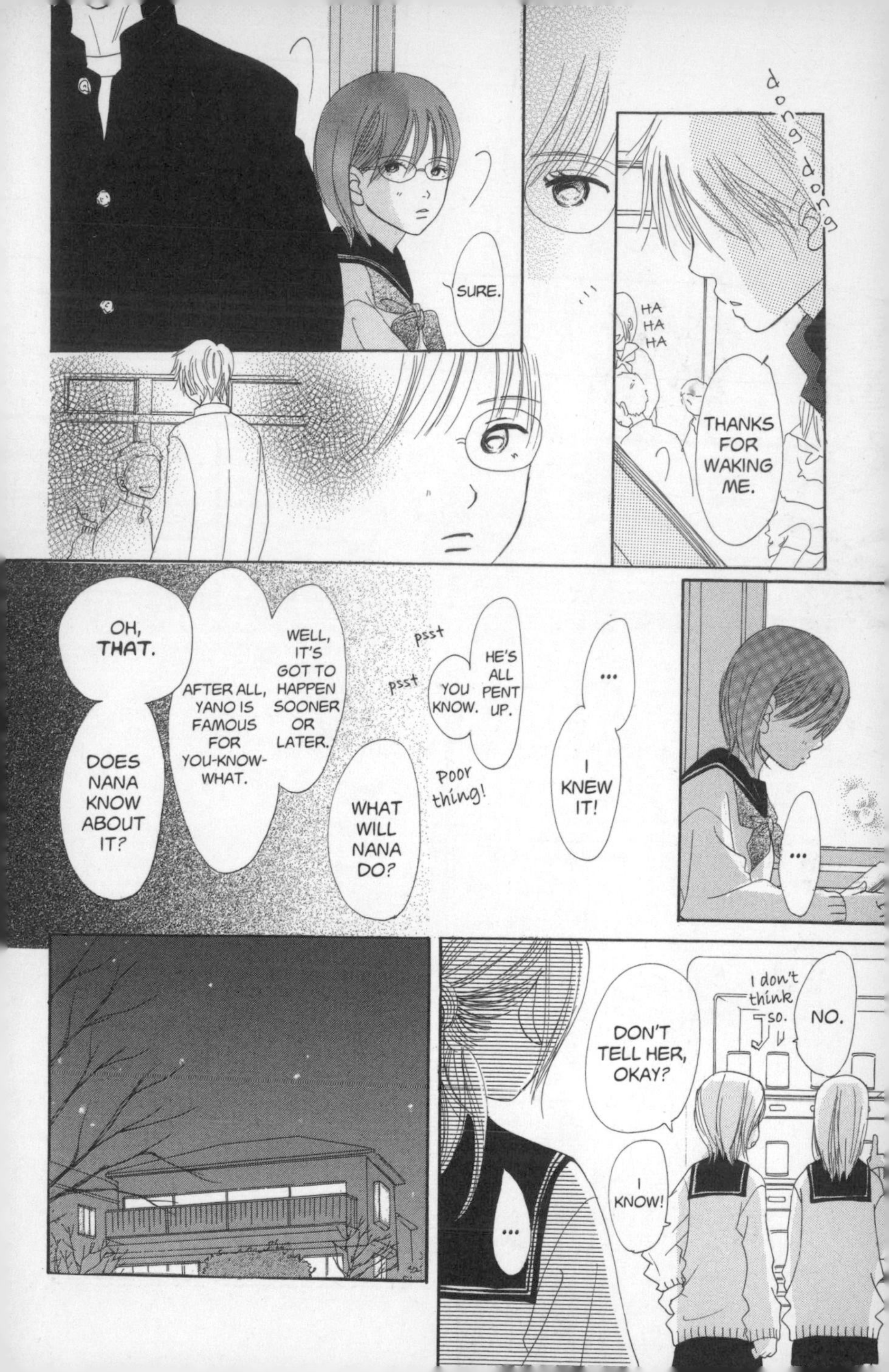
dong dong dong
HA HA HA
THANKS FOR WAKING ME.
SURE.
...
...
I KNEW IT!
HE'S ALL PENT UP.
YOU KNOW.
psst
psst
Poor thing!
WHAT WILL NANA DO?
WELL, IT'S GOT TO HAPPEN SOONER OR LATER.
AFTER ALL, YANO IS FAMOUS FOR YOU-KNOW-WHAT.
OH, THAT.
DOES NANA KNOW ABOUT IT?
NO.
I don't think so.
DON'T TELL HER, OKAY?
I KNOW!
...

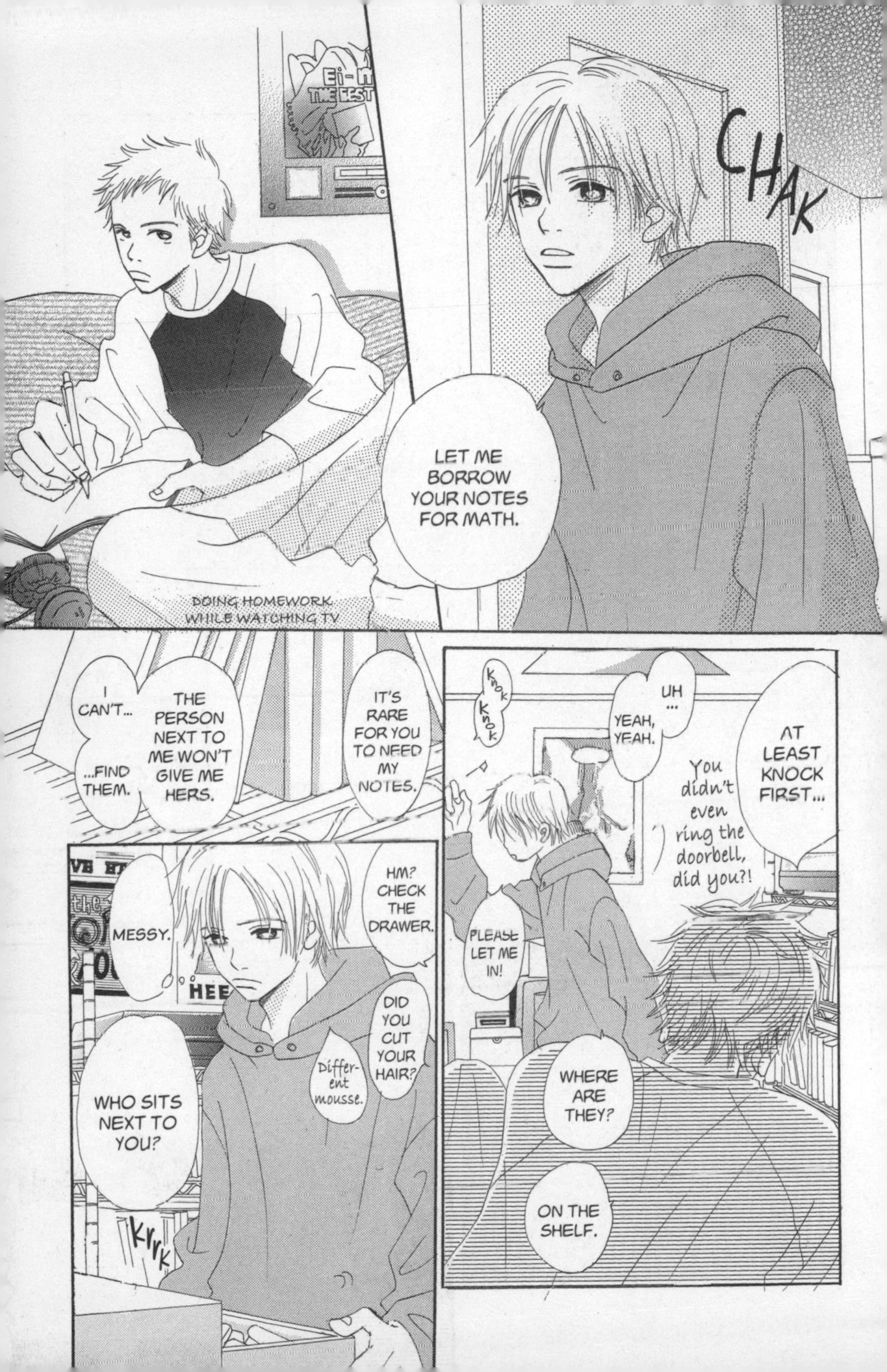
CHAK
LET ME BORROW YOUR NOTES FOR MATH.
DOING HOMEWORK WHILE WATCHING TV
AT LEAST KNOCK FIRST...
You didn't even ring the doorbell, did you?!
UH ... YEAH, YEAH.
Knock knock
PLEASE LET ME IN!
WHERE ARE THEY?
ON THE SHELF.
IT'S RARE FOR YOU TO NEED MY NOTES.
THE PERSON NEXT TO ME WON'T GIVE ME HERS.
I CAN'T...
...FIND THEM.
HM? CHECK THE DRAWER.
DID YOU CUT YOUR HAIR?
Differ-ent mousse.
MESSY.
WHO SITS NEXT TO YOU?
Krrk

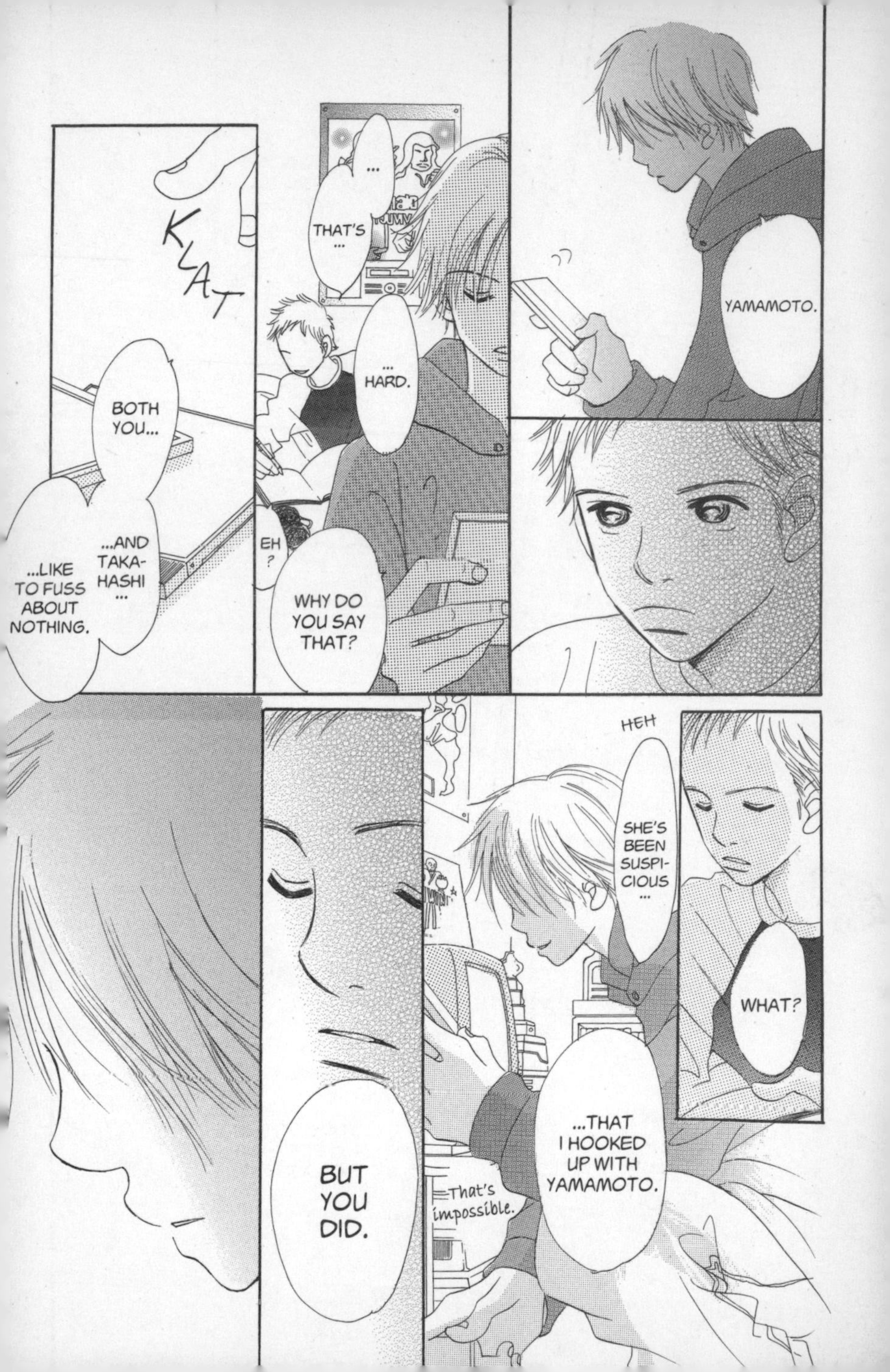
YAMAMOTO.
...
THAT'S ...
... HARD.
WHY DO YOU SAY THAT?
EH ?
KLAT
BOTH YOU...
...AND TAKA-HASHI ...
...LIKE TO FUSS ABOUT NOTHING.
HEH
SHE'S BEEN SUSPI-CIOUS ...
WHAT?
...THAT I HOOKED UP WITH YAMAMOTO.
That's impossible.
BUT YOU DID.

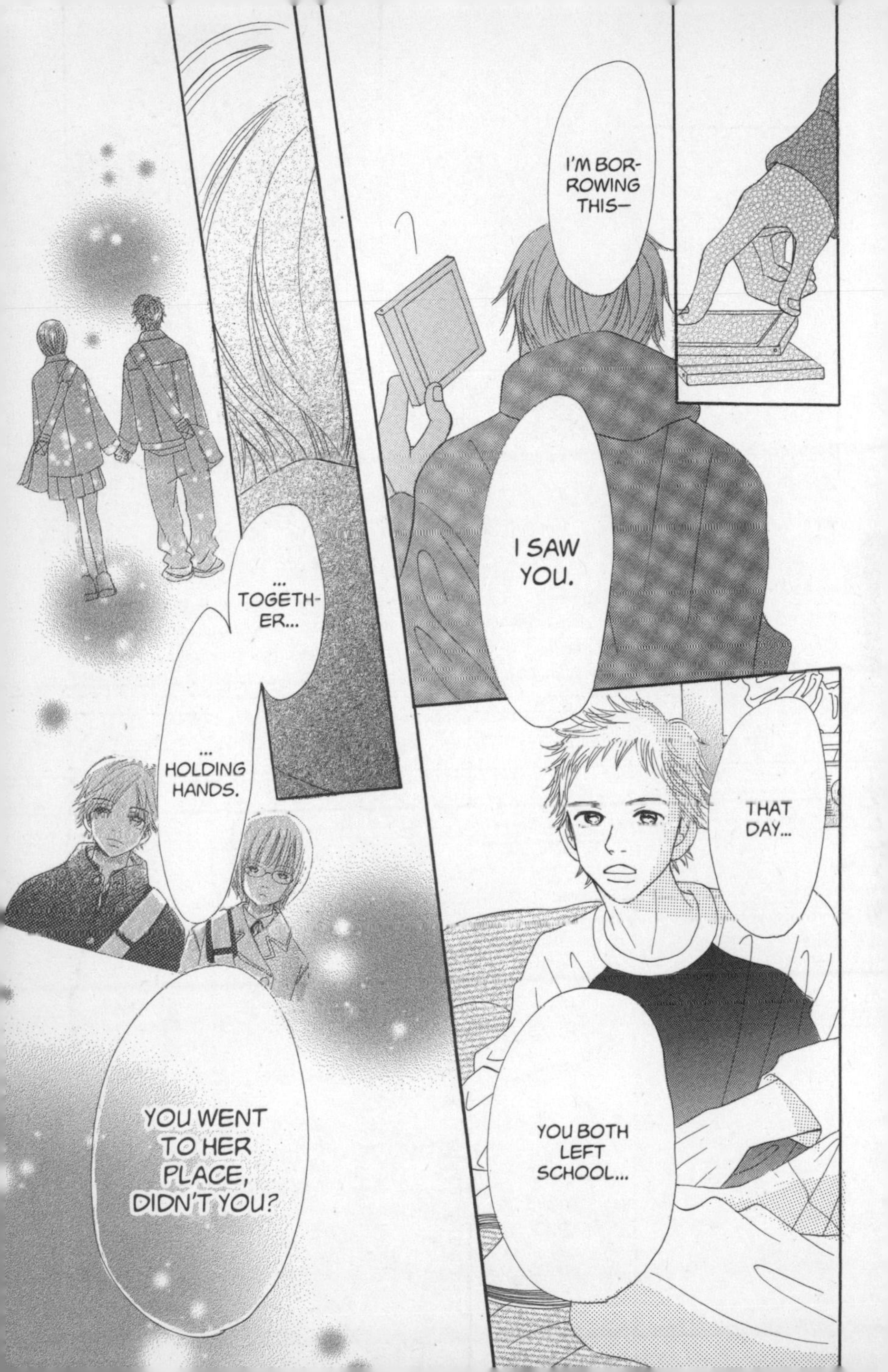
I'M BOR-ROWING THIS—
I SAW YOU.
THAT DAY...
YOU BOTH LEFT SCHOOL...
...TOGETHER...
...HOLDING HANDS.
YOU WENT TO HER PLACE, DIDN'T YOU?

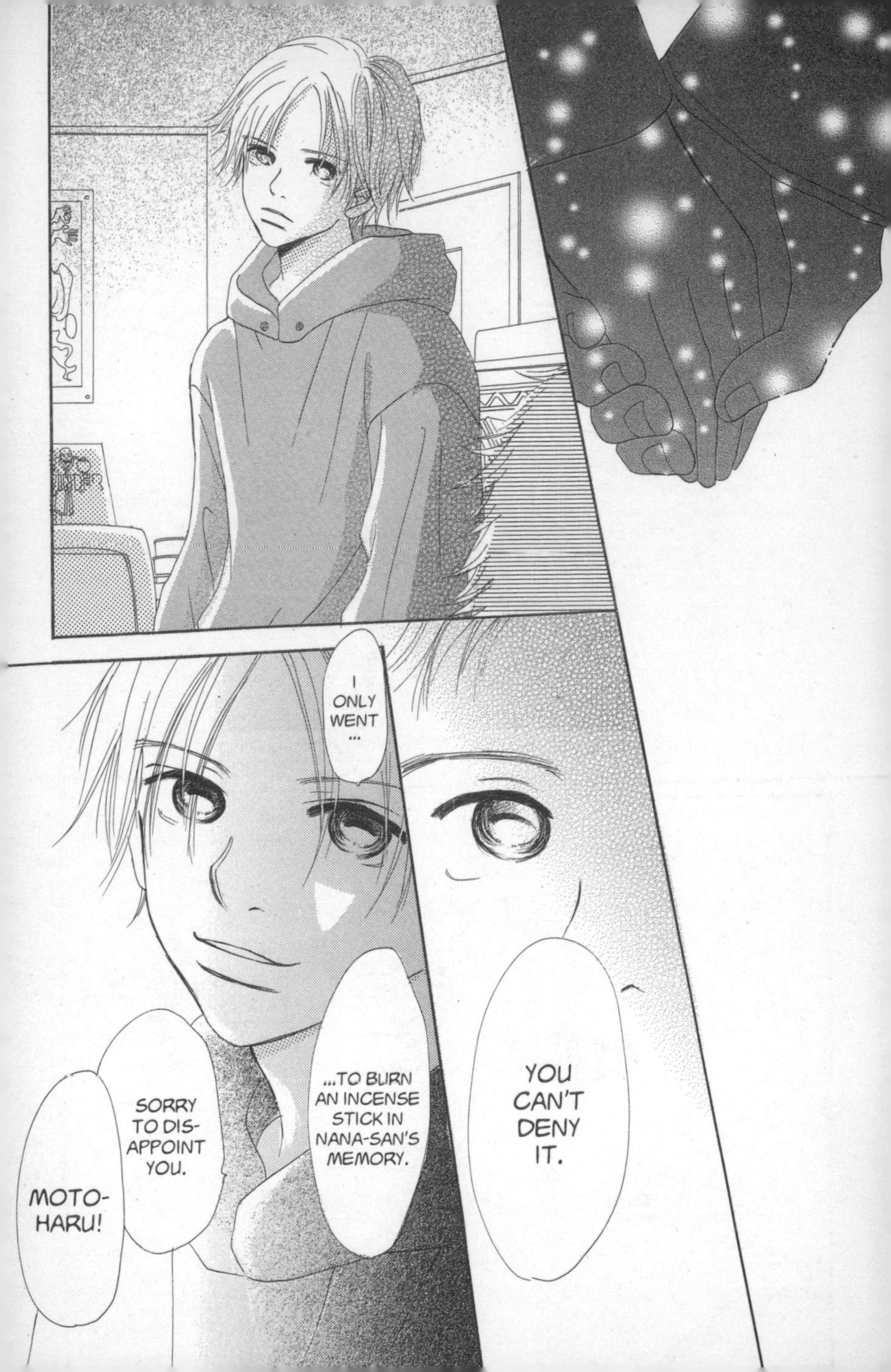
I ONLY WENT ...
YOU CAN'T DENY IT.
...TO BURN AN INCENSE STICK IN NANA-SAN'S MEMORY.
SORRY TO DIS-APPOINT YOU.
MOTO-HARU!

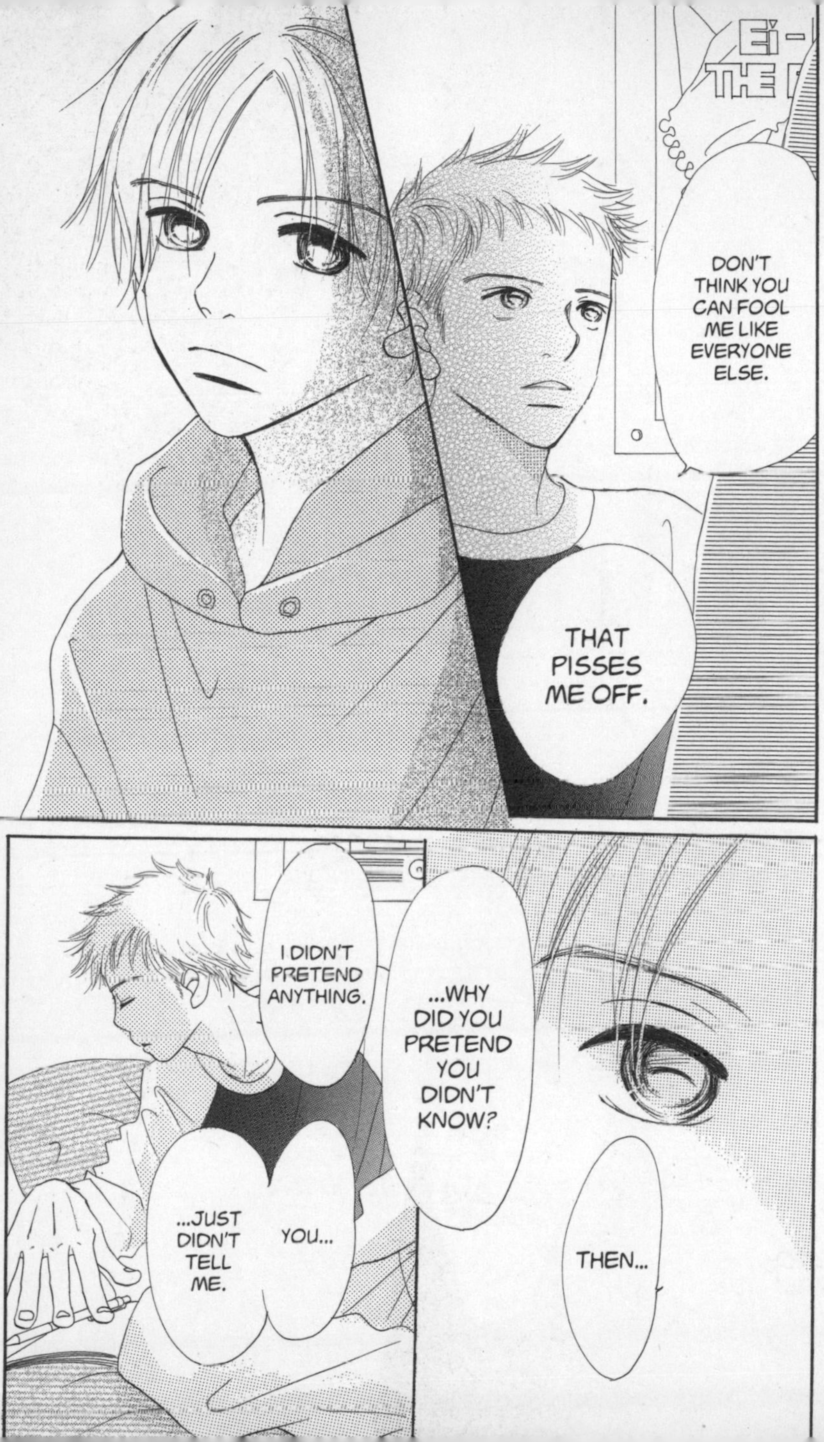
DON'T THINK YOU CAN FOOL ME LIKE EVERYONE ELSE.
THAT PISSES ME OFF.
THEN...
...WHY DID YOU PRETEND YOU DIDN'T KNOW?
I DIDN'T PRETEND ANYTHING.
YOU...
...JUST DIDN'T TELL ME.

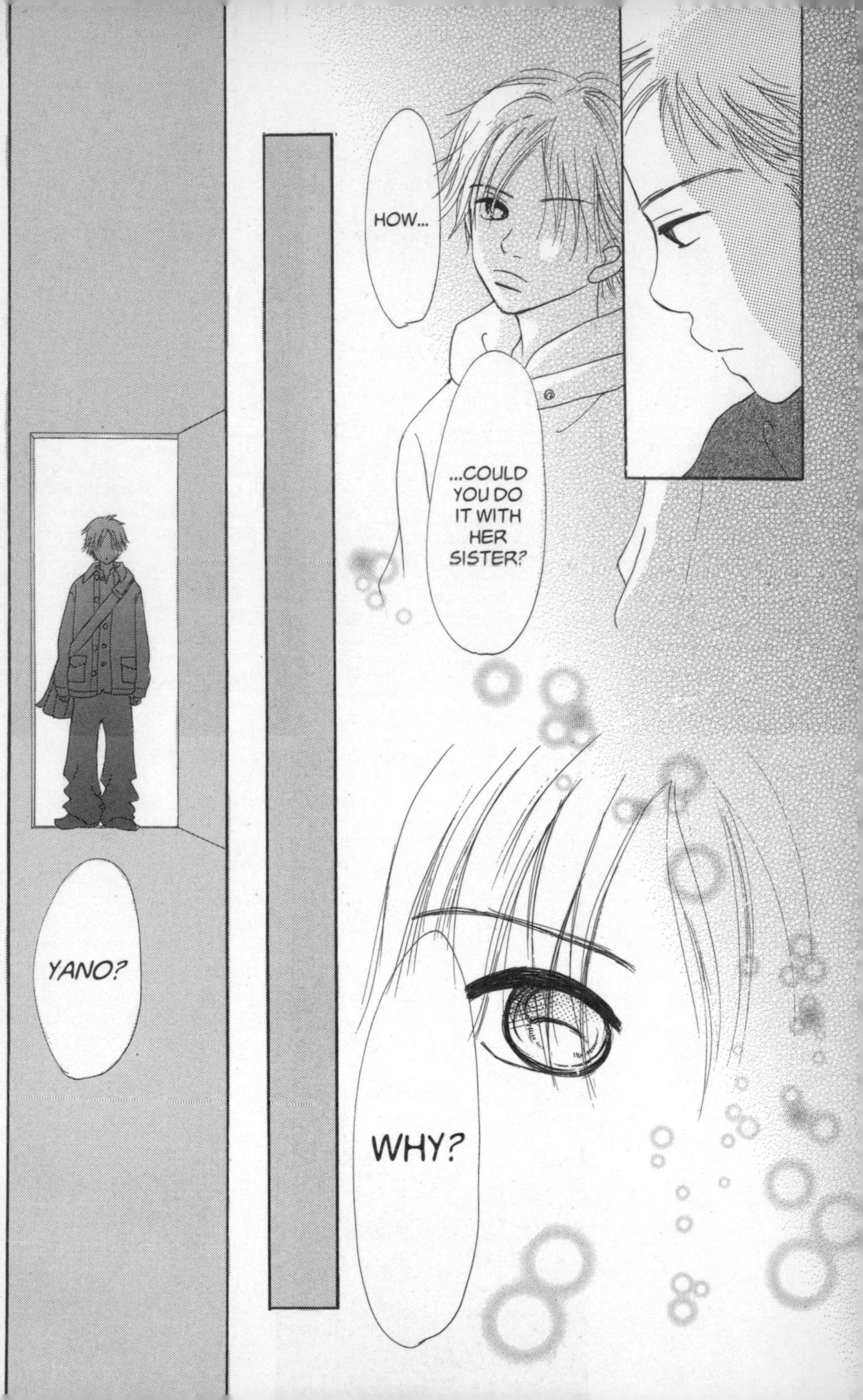
HOW...
...COULD YOU DO IT WITH HER SISTER?
WHY?
YANO?

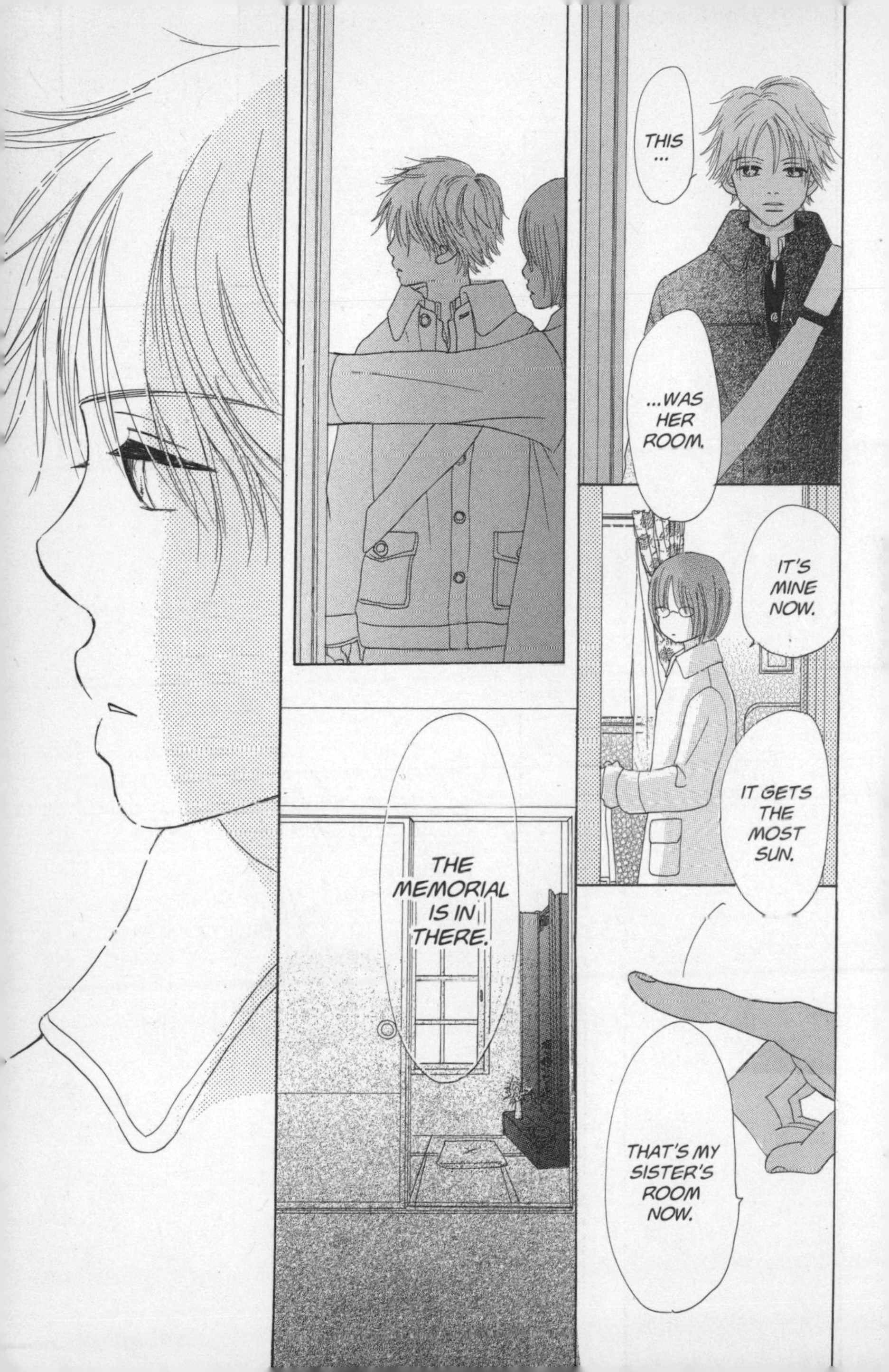
THIS ...
...WAS HER ROOM.
IT'S MINE NOW.
IT GETS THE MOST SUN.
THAT'S MY SISTER'S ROOM NOW.
THE MEMORIAL IS IN THERE.

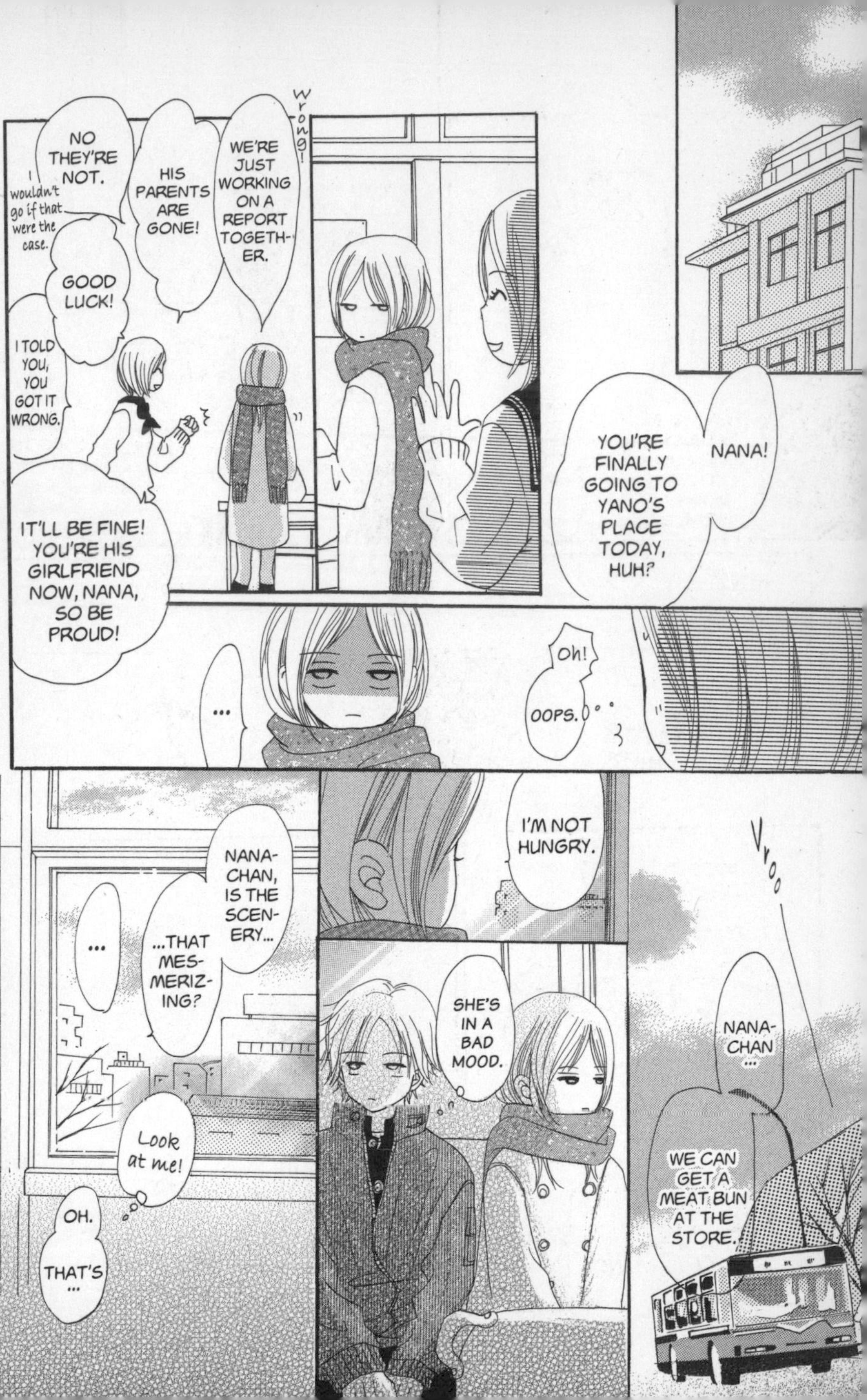
NANA!
YOU'RE FINALLY GOING TO YANO'S PLACE TODAY, HUH?
WE'RE JUST WORKING ON A REPORT TOGETH-ER.
Wrong!
HIS PARENTS ARE GONE!
NO THEY'RE NOT.
I wouldn't go if that were the case.
GOOD LUCK!
I TOLD YOU, YOU GOT IT WRONG.
IT'LL BE FINE! YOU'RE HIS GIRLFRIEND NOW, NANA, SO BE PROUD!
Oh!
OOPS.
...
Vrooo
NANA-CHAN...
WE CAN GET A MEAT BUN AT THE STORE.
I'M NOT HUNGRY.
SHE'S IN A BAD MOOD.
NANA-CHAN, IS THE SCEN-ERY...
...THAT MES-MERIZ-ING?
...
Look at me!
OH.
THAT'S...

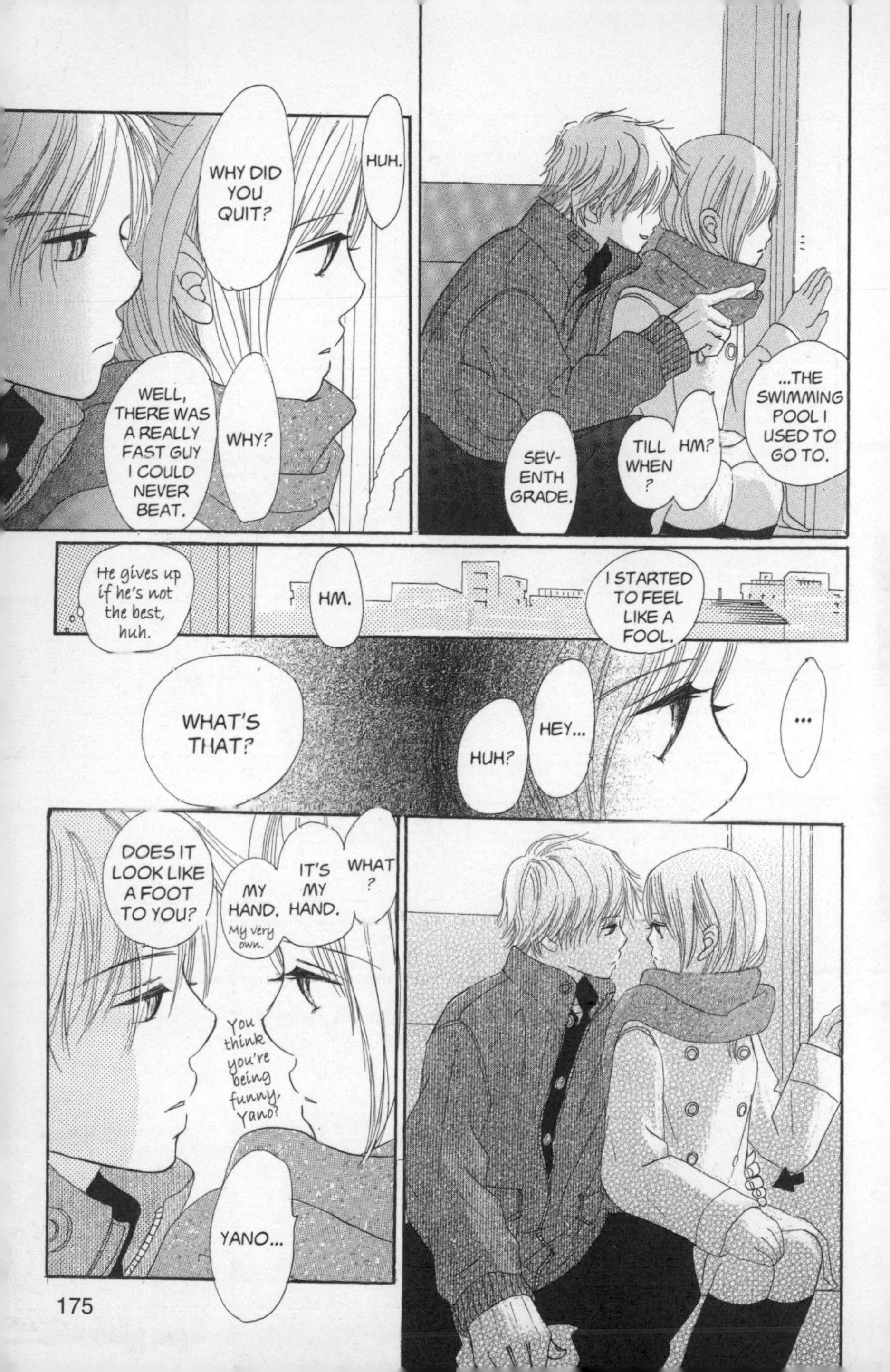
...THE SWIMMING POOL I USED TO GO TO.
HM?
TILL WHEN?
SEV-ENTH GRADE.
HUH.
WHY DID YOU QUIT?
WHY?
WELL, THERE WAS A REALLY FAST GUY I COULD NEVER BEAT.
I STARTED TO FEEL LIKE A FOOL.
HM.
He gives up if he's not the best, huh.
...
HEY...
HUH?
WHAT'S THAT?
WHAT?
IT'S MY HAND.
MY HAND.
My very own.
DOES IT LOOK LIKE A FOOT TO YOU?
You think you're being funny, Yano?
YANO...

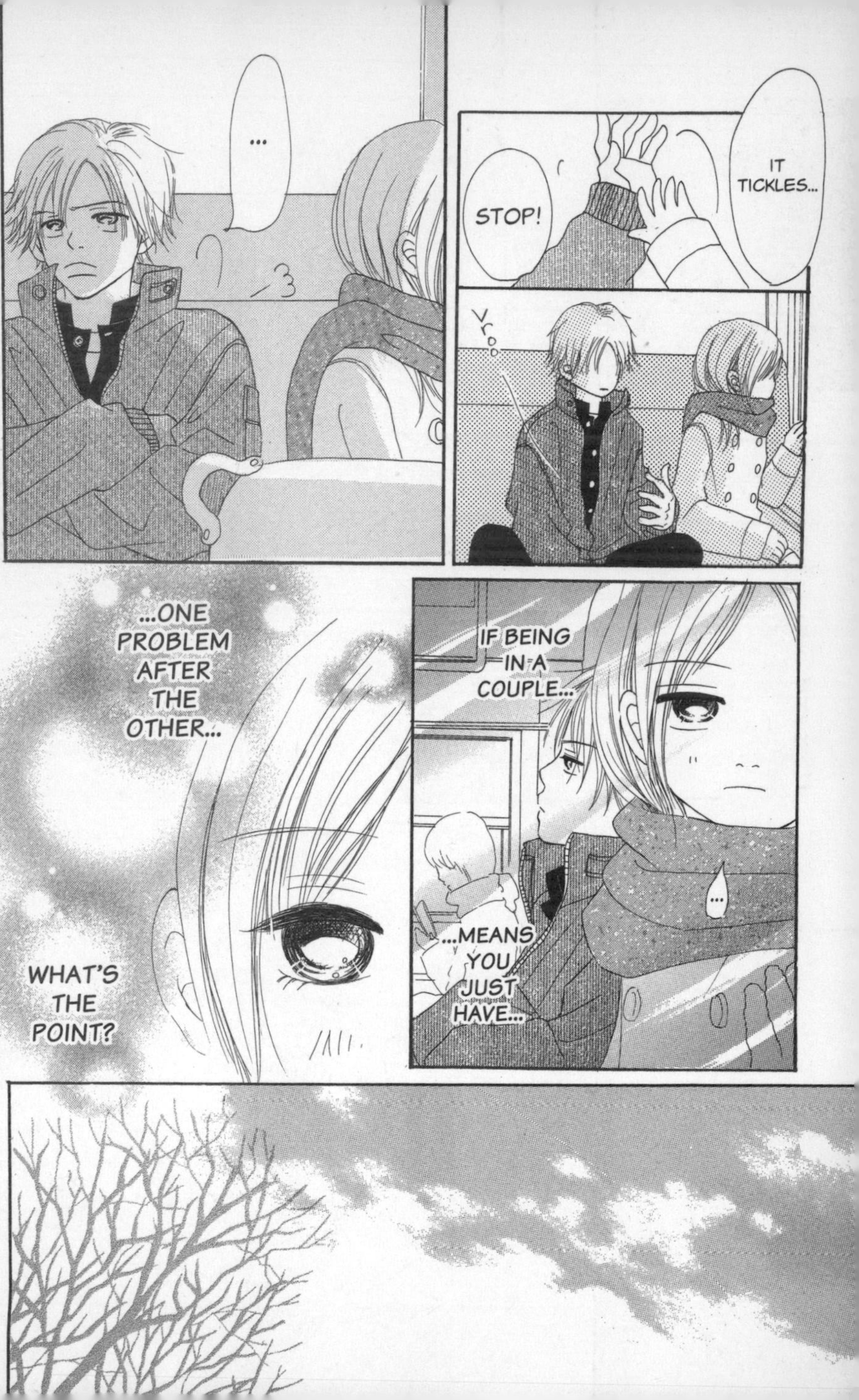

IT TICKLES...
STOP!
Vroo
...
IF BEING IN A COUPLE...
...
...MEANS YOU JUST HAVE...
...ONE PROBLEM AFTER THE OTHER...
WHAT'S THE POINT?

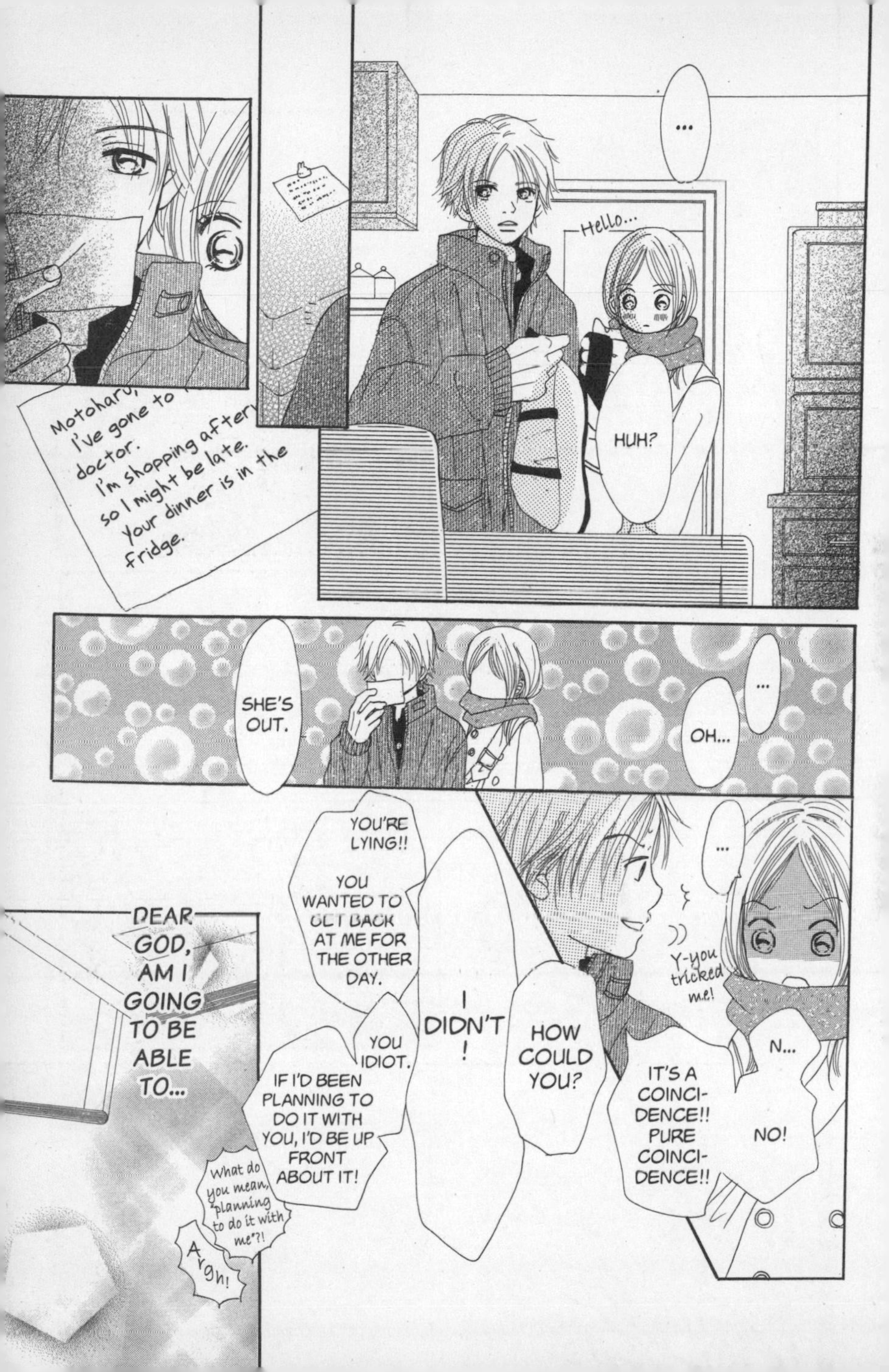
...
Hello...
HUH?
Motoharu, I've gone to t
doctor. I'm shopping after
so I might be late. Your dinner is in the fridge.
...
OH...
SHE'S OUT.
...
Y-you tricked me!
N...
NO!
IT'S A COINCIDENCE!! PURE COINCIDENCE!!
HOW COULD YOU?
I DIDN'T!
YOU'RE LYING!! YOU WANTED TO GET BACK AT ME FOR THE OTHER DAY.
YOU IDIOT.
IF I'D BEEN PLANNING TO DO IT WITH YOU, I'D BE UP FRONT ABOUT IT!
What do you mean, "planning to do it with me"?!
Argh!
DEAR GOD, AM I GOING TO BE ABLE TO...

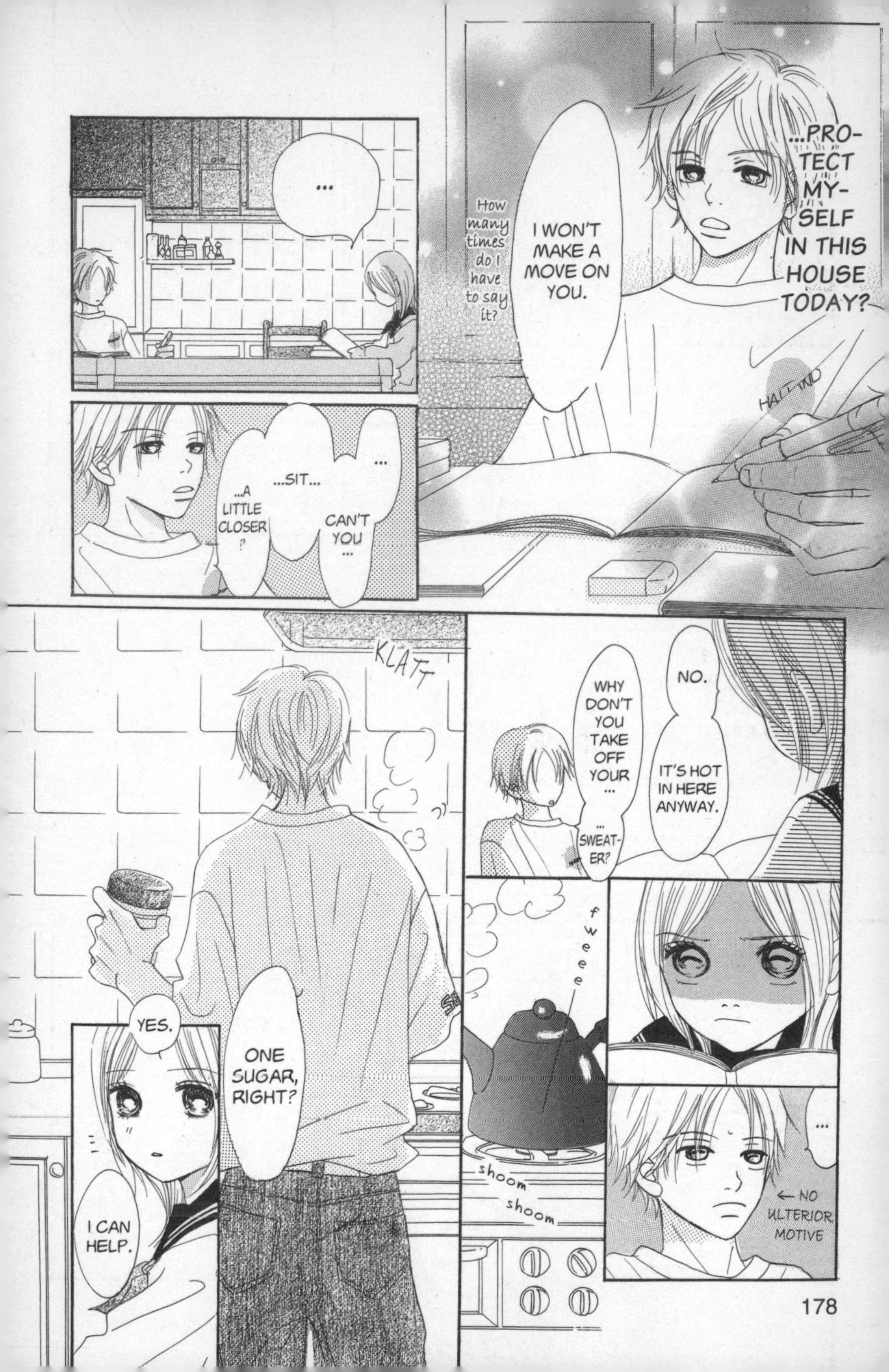
...PRO-TECT MY-SELF IN THIS HOUSE TODAY?
I WON'T MAKE A MOVE ON YOU.
How many times do I have to say it?
...
...
CAN'T YOU ...
...SIT...
...A LITTLE CLOSER?
NO.
IT'S HOT IN HERE ANYWAY.
WHY DON'T YOU TAKE OFF YOUR ...
... SWEAT-ER?
fweee
shoom shoom
...
← NO ULTERIOR MOTIVE
KLATT
ONE SUGAR, RIGHT?
YES.
I CAN HELP.

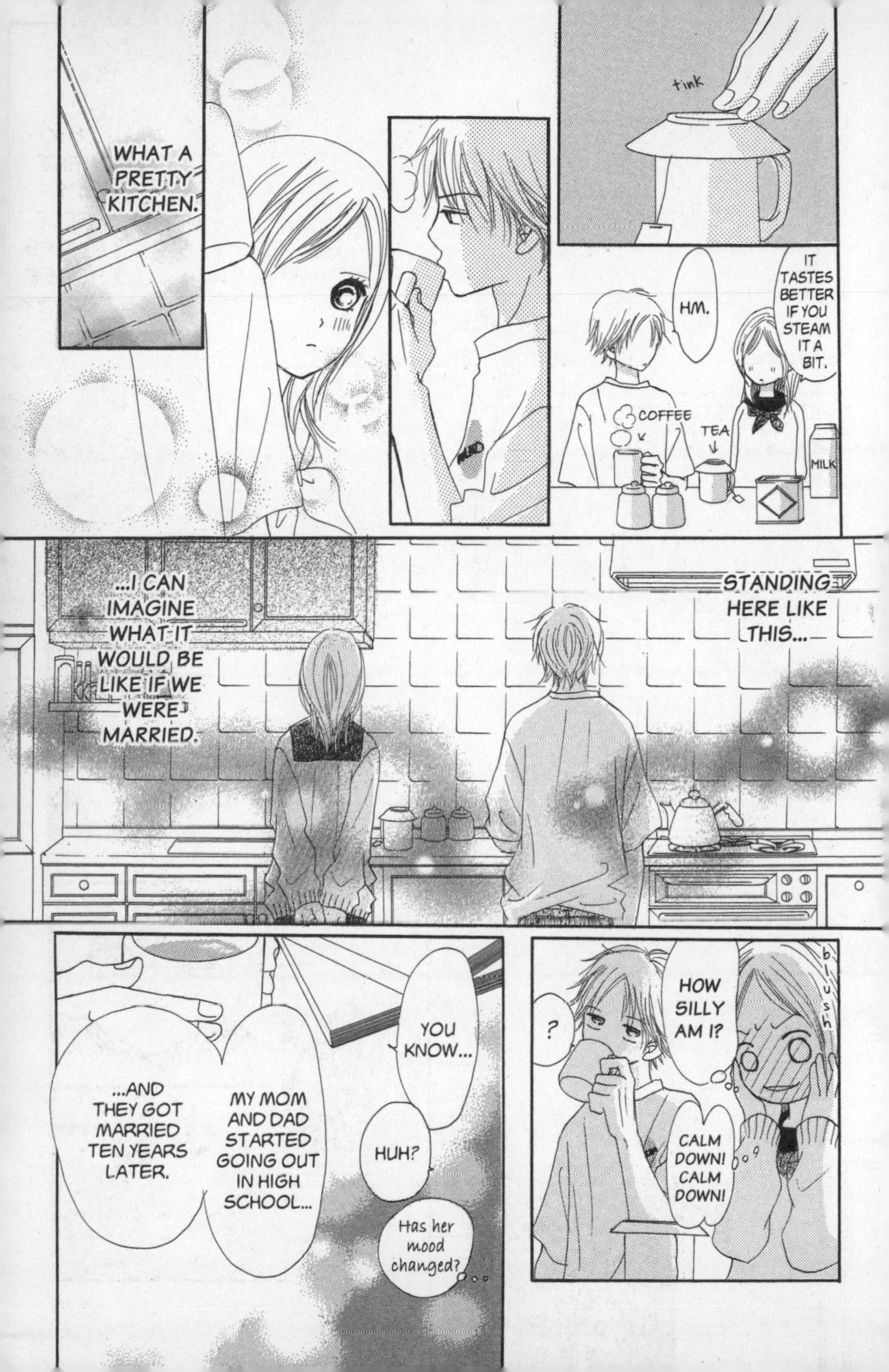
tink
IT TASTES BETTER IF YOU STEAM IT A BIT.
HM.
COFFEE
TEA
MILK
WHAT A PRETTY KITCHEN.
STANDING HERE LIKE THIS...
...I CAN IMAGINE WHAT IT WOULD BE LIKE IF WE WERE MARRIED.
blush
HOW SILLY AM I?
?
CALM DOWN! CALM DOWN!
YOU KNOW...
HUH?
Has her mood changed?
MY MOM AND DAD STARTED GOING OUT IN HIGH SCHOOL...
...AND THEY GOT MARRIED TEN YEARS LATER.

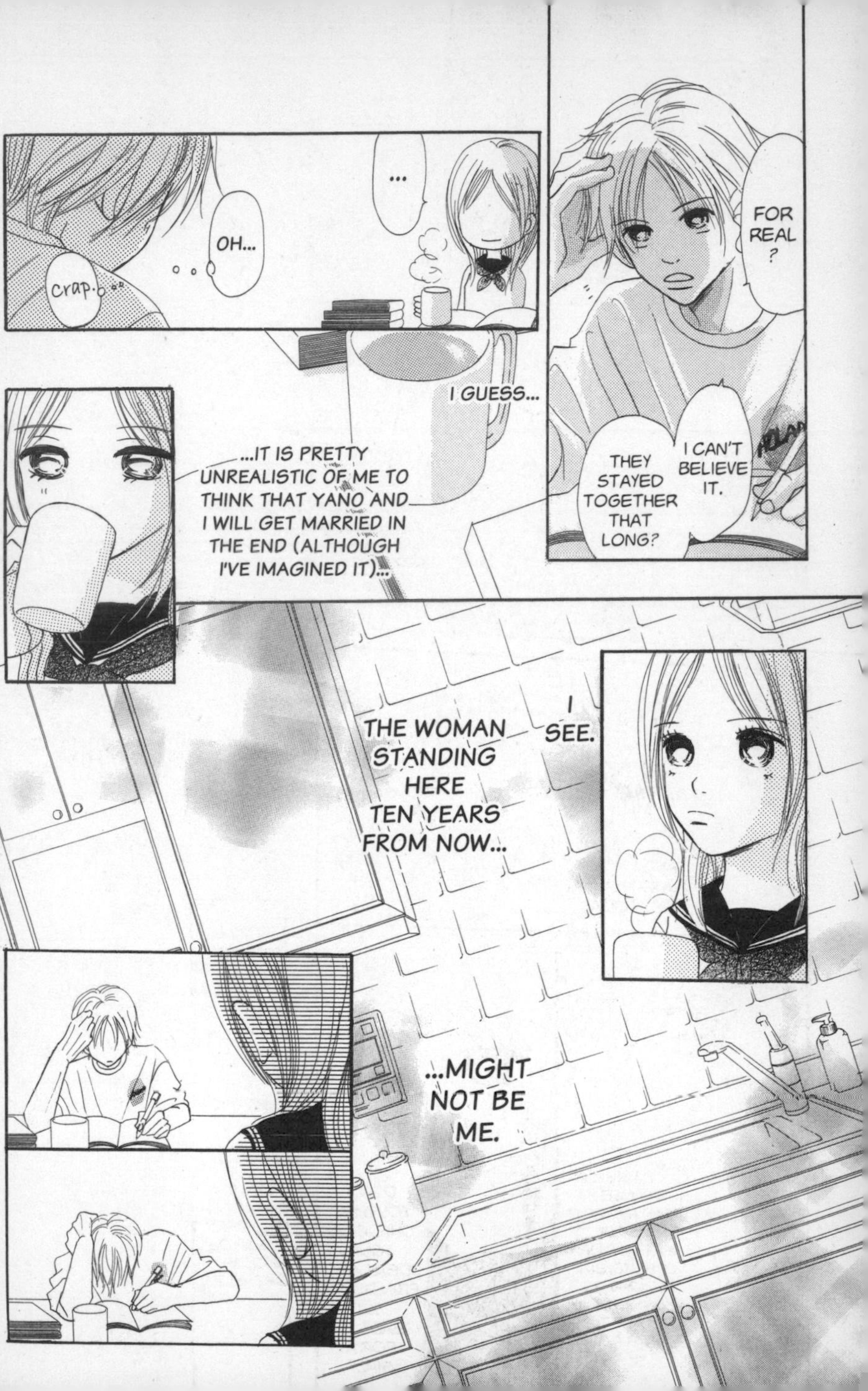
FOR REAL ?
I CAN'T BELIEVE IT.
THEY STAYED TOGETHER THAT LONG?
...
OH...
crap.
I GUESS...
...IT IS PRETTY UNREALISTIC OF ME TO THINK THAT YANO AND I WILL GET MARRIED IN THE END (ALTHOUGH I'VE IMAGINED IT)...
I SEE.
THE WOMAN STANDING HERE TEN YEARS FROM NOW...
...MIGHT NOT BE ME.

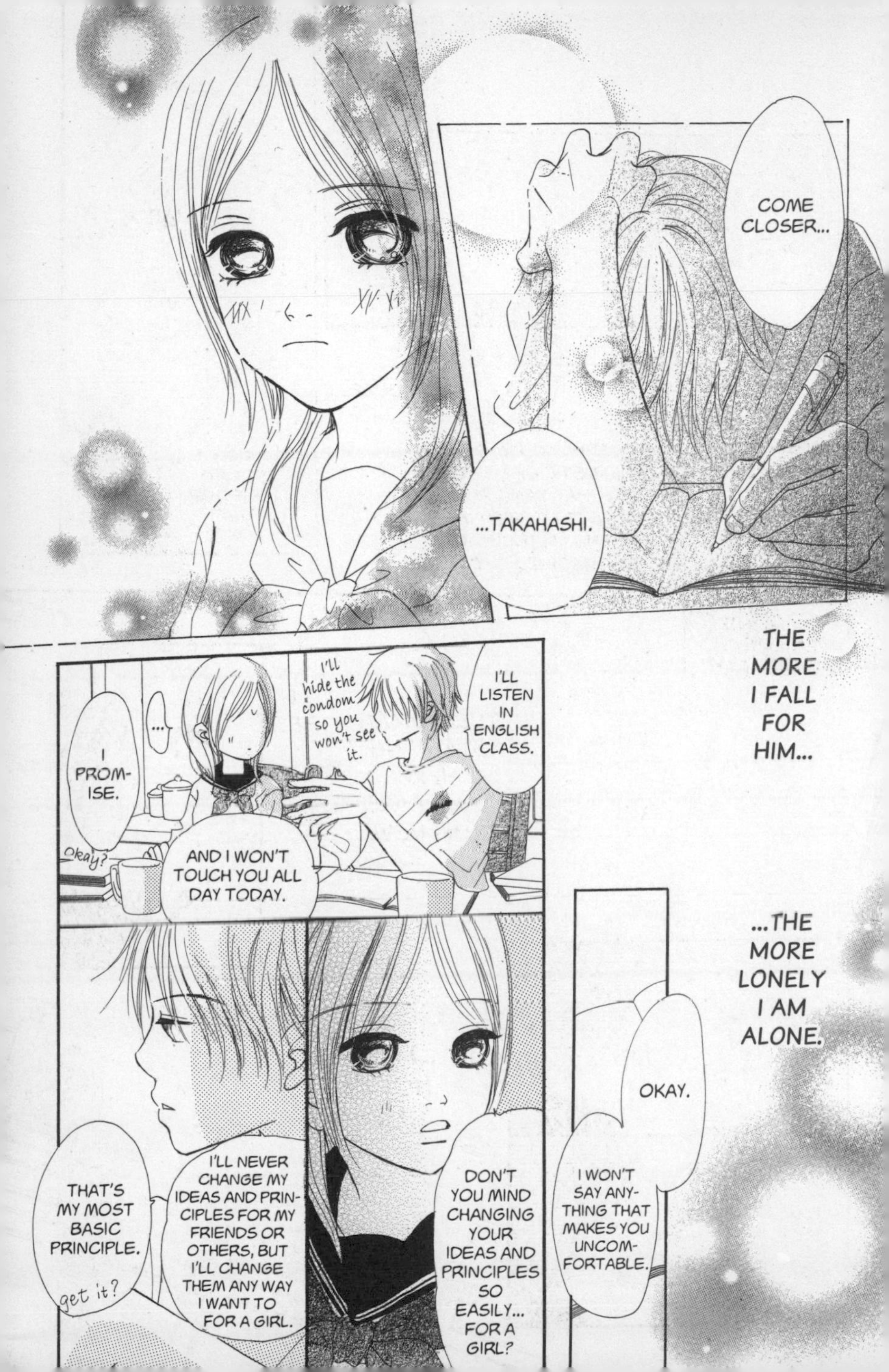
COME CLOSER...
...TAKAHASHI.
THE MORE I FALL FOR HIM...
I'LL LISTEN IN ENGLISH CLASS.
I'll hide the condom so you won't see it.
...
I PROMISE.
AND I WON'T TOUCH YOU ALL DAY TODAY.
Okay?
...THE MORE LONELY I AM ALONE.
OKAY.
I WON'T SAY ANYTHING THAT MAKES YOU UNCOMFORTABLE.
DON'T YOU MIND CHANGING YOUR IDEAS AND PRINCIPLES SO EASILY... FOR A GIRL?
I'LL NEVER CHANGE MY IDEAS AND PRINCIPLES FOR MY FRIENDS OR OTHERS, BUT I'LL CHANGE THEM ANY WAY I WANT TO FOR A GIRL.
THAT'S MY MOST BASIC PRINCIPLE.
get it?

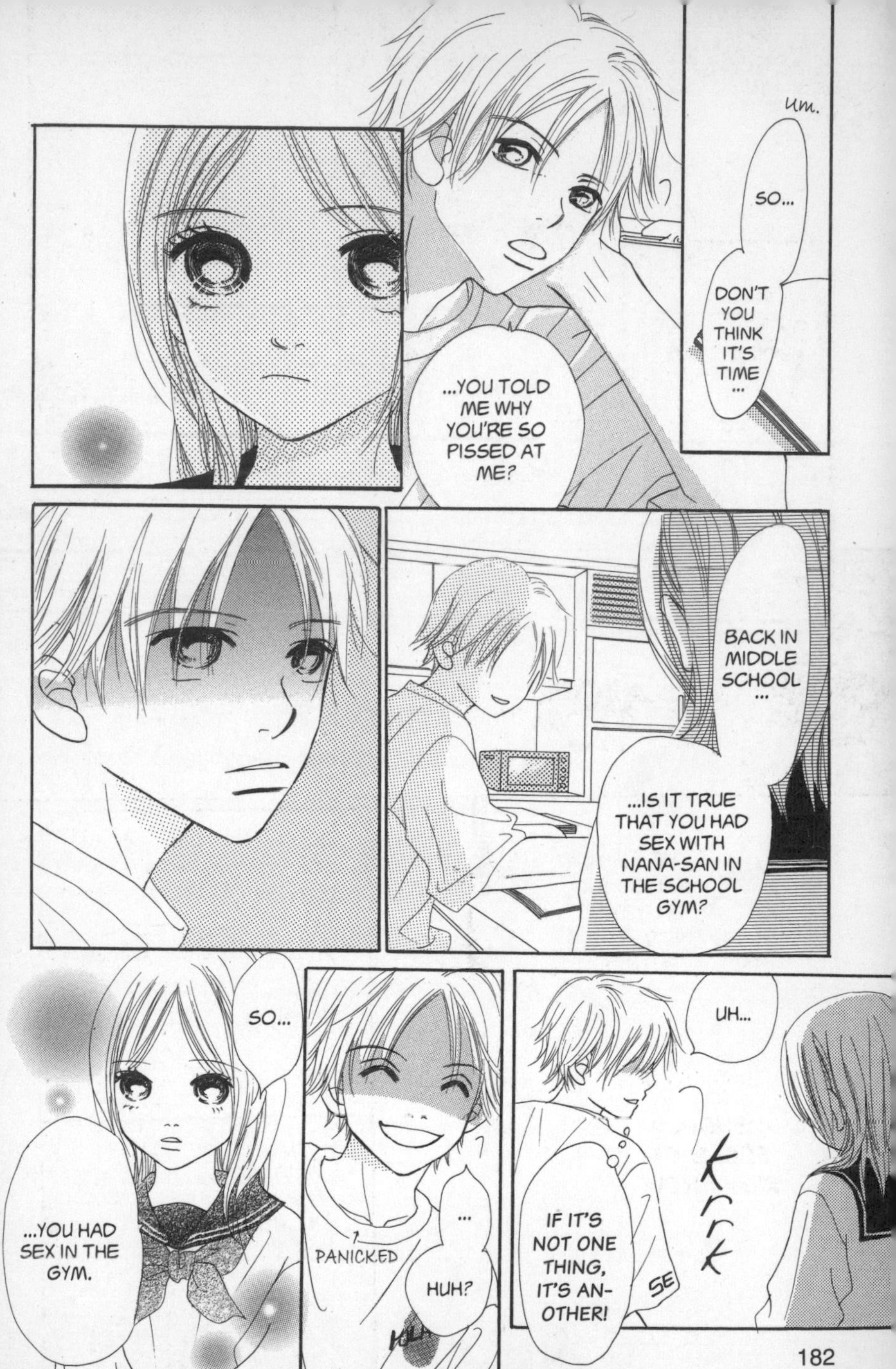
Um.
So...
Don't you think it's time ...
...You told me why you're so pissed at me?
Back in middle school ...
...Is it true that you had sex with Nana-san in the school gym?
Uh...
Krrk
If it's not one thing, it's an-other!
SE
...
Huh?
Panicked
So...
...You had sex in the gym.

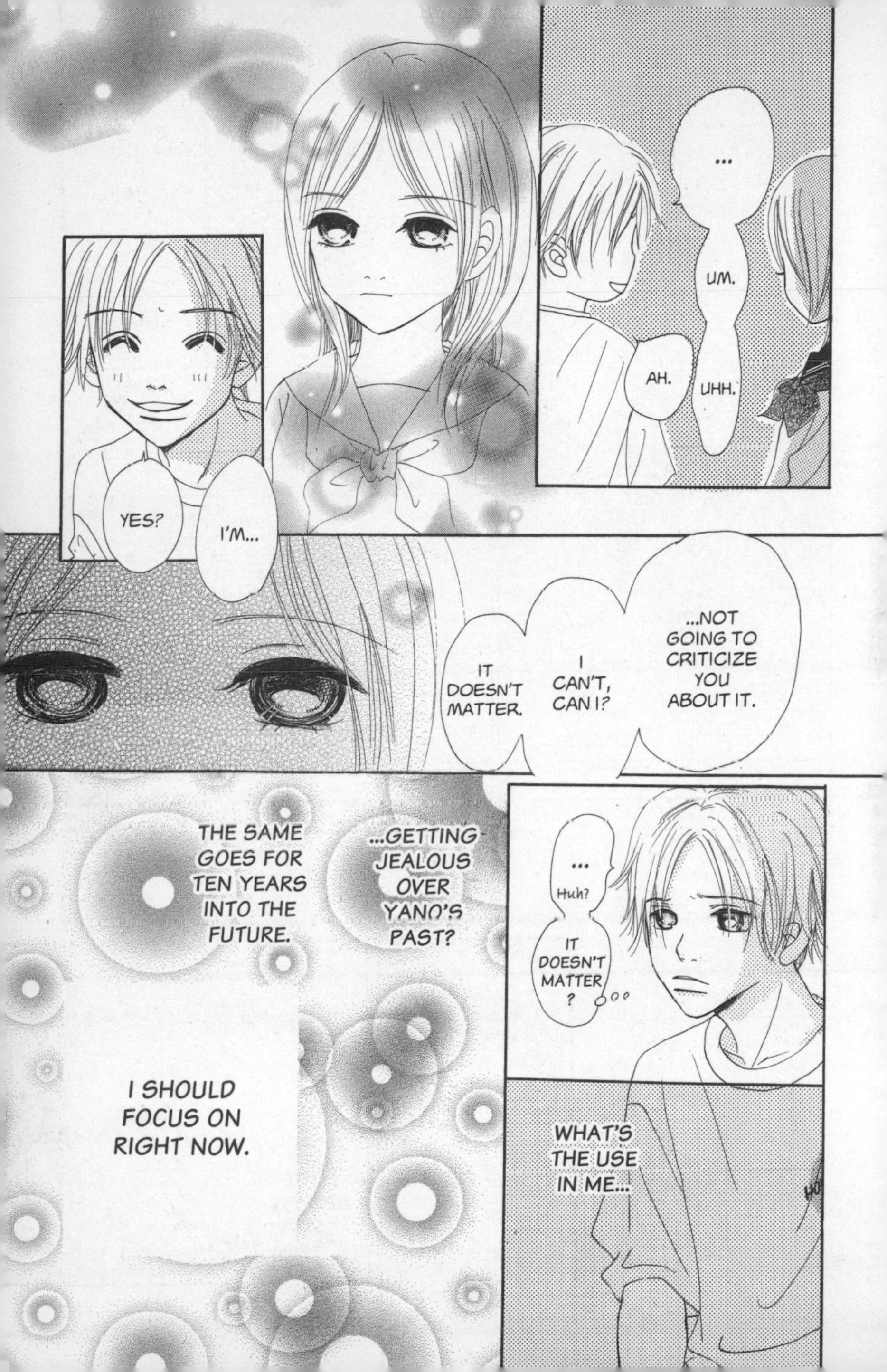
...
UM.
UHH.
AH.
I'M...
YES?
...NOT GOING TO CRITICIZE YOU ABOUT IT.
I CAN'T, CAN I?
IT DOESN'T MATTER.
...
Huh?
IT DOESN'T MATTER?
WHAT'S THE USE IN ME...
...GETTING JEALOUS OVER YANO'S PAST?
THE SAME GOES FOR TEN YEARS INTO THE FUTURE.
I SHOULD FOCUS ON RIGHT NOW.

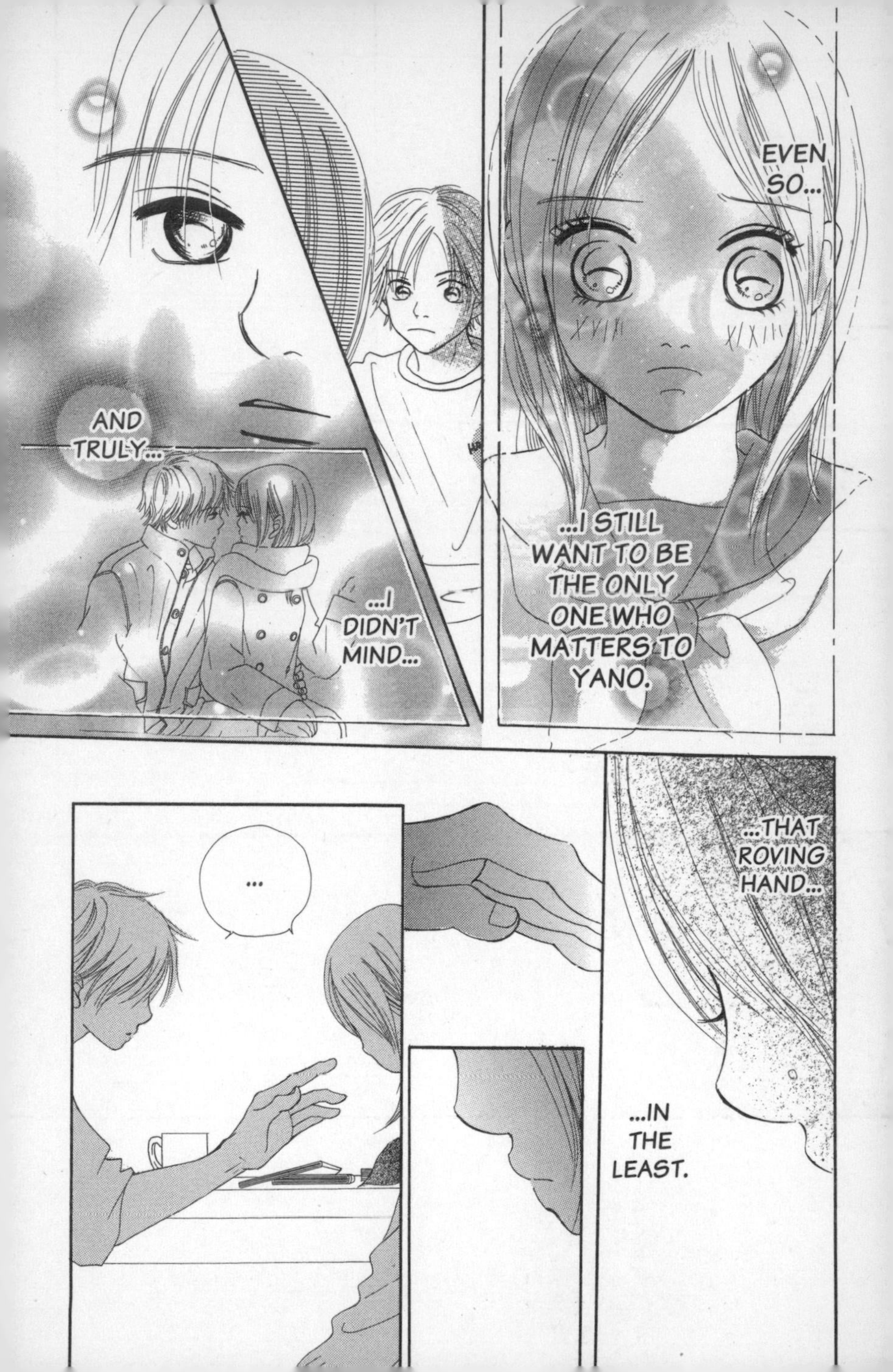
EVEN SO...
...I STILL WANT TO BE THE ONLY ONE WHO MATTERS TO YANO.
AND TRULY...
...I DIDN'T MIND...
...THAT ROVING HAND...
...IN THE LEAST.
...

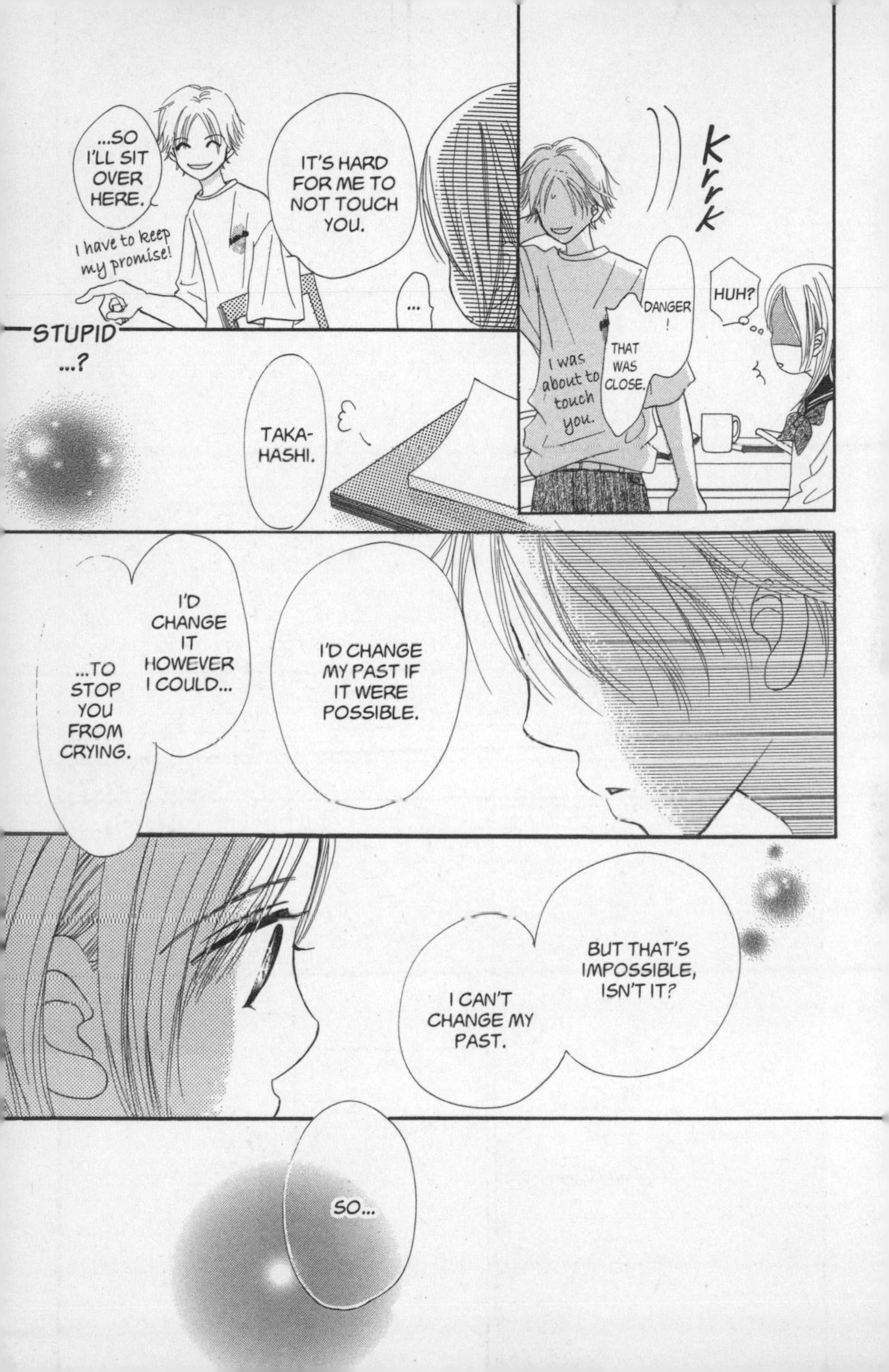
KRRK
HUH?
DANGER! THAT WAS CLOSE.
I was about to touch you.
IT'S HARD FOR ME TO NOT TOUCH YOU.
...
...SO I'LL SIT OVER HERE.
I have to keep my promise!
STUPID ...?
TAKA-HASHI.
I'D CHANGE MY PAST IF IT WERE POSSIBLE.
I'D CHANGE IT HOWEVER I COULD...
...TO STOP YOU FROM CRYING.
BUT THAT'S IMPOSSIBLE, ISN'T IT?
I CAN'T CHANGE MY PAST.
SO...

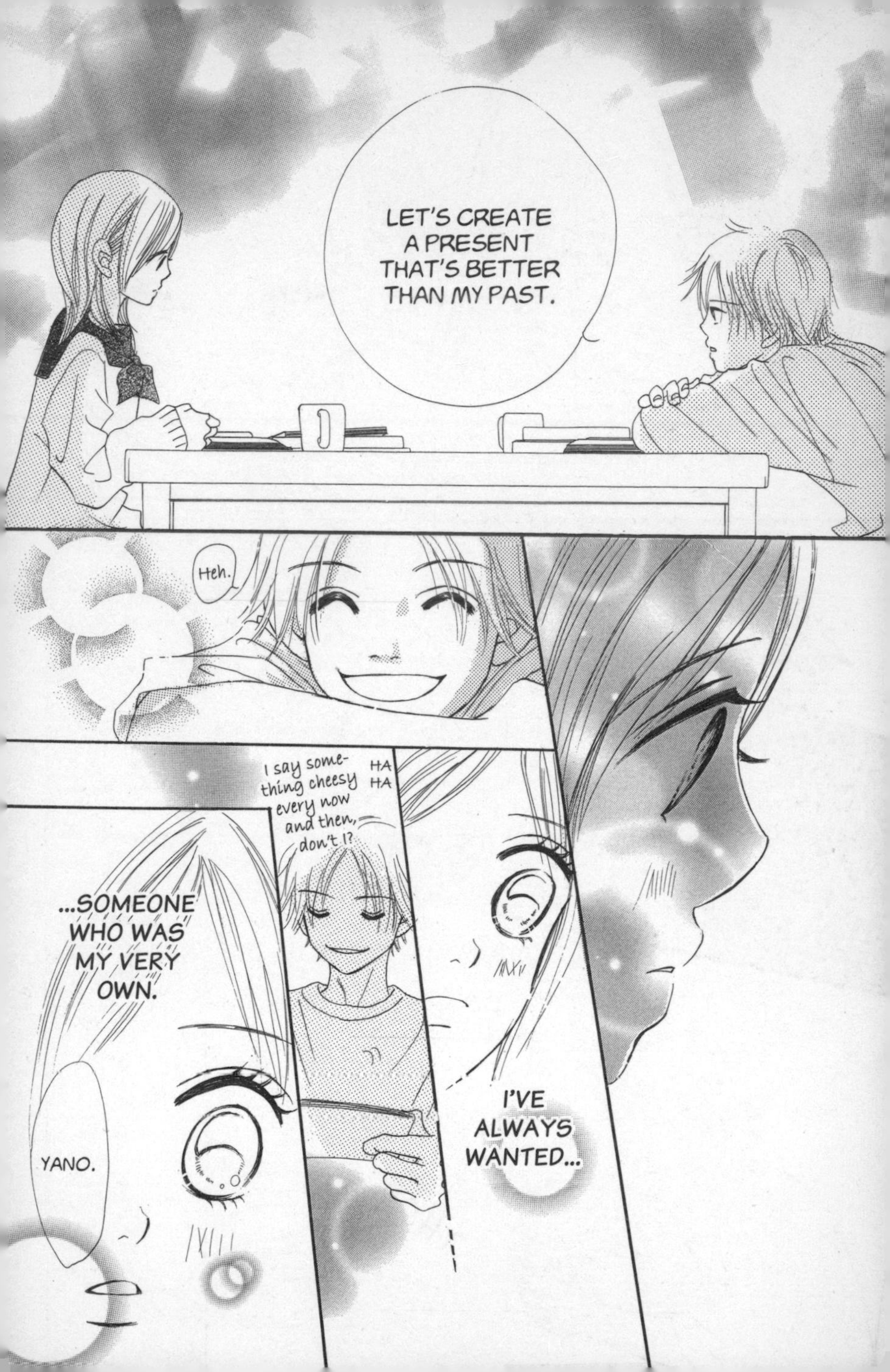
LET'S CREATE A PRESENT THAT'S BETTER THAN MY PAST.
Heh.
I say something cheesy every now and then, don't I?
HA HA
I'VE ALWAYS WANTED...
...SOMEONE WHO WAS MY VERY OWN.
YANO.

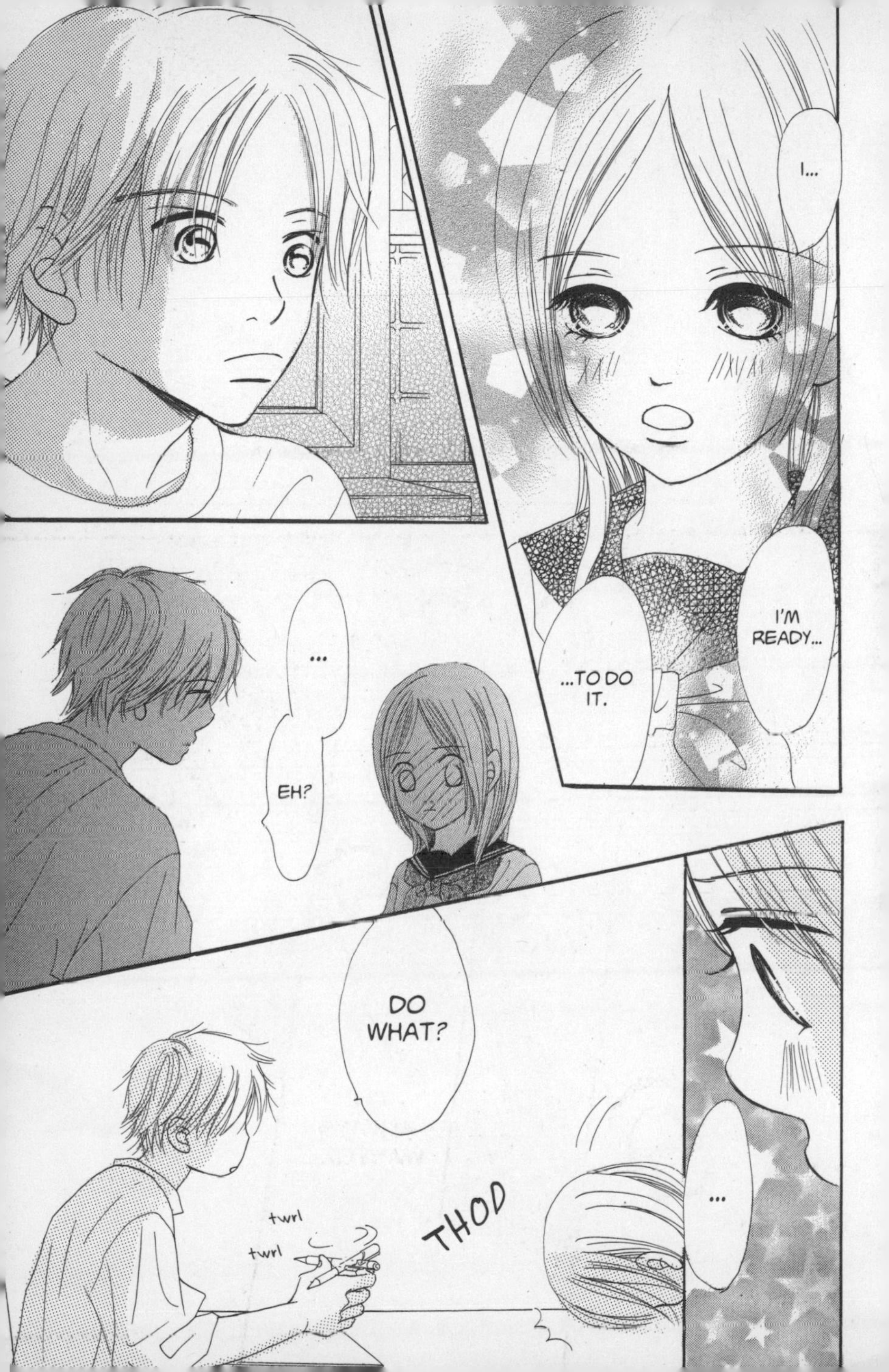
I...
I'M READY...
...TO DO IT.
...
EH?
...
DO WHAT?
THOD
twrl
twrl

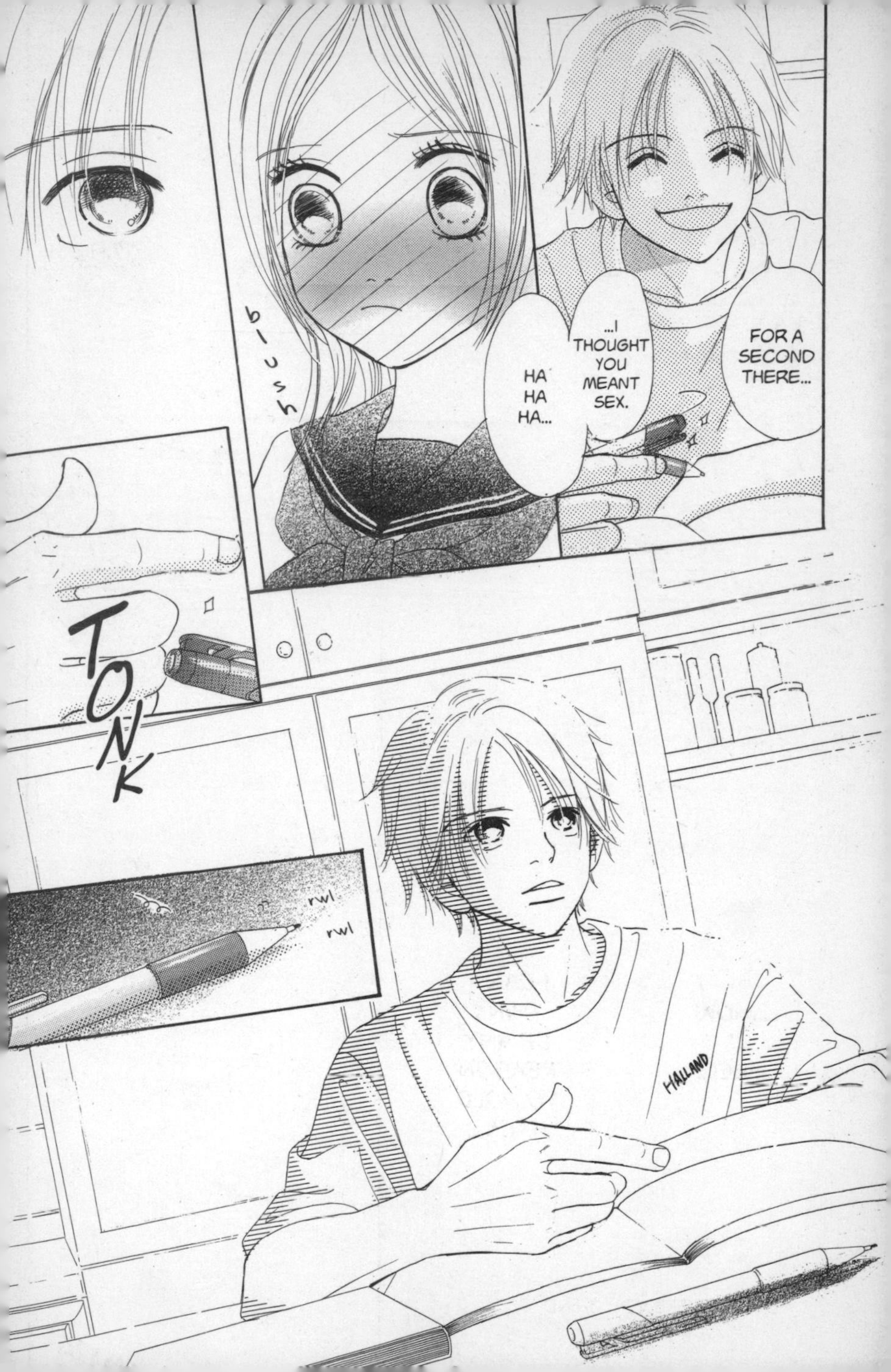
FOR A SECOND THERE...
...I THOUGHT YOU MEANT SEX.
HA HA HA...
blush
TONK
rwl
rwl
HALLAND

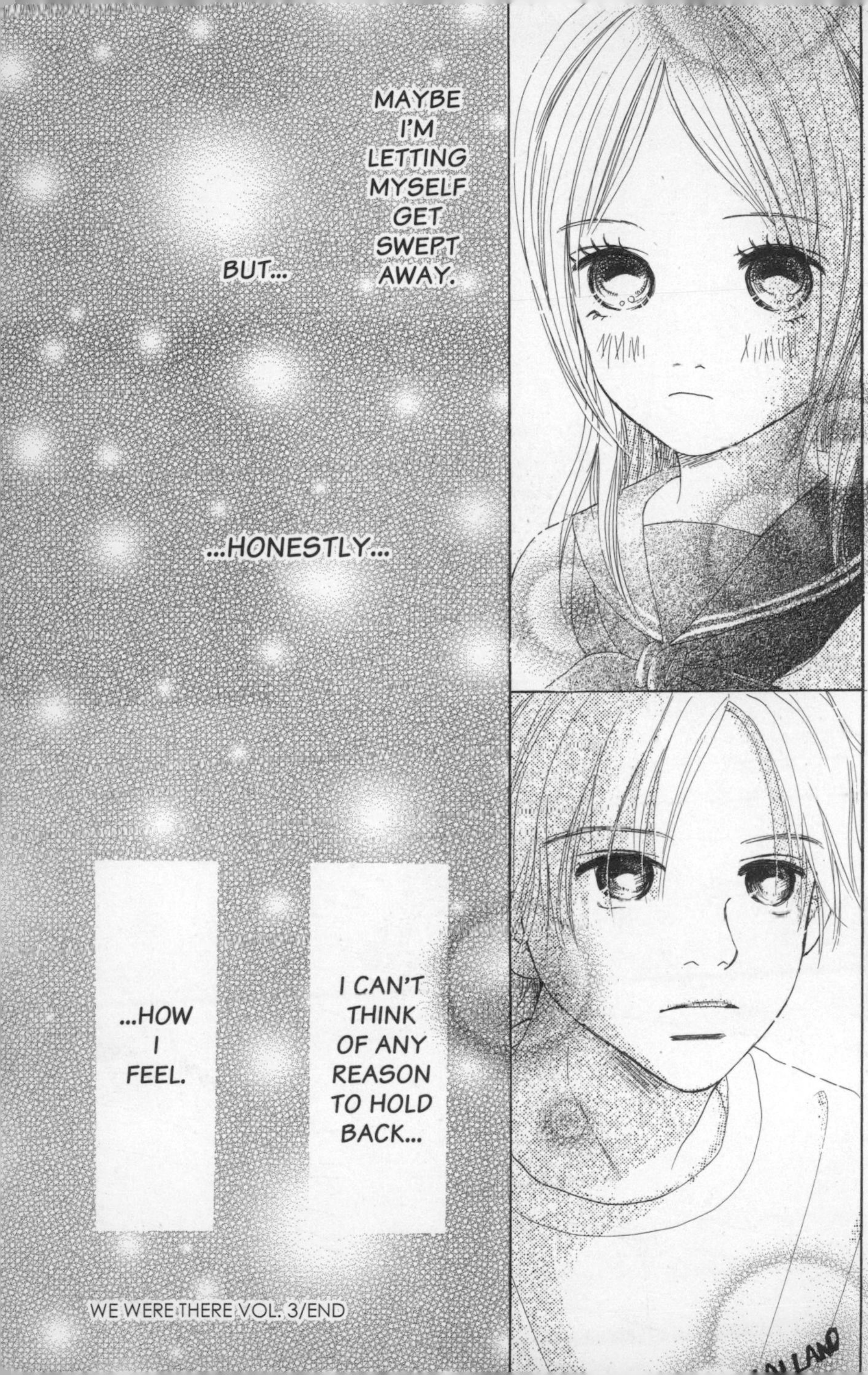
MAYBE I'M LETTING MYSELF GET SWEPT AWAY.
BUT...
...HONESTLY...
I CAN'T THINK OF ANY REASON TO HOLD BACK...
...HOW I FEEL.
WE WERE THERE VOL. 3/END

Notes

Honorifics

In Japan, people are usually addressed by their name followed by a suffix.
The suffix shows familiarity or respect, depending on the relationship.

Male (familiar): first or last name + kun
Female (familiar): first or last name + chan
Adult (polite): last name + san
Upperclassman (polite): last name + senpai
Teacher or professional: last name + sensei
Close friends or lovers: first name only, no suffix

Nana-chan vs. Nana-san

Nanami's nickname is "Nana-chan." Yano's ex-girlfriend
was a year older, so she was known as "Nana-san."

Terms

In Japan, it's traditional to offer incense sticks to the deceased at the
family altar in the house.

Fruit Milk is a flavored milk sold in Japan.

"Masa" is Masafumi's nickname.

Bakappuru, or "silly couple," is a Japanese slang term created from
baka (stupid) and *kappuru* (couple). It's used to indicate a loving couple
who seems annoying or extremely lovey-dovey to other people.

Yuki Obata's birthday is January 9. Her debut manga, *Raindrops*, won the Shogakukan Shinjin Comics Taisho Kasaku Award in 1998. Her current series, *We Were There* (*Bokura ga Ita*), won the 50th Shogakukan Manga Award and was adapted into an animated television series. She likes sweets, coffee, drinking with friends, and scary stories. Her hobby is browsing in bookshops.

Shojo Beat

We Were There
Vol. 3
The Shojo Beat Manga Edition

STORY & ART BY
YUKI OBATA

Adaptation/Nancy Thistlethwaite
Translation/Tetsuichiro Miyaki
Touch-up Art & Lettering/Inori Fukuda Trant
Design/Izumi Hirayama
Editor/Nancy Thistlethwaite

Editor in Chief, Books/Alvin Lu
Editor in Chief, Magazines/Marc Weidenbaum
VP, Publishing Licensing/Rika Inouye
VP, Sales & Product Marketing/Gonzalo Ferreyra
VP, Creative/Linda Espinosa
Publisher/Hyoe Narita

BOKURA GA ITA 3 by Yuuki OBATA © 2003 Yuuki OBATA
All rights reserved. Original Japanese edition
published in 2003 by Shogakukan Inc., Tokyo.
The stories, characters and incidents mentioned
in this publication are entirely fictional.

Printed in Canada

Published by VIZ Media, LLC
P.O. Box 77010
San Francisco, CA 94107

Shojo Beat Manga Edition
10 9 8 7 6 5 4 3 2 1
First printing, March 2009

VIZ
MEDIA
www.viz.com

store.viz.com